FIRE BENEATH OUR FEET

FIRE BENEATH OUR FEET

SHAYS' REBELLION AND ITS
CONSTITUTIONAL IMPACT

Rock Brynner, Ph.D.
Columbia University, 1993

DISTINCT PRESS

Fire Beneath Our Feet
Shays' Rebellion and its Constitutional Impact
Copyright © 1993 Rock Brynner

Summary: *Fire Beneath our Feet* makes sense of how the U.S. Constitution came into being. It explores how the collapse of the Confederation of States was avoided and the effects of Shays' Rebellion.

Library of Congress Control Number: 2018965679

1. Rock Brynner, 1949 - 2. History; Colonial Period 3. Revolution & Founding 4. Shays' Rebellion 1786 - 1787

Brynner, Rock 1949 -
Fire Beneath Our Feet: Shays' Rebellion and its Constitutional Impact

ISBN: 9781943103195

Printed in the United States of America
10 9 8 7 6 5 4 3 2 1

—

DISTINCT PRESS PUBLISHING

If you are interested in bulk ordering of paperback versions of this book, or professional review copies of this book because you intend to write a review in your publication, mention this book on your radio show or podcast, post to your blog or website, or request an article or interview, send your request to please contact us directly at sayhi@distinctpress.com

For more information visit
www.DistinctPress.com

ABSTRACT

This dissertation aims to demonstrate the determinative impact of Shays' Rebellion upon the drafting and ratification of the United States Constitution. While some historians have assumed a causal connection between the two events, and a few have disputed it, the question has not heretofore received a thorough examination.

"The Regulation" was a series of peaceable demonstrations that closed the court-houses in western Massachusetts between August and December, 1786, followed by one lethal confrontation at the Springfield Arsenal a month later. "Shays' Rebellion," however, was a deliberate misperception of the Regulation promoted by nationalists determined to supplant the Articles of Confederation with a consolidated federal government. By painting the Regulation in lurid colors that evoked the Leveller movement in England under Cromwell, the nationalists succeeded in alarming leaders and citizens throughout the United States with notions of imminent civil war and the re-distribution of private property. These citizens included George Washington: because of the exaggerated reports he received of Shays' Rebellion, he forsook retirement to attend the Constitutional Convention, bringing all his prestige to bear in favor of an empowered national government

During the Convention, and the subsequent process of constitutional ratification by the states, Shays' Rebellion continued to furnish an alarming illustration of the Confederation's inadequacies, and thereby provided the delegates in Philadelphia and at the ratifying conventions with a powerful motive for accepting the compromises implicit in the new Union.

CONTENTS

Preface   *I*
Abbreviated Titles   *V*
Introduction   1

PART ONE
THE REGULATION

Chapter One   13
Chapter Two   45
Chapter Three   75

PART TWO
THE NATIONALISTS' RESPONSE

Chapter Four   113
Chapter Five   147
Chapter Six   193

PART THREE
THE CONSTITUTIONAL IMPACT OF
SHAYS' REBELLION

Chapter Seven   237
Chapter Eight   275

Historiographic Essay   285
Bibliography   315
Appendix A   349
Appendix B   353

In memory of my mother
Virginia Gilmore (1919-1986)
and my father
Yul Brynner (1920-1985)

PREFACE

The origins, events, and constitutional consequences of Shays' Rebellion provide an expansive story composed of enduring themes in social, intellectual, and political history. Many of those themes emerged almost one hundred fifty years earlier during the first English Revolution, including popular sovereignty, parliamentary authority, and religious freedom. The vivid memory of that era, in literature and folk-lore, haunted post-revolutionary Americans. History, to rephrase James Joyce, was a nightmare from which they struggled to awake.

At first the broad contours of this story seemed to be shapeless, especially during a close examination of the passionate personalities that emerged from both the Regulation and its suppression. These were stolid individuals determined to defend their prerogatives, as they understood them - not hapless instruments of overriding historical forces. But the actions that they took grew out of a wealth of beliefs, mores, and convictions, and therein lay their connection to a much larger story than the post-war depression. It is also why they came to provide the means as well as a motive for the establishment of the United States Constitution.

During my research, this story began to take the shape of an hour-glass. From the broad array of ideas that erupted in England in the 1640s, the story is compressed through a narrow moment in western Massachusetts, from which it spreads out across the thirteen states during the formation and ratification of the Federal government. Those same themes of government and citizens' rights reverberated forward, from Cromwell's Commonwealth to the Massachusetts Commonwealth, against a background of revolution and its aftermath. Exaggerated reports of the Regulation confirmed the country's most dire expectations - expectations derived from the same republican ideology that had informed the War. It was these expectations, more than the number of men assembled or shots fired, that made the 'rebellion' seem so momentous. Those who sought to reconstruct the continental government succeeded in using these peaceful protests to cast a giant shadow, by holding them up close to the still fiery embers of Oliver Cromwell's Interregnum.

I owe a great debt to three of my professors at Columbia University for the patience and encouragment that they offered, along with their excellent advice and uncompromising standards: Richard Bushman, my dissertation advisor, Eric Foner, whose lectures on early American radicalism offered a grounding in the ideological environment of the era, and Alden Vaughan, whose lectures provided an invaluable historical background for the events of the 1780s. I am especially fortunate to have had the guidance of Prof. Bushman, who worked hard to set me on the right course when I was headed in quite another direction. From his criticisms and marginal notes I learned that the singular prose style shared by the better academic historians is neither a capricious tradition nor a collective idiosyncrasy, but a methodical solution for presenting a complex argument with its supporting evidence. I have also drawn inspiration from the fact that his own undergraduate advisor was the late Robert A. Feer, author of the most comprehensive exposition of Shays' Rebellion, who issued a challenge more than twenty years ago which this present study is intended to meet.

At Columbia, I am also indebted to Ene Sirvet, who has devoted many years to the study and publication of the John Jay Papers: she has given generously of her time and effort, with her advice and criticism. It was thanks to Ms. Sirvet that I met with her mentor, the late Richard B. Morris, who led me to recognize that the Regulators were not ideological radicals, nor merely debt-ridden farmers, and that the true character of their protests had been masked by the larger purposes of those who sought a new United States government.

Robert A. Gross at the College of William and Mary kindly offered an early manuscript of In Debt to Shays, a forthcoming collection of essays (including his own), which he edited. William Pencak at Pennsylvania State University has been particularly helpful with detailed criticism and lively discussion. And James Thomas Flexner was good enough to spend some time with me at the New-York Historical Society: his painstaking biography of George Washington suggested some of the arguments that I am making here.

Much of the research for this paper centered upon the documentary evidence of eighteenth-century Massachusetts and the extensive correspondence between the nationalists at the American Antiquarian Society, the Massachusetts Historical Society, the Houghton Library at Harvard University, the Massachusetts Archives, the Forbes Library in Northampton, the Springfield Gty Library, the Berkshire Athenaeum in Pittsfield, the Columbia Rare Books Library and the Microfilm Department, the New- York Historical Society, the New York Public Library, and the National Archives. I am very grateful for the assistance I have received from Joanne Chason and Joyce Tracy at the AAS, Patrick Flynn and Peter Drummey at the MHS, Elise Feeley at the Forbes, Ruth Degenhardt at the Berkshire Athenaeum, and Milton O. Gustafson at the National Archives. Unpublished tracts and other writings of Gerrard Winstanley and the Levellers were readily available at the British Library.

My thanks to the Houghton Library, Harvard Univeristy, and the Forbes Library, Northampton, Mass., for permission to publish extensive excerpts from William Manning's Key of Libberty and the Daniel Stebbins Journal, respectively. Finally, I gratefully acknowledge my debt to the many historians who devoted part of their lives to the era between the War of Independence and the adoption of the Constitution.

ABBREVIATED TITLES

Bowdoin-Temple Papers.
Bowdoin and Temple Papers. 2 vols. (Massachusetts Historical Society, *Collections, IX*, 7th Ser. [Boston, 1907] vol. 6).

Burnett, *Letters.*
Edmund C. Burnett. *Letters of Members of the Continental Congress.* 8 vols. Gloucester, Mass: Peter Smith, 1963 [orig. publ. 1934, Washington, D.C.: Carnegie Institution, 1934].

Elliott, ed., *Debates.*
Jonathan Elliot, ed. *Debates in the Several State Conventions on the Adoption of the Federal Constitution.* 5 vols. New York: Lippincott, 1888.

Farrand, ed., *Records.*
Max Farrand, ed. *Records of the Federal Convention of 1787.* 4 vols. New Haven: Yale University Press, 1937.

JCC.
U. S. Continental Congress. *Journals of the Continental Congress.* Worthington Chauncey Ford, *et al.*, eds. 34 vols. Washington, 1904-1937.

Jefferson Papers.
Julian P. Boyd, ed. *The Papers of Thomas Jefferson.* 17 vols. Princeton: Princeton University Press, 1950-1965.

Knox Papers.
The Papers of Henry Knox, Massachusetts Historical Society (microfilm).

Madison Papers.
William T. Hutchinson, Robert A. Rutland, and William M. E. Rachal, *et al.*, eds. *The Papers of James Madison.* 16 vols. Chicago: University of Chicago Press, 1977.

Papers of the Continental Congress.
U. S. Continental Congress. Papers of the Continental Congress. Library of Congress (microfilm.)

Washington Papers.
The Papers of George Washington. Library of Congress (microfilm).

Writings of Washington.
John C. Fitzpatrick, ed. *Writings of George Washington from the Original Manuscript Sources 1745-1799.* 39 vols. Washington: U. S. Government Printing Office, 1931-1944.

"I believe it is not generally known on what a perilous tenure we held our freedom and independence at that period. The flames of internal insurrection were ready to burst out in every quarter. . . and from one end to the other of the continent, we walked on ashes, concealing fire beneath our feet. . . ."

— James Wilson, Pennsylvania Ratifying
Convention, December 11th, 1787.[1]

"The most trifling events have been Magnified into Monstrious outrages "

— Uriah Forrest to Thomas Jefferson,
December 11th, 1787.[2]

1. Elliott, *Debates*, II, 521.
2. *Jefferson Papers*, XII, 416.

INTRODUCTION

This dissertation aims to demonstrate the determinative impact of Shays' Rebellion upon the drafting and ratification of the United States Constitution. The Regulation, as the "rebels" called their series of demonstrations, was not just a catalyst for the constitutional movement, nor merely a pretext, but the efficient cause of the Constitution's establishment. The credible threat of violence and redistribution of property provided by the nationalists' misrepresentations of the insurrection was a prerequisite element in their campaign for a strong central government. That threat accounted for the successful call for delegates to the Constitutional Convention, starting with its president, George Washington, who had retired unequivocally from public life until Shays' Rebellion. During the Convention it provided a crucial motive for achieving consensus and compromise, and held the delegates' feet to the fire by illustrating the failures of the Confederation. And, during the process of ratification, that threat foreshadowed the apparent consequences of anti-Federalism; at the same time, only by acceding to a Bill of Rights which addressed some Shaysite concerns were the Federalists able to achieve their goal.

Much as Japan's attack on Pearl Harbor enabled the Roosevelt administration to declare war against the Axis nations, Shays' Rebellion enabled Federalists to supplant the self-defeating alliance of states delineated in the Articles of Confederation with a fundamental law for the United States. An examination of the hard evidence and its ideological underpinnings demonstrates that Shays' Rebellion was the efficient cause of the formation and ratification of the Constitution.

"The Regulation" was a series of demonstrations that closed the court-houses in western Massachusetts between August and December, 1786, followed by one lethal confrontation at the Springfield Arsenal a month later.[1] "Shays' Rebellion," however, was a deliberate misperception of the Regulation promoted by such nationalists as General Henry Knox, Massachusetts Governor James Bowdoin, and merchant-financier Stephen Higginson.[2] The momentous impact of the insurrection did not lie in the military threat that it posed, but in that misperception. What made that misperception credible was the violent history of English civil war that was evoked by these mostly peaceable commotions. Shays' Rebellion forced the question of whether any republican government could be sustained; that is, whether common ground could be found between those who believed in a continuous, democratic referendum comparable to the familiar town meeting, and those who agreed with John Jay, that the country should be governed by the men who' owned it.[3] Put otherwise, should republican governance arise directly from the electorate, or be handed down to them by a mercantile élite?

As fundamental as that question was, the Regulation itself was only a brief, ineluctable phase in the chain of events that began with the Stamp Act and ended in the genesis of the American two-party system. It was also the ardent expression of a powerful idea conceived more than a century earlier, and fostered by republican thought: popular sovereignty, and in particular, representative government by the consent of the people. This was the ideological impulse that propelled Americans through the imperial crisis, the War of Independence, Shays' Rebellion, the drafting of

1. The reader who is entirely unacquainted with this subject may wish to turn to the account of the Regulation in Chapter Three before reading about its ideological origins and proximate causes in Chapters One and Two.

2. Where that eponymous misperception of the Regulation is the subject, rather than the protests themselves, the commotions are referred to here as "the rebellion," "the insurrection," or "the insurgency;" otherwise, they are referred to as "the Regulation," "the demonstrations," or "the protests."

3. "It being a favorite maxim with Mr. Jay," according to his son, "that those who own the country ought to govern it" William Jay, *Life of John Jay*, 2 vol. (New York, 1833), 1, 70.

the Constitution and the Bill of Rights, and on to the formation of a lasting loyal opposition. Only after that sequence of events can it be said that revolutionary settlement - a constitutional framework of sufficient stability to absorb challenges from within - had been reached.[4]

Like the Revolution itself, Shays' Rebellion was a crisis of representation. Though prompted by post-war economic hardship, the Regulation was not about paper money, or debt, or even land: it was about the inherent injustice of the revolutionary settlements embodied in the Massachusetts Constitution of 1780 and the Articles of Confederation, and particularly those injustices endured by the common soldiery upon returning home from the war. Among the major grievances was the specific manner in which taxes were assessed, collected, and spent by the Massachusetts government of James Bowdoin, as well as the Continental Congress (by way of supplementary funds). But Shays' Rebellion was not caused by the poll-tax, any more than the American Revolution was caused by the Tea Act; both were caused by a hunger for self-government.

The actual events of the insurrection did less to precipitate the drafting of the Federal Constitution than did the vivid colors in which they were depicted. Indeed, the enormous disparity between the first few peaceable demonstrations and the alarming descriptions they received clearly suggests the purposefulness with which the most overblown eventualities were being projected.

---

4. Murrin agreed that a "Revolution Settlement" is not complete until the time when "internal forces alone will not alter the regime or constitutional system in more than secondary details. . . . The American Revolution reached stability with the triumph of Jeffersonian government. . . ." John M. Murrin, "The Great Inversion, or Court versus Country: A Comparison of the Revolution Settlements in England (1688- 1721) and America (1776-1816)," in *Three British Revolutions: 1641 , 1688, 1776,* J. G. A. Pocock, ed. (Princeton, 1980), 378. See also John L. Brooke, "To the Quiet of the People: Revolutionary Settlements and Civil Unrest in Western Massachusetts, 1774-1789," *William and Mary Quarterly,* 3rd Ser., XLVI (July 1989), 425-462. Stephen Patterson observed that since "the party struggle was anterior to the challenge to America liberty, it absorbed imperial issues into a partisan context from the very first, and party conflict thrived symbiotically on imperial issues. . . ." Stephen E. Patterson, *Political Parties in Revolutionary Massachusetts* (Madison, 1973), 4.

Those who sought to establish a federal government succeeded masterfully in shaping the continental perception of the uprising, and its implications to a political culture deeply cognizant of the ephemeral nature of revolutionary governments.

The Regulation has usually been misconstrued to encompass the months and years of town and county petitions which preceded it, and the isolated acts of violence which followed it. By presenting those petitions as the first phase of rebellion, historians have dismissed the distinctive nature and purpose of the paramilitary protesters. By depicting the desperate supply raids of fleeing Regulators after the protests as a part of the larger movement, they have tarnished the pacific nature of the demonstrations. To overcome the effect of two centuries of such misrepresentation, one must take care to rectify the nomenclature applied to the protests initiated by Knox, Bowdoin, Higginson, and the Federalist historian, George Richards Minot. In fact, "Shays' Rebellion" was neither Daniel Shays's, nor a rebellion, but a widespread ritual of disobedience, firmly rooted in the tradition of moral economy in western Massachusetts.[5]

Even in an age distinguished by its dynamic exercise of political ideology, determining the cause for a given action is not simple, especially for an action as complex as the drafting of the Federal Constitution. Some historians have resorted to counterfactual conjecture; for example, "Would the Constitution still have emerged if Shays' Rebellion had never happened?" But such hypothetical musings are both unhelpful and misleading, since Shays' Rebellion was itself a consequence of the Revolutionary War. To find meaningful criteria for testing causality, the historian must turn to philosophy. In the case of Shays' Rebellion, rational idealism provides a particularly useful, analytic framework.

---

5. Dennis Dalton, Professor of Political Science at Columbia University, who served on the Defense Committee for this dissertation, objected to the description of Shays' Rebellion as "civil disobedience," or "a broad-based, popular political movement," arguing that the present study has not considered the criteria Political Science applies to such descriptions. Although I believe it can be demonstrated that the Regulation meets those criteria, at this stage I have deferred to his objections and omitted those specific phrases.

Historical processes, wrote R. G. Collingwood, "are not processes of mere events, but processes of actions, which have an
inner side, consisting of processes of thought; and what the historian is looking for is these processes of thought."[6] Aspects of an
event other than its cause might be addressed in other ways; then,
instead of seeking out those processes of thought, we might dwell,
for example, on statistical evidence. To determine when and how
subsistence farmers produced a sufficient surplus of crops to ini-
tiate a market economy, we might analyze the records of their
livestock holdings and manure yields. But we cannot learn why
those farmers acted as they did without understanding what they
thought and what they believed.

"When an historian asks 'Why did Brutus stab Caesar?'"
Collingwood continued, "he means 'What did Brutus think,
which made him decide to stab Caesar?' The cause of the event,
for him, means the thought in the mind of the person by whose
agency the event came about: and this is not something other than
the event, it is the inside of the event itself." Ultimately, wrote
Collingwood, "the history of thought, and therefore all history,
is the re-enactment of past thought in the historian's own mind."[7]

It is easier to identify the past thoughts of an individual au-
tocrat than those of a large, inarticulate crowd, marshalled by a
variety of leaders who shared only a few common aims among
a broad diversity of lesser motives. But the Constitutional Convention was caused only indirectly by Shaysite ideology: it arose
directly from the "process of thought" among the nationalist foes
of the Regulation, who saw in the commotions an opportunity to
achieve their goal of consolidating the Union. It is the historian's
good fortune that they executed their strategy by means of their
prolific correspondence; as a result, we can hold in our hands not
just evidence of the nationalists' intentions, but the very instruments whereby they effected their plan.

In eighteenth-century America, the causal relationship between
ideology and action is generally less equivocal than in other eras.
In Massachusetts, the rich heritage of political thought ranged

6. R. G. Collingwood, *The Idea of History* (New York, 1946), 214-215.
7. *Ibid.*, 215.

from sophisticated theories like those of Sidney and Harrington, to a heterogeneous, popular ideology rooted in town-meeting politics. In the case of Shays' Rebellion, the processes of thought behind the actions on both sides of the confrontation dated back more than a century to the only precedent for non-monarchical government in British history: the elimination of Charles I. That is why the dread of civil war was so prevalent throughout the Confederation period, and raised the ominous specter of an American Restoration. It was the dread of this historical process, embedded in folk-memory as well as learned essays, that gave Shays' Rebellion its menacing resonance.

So, for many who watched the Regulation unfold, nothing less was at issue than the capacity of the human race to prevail against the riptide of cyclical history and determine its own destiny. In the first paragraph of the *Federalist Papers*, Alexander Hamilton juxtaposed the issue of collective free will — self-determination — with the crisis of Shays' Rebellion and the circumstances from which it arose. "It seems to have been reserved to the people of this country," wrote Hamilton, "by their conduct and example, to decide the important question, whether societies of men are really capable or not, of establishing good government from reflection and choice, or whether they are forever destined to depend, for their political constitutions, on accident and force. If there be any truth in the remark, the crisis, at which we are arrived, may with propriety be regarded as the era in which that decision is made...."[8]

The causal relationship between Shays' Rebellion and the Constitution has been assumed by some historians and challenged by others, but it has never been thoroughly examined. This is in part, perhaps, because there was little apparent evidence of a direct ideological connection. Recently, though, as social historians began to examine history "from the bottom up," they have sought to understand the ideology of crowd actions and, as a result, they have discovered that the Regulators were not in fact a mob of

8. Alexander Hamilton et al., *The Federalist*, No. 1 (Philadelphia, 1977 [orig. publ. 1787]), 3. From other references in his essays, it is clear that Hamilton is alluding to Shays' Rebellion: see *The Federalist*, No. 6, 33, 37-38; see also below, 237.

"lawless banditti" responding mindlessly to the post-war depression.[9] By placing the Regulation in the broader context of colonial protest movements, they have uncovered a traditional moral economy at work. With this advancement, historians have freed themselves from two obsolete, related perspectives about the historical process. One of these perspectives is what E. P. Thompson called "the spasmodic view of popular history," according to which common folk intrude only intermittently as historical agents, usually by rioting.[10] The other is economic determinism, whereby the Regulation has been portrayed as a reaction to the depressed economy, with no regard for its underlying ideology.

Both these perspectives fail to address the most distinctive features of the Regulation. For five months, thousands of armed men marched in rank and file through towns all across Massachusetts; yet, on all the occasions when the men were mustered in a body, not one shot was fired, nor a single blow dealt. Even those historians who have recognized the importance of political ideology in the struggle for independence have overlooked this fact, and generally reverted to simplistic, economic assumptions to explain away the Regulation, in the face of overwhelming evidence that this was a broad-based movement founded upon traditional ideology.

It seems that the more closely historians have examined the Regulation itself, the less connection they have found to the Philadelphia Convention; that is because the connection was not apparent within the protests themselves. Robert Feer, author of the most comprehensive study of Shays' Rebellion, found no causal relationship at all between the two events. "In all likelihood," Feer wrote, "the Constitutional Convention would have met when it

---

9. "The central question which Rudd addresses [in *Ideology and Popular Protest*] is 'Where did the ideas bound up with popular protest come from?'" Harvey J. Kaye, "George Rudd, Social Historian," in George Rudd, *The Face of the Crowd: Studies in Revolution, Ideology and Popular Protest* (Atlantic Heights, N.J., 1988), 24.

10. E. P. Thompson, "The Moral Economy of the English Crowd in the Eighteenth Century," *Past and Present*, No. 50 (1971), 76.

did, the same document would have been drawn up, and it would have been ratified even if Shays's Rebellion had not taken place. If by a 'cause' we mean something necessary to the occurrence of a particular event, Shays's Rebellion was not a cause of the Constitution of the United States."[11] But he also noted that "there has never been a careful analysis of the evidence to see in what way Shays's Rebellion influenced the Constitution."[12]

The present study aims to meet that challenge. Given the consistent failure of Congress to compensate soldiers who were owed backpay and land bounties promised for as long as six years, Shays' Rebellion was not merely a consequence of the Revolutionary War, but an integral part of it. That Shays' Rebellion was truly the *sine qua non* of the Constitutional Convention becomes apparent from the extensive correspondence between those who recognized the structural inability of Congress to meet its own commitments, or to amend itself to do so. The chance of achieving constitutional reform, nationalists agreed, lay largely in the hands of Washington, whose unique prestige, either granted to or withheld from the Convention, would determine its success or its failure. Even with his personal involvement, it was, in Washington's words, "little short of a miracle, that the Delegates from so many different States . . . should unite in forming a system of national Government, so little liable to well founded objections."[13] Without his participation, the Philadelphia Convention would probably have had no more success than the Annapolis Convention eight months earlier, when only five states bothered to send delegates. And the key to bringing Washington out of retirement was an event that could excite in him the dread of an imminent collapse of all government. Shays' Rebellion was exactly that key.

Part One of this dissertation concerns the background, the or-

---

11. Robert Feer, "Shays's Rebellion and the Constitution: A Study in Causation," in *New England Quarterly* XLII No. 4 (1964), 410, 388. For his most comprehensive work, see Robert Feer, *Shays's Rebellion* (New York, 1988 [Harvard Ph.D. dissertation, 1958]).
12. Feer, "Shays's Rebellion . . .," NEQ, XLII (1969), 388.
13. Washington to Lafayette, 7 Feb., 1788, *Writings of Washington*, XXIX, 411.

igins, and the events of the Regulation itself. Part Two addresses the reactionary response to the commotions by the nationalists, especially Henry Knox, Stephen Higginson, and George Washington. Part Three demonstrates the impact of the Regulation upon the Philadelphia Convention, the formation of the Constitution, and its ratification with a Bill of Rights.

PART ONE
THE REGULATION

CHAPTER ONE

Popular Culture, Moral Economy, and the Ritual of Regulation: The Social and Ideological Origins of Shays' Rebellion

"I have heard some men say... that they dreaded an independence, fearing that it would produce civil wars."
— Tom Paine, *Common Sense*[1]

As the second half of the eighteenth century began, Massachusetts society was still a structured, hierarchical world clearly divided by class, in which every citizen's place could easily be ascertained: a man's status was assessed by the leisure he enjoyed, the education he had attained, and the clothing he wore. Compared to England, there were far fewer indolent paupers or wealthy noblemen; only a small minority of adult, white males were unfree, and fewer still owned virtual duchies like the estate of James Bowdoin. Within this truncated society, pews were carefully allocated, titles such as "Mister" or "Gentleman" were cautiously ascribed, and such luxuries as silver shoe-buckles were reserved to those whose status demanded a fashionable opulence.[2]

A variety of customs determined whether or not a citizen

---

1. Thomas Paine, *Common Sense* (New York, 1976 [orig. publ. Philadelphia, 1776]), 95.
2. See Gordon S. Wood, *The Radicalism of the American Revolution* (New York, 1992), 109. "A society like this," wrote Wood, "accentuated the difference between the few and the many, gentlefolk and commoners, and gave meaning to the age-old distinction between rulers and ruled." *Ibid.*, 73.

belonged to the lower classes or had been received into the gentry, where an intricate web of interests, duties, and patronage served to exclude all but the hardiest social climbers. It was not enough for a successful farmer to don a powdered wig and silk stockings if his knowledge of the classics was found wanting. An aristocratic bearing and a fine carriage could not earn him deference in the street if his conduct toward those above and below him did not conform to expectations. For while the class distinctions which set the gentry apart conferred many advantages, they also entailed significant social responsibilities. Noblesse oblige was no empty saw. Dependence was a reciprocal relationship, and those who rose above the laboring class were expected to institute their own paternalistic commitments before they were welcome among the established families and coteries. As Richard B. Morris put it, Massachusetts Bay was "the happy hunting ground for paternalistic controls over religion, morals, and usiness."[3] But with privilege came obligations, and only after they were met could any modicum of power be attained. Interlopers, especially commercial middlemen, who failed to rise to the occasion did not elevate their station or enhance their influence.

Gradually, the well-defined architecture of Massachusetts society began to erode, until the subtle gradations of social strata ceased to be meaningful. A variety of causes and events precipitated these social changes; foremost was the fact that the population itself was in flux. Society in Massachusetts, as in the other colonies, was being spread out toward the west. The eighteenth century brought a new wave of immigrants from Northern Ireland, Scotland, and North Britain, many of whom flowed directly past the coastal cities to unclaimed land in the west.[4] They were joined by residents from coastal re-

3. Richard B. Morris, *Government and Labor in Early America* (Boston, 1981), 55.

4. The town of Pelham, for example, where Daniel Shays lived, "was settled with people, chiefly from the North of Ireland. They were, of course, strict Presbyterians. They valued themselves much on being acquainted with the nice distinctions between orthodox and heterodox principles and practices. . . . A people generally possessing violent passions, which once disturbed, raged,

gions who had no particular affiliation to society in the east, and by 1780, new settlements in the counties west of Worcester outnumbered those in the east ten to one.[5] Thus a large part of the population there had little or no political affiliation with the Boston establishment.

In the west, at town meetings and taverns, churches and granaries, a fresh social consensus evolved. While not yet a distinct political culture, this western perspective bore little connection to the vertical and horizontal network of dependence and interest that stretched from Newburyport to Northampton, sustained and enhanced by royal prerogatives. This network provided a social trellis which, by its mutual observance, gave Massachusetts society its stability. While men of enormous wealth arose in the west — John Stoddard, Israel Williams, Joseph Hawley, and other river gods, who owned tens of thousands of acres — they gave little priority to the social nuances that stratified the east, even as they governed their civil courts with iron fists.[6] Though politically these great men generally adhered to the ruling hierarchy in Boston, their daily concerns better resembled those of the neighboring yeomen, with whom they formed separate networks of dependence and allegiance.

---

uncontrolled by the dictates of reason." Stephen Burroughs, *Memoirs of Stephen Burroughs* (Hanover, N. H., 1798 [Evans No. 33478]), 68.

5. For a close study of eighteenth-century emigration patterns from the British Isles to Massachusetts, see Bernard Bailyn, *Voyagers to the West* (New York, 1986), esp. Part IV, and David Hackett Fischer, *Albion's Seed: Four British Folkways in America* (New York, 1989), 605-673. For patterns of migration within Massachusetts, see Douglas Lamar Jones, *Village and Seaport: Migration and Society in Eighteenth-Century Massachusetts* (Hanover, N. H., 1981), 116.

6. Robert J. Taylor, *Western Massachusetts in the Revolution* (Providence, 1954), 11-24. Courts governed by the river-gods were "a monopoly of judicial placeholding 'in the form of a closed corporation;" ' John L. Brooke, "To the Quiet of the People: Revolutionary Settlements and Civil Unrest in Western Massachusetts, 1774-1789," *William and Mary Quarterly*, 3rd Ser., XLVI (July 1989), 436. See also Ronald K. Snell, "Ambitious of Honor and Places: The Magistracy of Hampshire County," in Bruce C. Daniels, ed., *Power and Status: Officeholding in Colonial America* (Middletown, CL, 1986), 17-36.

The social structure of Massachusetts buckled with the imperial crisis in 1764, when the plight shared by the colonial subjects came to outweigh the fine distinctions of class that separated them. A more egalitarian consensus blossomed, valuing the ardent patriot over the well-born gentleman. Taken together, the parliamentary taxes of the 1760s and 1770s were largely indiscriminate, impinging upon card-players, almanac-readers, rum-drinkers, and anyone who fancied sugar. And, with the Boston Massacre, it was a common cry that rose up across the colony. When the shared assumptions of monarchical society could no longer be sustained — when you could not be sure if your neighbor bore allegiance to the King — less fundamental differences in society were easily discounted.

As the Commonwealth coalesced for war, men of leisure became men of action and of commerce; and with the loss of leisure, their station in society was further eroded. "The gentry's distinctiveness," wrote Gordon S. Wood, "came from being independent in a world of dependencies, learned in a world only partially literate, and leisured in a world of laborers."[7] But the deepening crisis brought new interdependencies, as well as a shared political culture for all but the Loyalists. Long-standing networks of dependence lost their reliability, as the exigencies of war brought greater significance to local government.

The coalescence of patriots from all classes, and the new political culture they nurtured, led them to seek a common denominator. They found it in the popular ideology they shared. For beneath the contentious diversity of this dynamic, variegated, and stratified society lay a unifying rationale more powerful than its fragmented interests. This *mentalité*, inarticulate and unselfconscious, was composed of "deeply ingrained assumptions about politics," wrote Richard L. Bushman, "assumptions so old and so common that they were as

---

7. Wood, *op. cit.*, 34. Wood also observed that "no event in the eighteenth century accelerated the capitalistic development of America more than did the Revolutionary War." *Ibid.*, 248.

much feelings as ideas."[8] In fact they were both: to the extent that these assumptions were ideas that could be articulated, dissected, and discussed, they constituted what George Rudé called "the 'derived' element of popular ideology." To the extent that these assumptions were feelings, they made up what Rudd called "the 'inherent' element of popular ideology." Rudd's distinction is especially well-adapted for examining the social and ideological origins of Shays' Rebellion, and for fusing the social history of the post-Revolutionary era with its intellectual history.[9]

Both elements of popular political ideology in Massachusetts — ideas and feelings, political abstractions and home-grown truths — were bound up with the principles of republicanism, fervendy rehearsed in the 1770s, and every bit as germane to events in the 1780s. This colonial culture had brought a variety of folk traditions from across the British Isles, but they all descended from a single history, and much of their shared lore — both literate and unstudied — harked back to the only English antecedent for the elimination of monarchy: the Civil Wars of the 1640s and 1650s, and the

---

8. Richard L. Bushman, *King and People in Provincial Massachusetts* (Chapel Hill, 1985), 7.

9. Examining numerous riots and popular *actions* in eighteenth-century Europe, Rudd wrote, "But what of the motives that underlay them and the ideology — or *mentalité* — of those taking part . . .? Popular ideology is composed cf two elements of which the second, when occasion demands it, becomes superimposed on the first. The first, what I call the 'inherent' element, is the traditional body of ideas or attitudes arising within the experience or folk-memory cf the common-people; and the second, the 'derived' element, is that formed by the ideas borrowed from and transmitted by other groups, whether they are read in books, proclaimed from a pulpit or platform or village square, or passed on at street corners, in markets or in workshops: such ideas as . . . the Rights of Man and the Sovereignty of the People." George Rudd, *The Face of the Crowd: Studies in Revolution, Ideology and Popular Protest* (Atlantic Heights, NJ,, 1988), 1934. The distinction between these two 'elements' is hardly different from the contrast drawn by Herder two centuries earlier, between *Kultur des Volkes and Kultur der Gelehrten*; see J. G. Herder, *Ideen zur Philosophic der Geschichte*, 4 vols. (Riga/Leipzig, 1784-1791), esp. part 3. See also Peter Burke, *Popular Culture in Modern Europe* (New York, 1978), 8.

Commonwealth of Oliver Cromwell.[10]

The coastal communities were arguably more literate and communicative than western settlements, and so the element of popular ideology derived from political writings was more influential there. In the west, this literate ideology was secondary, superimposed upon what J. Winny called "the great hinterland of beliefs,"[11] But since both these elements were pertinent to Shays' Rebellion, they merit close examination.

The political tenets of more than a century of opposition to royal and ministerial absolutism informed the literate elements of this ideology. Popular sovereignty, the very ideology which had inspired Parliament in the 1640s, also drove the colonists to independence — and beyond that, to the anticipation of civil war in 1786. This language of revolution was enriched by an enduring vocabulary of parliamentary supremacy, with a grammar provided by opposition ideology. The writings of Lilbume, Harrington, Hobbes, Locke, Milton, Sidney, and Cato (Trenchard and Gordon) had all contributed to the evolving notion of popular sovereignty, and fostered a potent anti-ministerial sentiment that outlived the Revolution. As J. G. A. Pocock put it, drily: "The importance of the alternative ideology — the republican, commonwealth, or country tradition — is that it provided Americans with a radical but rather shallow explanation of why they could no longer be parliamentary Englishmen, and a rather profound understanding of what else they might become."[12]

---

10. Bushman observed that "The model for the American Revolution should have been the Glorious Revolution of 1688, the Revolution honored by all Britons, including colonials, as the culmination of their constitutional development. . . . Yet Americans . . . followed instead the bloody Puritan Revolution, when England had executed its king." Bushman, *op. cit.*, 5. For a comprehensive examination of the origins of folk traditions in Massachusetts, see Fischer, *op. cit.*, 13-207.

11. J. Winny, ed., *The Frame of Order* (London, 1957), 10.

12. J. G. A. Pocock, *Virtue, Commerce, and History* (Cambridge, 1985), 75. Pocock also observed that "This commonwealth or Country ideology . . . was on both sides of the Atlantic considerably better articulated than was the defense of existing practice, but in the American colonies it came to have an importance far greater than it ever possessed in Britain where it originated."

While these writings were more widely studied in the east, their tangible impact upon day-to-day political dialogue can be found throughout Massachusetts before, during, and after the imperial crisis. As early as 1754, for example, responding to a new excise tax, opponents framed their arguments in the language that Bolingbroke had used to Walpole for the same reason twenty years earlier. In 1772, the people of Hubbardston replied to the Boston's Committee of Correspondence in the political vernacular of popular sovereignty: "Rulers first Derive their Power from the Ruled by Certain Laws agreed upon by Ruler and Ruled. . . . The Ruled have a Right to Judge for themselves when Rulers Transgress." Altogether, more than 144 towns replied to the "Boston pamphlet." In a close analysis of those replies, Bushman found in them early evidence of "a network of political activists stretching from Boston to the remotest comers of the Province." While the writers were not usually dirt farmers in the western communities, key words like "tyranny" and "slavery" were on everyone's lips, and had been practiced for decades.[13]

Tyranny could take many forms, but the locus of oppres-

Ibid., 77

13. For the use of Bolingbroke, see Paul S. Boyer, "Borrowed Rhetoric: The Massachusetts Excise Controversy of 1754," in *William and Mary Quarterly,* 3rd. Sen, XXI (1964), 328-351. Bailyn wrote that "The arguments, the claims and counter-claims, the fears and apprehensions that fill the pamphlets, letters, newspapers, and state papers of the Revolutionary years had in fact been heard throughout the century." Bailyn, *Ideological Origins,* xi. The most thorough analysis of this ideological legacy remains Caroline Robbins, *The Eighteenth-Century Commonwealthmen: Studies in the Transmission, Development and Circumstance of English Liberal Thought from the Restoration of Charles II until the War with the Thirteen Colonies* (Cambridge, 1959). See also Pocock, *Virtue, Commerce, and History,* 77-88, and J. G. A. Pocock, "Machiavelli, Harrington, and English Political Ideologies in the Eighteenth Century," *William and Mary Quarterly,* 3rd. Sen, XXII (1965), 549-583. For the Hubbardston letter, and other examples of opposition language in western Massachusetts, see Richard L. Bushman, "Massachusetts Farmers and the Revolution," in *Society, Freedom, and Conscience: The American Revolution in Virginia, Massachusetts and New York,* Richard M. Jellison, ed. (New York, 1976), 77-84. "Tradition had created in the images of enslavement what amounted to a vernacular sociology," wrote Bushman, *ibid.,* 84.

sion was most often the court-house. In 1776, the town of Pittsfield appealed to the General Court for independent justices: "Since the suppression of [royal] government, we have lived in peace, love, safety, liberty and happiness. . . . We find ourselves in danger of . . . undergoing a yoke of oppression which we are no longer able to bear. . . ." Two years later the town of Lenox, in Berkshire, objected to property qualifications for voters of £60, whereby the proposed Massachusetts Constitution "declares Honest Poverty a Crime for which a large Number . . . who have fought and bled in their Countrys Cause are deprived of the above mentioned Rights (which is Tyranny). . . ." Even the motto in the ubiquitous seal of Massachusetts — *Ense petit placidam sub libertate* — came from Algernon Sidney, who had provided the colonials with "a textbook for revolution."[14]

The notion of political enslavement also preceded and outlasted the War of Independence, and was closely bound to popular feelings about what constituted fair representation; for, without the consent of the governed through legislative representation, enslavement was inevitable. The town of Athol, responding to the "Boston pamphlet," deplored English ministerial schemes for gain "at the expence of Enslaving a free and Loyal People." Bushman has noted that they were using the same language as the reply of Charles I to the Nine-

---

14. Letter from Pittsfield quoted in Taylor, *Western Massachusetts*, 89; "Return of Lenox," 20 May, 1788, in Robert J. Taylor, ed., *Massachusetts, Colony to Commonwealth: Documents on the Formation of Its Constitution, 1775-1780* (Chapel Hill, 1961), 59. See also Caroline Robbins, "Algernon Sidney's *Discourses Concerning Government: Textbook of Revolution,*" *William and Mary Quarterly*, 3rd. Ser., IV (1947), 267-296. For the Massachusetts seal (chosen at the Watertown Convention in 1775), see Chester N. Greenough, "Algernon Sidney and the Motto of the Commonwealth of Massachusetts," in *American Historical Association Proceedings LI* (1917 1918), 259-282. James Otis, Sr. had observed that he would have been accused of levelling and charged with sedition had he quoted from Sidney. James Otis, Sr., *A Vindication of the Conduct of the House of Representatives* (1762), 20, *University of Missouri Studies IV* (July 1929), 24n. "I can hardly consider the name of Algernon Sidney," wrote one historian, "as other than an American name — American in all its associations, and American in all its influences." R. C. Winthrop, quoted in Robbins, "Sidney's *Discourses,*" WMQ, 3rd. Ser., IV (1947), 296.

teen Propositions of 1642. Inadequate representation became "enslavement" whenever it was, in E. P. Thompson's words, "an outrage to . . . moral assumptions, quite as much as actual deprivation." The result was inevitably a political crisis.[15]

The crisis of representation which propelled Shays' Rebellion arose from the great disparity between expectation and reality in western Massachusetts, where citizens had long represented themselves in town meetings, deputizing and instructing advocates to vote on their behalf in the General Court. This sort of representation bore a much closer resemblance to Parliament in the seventeenth century than the eighteenth, leaning "toward the medieval forms of attorneyship in representation," rather than toward the concept which Edmund Burke expressed in 1774, of "a *deliberative* assembly of *one* nation, with *one* interest."[16] It was clearly the former that "Monitor" envisaged, writing in *The Massachusetts Spy* the same year, as he quoted Blackstone, the arch-Tory: "'The commons . . . consist of all such men of any property in the kingdom, as have not seats in the House of Lords; *every one* of which has a voice in parliament, either personally or by his representatives. . . . Here is the democracy or legal power of the people of Great Britain."[17] This was a restatement of the belief that, in Saxon times, the whole people had assembled together, and that Parliament was that same assembly in miniature: it also resembled what westerners had experienced in their annual town meetings each spring, still their model of government. Eventually western dissenters sought to move government closer to their own communities. In the

15. "Tradition had created in the images of enslavement what amounted to a vernacular sociology. . . ." Bushman, "Massachusetts Farmers . . .," *Society, Freedom, and Conscience*, 84. In the reply from the town of Athol, Bushman found the language of Charles I; *ibid.*, 84. See also the extensive evaluation of the notion of enslavement in Bushman, *King and People*, 176-210. Thompson, "The Moral Economy," *Past and Present* (1971), 77.
16. Bailyn, *Ideological Origins*, 164, 163.
17. "Monitor," *The Massachusetts Spy*, 18 Aug., 1774, in *American Political Writing during the Founding Era, 1760-1805*, Charles S. Hyneman and Donald S. Lutz, eds., 3 vols. (Indianapolis, 1983), 1, 278.

six months between August, 1786 and February, 1787, thir-
ty-three town and county petitions called for moving the state
capital out of Boston — a "country" concern, in every sense.[18]

"'All power corrupts' might have been a Country motto,"
wrote Pocock, effectively summing up the key Commonwealth writers — Harrington, Sidney, Trenchard and Gordon
— *and* the backcountry skepticism that had arisen in Massachusetts by 1786, when the cost of the war and the failure
of representation combined to produce protests verging upon
rebellion.[19] Similar mistrust of all legislative administration,
patronage, and placemen had always been central to the Real
Whigs' elective proposals. For James Harrington, the system
of representation through secret ballot laid out in *Oceana* — a
division of the republic into Saxon-like hundreds, with fre-
quent rotation of office — was tied to his notion of Agrarian
Law, whereby limitations could be placed upon wealth.[20]

With Harrington, the Agrarian Law was neither a symp-
tom nor a system of egalitarianism, as it was with Trenchard
and Gordon, whose reforms, proposed in *Cato's Letters* of the
1720s, must have seemed much more radical in the independent Commonwealth of Massachusetts than it did in the Province. "An Equality of Estate will give an Equality of Power;"
wrote Cato, "and an Equality of Power is a Commonwealth,
or Democracy. An *Agrarian* law, or something equivalent to
it, must make or find a suitable Disposition of Property; and
when that comes to be the case, there is no hindering a popular Form of Government."[21] While the writings of Harrington,

18. See Feer, *Shays's Rebellion*, Appendix B: Demands for Remedial Legislation, esp. 543-545.
19. Pocock, "Machiavelli, Harrington, and English Political Ideologies,"
WMQ, 3d. Ser., XXII (1965), 565.
20. For Harrington's complex ballot procedure, see "The Commonwealth of
Oceana," in *The Political Works of James Harrington*, J. G. A. Pocock, ed.
(Cambridge, 1977), esp 214-228, 241-250. See also "The Manner and Use of
the Ballot," *ibid.*, 362-367. The Agrarian is explained throughout *Oceana*.
21. John Trenchard and Thomas Gordon, Cato's Letters, 4 vols., 3rd. ed. (London, 1733 [orig. publ. 1721]), IV, 236, as quoted in Robbins, *Eighteenth-Century Commonwealthmen*, 125.

Sidney, and Trenchard and Gordon did not, wrote Robbins, "make those demands for social and economic equality which give to the Diggers and Winstanley considerable interest for a post-Marxian world," the language of Equality, Democracy, and Agrarian Law, which in the 1770s helped landowners to inspire a revolution, was a major cause for alarm a decade later.[22]

The impact of these political writings did not end with Independence. Many of Sidney's pronouncements — that no unjust law was legal, for example, and that parliamentary decisions should be referred back to the people — remained touchstones of post-Revolutionary political thought, as evidenced by the Massachusetts constitutional deliberations of 1778, 1780, and 1788.[23] At the time of Shays' Rebellion, Sidney was still remembered for his assertion that when a people rise up against unjust magistrates, it is not a rebellion at all.[24]

One of the principles of Sidney's *Discourses* most often recited in Massachusetts was his early opposition to the tyrannical threat of a Standing Army. Sidney was adopting the position put forth in *Oceana* by Harrington, who as early as 1656 had dared to challenge the New Model Army. For the next half century, this principle was universally defended by the Country party, though none was more insistent than John Trenchard, who had witnessed British garrisons while attending Trinity College, Dublin, in the 1680s, and whose tracts helped fuel the great confrontation over this issue between Parliament and William HIII, from 1697 to 1699.[25]

---

22. Robbins, "Algernon Sidney's *Discourses*," *WMQ*, 3rd. Ser., IV (1947), 272.

23. *Ibid.*, 280.

24. "If the laws of God and Men are therefore of no effect, when the Magistracy is left at liberty to break them . . . those Seditions, Tumults and Wars are justified by the Laws of God and Man." Quoted in Robbins, "Sidney's *Discourses*," *WMQ*, 3rd Ser., IV (1947), 292.

25. John Trenchard and Walter Moyle, "An Argument Shewing, That a Standing Army is inconsistent with a Free Government, and absolutely destructive to the Constitution of the English Monarchy," in *A Collection of State Tracts, published during the Reign of King William III . . .*, 2 vols. (London, 1706 [orig. publ. 1697]), II, 564-584. See also [John Somers] "A Letter, ballancing

The citizen's lot was enslavement, argued Trenchard, "whilst a Standing Army must be kept up to prey upon our Entrails, and which must in the hands of an ill Prince . . . infallibly destroy our Constitution From the day you set them up, you set up your Masters. . . . It is the Conquest of the Nation in the silentest, shortest, and surest way."[26] In 1786, when Governor James Bowdoin and General Henry Knox raised troops to defeat peaceful protesters, this warning rang just as true as it had in the 1770s.[27]

This apprehension was widespread and profound. The Articles of Confederation specified that no "vessels of war shall be kept up in time of peace by any state . . . nor shall any body of forces be kept up in any state, in time of peace. . . ."[28] While limited provisions were made for militias and the maintenance of forts, the Articles nonetheless incorporated the antimilitarist ideology of the Real Whigs, who defended the right of a people to rise up against their own government. As long as the Articles were the basis of American govern-

---

the Necessity of keeping a Land-Force in times of Peace, with the dangers that may follow on it," ibid.,585-589; "A Letter from the Author of the Argument against a Standing Army, to the Author of the Ballancing Letter," ibid., 590-594; "A Short History of Standing Armies in England," *ibid.*, 656-677. "For Trenchard and his friends," wrote Lois Schwoerer, "the issue was a political one. . .. [They] argued that an army would alter the separation and balance which they saw among the parts of government. . . ." Lois G. Schwoerer, *"No Standing Armies!": The Antimilitary Ideology in Seventeenth Century England* (Baltimore, 1974), 180.

26. Trenchard, "An Argument Shewing . . .," in *A Collection of State Tracts*, II, 567, 581.

27. In early 1776, Samuel Adams restated Trenchard's argument wholecloth, declaring "A Standing Army, however necessary it may be at some times, is always dangerous to the Liberties of the People. Soldiers are apt to consider themselves as a Body distinct from the rest of the Citizens....They soon become attached to their officers and disposed to yield implicit obedience to their Commands. Such a Power should be watched with a jealous Eye." 27. Samuel Adams to Joseph Warren, 7 Jan., 1776, Warren-Adams Letters.. ., *Massachusetts Historical Society Collections*, LXXII-LXXIII, 2 vols.(Boston, 1917-1925),1, 197-198.

28. "The Articles of Confederation," Article VI, 4, Henry Steele Commager, ed., *Documents of American History*, 2 vols. (Englewood Cliffs, N.J.,1972),I, 112.

ment, the Continental Congress was constitutionally unable to protect its arsenal at Springfield from insurrection — much less provide Knox with the permanent military establishment he so badly wanted.

After the Boston Massacre, wrote John Adams, "Cato's Letters ... and all the writings of Trenchard and Gordon, Mrs. Macauley's *History*, Burgh's *Political Disquisitions*, Clarendon's *History of the Civil War*, and all the writings relevant to the revolutions of England became fashionable reading."[29] Then, with the end of the War, there was no more doubt: a new age had begun, an era that repudiated the key symbols of almost every known government for a thousand years. Every European history that Americans had read and every folktale they had heard contained the same archetypes: but now the world that they had made for themselves was something new, bereft of king, queen, prince, prime minister, parliament, archbishop, duke, baron, and earl; the very words had been swept from their daily vocabulary. This new world they were inventing was not only unprecedented, it was also unfamiliar. Events could no longer be perceived in customary contexts, and so traditional covenants of trust in authority did not hold.

In the absence of other familiar landmarks in society, what remained were the ideologies that had crystallized before and during the War. But while new political priorities in the east called for the maintenance of an authoritative government, the political landscape in the backcountry had changed less since the 1770s. And whereas a standing army and a hereditary aristocracy were anathema throughout Massachusetts, only in the west was adequate representation still a concern under the

---

29. John Adams to Jedediah Morse, 15 Jan., 1816, Charles Francis Adams, ed., *Works of John Adams*, 10 vols. (Boston, 1850-1856), X, 202-203. To Americans, wrote Pocock, the republican ideology expressed in that literature "came to have an importance far greater than it ever possessed in Britain where it originated." Pocock, *Virtue, Commerce, and History*, 77. This same ideology continued to express itself in Shays' Rebellion, and the perception that it represented the beginning of civil war.

Constitution of 1780, where the spirit of radical Whiggism remained a widespread presumption.[30]

These and most other elements of political ideology derived directly from events in England a hundred and fifty years earlier — on both ends of the political spectrum. Since the Puritan Revolution was the only precedent for the disposal of monarchy, the horrifying implication was that the continental government might represent nothing more than an American interregnum. Although few expected that George III would be supplanted swiftly, the notion of a military dictatorship followed by an American king lurked in the shadows of the political culture.[31]

Indeed, the implications of history did not bode well for republican liberties. Ominously, most of the ideologues who had inspired the Revolution had also expressed their belief in historical inevitability. Even John Trenchard seemed to concur with Giambattista Vico, his contemporary, in this conviction. "Let us flatter our selves as much as we please," he wrote in one of his best known tracts, "what happen'd yesterday will come to pass again, and the same Causes will produce like Effects in all Ages."[32] This belief in the cyclical nature of history was weli expressed by the Philosophe Charles Pinot Duclos. "The theatre of the world supplies only a certain number of scenes, which are perpetually coming over again in one constant train of succession. . . . Things past should instruct us in relation to things to come, the knowledge of history is no

---

30. Perhaps because the town meeting was more central to western politics, a democratic disposition was quicker to emerge there, out of the Whig tradition. "New democrat is but old Whig writ large . . .," wrote Pocock, in *Virtue, Commerce, and History*, 88.

31. When, in the "Proclamation of Rebellion," authored by Samuel Adams, Bowdoin accused the insurgents of plotting to "form their adherents into regular military companies properly officered to thereby establish in this Commonwealth a standing force . . .," he was evincing the memory, not of British troops quartered in Boston, but of Cromwell's rebellious New Model Army. *JCC*, XXXII, 104.

32. John Trenchard, "An Argument shewing . . .," in *A Collection of State Tracts*, II, 566.

other than an anticipated experience."[33]

If history were to repeat itself, then the American Revolution would be followed by years of civil war between the officers of a Standing Army that refused to disband, like Lilbume and the Levellers, and troops recruited by an unrepresentative General Court, like Parliament. The Senate, representing property, would be abolished, thus ending the mixed government to which, Corinne C. Weston wrote, "English thinkers attributed the peculiar excellence of their government."[34]

If "what happen'd yesterday will come to pass again," then some malcontents could be expected to go beyond the Levellers and, like Winstanley and the Diggers, call for agrarian laws to redivide all real property.[35] The Levellers, according to Christopher Hill, "sharply differentiated themselves from the Diggers who advocated a communist programme and began communal cultivation."[36] Winstanley's "communism was an effort to envisage a different kind of social system," wrote George H. Sabine. "His argument is that the common land is

33. Charles Pinot Duclos, *The History of Lewis XI, King of France* . . . 2 vols. (London, 1746), I, xi-x. Following the Great Awakening, wrote Stow Persons, "the new view of history which came into vogue among conservative thinkers . . . found the source of historical dynamics in the operation of the universal moral law, the effect of which upon history was an endless cyclical movement analagous to the life cycle of the individual organism." Stow Persons, "The Cyclical Theory of History in Eighteenth-Century America," *American Quarterly* VI (1954), 152. See also Rutherford E. Deimage, "The American Idea of Progress, 1750-1800," in *Proceedings of the American Philosophical Society*, XCI (Philadelphia, 1947), 307-314.
34. Corinne Comstock Weston, *English Constitutional Theory and the House of Lords, 1556-1832* (New York, 1965), 1.
35. "The Levellers . . . ." wrote George H. Sabine, "were in principle democrats." George H. Sabine, ed., *The Works of Gerrard Winstanley: With an Appendix of Documents relating to the Digger Movement* (New York, 1965), 53. See also Lewis H. Berens, *The Digger Movement in the Days of the Commonwealth: As Revealed in the Writings of Gerrard Winstanley* (London, 1961 [orig. publ. 1906]).
36. Christopher Hill, *The Century of Revolution, 1603-1714* (New York and London, 1980), 111; see also Christopher Hill, *Puritanism and Revolution: Studies in Interpretation of the English Revolution of the 17th Century* (New York, 1986), esp. 154-193, 267-302; and Richard Ollard, *This War Without An Enemy: A History of the English Civil Wars* (London, 1976), 204.

commonly owned."[37] In *The Law of Freedom*, addressed to Cromwell in 1651, Winstanley had proclaimed the people's right to divide and share the Royalists' property by Agrarian Law: "So that whatever is recovered by a joynt consent of the Commoners: therefore it is all equity. That all the Commoners who assisted you: should be set free from the Conqueror's power with you; as David's Law was: *The spoyl shall be divided between them who went to war, and them who stayd at home.*"[38]

Ultimately, it was thought, such excessive democracy would lead inexorably back to monarchy. This might be forestalled for a period of years: after all, Cromwell had defeated Charles II at Worcester. The government might sustain itself for a time, as the Long Parliament had done, by selling its land to the highest bidder; in fact, Congress sold off a million acres to General Rufus Putnam and his Ohio Company.[39] Still, Cromwell's Interregnum, the only precedent for the American Revolution, had ended in monarchy after a decade, a fact of haunting significance ten years after the Declaration of Independence. If the laws of nature were "uniform and invari-

---

37. Sabine, ed., *Winstanley*, 53. For a thorough study of Winstanley's ideology compared to that of the Levellers, as well as its relation back to Thomas More's humanistic communism and forward to the dialectic of Marx and Engeis, see T. Wilson Hayes, *Winstanley the Digger: A Literary Analysis of Radical Ideas in the English Revolution* (Cambridge, Mass., 1979), esp. 2, 124, 189-190, 199.

38. Gerrard Winstanley, *The Law of Freedomin a Platform: Or, True Magistracy Restored* (London, 1651 [British Museum, P. M., E. 655]), 4. [Winstanley's italics.] See also Gerrard Winstanley et al., *The True Levellers Standard Advanced: Or The State of Community opened, and Presented to the Sons of Men* (London, 1649 [British Museum, P. M., E. 552(5)]). In his pivotal letter to Washington about Shaysite rebels on October 28, 1786, Knox was explicitly evoking the Diggers' threatening ideology. "Their creed is, 'That the property of the United States has been protected from confiscation of Britain by the joint exertions of all, and therefore ought to be the common property of all. and he that attempts opposition to this creed is an enemy to equity and justice, and ought to be swept from off the face of the earth. . . .' In a word, they are determined to annihilate all debts, public and private, and have agrarian Laws. . . ." For the full letter, see Appendix B.

39. Putnam was Daniel Shays commander during the war, and his adversary during the Regulation; see Chapter Three below.

able," as Otis believed, then historical inevitability dictated that the Commonwealth would end with military dictatorship, followed by the restoration of monarchy about ten years after its elimination, i.e., sometime around 1786.[40]

It may be easy to exaggerate the parallels between England under the Protectorate and America under the Articles; nonetheless, a great historical resonance echoed forward from the former to the latter, since so many of the issues that arose when Charles I was disposed of naturally reappeared when George HI lost his authority over America. Thanks partly to the constant efforts of Thomas Hollis to supply the complete Whig canon, the libraries of Massachusetts were filled with arguments derived from numerous sources against a Standing Army, or so-called Peace Establishment — even as Shays' Rebellion appeared to confront the Continental Congress with an urgent need for exactly that.[41]

The inherent elements of popular political ideology played a much larger role in western Massachusetts than the element derived from literature. This latent ideology was an inchoate, secular system of beliefs that stemmed from principles so fundamental to Protestant republicanism that neither the Congregational merchant nor the Baptist yeoman could dispute them: popular sovereignty, the sanctity of private property, and the supremacy of the law.[42] These principles had

---

40. James Otis, as quoted in Bailyn, *Ideological Origins*, 85. In 1784, Samuel Adams, the firebrand of '76 who became a fierce opponent of western protest, wrote that "the Commonwealth of England lasted twelve years and then the exiled King was restored with all the Rage and Madness of Royalty! — A Caution to the Citizens of the United States zealously to counteract the Hopes our Enemies entertain. . . Samuel Adams to Richard Henry Lee, 23 Dec., 1784, *The Writings of Samuel Adams*, Harry A. Cushing, ed., 4 vols.(New York, 1904-1908), IV, 312.

41. See Caroline Robbins, "The Strenuous Whig, Thomas Hollis of Lincoln's Inn," *William and Mary Quarterly*, 3rd Ser., VII (1950), 406453; see also Schwoerer, "No Standing Armies!", 195-199, and H. Trevor Colboum, *The Lamp of Experience: Whig History and the Intellectual Origins of the American Revolution* (Chapel Hill, N.C., 1965), 200-232.

42. Edward S. Morgan, *Inventing the People: The Rise of Popular Sovereignty in England and America* (New York, 1988) offers a comprehensive overview

evolved inexorably from Martin Luther's enshrinement of the individual conscience.[43] In eighteenth-century America, the Great Awakening went far to promulgate the precepts of individualism. At the core of Massachusetts' popular ideology was the conviction that every man was king of his castle, as well as his own priest, and thus all must be governed, taxed, and tithed by their own consent.

Just how traditions of English plebeian culture were transmitted to America has been examined by Alfred F. Young, who saw other processes at work beyond straightforward importation, retention, and usage: one is "a kind of holding pattern process in which customs and traditions migrate, are 'stored,' and not put into practice until they are functional."[44] Young demonstrated this process with the enduring figure of Cromwell in Revolutionary Massachusetts, which showed the ambivalence that colonial culture had sustained toward the trauma of regicide. As late as Cotton Mather's time, the Puritans admired Cromwell, but with the Radical Whigs' growing suspicion of standing armies, some influential figures of eighteenth-century society came to revile the Protector, even while others, including James Otis, bore Cromwell a sneaking admiration. Just months before Shays' Rebellion erupted, John Adams visited Worcester in England, and declared

---

of how these principles evolved, beginning with the English Civil Wars.

43. "Whatever your heart clings to and confides in, that is really your God." Martin Luther, "The First Commandment," *The Large Catechism*, Part I. A vigorous example of this inherent belief appears in "The Key of Libberty," by William Manning, who argued that man "has implanted in him a sence of Right & Rong, so that if he would always follow the dictates of Contiance & consider the advantages of Society & mutual assistance he would need no other Law or Government" See William Manning, *The Key of Libberty. Shewing the Causes why a free government has always Failed, and a Remidy against it. Adresed to the Republicans, Farmers, Mecanicks, & Labourers in the United States of America by a Labourer. Finished February the 20th, 1798*, reprinted in Samuel E. Morison, "*William Manning's The Key of Libberty*," *William and Mary Quarterly*, 3rd Ser., XIII (Jan. 1956), 214.

44. Alfred F. Young, "English Plebeian Culture and Eighteenth-Century American Radicalism," in *The Origins of Anglo-American Radicalism*, Margaret Jacob and James Jacob, eds. (London, 1984), 185-212; quotation on 189.

Cromwell's battlefield "holy ground."[45] Still, most British and Loyalists alike meant to insult the colonists by describing them as "the descendants of Oliver Cromwell, who truly inherited the spirit which was the occasion of so much bloodshed. . . ."[46]

Throughout New England generally, "Cromwell survived in a folk tradition devoid of the negative features. . . . People referred to him as Oliver . . . and . . . named their children after him."[47] Cromwell, Connecticut testifies to the belief that Cromwell had meant to settle near Saybrook; just after the Stamp Act, some New Light churches in that state, mocking the loyal Anglicans, read together outloud the prayer: "We beseech thee, O Cromwell . . ., deliver us." By the 1770s, the pseudonym of 'Joyce, Jun.,' a reference to one of Charles I executioners, began appearing frequently, even in Boston.[48]

The most explosive assumption embedded in popular ideology was the emerging notion of equality as proclaimed in the Declaration of Independence, and codified in the Massachusetts Constitution: "All men are born free and equal, and have certain natural, essential and inalienable rights." Wood noted that such egalitarianism "was perhaps latent in republican thought;" it was also implied in the contractual agreement between the ruler and the ruled that Hubbardston had asserted. From the pulpit, ministers insisted in sermons (often reprinted in the press) that rulers were "of the same species . . . and by nature equal" with their "fellow-men."[49] In the

---

45. John Adams, 4 and 10 Apr., 1786, *The Diary of John Adams*, in, 185.

46. Letter from a surgeon of one of His Majesty's ships at Boston, 26 May, 1775, in Henry Steele Commager and Richard B. Morris, eds., *The Spirit of 976: The Story of the American Revolution as told by its Participants* (New York, 1958), 152-153.

47. Young, "English Plebeian Culture," 195, 197.

48. Ibid.,195, 197, 198-199. For more on the memory of Cromwell, see Peter Shaw, *American Patriots and the Ritual of Revolution* (Cambridge, Mass., 1981), 178, 189-195.

49. Article I, Constitution of 1780, in Taylor, ed., *Massachusetts Documents*, 128. "Equality became so potent for Americans because it came to mean that everyone was really the same as everyone else, not just at birth, not in talent or property or wealth, and not just in some transcendental religious sense of

early 1780s, this potent doctrine was most often expressed in anti-aristocratic rhetoric against the Society of the Cincinnati and in petitions calling for the dissolution of the Massachusetts Senate.[50]

The crisis of representation that caused Shays' Rebellion was precipitated by the post-war depression. This was true not only at the state level, but also at the Continental level, where the vacuum of authority after Washington's "oath of retirement" could hardly be filled by Congress, which for eight years had repeatedly broken faith with the soldiery; or by Knox, the subsequent commander of the Continental Army, whose mandate was to dismantle the American forces. Washington's absence was sorely felt throughout the civilian population, but all the more so, naturally, among the Revolutionary soldiers, for whom Washington had served as a powerful advocate before Congress; indeed, with his retirement, the veterans lost their most impassioned representative in the Continental government.[51] In fact they had no other: all

the equality of all souls. Ordinary Americans came to believe that no one in a basic down-to-earth and day-in-and-day-out manner was really better than anyone else. That was equality as no other nation has ever quite had it" Wood, *op. cit.*, 234. This equality is very different from Locke's, who wrote that "Age or Virtue may give Men a just Precedency: *Excellency of Parts and Merit* may place others above the Common Level: *Birth* may subject some, and *Alliance* or *Benefits* others, to pay an Observance to those to whom Nature, Gratitude or other Respects may have made it due; and yet all this consists with the *Equality*, which all Men are in, in respect of Jurisdiction or Dominion one over another. . . ." John Locke, *Two Treatises of Government*, ed. Peter Laslett (Cambridge, 1960), Section 54. For Hubbardston letter, see above, 16. Samuel Cooke, "A Sermon Preached at Cambridge in the Audience of His Honor Thomas Hutchinson, Esq . .," (Boston, 1770), in John W. Thornton, ed., *The Pulpit of the American Revolution: Or, the Political Sermons of the Period of 1776* (Boston, 1860), 162, 163.

50. For a study of later anti-aristocratic feeling in the west, see Saul Cornell, "Aristocracy Assailed: The Ideology of Backcountry Anti-Federalism," in *Journal of American History LXXVI* (1990), esp. 1162. For the Cincinnati, see below, 41, 45-48.

51. For Washington's role as a national archetype during the Revolution and beyond, see Barry Schwartz, *George Washington: The Making of an American Symbol* (New York, 1987). See also below, Chapter Six.

eighteen Massachusetts delegates to Congress between 1780 and 1785 were from, or allied to, the commercial-cosmopolitan towns.[52] These were the veterans who gave Shays' Rebellion its paramilitary character, distinguishing it from all other agrarian protests. From their "Form of Enlistment" to their sprig of hemlock, the rebels affected a regimental, revolutionary appearance — until the first cannon was fired in their direction.[53] In the absence of any effective, established representation, the dissidents were determined to represent their own interests, in quasi-military array.

"The rising of 1786," wrote J. R. Pole, "demonstrated with cruel violence that something had gone wrong with the very institutions of representation which the people of the Bay Colony had fought to defend and had agreed, by conference, to maintain."[54] Pole chronicled thoroughly a decade of evidence that "something had gone wrong" with systems of political representation, as he traced western discontent back to the Act of 1776 whereby representation in the House was shifted from equality between towns to population ratios, and "the number of members . . . rose from 201 to 226, the increase from the seaboard being enough to account for the whole difference."[55] The deterioration of western representation continued in 1778, after the rejection of the draft constitution, with the notion introduced by *The Essex Result* that the House was to represent persons, and the Senate to represent property — a concept which was then embodied in the Constitution of 1780.[56]

---

52. Van Beck Hall, *Politics without Parties: Massachusetts, 1780-1791* (Pittsburgh, 1972), 144.

53. The Regulators' "Form of Enlistment," committing the prospective rebel to three months' service in "Col. Hazleton's Regiment of Regulators, in order for the surpressing of tyrannical government in the Massachusetts State," 189 M.A., 429; see below, 74 n.22.

54. J. R. Pole, *Political Representation in England and the Origins of the American Republic* (New York, 1966), 227.

55 *Ibid.*, 175.

56. *Ibid.*, 189. [Theophilus Parsons], "The Essex Result," Taylor, ed., *Massachusetts Documents*, 73-89. "The House of Representatives is intended as the Representative of the Persons, and the Senate, of the property of the Common Wealth;" from "An Address of the Constitutional Convention, to their Constit-

With the passage of this new Constitution, despite some concessions to democratic principles, the west suffered a variety of setbacks in political representation. For example, although property qualifications were suspended for the selection of delegates to draft the Constitution, placing the Convention "on a wider basis of representation than the government [thereby] established," the Convention was allowed to determine its own method of ratification, which lead to a powerful sense in the west that the new frame of government was foisted upon them — as indeed appears to have been the case.[57]

"In a sense," wrote Pole, "the whole problem of the Constitution was the problem of representation."[58] To the yeomen, the whittling away of their representation under the new Constitution seemed the perfect demonstration of eastern chicanery. Senate seats, for example, "were to be distributed among the county districts, not on the basis of population, but of public taxes paid in the county," thereby assuring the Senate's bias in favor of eastern property.[59] At the same time came the exclusion of towns with less than 150 rateable polls, which meant that towns of approximately 600 residents or less were completely disenfranchised. By its demand that voters possess £3 worth of personalty in rare Massachusetts silver, the Constitution effectively raised the property qualification by 12.5 per cent.[60]

---

uents, 1780," introducing the Constitution of 1780, *ibid.*, 125.

57. Pole, *op. cit.*, 191. In a close examination of the hurried and skewed ratification procedure that fostered significant western distrust, Morison determined that "it is hard not to come to the conclusion that there was not a two-thirds majority for at least two articles of the constitution, and that the Convention deliberately juggled the returns in order to make it appear that there was." Samuel Eliot Morison, "The Struggle over the Adoption of the Constitution of Massachusetts, 1780," *American Historical Association Proceedings L* (Boston, 1917), 353-411.

58. Pole, *op. cit.*, 192.

59. *Ibid.*, 194.

60. *Ibid.*, 209. Taylor estimated the increase in property qualification under the charter at 17%; Taylor, *Western Massachusetts*, 142-143.

Although the west had always benefited theoretically from equal representation of towns in the General Court, in reality the smaller towns had often been unable to afford the cost of representation; according to figures cited in 1755 by William Douglass, between 33 and 40 percent of towns in Hampshire between 1728 and 1748 failed to send members to the General Court.[61] This is not surprising, since in 1748 each town that sent a representative was assessed in the province tax the 30s. per day paid out by the General Court, plus 30s. per twenty miles traveled. So the cost for each representative from Pittsfield, for example, was about £135 for a two-month session — and in winter the representative might be out of pocket for extra travel-time. Until the 1760s, the concerns of the province were rarely that important to the towns, except to the wealthier and more conservative inhabitants, especially the river gods. Since they alone could afford the time and cost of elective office, they monopolized local and provincial representation in their regions throughout much of the eighteenth century. Israel Williams, for example, was a selectman for Hatfield from 1732 to 1763, and throughout about half those years he also served as representative in the General Court.[62]

"What troubled westerners most," wrote Robert J. Taylor, "was that their votes were not doing them any good. . . . Towns might instruct their representatives, but if they abided by their instructions the resulting bills would not get by the Senate."[63] While the west did not yet represent a political interest group and, because of its commercial-cosmopolitan centers, did not vote as a uniform bloc, it was gradually becoming clear that

---

61. William Douglass, *A Summary, Historical and Political, of the First Planting, Progressive Imrovements, and Present State of the British Settlements in North America*, 2 vols. (Boston, 1755), 1, 515, 535, as quoted in Taylor, *Western Massachusetts*, 34.

62. From 1760 through 1766 Williams was also a member of the Governor's Council; Taylor, *Western Massachusetts*, 14. Williams held other offices as well, including Chief Justice of the Inferior Court of Common Pleas, and Judge of Probate for Hampshire County; Ellen E. Brennan, *Plural Office-Holding in Massachusetts, 1760-1780: Its Relation to the "Separation" of Departments of Government* (Chapel Hill, 1945), 35.

63. Taylor, *Western Massachusetts*, 143.

some political coherence would be necessary to counter sophisticated, eastern chicanery and arrive at fair representation. To the western eye, such machinations may have seemed all the worse because of the unabashed defense they were given in the "Address" accompanying the Constitution, signed only by James Bowdoin, the President of the Constitutional Convention - a fact which may have contributed to the western hostility he experienced six years later as Governor. The "Address" declared frankly its intention to exclude those "who are but just entering into a business, or whose Idleness of Life and profligacy of manners will forever bar them from acquiring and possessing Property . . . who will pay less regard to the Rights of Property because they have nothing to lose."[64] "The return of Worcester . . . gives the deliberate voice of western Massachusetts on this question of representation," wrote Samuel Eliot Morison, about the response to the new draft Constitution. "Failure of the Convention to heed their demands was one cause of Shays' Rebellion,"[65] In 1786, "no taxation without representation" was an inherent element of the popular ideology, as it had been twenty years earlier.

Pole's convincing analysis of republican disillusionment does not preclude other interpretations of the broader situation in the west, based upon the dimming traditions of patronage: the paternalistic responsibility of the governing class to the governed, based upon a code of honor.[66] It is entirely compatible, for example, with Alan Taylor's thesis that throughout the revolutionary and post-revolutionary years there had been a progressive failure of the protection covenant, whereby "the yeomanry expected political leadership . . . from gentlemean

---

64. "An Address of the Constitutional Convention," Taylor, ed., *Massachusetts, Colony to Commonwealth*, 125.

65. Morison, "Struggle over the . . . Constitution," *AHA Proceedings* (1917), 388.

66. Wood wrote that "Honor made sense only in an unequal society Honor was exclusive, heroic, and elitist, and it presumed a world very different from the world that was emerging and from our own, a hierarchical world in which a few could unabashedly claim a moral superiority over the rest" Wood, *op. cit.*, 40.

with the requisite social standing, wealth, education, and external contacts to successfully conduct county, state, and national governance."[67] Looking back at the failures of this neo-feudal representation in the monarchical political culture, Bushman wrote that "enough incidents occurred to demonstrate the capacity of ordinary people to take the law into their own hands. They readily suspended allegiance when they believed their rulers were failing in their obligations. Riots usually struck at something or someone other than government, but . . . the crowd's anger usually in time enveloped rulers."[68] According to this contractual interpretation, "the ambiguity in the protection covenant justified both the stifling of dissent and shameless resistance." Beginning in 1764, Parliamentary taxation effectively junked the colonial assemblies; "politics," wrote Bushman, "therefore moved into the streets."[69]

Such "politics out of doors" evolved naturally from another inherent element of traditional, popular ideology: moral economy, or collective action as a method of political and economic regulation.[70] In a hierarchical society dominated by

67. Alan Taylor, "Regulators and White Indians: Forms of Agrarian Resistance in Post-Revolutionary New England," in Robert A. Gross and Frederick Allis, eds., *In Debt to Shays: The Legacy of an Agrarian Rebellion* (forthcoming), n.p. I am grateful to Prof. Gross for sharing this manuscript with me prior to publication. For more on the protection covenant, see Bushman, *King and People*, 37.

68. Bushman, *King and People*, 43-44.

69. Bushman, *King and People*, 37, 182. See also the extensive evaluation of the notion of enslavement in ibid., 176-210.

70. E. P. Thompson offered the clearest definition of moral economy in his pioneering essay on the subject. "These grievances [against excessive prices] operated within a popular consensus as to what were legitimate and what were illegitimate practices in marketing, milling, baking, etc. This in its turn was grounded upon a consistent traditional view of social norms and obligations, of the proper economic functions of several parties within the community, which, taken together, can be said to constitute the moral economy of the poor. An outrage to these moral assumptions, quite as much as actual deprivation, was the usual occasion for direct action." Thompson, "The Moral Economy," *Past and Present* (1971), 77 [my italics]. See also Eric Hobsbawm, *Primitive Rebels* (New York, 1959), 10. In recent years, several American historians have applied the analytic tools of contemporary British social historians, notably Eric Foner, *Tom Paine and Revolutionary America* (New York, 1976), 145-182;

paternalism, dependence, and subordination, the political and economic relationship between "those that Labour for a Living & those that git a Living without Bodily Labour . . .," in William Manning's words, was governed by the protection convenant.[71] In England, Thompson wrote, "the paternalist model existed in an eroded body of Statute law, as well as common law and custom. It was the model which, very often, informed the actions of Government in times of emergency until the 1770s."[72] During economic crises, if the patrician class failed to honor the plebians' subordination with the expected "corresponding return," by lowering prices, the people would take to the streets. Their purpose, however, was not to challenge traditional values, but to uphold them. "Often," wrote Wood, "the crowds acted to support traditional customs and moral relationships against changes brought on by new impersonal market conditions, maintaining by force, for example, customary prices and the traditional ways of distributing goods against the perceived forestalling and gouging practiced by unscrupulous shopkeepers and middlemen. . . . [Thus they] made their power felt temporarily in a political system that was otherwise largely immune to their influence. . . ."[73]

Collective action as a means of price regulation, usually against profiteering "engrossers and forestalled," was a common feature of eighteenth-century Anglo-American society, just as it was a means of wage regulation and political expression.[74] Throughout the Revolution, such scenes of "taxation

Ruth Bogin, "Petitioning and the New Moral Economy of Post-Revolutionary America," *William and Mary Quarterly*, 3rd Ser., XLV, No. 3 (1988), 391425; and John L. Brooke, "A Deacon's Orthodoxy; Religion, Class, and the Moral Economy of Shays's Rebellion," in Gross and Allis, eds., *In Debt to Shays* (forthcoming).

71. William Manning cited this distinction first among "the Causes that ruen Republicks. . . ." Morison, "Manning's *Key of Libberty*," *WMQ*, 3rd. Ser., XIII (1956), 212.

72. Thompson, *op. cit.*, 83.

73. Wood, *op. cit.*, 90.

74. See Ruth Bogin, "Petitioning and the New Moral Economy," *WMQ*, 3rd Ser., XLV (1988), 391425, and John L. Brooke, "A Deacon's Orthodoxy,"

populaire" were common, particularly in New England, wrote Eric Foner, "with its tradition of corporate Puritan wealth."[75] A striking example of this kind of regulation took place in 1776 near Springfiel, later in the central arena of Shay's Rebellion. Because of the issue involved — moral economy, extra-legal regulation by crowds, fair practice, and paper money — the case of merchant Samuel Colton offers a telling precedent of the popular ideology that informed the Shaysite Regulation a decade later.[76]

In Longmeadow, Massachusetts, at the time of the Declaration of Independence, crowds had repeatedly gathered to express their support for Congress's Continental Association, and their outrage at certain local merchants who refused to accept the paper money newly issued by Congress.By demanding hard money instead of the depreciating paper, these merchants, the crowds insisted, were effectively raising the price of certain goods imported from the West Indies. On July 11, 1776, one such crowd delivered a note to the firm of Jonathan and Hezekiah Hale, declaring that "we find you guilty of wrong behaviour in selling at extravagant prices. . . . This conduct plainly tends to undervalue paper Currency which is very detrimental to the Liberties of America."[77] Within an hour, the Hales capitulated.

Gross and Allis, eds., *In Debt to Shays*, n.p. For an examination of price controls during the Revolution, see Barbara Clark Smith, "The Politics of Price Control in Revolutionary Massachusetts" (Yale Ph.D. dissertation, 1983). For a thorough study of early collective action to regulate wages, see Morris's chapter on "Concerted Action among Workers," *Government and Labor in Early America*, 136-207. For the political impact of pre-Revolutionary crowds, see Pauline Maier, *From Resistance to Revolution: Colonial Radicals and the Development of American Opposition to Britain*, 1765-1776 (New York, 1972), esp. 3-42.

75. "Massachusetts was the scene not only of 'well-nigh universal' demands by urbanites for control of food prices, but of direct actions against merchants. . . ." Foner, *op. cit.*, 151.

76. I owe this account of Samuel Colton's ordeal to Barbara Clark Smith, *After the Revolution: The Smithsonian History of Everday Life in the Eighteenth Century* (New York, 1985).

77. From the Diary of Rev. Stephen Williams, 11 July, 1776, bk. 9, 117, quoted in Smith, *After the Revolution*, 35.

However, Samuel Colton, another merchant who had received the same ultimatum, did not. "Like most 'River Gods' in the valley," wrote Barbara Clark Smith, "Colton had little sympathy for a movement that promoted popular political activity instead of leaving control in the hands of wealthy and prominent men."[78] So, at midnight, several members of the crowd led by Nathaniel Ely, a Congregational deacon, blackened their faces, wrapped themselves in Indian blankets, and broke into the Colton shop adjoining his mansion, where they ignored the valuable farm tools and textiles, and seized only a particular stock of goods imported from the West Indies: rum, molasses, sugar, and salt. "The crowd delivered their prize to the town clerk — another Colton — who openly sold it over the months that followed" at fair price. Eventually, Nathaniel Ely "offered the proceeds from these sales to Samuel Colton and, when the merchant refused the money, simply left it on a table at Colton's house."[79] Since crowds had already closed down the courts of justice, Colton had no legal recourse. Six months later, after Massachusetts was rid of its royal Governor, the General Court enacted wage and price controls.[80]

In 1780, Colton took Ely and two other raiders to court for theft. In a lengthy petition, one hundred twenty-six of Ely's neighbors sided with the raiders, and signed a petition seeking immunity from prosecution on their behalf. The argument they offered was that, "'All power having originated from the Body of the People,' . . . in times of crisis, power 'reverted back to its Source and Fountain. . . .' The people had acted 'to hinder some Members of the Community from acting contrary to the General Welfare. . . .' In February, 1781, the General Court voted to indemnify the raiders against Samuel Colton's lawsuits."[81]

---

78. *Ibid.*, 33, 36.
79. *Ibid.*, 4.
80. *Acts and Resolves, Public and Private, of the Province of Massachusetts Bay*, 21 vols. (Boston, 1869- 1922), V, 583-589.
81. Smith, *After the Revolution*, 39. Quotations are from the "Petition of Nathaniel Ely, Festus Colton, and Azariah Woolworth, December 15, 1780," 231 M. A. 136-139.

"In charging him with Toryism," wrote Smith, "the raiders did not claim that Colton had rooted for the British; they claimed he had acted like a merchant instead of a neighbor."[82] One would be hard pressed to find a better example of moral economy in eighteenth-century America. This was popular ideology in action. According to their petition, the crowd had seized the goods to prevent Colton from selling them "in a Manner as essentially to injure the whole." The inherent belief that the community's welfare took precedence over the right of private property was at the heart of Shays' Rebellion.[83]

Popular actions such as this posed no threat to the social hierarchy, for they were, in Pauline Maier's words, "*extra-institutional* in character more often than they were anti-institutional."[84] They were "commonly viewed as momentary releases within the political system," wrote Wood, "temporary 'Thunder Gusts' that 'do more Good than Harm' in clearing the political atmosphere. Far from being symptoms of the breakdown of traditional authority, the behavior of the mobs indicated that the customary mechanisms of social control in the society were still working."[85]

Likewise, Shays' Rebellion, in John L. Brooke's words, "was rooted in the old organic culture of the orthodox communities. . . . Rather than a harbinger of the democratic politics of interest of the century to come, the Regulation was a final expression of a corporate political culture, wherein 'the body of the people' rose to 'regulate' the relationship between rulers and the ruled, and to defend an ancient and eroding conception of a moral economy."[86]

---

82. Smith, *After the Revolution*, 40.
83. *Ibid.*, 39. For community welfare as the motive of Shays' Rebellion, see Regulator Adam Wheeler's open letter below, 76-77.
84. Maier, *op. cit.*, 5.
85. Wood, *op. cit.*, 90. After receiving alarming reports about Shays' Rebellion, Jefferson wrote to Madison that "a little rebellion now and then is a good thing, and as necessary in the political world as storms in the physical." Thomas Jefferson to James Madison, 30 Jan., 1787, in *Jefferson Papers*, XI, 93.
86. John L. Brooke, "A Deacon's Orthodoxy," *In Debt to Shays*, 3. Wood noted that "even the recurrent mobbing and rioting of Anglo-American society, which seem to be challenges to the structure of authority, were in fact ultimate-

By the 1780s, as commercialism progressively depersonalized social relations, two political cultures had evolved. In
the east and throughout the mercantile community, unabashed
commercial interests had produced a contractual, capitalistic
attitude toward private property and mutual obligation: written commitments outweighed any economic or social exigencies. In the west, those who upheld the traditional, inherent
popular ideology and viewed society as an organic body of
citizens, continued to value the well-being of the community
over individual profit.

Many commonplace notions were transformed by Independence, and none more so than "the sovereignty of the people." Did the slogans of Sidney mean that "Seditions, Tumults
and Wars" could always be justified by the dissatisfaction of
a large crowd? Did not the election of representatives from
among the people confer to them some measure of authority
over the people? There were no ready answers to these dilem-
mas. Revolutionary settlement, which Brooke defines as "the
stable structure of constitutional framework and civil institutions that is the outcome of . . . a [revolutionary] transformation," had not yet been achieved by the summer of 1786, when
protesters first marched to the court-house steps of western
Massachusetts.[87] The demonstrators could well have given

---

ly testimonies to the paternalism and personal organization of that society. .
. . The riots took place within the existing structure of authority and tended
to reinforce that structure even as they defied it; often they grew out of folk
festivals and traditional popular rites and had much in common with them. . . .
Such rituals momentarily allowed humble people to overcome their feelings of
inferiority and subordination find to control the release of their pent-up anger
and hostility. . . . Although the crowds usually acted outside the bounds of law
and of existing institutions, they were not necessarily anti-authoritarian. The
mobs' actions often enjoyed widespread support in the local community, and
in fact were condoned or at least tolerated by many gentlemen who remained
confident of their paternal hegemony and who often wanted to separate themselves from crass and greedy tradesmen and moneymakers. . . . The mobs often
showed remarkable restraint, pinpointing their objectives with extraordinary
care, and limiting themselves to the intimidation of particular persons and to
the selective destruction of property." Wood, *op. cit.*, 89-90.
87. Brooke, "To the Quiet of the People: Revolutionary Settlements . . .,"
WMQ, 3rd Ser., XLVI (1989).

Samuel Adams (who vehemently opposed the Regulation) the explanation he had offered the English a decade earlier: "We boast of our freedom, and we have your example for it. We talk the language we have always heard you speak."[88]

Because the Shaysites carried arms and marched in step as they closed the courts, it has been universally assumed that they were yeomen armed specifically for warlike action. But in four months of protests, the embodied protesters never committed a single violent act, even after cannon were fired upon them.[89] The possibility deserves to be explored, then, that Shays' Rebellion was not a rebellion of armed yeomen, but a traditional crowd action performed by veteran soldiers accustomed to military display, and united by common interests — much like the organization of Revolutionary officers formed by Knox, called the Society of the Cincinnati. This interpretation offers a more consistent explanation of the events than those influenced by Minot, the Federalist historian, who explained the Regulators' motives by simple economic determinism.

In a ritualistic confrontation on the court-house steps, two political cultures met head-on, one filled with dreaded apprehension of a civil war, the other with well-rehearsed demands for a government of the people. Both parties believed they embodied the true spirit of the Revolution, because they both represented widely-held but conflicting perspectives of what the Revolution had been fought for. Both harbored mutual, exaggerated suspicions of each other's ambitions.[90] These

---

88. Adams quoted in Edwin G. Burrows and Michael Wallace, "The American Revolution: The Ideology and Psychology of National Liberation," *Perspectives in American History* VI (1972), 198.

89. It is true that isolated raiding parties, like that of Perez Hamlin, used violence to take hostages and seize supplies. But such attacks were utterly unrepresentative of the Regulation, as were the occasional threats called out by some demonstrators.

90. "Is it possible," David Brion Davis suggested, "that the circumstances of the Revolution conditioned Americans to think of resistance to a dark, subversive force as the essential ingredient of their national identity?" David Brion Davis, *Slave Power Conspiracy and the Paranoid Style* (Baton Rouge, 1969), 29.

two opposing perspectives of civil government, the contractual and the organic, collided in western Massachusetts, in what one side declared was an obstruction of justice, and the other maintained was a traditional regulation of the judiciary by veteran soldiers. Only with the ratification of the Federal Constitution three years later was an uneasy synthesis of these two parties finally achieved.

CHAPTER TWO

The Circumstances that Precipitated the Regulation

"Under all these circumstances the peopel were drove to the gratest extremity. Many countyes took to Conventions, Remonstrances & petition to a Corte where they were not halfe represented."

— William Manning, *The Key of Libberty*[1]

66 When ever Revolutions are brought about & free government established," wrote William Manning, the yeoman-philosopher of Billerica, Massachusetts, "it is by the influence of a few feeding men, who after they have obtained their object (like other men) can neaver receiv compensation & honours anough from the people for their services, & the people being brought up from their uths to reverance & respect such men they go on old ways & neglect to search & see for themselves & take care of their own interists."[2]

"The Key of Libberty," Manning's remarkable essay on the necessity of political parties, offers a cogent, contemporaneous expression of the political motives behind "the Shais afaire." Yet, perhaps because it was written a decade later, it has been overlooked by historians writing about the Regula-

---

1. Morison, "Manning's *Key of Libberty*," *WMQ*, 3rd Ser., XIII (1956), 242. Manning's important observations about "the Shais afaire" have never been cited in any study published about Shays' Rebellion.
2. *Ibid.*, 221.

tion, who have instead combed through the many town petitions of 1786, and assumed that they manifested the Regulators' grievances.[3]

The specific issues which provoked the Regulation were tangled together, and unweaving them for close scrutiny may obscure the collective impression they made upon rural westerners: that they had lost their right to self-governance through the political manipulation of eastern, monied interests. Nevertheless, those issues, addressed in this chapter, were: antipathy to the Cincinnati officers, who had procured benefits (five years' pay and Ohio land), when the common soldiery received little or nothing that they had been promised upon enlisting; excessive taxation, demanded in specie when none was available, without the customary relief afforded by paper money; and, as lawsuits multiplied exponentially, the costs and practices of the lower courts. Had a political remedy been available to the under-represented westerners, these immediate circumstances would not have led to the Regulation; indeed, all the Regulators sought was a chance to vote Hancock back into office and win more seats in the General Court, before their farms were seized by the courts. For that reason, Manning's essay rightly emphasized the political grievances over the economic, and provides an important link between Shays' Rebellion and the genesis of Jefferson's Republican party out of the ashes of anti-Federalist ideology.[4]

The upper-class practice of forming professional Associations, Manning observed, compelled the laboring class to

---

3. While the petitions pleaded issues that aggravated the Regulators' situation — the urgent need for a circulating medium, for example, and the presence of the General Court in Boston — they themselves did not press these points, but concentrated on the postponement of property seizures until after the next gubernatorial elections, as well as judicial reform.

4. Bums wrote of "The Key of Libberty," that "if leaders such as Adams and Jefferson failed to understand the strategy of national parties, could anyone else have done so? We know of only one man who did — William Manning." James McGregor Bums, *The Vineyard of Liberty* (New York, 1982), 139. For a thorough discussion of the subtle connotations of "anti-Federalist" and "Antifederalist," see Forrest McDonald, "The Anti-Federalists, 1781-1789," *Wisconsin Magazine of History*, 46 (Spring 1963), 206-214.

do likewise.[5] The most dangerous of these "Aristocraticle" Societies, according to Manning, was the Society of the Cincinnati, which served the common cause of veteran officers, especially by securing land for them from Congress, west of the Ohio River. Manning's remedy was for an educated populace to form a similar combination. "I propose a Sociaty of Labourers to be formed as near after the ordir of the Cincinati as the largeness of their numbers will admit of. The Sociaty to be composed of all the Republicans & Labourers of the United States."[6]

Manning's balanced assessment of the western protests faulted the citizens for overlooking their political responsibilities, and at the same time lay much of the blame on Governor Bowdoin's response to the situation. But he made it clear that this was first and foremost a crisis of representation, and thus avoided the economic determinism of Minot's account. "This Shais afair neaver would have hapned," wrote Manning, "if the peopel had bin posesed of a true knowledge of their Rights, Dutyes, & Interests, or if the government had done their duty according to the oaths they ware under, & if they had have had such a govenour as Hancok at that time." Manning did not disguise his admiration for Hancock, or his worldweary disdain for warmongers. "Even after the Corts ware stoped [Hancock] would have Settled the hole afare for less than a thousand dollers. But as it was maniged it cost the State seaveral hundred thousands dollers, & this is always the way in wars. The few that are imployed to manage them make them as costly as posable. . . ."[7]

---

5. "As Manning shrewdly observed," Morison wrote, "the upper classes of the community, the merchants, lawyers, ministers and physicians, all had their associations, through which they obtained favorable legislation and a friendly press." Morison, "Manning's *Key of Libberty*," *WMQ*, 3rd Ser., XIII (1956), 207.

6. *Ibid.*, 248.

7. "The peopel being ignorant that all their help lay in being fully and fairly represented in the Legeslature," explained Manning, "many towns neglected to send Representitives in ordir to save the cost, so that the few ondly ware represented at cort, with an Aristocratical Bodoin as Govenour at their head." *Ibid.*, 243.

Manning made a number of important observations that connect the Cincinnati directly to the first stirrings of the Federalist movement in the Bay state.[8] He also made the remarkable observation that "When the Shais affair happened in Masachusets it was heded by one of this ordir & many of the rest of them put under pay to surpress it."[9] While there is no evidence to corroborate his assertion that Shays, Day, Parsons, Wheeler, or any other leaders of the demonstrations actually belonged to the Cincinnati, the convivial conversation which General Putnam reported having with his former Captain Shays, just when the protests turned ugly, suggests far more cooperation between the leadership of the two opposing parties than has heretofore been allowed.[10] "If the mater was sarched to the bottom," Manning insisted, "it would be found that some of the ordir of Cincinaty have bin at the bottom" of every contemporary military adventure, including Shays' Rebellion.[11]

The citizens' antipathy to the Massachusetts officers dated back to the beginning of the War. In December, 1775, the town of Cambridge had petitioned the General Court to complain of "the large stipends granted to officers, and some others, (except soldiers) in the American service; which stipends, at the lowest, were so high, that the knowledge thereof chilled

---

8. "Toards the close of the late War the Officers of the Continental army were considerably borne upon, by not being paid according to contract, & many of them thought they ware not notified anough in the framing the State Constitutions. At the close of the War they formed themselves into a Sociaty by the name of Cincinaty. . . . From that time their was a continual noys & wrighting from one end of the Continent to the other against the badness of publick credit, & the weekness & insefitiancy of the Federal Government" *Ibid.*, 223-224.
9. *Ibid.*, 224.
10. For more on this, see Chapter Three below. The very fact that Putnam did not immediately seize Shays while there was a warrant for his arrest for treason demonstrates a curious complicity between the two sides. See General Rufus Putnam to Governor James Bowdoin, Rutland, 8 Jan., 1787, typescript in Shays' Rebellion Box, AAS. For proof that Putnam and Shays socialized during the war, see 22 Feb., 1780, in Benjamin Gilbert, *A Citizen-Soldier in the American Revolution: The Diary of Benjamin Gilbert in Massachusetts and New York*, Rebecca D. Symmes, ed. (Cooperstown, N. Y., 1980), 65.
11. Morison, "Manning's *Key of Libberty*," *WMQ*, 3rd Ser.. XIII (1956), 243.

the hearts of the commonality. That the distresses of America should prove a harvest to some, and famine to others, this we deprecate."[12] Eleven years later, that harvest came in for Massachusetts' 480 former officers (albeit in depreciating paper, which the Ohio Company successfully converted to land); but among the 68,000 or so retired soldiery, the famine was widespread — and not only rhetorically.[13] Military pensions for officers but not enlisted men, and the underlying question of class, created a lasting social schism after die war. This polarization has sometimes been discounted as a major factor in Shays' Rebellion, mostly because military matters were not addressed by the town petitions of 1786.[14] But the Regulation itself, unlike the towns' convention movement, was military in character, manned and managed by the veteran soldiers; key participants and witnesses, including Manning, Daniel Stebbins, and Shays himself reiterated the grievances shared by the unpaid soldiery of the Revolutionary War. In fact, since Washington himself, upon his retirement, had defended the favored treatment of officers, it is not clear to whom the common soldiers would have directed their grievances: certainly not "the General's General," Secretary of War Knox, founder of the Cincinnati.[15]

---

12. Petition of the town of Cambridge, 27 Dec., 1775, in Peter Force, ed., *American Archives*, 9 vols., 4th Ser. (Washington, 1837-1853) IV, 1245.

13. These estimates appear in Sidney Kaplan, "Rank and Status among Massachusetts Continental Officers," *American Historical Review*, LVI (1951), 319. The population of Massachusetts in 1786 was 357,000, according to Evarts B. Greene and Virginia D. Harrington, *The American Population before the Federal Census of 1790* (New York, 1932).

14. There were exceptions: the petition of Lee, in Berkshire, complained "that Men who never took an active Part in the Defence of their Country in the Late War, are allowed to hold any post of Honour or Profit." Petition of Lee, 30 Sep., 1786, Shays* Rebellion Box, AAS.

15. For Manning and Stebbins on this point, see below, 52-53; for Shays* complaint, see below, 79-80. Jonathan Smith called the protests "a movement organized and sustained by revolutionary soldiers They had special grievances. Many of their debts had been contracted while they were absent in the service The state was owing them large sums of money for back pay and allowances," even as it demanded taxes in specie Jonathan Smith, "The Depression of 1785 and Shays' Rebellion," *William and Mary Quarterly*, 3rd Ser., V (Jan. 1948

The eight-year effort by Revolutionary officers to obtain pensions has been thoroughly chronicled by Sidney Kaplan; in Massachusetts, this was a pitched battle.[16] The Bay state had contributed one-fifth of the commissioned personnel of the army, and yet public sentiment remained firmly opposed to giving them half-pay for life, or to commuting this to full pay for five years, or lastly, to supplying Congress with a supplementary fund to pay for the commutation.[17] In fact, at the start of the Regulation, Knox reported to Congress that "the granting of the supplementary funds to the United States appears to have been the immediate cause of its bursting forth. . . ."[18]

[orig. publ. 1905]), 88.

"With regard to a distinction between officers and soldiers . . .," wrote Washington, "the uniform experience of every nation of the world, combined with our own, proves the utility and propriety of the descrimination. . . .. In some lines, the soldiers have perhaps generally had as ample a compensation for their services, by the large bounties which have been paid to them, as their officers will receive in the proposed commutation; in others, if, besides the donations of lands... we take into estimate the douceurs many of the soldiers have received, and the gratuity of one year's full pay, which is promised to all, possibly their situation ... will not be deemed less eligible than that of the officers." Washington, Circular Letter, 8 June, 1783, *Writings of Washington*, X, 262.

16. Sidney Kaplan, "Veteran Officers and Politics in Massachusetts, 1783-1787," *William and Mary Quarterly*, 3rd Ser., IX (Jan. 1952), 29-57; Kaplan, "Pay Pension, and Power: Economic Grievances of the Massachusetts Officers of the Revolution," in *Boston Public Library Quarterly*, III (1951), 15-34, 127-142; and Kaplan, "Rank and Status among Massachusetts Continental Officers," *American Historical Review* LVI (1951), 319-326.

17. For the proportion of Continental officers from Massachusetts, see Kaplan, "Pay, Pension and Power," BPLQ III (1951), 15. Late in 1782, more than 34 petitions were submitted by towns in western Massachusetts, protesting half-pay and commutation. Kaplan, "Veteran Officers and Politics," *WMQ* 3rd. Ser., IX (1952), 37. See also George Richards Minot, *The History of the Insurrections in Massachusetts in the Year 1786 and the Rebellion Consequent Thereon*, 2nd ed. (Boston, 1810), 17-18.

18. Knox to Congress, Springfield 3 Oct, 1786, *JCC*, XXXI, 753. The General Court had granted the additional money to Congress in July, 1786, the month before Shays' Rebellion began. It is not clear that the supplementary fund was "the immediate cause" of the protests (or whether the fund would have gone to the officers, as the population feared, or to pay interest on the foreign debt, as nationalists wanted); still, it is clear that, from the start, Knox linked the

When the Revolutionary War began, the Massachusetts Line was known throughout the Army for the egalitarian relations that prevailed between officers and soldiers. One Pennsylvania soldier remembered seeing Colonel Rufus Putnam, then chief engineer of the army, carrying his own ration of meat to his quarters, and remarked that "so far from aiming at a deportment which might raise them above their privates . . . the [Massachusetts officers'] object was, by humility, to preserve the existing blessing of equality."[19] But early in the course of the war that began to change, under direct orders from General Washington, who warned Congress in September, 1775 that the officers' inadequate pay was "one great source of that Familiarity between the Officers and Men, which is incompatible with Subordination and Discipline;" a month later he advised General Heath to choose officers for the Massachusetts Line who had not "placed themselves upon a level with the common Soldiery."[20] "Before the war was well under way," wrote Kaplan, "the equalitarian tendencies in the Massachusetts civil and military background, if not completely obliterated, were effectively throttled," rendering the officers' corps "a distinct social and economic entity in conscious pursuit of its special interest."[21]

When the officers received the swiftly depreciating certificates of commutation, Kaplan wrote elsewhere, the Continental Certificates seemed nothing more than "a token . . . of the future contempt of one's neighbors and friends," not least of all because the bonus made them pensioners.[22] After the failure of the Newburgh Petition, two strategies were devised by Massachusetts Generals Knox and Putnam to soften the officers' return to civilian life: the Society of the Cincinnati, and the Ohio Company.[23] Both schemes further alienated the

---

protests directly to national issues.
19. Alexander Graydon, quoted in Kaplan, "Rank and Status," *AHR*, LVI (1951), 321.
20. *Ibid.*, 325.
21. *Ibid.*, 326.
22. Kaplan, "Veteran Officers and Politics," *WMQ*, 3rd. Ser., IX (1952), 30.
23. "Ninety percent of the two hundred and eighty-eight officers who signed

officers from the general population.

In 1783, when it was clear that the army would soon be dismissed, Knox produced an eight-page draft of a constitution for a hereditary order of Revolutionary officers, which he called "The Institution of the Society of the Cincinnati."[24] Part of his purpose was to continue the fight for commutation after the officers had been dismissed. But the "Institution" adopted by the states' officers that May made it clear that Knox had larger things in mind, declaring that the Cincinnati had an "unalterable determination to promote and cherish between the states, that union and national honor so essentially necessary to their happiness, and the future dignity of the America empire."[25] Knox wrote to General Benjamin Lincoln the same week that "the sole objects are the union of the states as far as the humble influence of the officers may intend."[26] But another object was to create an hereditary, national organization that would outlive the veterans, with future membership limited by primogeniture — the most controversial aspect of the Cincinnati. In the long run, though, even the addition of

---

the Newburgh Petition were members of the Cincinnati from Massachusetts and Connecticut." Archer Butler Hulbert, ed., *The Records of the Original Proceedings of the Ohio Company* (Marietta, 1917), xli.

24. "The Institution" is reprinted in Francis S. Drake, *Memorials of the Society of the Cincinnati of Massachusetts* (Boston, 1873). Knox had been preparing this plan for a long time. Seven years earlier, in September 1776, John Adams had seen Knox and Washington dining with others in New York and, as he reported to Thomas Jefferson, "in the course of the conversation . . . [Knox] said he should wish for some ribbon to wear in his hat, or in his button hole, to be transmitted to his descendants as a badge and a proof that he had fought in defence of their liberties. He spoke of it in such precise terms as shewed he had revolved it in his mind before." Jefferson Diary, 16 Mar., 1788, *Jefferson Papers*, XIII, 11.

25. William S. Thomas, *The Society of the Cincinnati*, 1783-1935 (New York, 1935), 24-32.

26. Knox to Lincoln, 21 May, 1783, as quoted in Minor Myers, Jr., *A History of the Society of the Cincinnati* (Charlottesville, 1983), 29. Forrest McDonald pointed out that, apart from Congress itself, the Society of the Cincinnati was virtually the only existing national organization. Forrest McDonald, *E Pluribus Unum* (Boston, 1965), 33.

Washington as the Society's President did not make this ersatz aristocracy of officers more palatable to the unpaid private soldiers. They were mustered out in June, leaving the Continental Army with a company of only eighty men and an arsenal of weapons.

There were already predictable tensions between officers and the enlisted men. The day that news of formal peace with Britain arrived at Newburgh, April 16, 1783, Knox wrote to Washington that there was growing discontent among the privates and non-commissioned officers in the Connecticut line, where the soldiers wanted the same five years' pay that officers received. According to Merrill Jensen, Knox said that "this was a new claim, and that others might spring up. The sooner the 'war men,' the men enlisted for the duration, were discharged, the better." General Nathanael Greene reported that the news of discontent among the northern troops was spreading, "and threatens a convulsion."[27] There were other accounts of widespread unrest when, two weeks after the Cincinnati was founded, Congress furloughed all non-commissioned officers and 'war men.'[28]

In Massachusetts, where there were more than three hundred members of the officers' Society led by Knox and Lincoln, public outrage with the Cincinnati grew smoothly out of the anti-commutation sentiment, especially after the *Independent Chronicle* reprinted extracts of Aedanus Burke's anti-aristocratic pamphlet, *Considerations on the Order or Society of Cincinnati*.[29] By early 1784, James Warren wrote to John Adams, "nothing seems to be a more General Subject of Conversation than the Cincinnati Clubb. People seem not

---

27. Quoted in Merrill Jensen, *The New Nation* (New York, 1950), 80.

28. May 26, 1783, *JCC*, XXIV, 364-365.

29. *Independent Chronicle*, April 8, May 6, 1784. The *Chronicle* continued printing articles concerning the Cincinnati every week in April, as well as May 6 and June 3; see also *Massachusetts Spy*, May 13, May 27, 1784. Ædanus Burke [Cassius, *pseud.*], *Considerations on the Order or Society of Cincinnati* (Hartford [1783?], 1784). See also Edgar Erskine Hume, "Early Opposition to the Cincinnati," *Americana*, XXX (1936), 597-638, and Wallace Evans Davies, "The Society of Cincinnati in New England, 1783-1800," *William and Mary Quarterly*, 3rd Ser., V (Jan. 1948), 3-25.

to have considered the nature and dangerous tendency of the Institution till they were roused and alarmed by a Pamphlet wrote . . . by Mr. Burke. . . . People in N. England more especially, have manifested great uneasiness at the half pay for Life to the Officers of the Army, since commuted for five years pay; but the uneasiness seemed to be subsiding till Irritated to fresh resentment by this Insitution. County Conventions and Town Meetings are now frequently expressing their Resentments and determinations for the Commutations."[30] In February 1784, Knox admitted to Washington, the Society's president, that "sentiment was universally hostile throughout the section."[31] In March, the General Court condemned the Society, when a committee of both houses insisted that the Cincinnati "savors of a disposition aspiring to become independent of lawful and constitutional authority," and could become "destructive of the liberties of the State; and the existence of their free constitutions."[32] In April, Greene wrote to Washington about "the uproar that is raised against the Cincinnati. . . . If this is done away with, the whole tide of abuse will run against commutation." Greene added perceptively that "the public seem to want something in New England to quarrel with the officers about; remove one thing, and they will soon find another."[33] John Adams, in turn, wrote to Lafayette that the Cincinnati represented "the first step taken to deface the beauty of our temple of liberty."[34] Even Stephen Higginson, the Salem merchant, saw that the Society was "most clearly anti republican, & while our People remain

---

30. James Warren to John Adams, March 10, 1784, "Warren-Adams Letters," 2 vols., *MHS Collections* LXXIII (1925), H, 237-238.

31. Davies, *op. cit.*, 4.

32. Quoted in Davies, *op. cit.*, 12. See the Journal of the Senate of the Commonwealth of Massachusetts 1783-1784, IV, 339, 366, and the Journal of the House of Representatives (May 1783 to March 1784), IV, 389, 420, Massachusetts State Library. See also Hume, "Early Opposition," *Americana* (1936), 612.

33. Nathaniel Greene to George Washington, 22 Apr., 1784, *General Washington's Correspondence Concerning The Society of the Cincinnati*, Edgar Erskine Hume, ed., (Baltimore, 1941), 142.

34. Davies, *op. cit.*, 11.

attached to the present Constitution, they cannot but be averse to every thing of the kind."[35]

At its first general meeting in Philadelphia in May, 1784, the Society acquiesced to Washington's demand for fundamental changes in its charter. "They abolished all inherited eligibility, honorary membership and correspondence among societies," and agreed to seek charters from their respective legislatures, but, according to Wallace Evans Davies, "in Massachusetts the society did not dare apply for a charter as proposed."[36] Notwithstanding the revisions in the Institution, hostility toward the Cincinnati in Massachusetts continued for years.[37]

Ultimately, it was the officers of the Cincinnati who collaborated over a period of months to crush Shays' Rebellion.[38] While it is also true, as Robert J. Taylor wrote, that "the backbone of the insurgent faction was former officers and soldiers in the Revolutionary War," no one above the rank of captain participated in the Regulation.[39] It seems that most of the captains who helped coordinate the demonstrations, like Daniel Shays and Luke Day, shared the economic plight of the privates, rather than the opportunities of the ranking officers. Perhaps they had not completed the three years of service required to join the Society; or perhaps they could not afford the Cincinnati's initition fee of one month's pay — or, for that matter, the membership dues of the Masonic Lodges. And

---

35. Stephen Higginson to Elbridge Gerry, Boston, 28 Apr., 1784, Elbridge Gerry Papers, New-York Historical Society.

36. Davies, *op. cit.*, 15.

37. *Ibid.*, 17; see also James Warren to John Adams, May 18, 1787, "Warren-Adams Letters," 2 vols., *MHS Collections* LXXIII (1925), II, 291.

38. Kaplan wrote that "a handful of veteran Massachusetts officers of the Continental Line, who had kept up their battlefield friendships as members of the . . . Cincinnati, the Ohio Company . . ., and the Order of . . . Masonry." Kaplan, "Veteran Officers and Politics," *WMQ*, 3rd. Ser., IX (1952), 29.

39. Taylor, *Western Massachusetts*, 149. Taylor notes that among Robert Treat Paine's "Black List of Insurgents," "about one fourth of the men named . . . had been officers in the Revolution." *Ibid.* Kaplan counts two Majors and two Lieutenants among the Regulators whose "names crop up in print," but their participation is not certain; Kaplan, "Veteran Officers and Politics," *WMQ*, 3rd. Ser., DC (1952), 51.

perhaps for that reason they felt all the more alienated from the administration of "the Aristocratical Bodoin," as Manning called the Governor, and the Cincinnati generals of Massachusetts — Knox, Lincoln, Shepherd, Putnam, and Tupper, among others — who served Bowdoin during the Regulation.[40]

The Ohio Company was Rufus Putnam's contribution to the cause of the veteran officers, with Knox's assistance.[41] In September 1783, after taking command of the rump of the Continental Army, Knox wrote to Washington that "I am daily solicited for information respecting the progress of the officers' petition for a new state westward of the Ohio. . . . The officers in a very few years would make the finest settlement on the frontiers, and form a strong barrier against the barbarians."[42] Toward this effort, Washington Lodge No. 10 and the American Union Lodge provided a valuable basis for trust, coordination, and lobbying.[43] At the former, where two hundred and fifty Massachusetts officers were members, Putnam, together with Generals Pickering and Huntington, conceived of the Ohio Company.[44]

---

40. Antipathy and distrust toward Bowdoin, along with the popularity of the (temporarily) retired Hancock played a large role in the escalation of events. See below, Chapter Five.

41. "Putnam's scheme of 1783 and its later outgrowth, the Ohio Company of 1786 — both the creations of the Massachusetts corps — were fashioned as levers to move Congress to keep its promises" of land bounties. Kaplan, "Veteran Officers and Politics," *WMQ*, 3rd. Ser., DC (1952), 33.

42. Knox to Washington, West Point, 17 Sept., 1783, Drake, *Correspondence of Knox*, 85.

43. Kaplan wrote that "a good many of the Massachusetts officers had already come together in the fraternal lodges of Free and Accepted Masonry. . . . By 1783 . . . , one out of every twenty-five Bostonians was a Mason." Kaplan, "Veteran Officers and Politics," *WMQ*, 3rd.Ser., IX (1952), 31.

44. Putnam had already hoped to settle western land along the Mississippi after the Seven Years War, with his fellow associates in the Company of Military Adventurers. See "Rufus Putnam's Journal," in A.C. Bates, ed., *The Two Putnams, Israel and Rufus, in the Havana Expedition 1762 and in the Mississippi River Exploration 1772-73* (Hartford, 1931), 143-262."The establishment of the Ohio Company settlement on the banks of the Ohio was the migration American Union Lodge." Hulbert, ed., *op. cit.*, xliv.

Putnam was a busy man. Although he was one of the delegates chosen by Massachusetts to the first meeting of the Cincinnati in May, 1784, he sent his apologies to Washington, explaining that "the settlement of the Ohio country, Sir, engrosses many of my thoughts." Thousands of veterans had asked him, "when are we going to the Ohio?"[45] For more than a year Congress failed to act upon the officers' petition of June 16, 1784. So, in January 1786, Putnam and General Benjamin Tupper decided to form the Ohio Company, to raise a large fund of Continental Certificates.[46] In fact, it was not until the Philadelphia Convention was under way that Congress gave serious consideration to the Ohio Company's offer to buy the land.[47] By no coincidence, the Northwest Ordinance was passed in the same week that the offer was accepted. Although the land bounties promised to the enlisting soldiery still had not been granted, one million acres were sold to the Ohio Company by Congress.[48] The officers had finally found

---

45. As quoted in Kaplan, "Veteran Officers and Politics," *WMQ*, 3rd. Ser., DC (1952), 41. See also *Washington's Correspondence Concerning The Cincinnati*, Hume, ed., 128.Washington wrote to Putnam that he had "dwelt upon the arguments you have used to shew the propriety of a speedy decision. Every member [of Congress] with whom I conversed acquiesed in the justice of the petition . . . but plead the want of cession of the Land to act upon." George Washington to Rufus Putnam, 2 June, 1784, Worthington Chauncey Ford, *Writings of George Washington*, 14 vols. (New York, 1889-1893) X, 391 392. Jefferson's "Ordinance for Ascertaining and Disposing of Lands," reiterating the land promised to the officers and soldiers, had been reported to Congress in May, but not yet acted upon; 28 May, 1784, *JCC*, XXVII, 446-453.

46. See Charles S. Hall, *The Life and Letters of Samuel Holden Parsons: Major General in the Continental Army and Chief Judge of the Northwestern Territory* (Binghamton, 1905), 496. Both Putnam and Tupper played significant roles in the military response to Shays' Rebellion. See Minot, *History*, 117, and General Rufus Putnam to Governor James Bowdoin, Rutland, 8 Jan., 1787, typescript in Shays' Rebellion Box, AAS.

47. "Congress had long been dreaming dreams of the money to be obtained from these lands. . .," wrote Edmund C. Burnett. With Putnam's offer, "real money, so it seemed, and lots of it was actually dangling before their eyes." Edmund C. Burnett, *The Continental Congress* (New York, 1941), 683.

48. As Commager wrote, "the immediate impulse for the Ordinance of 1787 came from a group of land speculators, members of the Ohio Company of Associates and of the Society of the Cincinnati, who wished to establish colo-

someone who would accept Continental notes at face value.[49]

In March, 1786, Putnam and his associates advertised in the press, announcing a meeting of veterans' delegates at the Bunch of Grapes Tavern in Boston, to form the Ohio Company.[50] When the Regulation erupted six months later, Reverend Manasseh Cutler, one of the co-founders of the Ohio Company, wrote that "these commotions will tend to promote our plan and incline well disposed persons to become adventurers, for who would wish to live under a Government subject to such tumults and confusions?"[51]

Thus both the Ohio Company and the Society of the Cincinnati welcomed Shays' Rebellion: the former because it might enlarge their Association, and the latter because it would represent an opportunity to improve their standing across the state, by quashing the threat of civil war.

Such was the officers' situation after the war. But for those who had served as common soldiers, circumstances were dire.[52] Their former officers appeared to have turned

---

nies in the Ohio country . . . [and] succeeded in lobbying through a moribund Congress the famous Ordinance." Commager, ed., *Documents of American History*, 1, 128. "Since the Treasury received depreciated certificates of indebtedness at par," wrote Rohrbough, "the Ohio Associates paid less than ten cents per acre." Malcolm J. Rohrbough, *The Land Office Business: The Settlement and Administration of American Public Lands, 1789-1837* (New York, 1968), 11. "The auction system of sale of wilderness land was in direct opposition to the pioneering process. . . . This was rank imperialism." Henry Tatter, "State and Federal Land Policy during the Confederation Period," *Agricultural History IX* (1935), 185.

49. By this time, most of the common soldiery had parted with their Continental Certificates at vastly lower values. The certificates were purchased and collected by speculators who were relying upon influential financiers to persuade Congress to pay full value for the paper; with Hamilton's funding plan, this became a reality. But for most of the soldiers, the expression "not worth a Continental" still held.

50. The Company's Articles were printed on the first page of the *Massachusetts Centinel*, 11 Mar., 1786.

51. Quoted in Kaplan, "Veteran Officers and Politics," *WMQ*, 3rd. Ser., IX (1952), 43.

52. Some soldiers got home by begging. . . ." For this and more, see Charles Royster, *A Revolutionary People At War: The Continental Army and the American Character, 1775-1783* (Chapel Hill, N.C., 1979), 352.

their backs on them, and they had no basis for organization among themselves: they were not welcome in the Cincinnati, nor could they afford membership in the Masonic Lodges. While the Ohio Company offered 100 acres for privates (scaled up to 1,100 acres for major generals), few had kept their Certificates, or could afford the cost of relocating with their families and settling so far from their homes.[53] True, as Washington had observed, the soldiers had originally been recruited by means of generous bounties.[54] But that was six years and many hungry months earlier; the common soldier, returning to his farm, would have liked to think of himself as Cincinnatus, too. The veteran privates "insisted that their genteel rulers perverted the Revolution for their own benefit," wrote Alan Taylor, "and deprived the poor soldiery of their just pay by embezzling tax receipts."[55]

"The poore Soldiers . . .," wrote William Manning in another essay, "had waited two or three years for their pay & then Discharged and Sent home to their Needy fameleys with nothing but Cirtificates. . . . the same Government (by Compelling them to pay their private Debts and taxes in hard Money) obliged them to Sell their publick Securityes for what they would fetch." In parting with most of their Continental certificates at radically discounted values, the soldiers "acted More Like Persons beset with Robers & prudently delivered up their purses Rather than, their Lives."[56] Manning's description is

53. Kaplan, "Veteran Officers and Politics," *WMQ*, 3rd. Ser., IX (1952), 33.

54. In February 1777, Knox wrote to Washington from Springfield that he was "surprised at the very extraordinary bounty offered by the State ($86 1/2) for recruits. . . . enlistments in this town have been exceedingly rapid. . ." Noah Brooks, *Henry Knox, A Soldier of the Revolution* (New York, 1900), 87.

55. Alan Taylor, *Liberty Men and Great Proprietors* (Chapel Hill, N.C., 1990), 102.

56. [William Manning] "Some proposals for Makeing Restitution to the Original Creditors of Government and to helpe the Continant to a Medium of trade, Subscribed to the consideration of a Member of the State Lejeslator of Masachusets February the 6th, 1790." MS Am 880.10, Houghton Library, Harvard University. See also Ruth Bogin,"Measures So Glaringly Unjust:" A Response to Hamilton's Funding Plan By William Manning," *William and Mary Quarterly*, 3rd Ser. XLVI (Apr.1989), 304-314. One of the few accounts that relates Shays' Rebellion directly to the veterans' plight is in Richard Severe and Lewis

confirmed by Daniel Stebbins, an eyewitness to the Springfield commotions, as the motive for the Regulation: "It is not pretended that SHAYS had any expectation or even desire of establishing himself at the head of Government as an arbitrary military chief, but only to proceed so far as to secure the Just right of the Soldiers, by whose powers, under Washington and a wise Providence, our Independence had been achieved. . . . But remember the steps of Oliver Cromwell at reform? there was no stopping place short of the supreme head of Government."[57]

Nothing better illustrated the plight of the ill-used veteran than "the well-publicized case of Timothy Bigelow," wrote David P. Szatmary, "an indebted Massachusetts farmer and Revolutionary War veteran who died in a damp cell of the Worcester County Jail."[58] While there are questions as to whether Bigelow's debts were war-related, the fact that Worcester's great war hero lay fading in a jail that "rivalled anything in Dickens," according to historian Richard B. Morris, was a sententious illustration of the society to which the veterans had returned.[59]

Milford, *The Wages of War: When America's Soldiers Came Home from Valley Forge to Vietnam* (New York, 1984), 19-79.

57. Daniel Stebbins's Notebook — "Reminiscences, 1845," 45, Forbes Library; for more of this much neglected account, see below, 82-98. Bellamy rightly attributed the cause of the demonstrations to the "great multitude of returned soldiers with which the state was at the time filled, men generally destitute, unemployed and averse to labor . . . feeling themselves aggrieved by a neglectful and thankless country. . . . The insurgent soldiery still held together wonderfully and in a manner that would be impossible to understand without taking into account the peculiar material that composed it" Edward Bellamy, *The Duke of Stockbridge* (Cambridge, Ma., 1962), 264.

58. David Szatmary, *Shays' Rebellion* (Amherst, 1980), 35. In the county prison logs, Bigelow was imprisoned repeatedly until released "By Deth," 1 Apr., 1789. See Worcester County Jail Records, AAS.

59. Robert A. Gross, in conversation, cast doubt on the nature of Bigelow's debts. Richard B. Morris, "Insurrection in Massachusetts," in Daniel Aaron, ed., *America in Crisis* (New York, 1952), 24. See also Charles A. Chase on Bigelow, in John Noble, "A Few Notes on Shays Rebellion," in *Proceedings of the American Antiquarian Society* XV (1902-3), 120-121. Recently, William Pencak has disputed the view that the Shaysites represented the veterans' interests; see below, 74.

"Whereas we have a Constitutional Right to Assemble at all times in an Orderly & peaceably Manner," began the petition from Methuen, "to Consult upon the Common good; and Request of the Legislative body, by way of Remonstrance, Redress of the wrongs done us, or Grievances we Suffer. . . ."[60] The key phrase was "the common good," which, to westerners, recalled the organic, political culture of the protection covenant with which they were familiar. That covenant was widely abrogated after the Revolution, as westerners were coming to understand: still, premodern farmers could not see how the gentry would benefit from the economic destruction of the common citizenry by ignoring their patriarchal obligations. But "insted of fatherly councals & admonitions," wrote Manning, "the dog of war was let loose upon them & they ware declared in a state of Insurrection & Rebellion."[61]

Books can be and have been written about the key issues presented in the petitions: paper money and other tender laws, tax relief, judicial reform, and the relocation of the General Court out of Boston to remedy western underrepresentation. These town and county petitions of the 1780s have been analyzed by many historians, first by Minot, most thoroughly by Van Beck Hall, and most recently by David Szatmary.[62] While there is little to add to the work that they have done, a review of the key issues raised by the petitions is necessary to grasp the political and economic woes besetting western yeomen,

60. "The Petition of the Inhabitants of the Town of Methuen," Oct. 2, 1786, AAS, citing the Constitution of 1780, Art I, II XIX, which specifically protected the right of the people "to assemble to consult upon the common good;" in Taylor, ed., *Massachusetts Documents*, 130. See the open letter from Regulator Adam Wheeler, who insisted the courts were causing "great damage . . . to the Community at large;" below 76-77. The paternalism inherent in the Constitution echoed the notion expressed in 1645 by John Winthrop: "This covenant between you and us is . . . that we shall govern you and judge your causes by the rules of Gods laws and our own." John Winthrop, "Oration of 1645," quoted in Perry Miller, *The New England Mind: The Seventeeth Century* (Cambridge, Mass., 1939), 426.

61. Morison, "Manning's *Key of Libberty*," *WMQ*, 3rd Ser., XIII (1956), 242.

62. Van Beck Hall, *Politics without Parties: Massachusetts, 1780-1791* (Pittsburgh, 1972); Szatmary, *Shays' Rebellion*, 37-55. See also Robert Feer, *Shays's Rebellion*, 46-86, 530-546.

which neither Hancock nor Bowdoin addressed until after the Regulation. Foremost among these was the scarcity of specie, exacerbated by the post-war elimination of paper money, and the consequent need for a Tender Act to legitimize barter.

Few historians have summarized the origins of "the money problem" more succinctly than Manning. "At the close of the late war with Brittan," wrote Manning, "although our paper money had dyed away, & left the peopel grately in debt by it, & a large publick det on us by the war, Yet their was a large quantity of hard mony amongue us sefitient for a Medium.[63] But for want of a proper regulation of trade, & the prices of Labour & produce being higher here than in other cuntryes, our marchents shiped it off lode after load by the hundred thousand dollars together untill their was but little left."[64]

The complex and tortuous history of eighteenth-century monetary policy in Massachusetts has been ably outlined by Joseph A. Ernst. "From the 1690's on . . . the merchants were instrumental in abolishing currency finance and banks-of-issue . . . and in substituting a specie currency and a system of funded debt. . . ." Wartime exigencies led to the reintroduction of paper money; but thereafter, with the political clout restored to the "great-merchant class" by the Constitution of 1780, mercantilists brought about "a return to hard money, public loans, and heavy taxes — thus setting the stage for the Massachusetts insurrections in 1786."[65]

Paper money was certainly not, *prima facie*, a preposterous solution to the shortage of specie, even from the mercantile perspective. Adam Smith had endorsed the circulation of tender notes, though Tom Paine did not; paper money offered the

---

63. The influx of bullion from Cuba accounted for the large quantity of hard money. James Swan estimated the quantity of gold and silver in Massachusetts had doubled or trebled between 1774 and 1780; James Swan, *National Arithmetick . . .* (Boston, 1786), 82. See also Richard Buel, Jr., "The Public Creditor Interest in Massachusetts Politics 1780-1786," in Allis and Gross, eds., *In Debt to Shays* (forthcoming), n.p., n.16.

64. Morison, "Manning's *Key of Libberty*;' *WMQ*, 3rd Ser., Xm (1956), 242.

65. Joseph A. Ernst, "Shays's Rebellion in Long Perspective: The Merchants and the 'Money Question,'" in Gross and Allis, eds., *In Debt to Shays* (forthcoming), n.p.

merchants economic stability, wrote Bailyn, by "providing a medium of exchange but also of creating sources of credit necessary for the growth of an underdeveloped economy and a stable system of public finance for otherwise resourceless governments."[66] But merchants had both ideological and practical justifications for rejecting paper, including "the corruption of public virtue," and the need for coin to pay English merchants who spitefully demanded specie after the war, creating a "chain of debt" that stretched from Britain to Boston to Berkshire.[67] Others, like George Washington, objected mostly to the susceptibility of paper money to speculation and depreciation.[68]

In the mid-eighteenth century, many country folk were subsistence farmers, not far removed culturally and economically from the European peasantry.[69] They relied upon merchants only for such commodities as window-glazing, buttons, ribbons, and shoebuckles; luxuries, if you will, that

---

66. Adam Smith, *An Enquiry into the Nature and Causes of The Wealth of Nations*, 2 vols. (London, 1904 [orig. publ. 1776]) [Book II, ch. 2], I, 275-7; Bernard Bailyn, *Faces of Revolution: Personalities and Themes in the Struggle for American Independence* (New York, 1990) 188. Tom Paine's excoriation of "the evils of paper money" was printed in the *Massachusetts Centinel*, May 24, 1784. E. James Ferguson wrote that "except for New England, where depreciation had given it a bad name, paper money was the 'ancient system,' which had long served well the needs of trade and the ordinary processes of government. . . . In time of war, all the colonies but one were fully prepared to adopt the methods of currency finance as the only way of meeting an emergency" E. James Ferguson, "Currency Finance: An Interpretation of Colonial Monetary Practices," *William and Mary Quarterly*, 3rd Ser., X (April 1953), 180.
67. Szatmary, *op.cit.*, 19-36. Wrote Wood, "The established gentry considered attacks on their patrimonial wealth by debtors promoting paper money and other forms of debt relief to be dishonest and unjust public evils that threatened not merely their personal well-being but the bonds that held the traditional society together...." Wood, *op.cit.*, 70.
68. George Washington to Thomas Stone, 18 Feb., 1787, *Writings of Washington*, XXIX, 164-165.
69. Anthropologists have argued that some Revolutionary farmers can accurately be termed peasants, since "many of them are only a generation or two removed from the European countryside." Joel Halpem and John Brode, "Peasant Society," in Bernard Siegel and Alan Beales, eds., *The Biennial Review of Anthropology*, 1967 (Stanford, 1967), 58. Cited by Szatmary, *op.cit.*, 6.

they cherished but did not strictly require.[70] During the war, however, the necessity of supplying three armies with beef, blankets, wagons, and rum made market-farmers out of these husbandmen. At the same time, New England profiteers, who had traditionally conducted much of their own foreign trade in barter, were beginning to establish the depersonalized economic culture that presaged the end of the moral economy.[71]

The first petition for paper money after the war came from Templeton, Worcester County, in September 1783, asking for Congress to emit a currency.[72] Three years later, delegates from forty-one towns in Worcester petitioned the General Court, stressing that the paucity of currency "subjects the inhabitants to the greatest inconveniences. The people in general are extremely embarrassed with public and private debts — no money can be obtained by the sale or mortgage of real estate. The produce of the present year & the remainder of our cattle, even if we were to sell the whole, are totally inadequate to the present demands for money. . . ."[73] Between 1782 and 1786, fifty-eight town and county conventions, seeking relief from the credit crisis, called for a Tender Act or the circulation of paper money, without satisfaction from the General Court.[74]

---

70. Robert E. Mutch, "Yeoman and merchant in pre-industrial America: eighteenth-century Massachusetts as a case study," *Societas: A Review of Social History* (Autumn 1977), 297-298.

71. In England this process had begun decades earlier, as described by Joyce Appleby, "The Moral Economy in Retreat," *Economic Thought and Ideology in Seventeenth Century England* (Princeton, 1978), 52-72. See also Robert A. East, "Massachusetts Conservatives in the Critical Period," *Era of American Revolution*, Richard B Morris, ed. (New York, 1939), 354.

72. The petition pleaded for "the Emition of a paper Currency Sufficient for a Circulating medium . . . the Said paper a Tender in all Payments."188 M. A. 426, as cited by Feer, *Shays's Rebellion*, 117.

73. Worcester County Petition, AAS, Shays' Rebellion Box, Folder 1. See also the petition from Methuen, Oct 1786: "The want of a circulating medium has so stagnated business of all kinds among us, that unless Speedily remedied, will involve the greater part of the people among us in a state of bankruptcy." *Ibid.*

74. Feer, *Shays's Rebellion*, Appendix B, 540-546. Jonathan Smith describes a typical transaction in the absence of currency. "The farmer who wanted cloth

Massachusetts itself eschewed Continental money, and continued to require the payment of taxes in specie through 1786, aiming to establish the state's public credit.[75] But there was no specie, nor was there a mint anywhere in America producing coin; for this reason alone, Bowdoin's attempt to rapidly retire the state's huge debt — some twenty times greater than the total value of its real and personal property — was politically and economically ill-advised.[76] And, in succeeding Hancock, he had a tough act to follow. Hancock, forever seeking the voters' approval, had reduced taxes from their war-time high of £1,000,000 each year from 1781 to 1783, to £140,000 in 1784, and to zero in 1785 (relying tenuously upon impost and excises). Hancock then suffered a prudent attack of gout and resigned before the 1785 election, only to return to Congress two months later to seek the Presidency.[77]

The following year, Bowdoin's General Court called for £311,411 in specie, the largest levy yet in peacetime America.[78] If that was not enough cause for protest, one-third of that

---

or groceries had to pay for them in produce. But first he must find someone who wanted his hay or corn and had the cloth or groceries to exchange for them. This often it was impossible to do." Jonathan Smith, *op. cit.*, 79. It should be noted that both Springfield and Hatfield were opposed to paper money; Taylor, *Western Massachusetts*, 140.

75. "Massachusetts had shown a strong disposition to establish its own public credit from the moment the Constitution of 1780 had been ratified." Buel, Jr. "The Public Creditor Interest," Allis and Gross, eds., *In Debt to Shays* (forthcoming), n.p.

76. "The few coins in circulation ...," wrote Smith, "were the issues of different countries, and their value was uncertain and constantly fluctuating." Jonathan Smith, *op. cit.*, 79. According to one historian, in 1780 "the valuation of Massachusetts was but $11,000,000, while its nominal debt was $200,000,000." Alden Bradford, *History of Massachusetts* (Boston, 1835), 295.

77. This is an abridged account of Hancock's ambivalent maneuverings. See Herbert S. Allen, *John Hancock: Patriot in Purple* (New York, 1953), 315-322, and Burnett, *The Continental Congress*, 640, 648. For a thorough account of this election, see William M. Fowler, Jr., "The Massachusetts Election of 1785: A Triumph of Virtue," Essex Institute, *Historical Collections*, CXI, (1975), 290-304.

78. Buel wrote that "in levying a heavy specie tax just when most of the specie... had drained out..., the Massachusetts General Court acted with about as much finesse as Parliament when it provoked the Stamp Act riots in 1765."

levy was apportioned for the redemption of the state's army notes, which the penniless soldiers had long since sold for a song to speculators, directly or indirectly. Now they were being taxed to pay for their own discounted paychecks, at par.[79] Bowdoin's negligible popularity in the west had been further tarnished when he became the first President of the Massachusetts Bank, which some held responsible for the shortage of currency, as protested by one letter to the *Massachusetts Centinel*: "Has not the BANK been the means of sending from this state more SPECIE, than would otherwise have gone, by bringing it all to a *point*, from whence it could easily be extracted? . . . If the BANK continues, [will] there remain a SINGLE DOLLAR in this Commonwealth?"[80]

While Bowdoin's unprecedented levy in unobtainable specie was certainly the greatest source of grief to the agrarian community, it is not accurate to call Shays' Rebellion a tax protest, as many have done. By failing to differentiate between the four months of paramilitary protests and the civil petitions that preceded them, most historians have forgotten

---

Buel's essay explains the foreign trade pressures with Holland and France that that led Court to such a drastic levy. Buel, *op.cit.* Still, "the legislature's whole fiscal program was directed rather by whimsy than by an appraisal of the people's ability to pay." Taylor, *Western Massachusetts*, 129.

79. H. James Henderson, "Taxation and Political Culture: Massachusetts and Virginia, 1760-1800," *William and Mary Quarterly*, 3rd Ser., XLVII (Jan. 1990), 105-108. "The most remarkable thing about the Revenue Act of 1786 was that the General Court even contemplated so heavy a tax." *Ibid.*, 108. On the same page, Henderson exemplified the economic determinism of many who have written about the Regulation." Had the poll tax been aimed at the laboring poor to the advantage of the propertied segment of the community, then the poor pollpayers of Gloucester, who contributed 40 percent of the taxes of that impoverished coastal town, should have joined the insurrection." But the Regulation was actually about the western veterans' inability to affect economic policy, owing to underrepresentation in the House and virtual exclusion from the Senate, which could veto House bills; see above, 28-31.

80. Bowdoin's election as Bank President was announced in the *Massachusetts Centinel*, 27 Mar., 1784, along with Directors Stephen Higginson, Edward Payne, George Cabot, and John Lowell, among others. For the Bank Directors' central role in financing the Cincinnati officers who defeated the Regulators, see below, 168 n.129. Quotation from "Queries," *Massachusetts Centinel*, 30 Apr., 1785.

that, as a body, the Regulation made only one consistent, specific demand throughout the commotions: to postpone the sitting of the courts until the next election. That demand had appeared in only six of more than one hundred town and county petitions written between 1782 and 1787.[81] The Regulators did not seek out tax collectors or judges to harass them, nor did they burn them in effigy, as they had done during the Stamp Act Crisis. There was none of the 'rough music' associated with Revolutionary crowd actions: no tar-and-feather treatment, or skimmington, or other indignities. No property was stolen, defaced, or damaged, and nothing resembling the particular, personal regulation of Samuel Colton reoccured.[82] Even after *habeus corpus* was suspended on November 15, 1786, the well-disciplined protesters directed their efforts, if not their words, only against the sessions of the courts.[83]

Doubtless, among the thousands of men who collected in towns from Pittsfield to Cambridge, some did complain about taxes, as did a considerable number of petitions.[84] There were also those among the demonstrators who garrulously exceeded the Regulators' singular mandate — especially at night in the taverns, often to pro-Bowdoin militiamen and spies.[85] As

---

81. Feer, *Shays's Rebellion*, Appendix B: "Demands for Remedial Legislation," 540-546.

82. For the Colton Regulation, see above, 34-36.

83. After Bowdoin suspended *habeas corpus* and issued a general search warrant, the tenor of the Regulation began to change, and other demands from Regulators appeared, often similar to those of previous petitions; their actions, however, remained aimed against the courts. See, for example, " An Address to the People of the Several towns in the County of Hampshire from the body now at Arms," signed by Daniel Gray, Worcester, 7 Dec., 1786, 189 M. A. 297.

84. "The Petition of eighteen towns in the county of middlesex," 3 Nov., 1786, Shays' Rebllion Box, AAS.

85. There is ample evidence of intelligence-gathering among the Regulators, including some organized by Isaiah Thomas. "*Government* are much pleased with my Correspondent at Worcester . . . in investigating the *Plans, Movements, Hopes and Fears of the Insurgents.*" "A Sincere Friend" to Isaiah Thomas, 8 Dec., 1786, Shays' Rebellion, AAS. "The Expences of keeping out Spies is Considerable which I have promised to pay soon." Timothy Newell to Benjamin Lincoln, Great Barrington, 30 Apr., 1787, Wetmore Family Collection, Yale University Library. These examples and more cited in Feer, *Shays's Re-*

well, some threats and pleas about taxes sent to the governor at the time of the demonstrations were ascribed to Regulators.[86] And there were two reports, from Exeter, New Hampshire and Springfield, three days apart, "that some were demanding 'an equal distribution of property' or 'the annihilation of debts,' while 'all of them exclaimed against law and government.'"[87] These alarming threats, though out of character with the protests, may have been just what the more timorous government-men expected to hear from the whole crowd. Maybe it was just a case of the squeaky wheel getting more ink. Or perhaps those threats were exactly what Knox *wanted* to hear on his visits to Springfield in September and October, 1786.[88]

The cost of litigation set by the General Court's fee schedule had increased significantly, just when the number of suits brought to court surged, and this was a continuous grievance in the west. The fee schedule was especially loathsome as it applied to small claims brought before the Court of Common Pleas, where a lawsuit to recover £5 might cost half again as much in court costs, even before the lawyer's fees. This postwar gouging, legitimized by the General Court, constituted an

---

bellion, 306 n.1. For the role of Major William North as an *agent provocateur* acting on Knox's behalf, see below, Chapter Four.

86. "Wee Country men will not pay taxes, as the think If you Dont lower the taxes we'll pull down the town house about you ears We Country men will not be imposed on. We fought of our Libery as well as you did. . . ." From an anonymous letter to Governor Bowdoin, n.d., cited in Burns, *The Vineyard of Liberty*, 14.

87. William Plumer to John Hale, 20 Sept, 1786, *Colonial Society of Massachusetts Transactions*, 11 (1906-7), 392; cited in Jackson Turner Main, *The Antifederalists: Critics of the Constitution* (Chapel Hill, 1961), 67. *The New Hampshire Gazette*, 28 Sept, 1786 offered an account of the commotions, including these reports, reprinted in *Boston Magazine* (Sep., Oct. 1786), HI, 401-404; as quoted in Richard B. Morris, ed., *Basic Documents on the Confederation and Constitution* (New York, 1970), 148-152. The Exeter "uprising" ended on 23 Sept.,1786, and the Springfield Regulation was three days later, more than a hundred miles away; it is unlikely any veterans took part in both demonstrations. Knox used the language of these atypical threats in his letter to Washington; see Appendix B, below.

88. See below, Chapter Four.

intolerable breach of faith.[89]

To protect themselves from suits which they could not afford to settle, debtors lodged defensive countersuits; the result was a daisy-chain of litigation. Scenes like that at the home of prominent lawyer Dwight Foster of Brookfield, as depicted by Jonathan Smith from local accounts, were not uncommon. "His office was thronged from early morning to late at night by creditors seeking to collect their dues, and by angry debtors, invoking his services to defend them in the courts. The fence on both sides of the road leading to his house were, during the daylight, lined with the carriages of his clients." At court, "mortgages were foreclosed, and debtors were imprisoned and even sold into servitude. . . . Unable to pay for seed and stock and tools, farmers were thrown into jail or sold out to service. Except for the clothes on the debtor's back, no property was exempt from seizure or execution. There was no homestead exemption, and property at execution brought nothing approaching its real value."[90]

The public opinion of the judicial process was almost uniformly scornful, and many petitions sought to wrest control of the judiciary out of Boston's control: to secure the prerogative to appoint judges, fix their salaries, limit their tenure, and provide for their removal.[91] The citizens' resentment made

---

89. Morris wrote that "the legal profession which had hailed the common law as the guardian of constitutional rights now defended it as the creditor's privilege. . . ." This change of perception and reality came at a time when there was "one lawsuit for the head of about every family in [Worcester] County." Morris, "Insurrection in Massachusetts," 26.

90. Jonathan Smith, *op. cit.*, 82.

91. "Radical criticisms of the court structure," wrote Barbara Karsky, "were yet another reflection of the desire to extend democracy at the local level and to increase popular autonomy in government, for they would have given the work of the Probate Court and the Registry of Deeds to town clerks and replaced the Court of Common Pleas by committees of arbitration, working with elected rather than appointed justices of the peace." Barbara Karsky, "Agrarian Radicalism in the Late Revolutionary Period (1780-1795)," *New Wines in Old Skins: A Comparative View of Socio-Political Structures and Values Affecting the American Revolution*, Erich Angermann, Marie-Louise Flings, Hermann Wellenreuther, eds. (Stuttgart, 1976), 93. See also Dirk Hoerder, "Socio-Political Structures and Popular Ideology," *ibid.*, 57-58.

little distinction between judges and lawyers. As Manning explained it, lawyers "are nither Juditial nor Executive officers, but a kind of Mule ordir, ingendered by, & many times overawing both. This ordir of men git their living intirely from the quairils Follyes disputes & destreses of the Many & the intricacy of our Laws, & it is from the arts & doings of these men, that the Juditial & Executive officers are furnished with the chief of their bisness & imploy. Consequently they are bound together by the strongest bonds of union."[92]

"The most intolerable torment you can inflict on any man," said one letter to the *Massachusetts Centinel*, "is to command him TO GO TO LAW; than which, through the *insolence and avarice* of lawyers, the easiness of appeals and continuances, and sometimes the ignorance of juries, no torment can be more severe or more painful."[93] A ditty in the *Boston Gazette* about lawyers expressed the same opinion of the judiciary found in a majority of petitions in 1786:

Like Drones they fatten on the Lab'rers Toil,
Defraud the Widow and the Orphans spoil.[94]

Another specific issue frequently mentioned in petitions was the proposal that "the General Court may be Removed out of the Town of Boston to Set in Some other Convenient and Propper Place within the Commonwealth."[95] This proposal, which headed the list in several petitions, best illustrated western malaise about underrepresentation; it was also whistling in the wind.[96] In fact, western settlements were as

92. Morison, "Manning's Key of Libberty," *WMQ*, 3rd Ser., XIII (1956), 242.
93. "A letter to Tyrants," from "Apollo," *Massachusetts Centinel*, 10 May, 1786. See also the series of letters to and from "A Lawyer," *ibid.*, Apr., May 1786.
94. "Aristides," in the *Boston Gazette*, 17 Apr., 1786, as quoted in Main, *Antifederalists*, 57 n.50, where Main offers a dozen similar examples from newspapers, petitions, and correspondence.
95. "The Petition of us the Inhabitants of the Town of Plympton," 19 Feb., 1787, Shays' Rebellion Box, AAS.
96. See for example the Petitions of Worcester and Middlesex Counties, and the "Answer of the Committee of Both Houses to Petitions," 27 Oct., 1786,

isolated politically as they were geographically. New communities had first to achieve the right to representation — no mean feat; then, they had to pay the substantial cost of their representatives' travel and lodging. Many towns continued to rely upon the political interests of the 'great men' in their area, who no doubt made their trips to Boston profitable.[97] These same towns, mostly in the Connecticut River Valley, remained placid and largely pro-Bowdoin in 1786, compared to other western towns.

Taken together with other non-economic demands — for example, the elimination of the Senate, and local appointment of magistrates — this call for moving the General Court westward makes it clear that political representation was a primary concern to the petitioning bodies, if not as pressing as the need for currency. Though the Court was hardly prepared to relocate, it is interesting to speculate that, if the state government had moved west, and the Ratification Convention of 1788 had followed it, chances are that the Federal Constitution would have been rejected by Massachusetts, and perhaps, as a consequence, by the remaining states. While this is conjectural, it is hardly farfetched, given the Federalists' slim majority.[98]

Some petitions, like that of Lee, called directly for revisions of the Constitution; many others expressed similar, fundamental discontent with Massachusetts government. As Morison demonstrated, a majority of citizens had actually opposed the Constitution of 1780, and its first six years of operation had probably not changed that majority's mind.[99] This

---

Shays' Rebellion Box, AAS.

97. See above, 29-30.

98. In Massachusetts, the majority in favor of ratification was only nineteen; see below, Chapter Seven. Main wrote that "the victory of the Federalists [in Massachusetts] had been due to a number of factors. First, a large number of the towns (over fifty) did not send delegates to the [Ratification] Convention, and of these, two-thirds would probably have been Antifederal." Main, *The Antifederalists*, 209. That difference alone would have defeated ratification.

99. "An examination of the Convention's methods of tabulating the popular vote raises the suspicion that the two-thirds majority was manufactured," wrote Morison, who doubted whether "the constitution of Massachusetts, now in force almost 137 years, was ever legally ratified." It appears, he added, that

underlying dissatisfaction with the framework of government was closely tied to a very profound, personal enmity toward Bowdoin, a point rarely noted by historians.[100] There can be no doubt that, given the opportunity, western towns would have effected numerous, significant constitutional revisions. At the same time, there is no evidence that the conventions sought a complete overthrow of the government.

Nonetheless, the very existence of these petitioning conventions caused considerable anxiety in Boston. Some of the radical views that Knox and others attributed to the demonstrators echoed Tom Paine's pamphlet *Public Good*, published just five years earlier, which argued that the west could not belong to the several States, since "the vacant territory is their property collectively." Among conservatives, A. Owen Aldridge wrote, "innuendos and insinuations in published attacks implied, that the sympathies of the author lay with the leveling doctrine."[101]

Years before the first court-closing in Northampton, Samuel Adams, whom Tories in the 1770s had called the "would-be Cromwell," was opposed to conventions, and he continued to defend the Constitution — which he and his cousin John had drafted, together with Bowdoin — until the end of his life. But despite the right guaranteed to citizens by that Constitution to convene and petition, Adams argued as early as 1784

"the Convention deliberately juggled the returns in order to make it appear that there was." Morison, "The Struggle over the Constitution," *AHA Proceedings, L* (Boston, 1917), 354, 400.

100. "The insurgents at Worcester had formed a procession, at which were carried the effigies of the Governor and Lieut. Governor, whose characters were treated with every kind of indignity and insult." *Massachusetts Centinel*, 13 Dec., 1786. But, *pace* Pencak, there is no mention of the effigies being burned; see William Pencak, "'The Fine Theoretic Government of Massachusetts is Prostrated to the Earth:' The Response to Shays' Rebellion," in Allis and Gross, eds., *In Debt to Shays* (forthcoming), n.p.

101. Thomas Paine, "Public Good," *The Complete Writings of Thomas Paine*, Philip S.Foner, ed., 2 vols. (New York, 1945), II, 332. Paine went on to add, with prescience, that "the several states will, sooner or later, see the convenience, if not the necessity of... electing a Continental convention, for the purpose of forming a Continental constitution." *Ibid.* A. Owen Aldridge, *Thomas Paine's American Ideology* (Newark, 1984), 96.

that such conventions threatened the very survival of the Massachusetts government. "Bodies of men, under any denomination whatever," wrote Adams, "who convene themselves for the purposes of deliberating upon and adopting measures which are cognizable by legislatures only will, if continued, bring legislatures to contempt and dissolution."[102] Incredibly, in his adoration of the Constitution and ignorance of western realities, Adams blamed the state's problems, among other things, on "the too great profusion of money."[103] By the time Bowdoin was elected, Adams had become his closest political ally and most articulte hard-liner, as a member of his council, then as the first senator to whom the Governor turned when the courts of Worcester and Hampshire were stopped. For the next year, in proclamations, Circular Letters, and in the press, Adams spoke for Bowdoin, not as an apologist, but as an aggressive, political defender of order against the "state of Nature" in the west, though his understanding of this condition owed more, it seems, to Hobbes than to Locke.[104]

The petitions of 1786 illustrate the conditions that plagued Massachusetts, as well as the traditional and constitutional means by which westerners sought to solve them.[105] Undoubtedly these conditions precipitated the Regulation; but, as the single, consistent demand of the Shaysites made clear, the pro-

102. "Would-be Cromwell," in John J. Miller, *Sam Adams: Pioneer in Propaganda* (Boston, 1936), 343. Much of this exposition I owe to William Pencak, "Samuel Adams and Shays's Rebellion," in *New England Quarterly* LXI (1989), 63-74. Quotation from Samuel Adams to Noah Webster, 30 Apr., 1784, in *ibid.*, 66.

103. *Ibid.*, 70-71.

104. George Mace explained that "Locke unfairly criticized . . . Hobbes's 'a state of nature,' insisting upon a distinction between a state of nature and a state of war . . . Hobbes and Locke . . . can be seen to disagree sharply on the essence of the state of nature. For Hobbes this condition will always be characterized by an attendant condition of war." George Mace, *Locke, Hobbes, and the Federalist Papers: An Essay on the Genesis of the American Political Heritage* (Caibondale, Illinois, 1979), 52.

105. Ruth Bogin wrote: "The idea that popular movements could use political action to gain control of their economic circumstances developed as part of the transition from the earlier moral economy." Bogin, "Petitioning and the New Moral Economy," WMQ, 3rd Ser., XV (1988), 423.

tests aimed to correct those conditions by eliminating Bowdoin in the election of 1787, rather than by pleading their case before him. From the beginning almost to the end, the Regulation was intended as merely a holding operation, aimed at delaying the seizure of property at least until Hancock could be returned to office, when the veteran enlisted men expected they could obtain satisfaction.

The Regulators saw themselves not so much as debtors as they did creditors of the state and the Confederation: if Massachusetts would not accept Continental certificates, why then should they? Had the Boston politicians and mercantilists made reasonable adjustments for post-war economic conditions, according to traditions which, though unwritten, were nonetheless enshrined, the Regulation might not have been necessary. Instead, Bowdoin's government, acting from a variety of conservative, fiscal motives, deliberately disregarded the genuine grievances, political and economic, of the impoverished 'war-men,' and berated the westerners for their 'levelling' tendencies. In truth, it was the General Court, and not the Regulators, who had abandoned the protection covenant.

CHAPTER THREE

The Regulation

"The people now in arms, in defence of their lives and liberties, will quietly return to their respective habitations, patiently waiting and hoping for constitutional relief from the burdens they now labour under. . . ."
— Daniel Shays to Benjamin Lincoln[1]

I n the last two hundred years, a galaxy of distinguished historians has scrutinized and retold the events of the Regulation, ostensibly rendering any further account redundant. The earliest narrative, published less than a year after the Regulation ended, was by George Richards Minot, first clerk of the Massachusetts House of Representatives under the Constitution of 1780, was remarkably thorough and deceptively even-handed, considering that it was produced to dispel "many misconceived ideas, tending to the discredit of the country," especially overseas.[2] At the age of twenty-nine, Minot was also concerned enough with his own social standing to assiduously avoid offending those who might influence his career: he noted in his diary that, before publication, he had "showed the History to the principal actors in the suppression of the

1. Daniel Shays "To the Honourable Major-General Lincoln," *Worcester Magazine*, Feb. 1787, as quoted in Michael Lienesch, "Reinterpreting Rebellion: The Influence of Shays's Rebellion on American Political Thought," *In Debt to Shays*, Gross and Allis, eds. (forthcoming), n.p.
2. Minot, *History*, iii. For historians who have examined the Regulation, see "Historiographic Essay" below, 261-290.

insurrections, in order that they might object to anything relative to their conduct, before it appeared in print . . ."[3] Possibly as a result of the admiration his manuscript received, Minot went on to become the clerk for the Massachusetts Ratification Convention.[4] Writing with a deadline more suited, perhaps, to a journalist than an historian, and from motives that were frankly political, Minot nonetheless offered what is still the most influential account of Shays' Rebellion, initiating an imperfect tradition that set the tone for most scholarship in the next two centuries.[5]

The most comprehensive study, by Robert Feer, leaves subsequent historians precious little to add.[6] Although he missed one or two important contemporary sources, Feer omitted little of what he found in his exhaustive research. The result is an invaluable trove of information for scholars, offering evidence to support virtually any historiographic argument. Indeed, that is the major problem with Feer's study, and to a lesser extent, with David Szatmary's admirable work.[7] Szatmary's analysis emphasized the broader context of the

3. Diary of George Richards Minot, 9 June, 1787, Theodore Sedgwick Papers, MHS. That Minot was concerned about offending then Governor Hancock by overpraising former Governor Bowdoin is clear from his next remark: "Mr. _____ thinks I have extricated myself very well from the danger of incurring the resentment of the jarring administrations, which any improper comparison between them, or decisive eulogium of either, would have inevitably drawn upon me." *Ibid.*

4. Later, Washington provided Minot with a publicist's dream review. "The series of events, which followed from the conclusion of the war, forms a link of no ordinary magnitude in the chain of the American Annals. That portion of domestic History . . . deserved to be discussed. I always feel a singular satisfaction in discovering proofs of talents and patriotism in those who are soon to take the parts of the generation, which is now hastening to leave the stage." Washington to Minot, 28 Aug., 1788, *Writings of Washington*, XXX, 65.

5. Recently, Robert Gross has rightly called Minot's account "a very sophisticated work, well beyond the crude polemics of the day," but acknowledged that "he had never lost sight of his central purpose," which was "to vindicate the Commonwealth and the cause of republicanism " Robert A. Gross, "The Uninvited Guest: Daniel Shays and the Constitution," *In Debt to Shays* (forthcoming), n.p.

6. Feer, *Shays's Rebellion* (New York, 1988).

7. Szatmary, *Shays' Rebellion* (Amherst, 1980).

protests and their suppression, but brought little focus to the key events of the Regulation itself. The outcome tends to confound the actual court-closings with the four years of economic distress and remonstrance which precipitated them: even though Szatmary carefully charted the progression from petition to armed rebellion, the spectrum of his narrative tends to blur the distinction.

To recognize the characteristically peaceable nature of the Regulation, it is necessary to separate the events of the demonstration from the petitions which preceded them and the scattered acts of (mostly) defensive violence that followed. This is not just an academic exercise: only when the court-closings are carved out from the peripheral activities and examined on their own can one identify the Regulators' goals from their actions, and see how far the nationalists went to exaggerate those goals in order to achieve their own. For reasons already explained, many people genuinely anticipated civil war. In the weeks before the Regulation began, letters to the *Independent Chronicle* warned that anarchy would open the door for the "enterprises of a modem Cromwell," and perhaps establish "a dreadful despotism of public freedom."[8] While the Regulation may have seemed to fill the bill, in fact the scenes at the court-houses were more like street theater than civil war, but when extraneous acts of violence are counted in, this important fact is lost.

Some accounts of the Regulation begin four years earlier, with the agitations of Samuel Ely. While the notion of stopping the court, and even some of the participants (notably Captain Reuben Dickinson) were the same, the Ely "rebellion" did not belong to the sequence of events of 1786. Ely had hardly invented judicial regulation: courts in western Massachusetts had already been closed regularly by popular *actions* from 1774 until 1782.[9] Rather, this was a political technique that he

---

8. (Boston) *Independent Chronicle*, 1 June, 31 Aug., 1786.
9. For Ely, who has been omitted here, see, for example, Szatmary, *Shays' Rebellion*, 56; Feer, Shays's Rebellion 142-164; and Alden T. Vaughan, "The 'Horrid and Unnatural Rebellion' of Daniel Shays," *American Heritage* XXVII, No. 4 (June 1966), 51. The most thorough account of Ely's commotions

seems to have adopted just to save his own hide.

A narrow focus upon the events that took place between August, 1786 and January, 1787 reveals a consistent pattern of disciplined ritual, designed to achieve a single, extra-constitutional goal: to postpone property seizures by the courts until the next elections, and improve their representation.[10] They shared with the larger movement of town and county petitions the greater goal of achieving revisions of the Constitution which had been forced upon them: a petition from Worcester, according to Minot, "prayed that the sense of all the towns . . . might be taken, respecting the necessity of revising the constitution. . . ." Thomas Grover listed the Regulator grievances to the *Hampshire Herald*, insisting first that the General Court must be moved from Boston, and second, that "a revision of the Constitution is absolutely necessary." Regulation leader Eli Parsons urged his "Friends and Fellow Sufferers" not to "support a constitution . . . which your common sense and your consciences declare to be iniquitous and

---

is Robert E. Moody, "Samuel Ely," *New England Quarterly*, V (Jan. 1932), 105-134. Daniel Stebbins noted that Samuel Ely "left behind him the 'seeds of rebellion' deeply implanted in the bosoms of an infuriated mob who seemed to have [espoused?] the sentiment of 'no compromise but at the Cannon's Mouth' and doctrine that insurrections against Government were both useful and necessary " Daniel Stebbins Notebook,1, 41, Forbes Library.(The present study also disregards the North Carolina Regulation of 1771-1776 as irrelevant to Massachusetts, which had long established its own tradition of Regulation; there is no evidence whatsoever linking the two movements.) For court closings from 1774 to 1780 in Berkshire, first urged by Joseph Hawley of Northampton, then sustained by the Berkshire Constitutionalists, see Taylor, *Western Massachusetts*, 76; for Hampshire, *ibid.*, 87; for Pittsfield, *ibid.*, 91; Great Barrington, *ibid.*, 98 "When a majority of the inhabitants of Berkshire County grew impatient at the failure of the state to adopt a new constitution, in which they hoped especially to see the court system revised, they defied the power of government that held office from 1775 to 1780. Their principal act of defiance was to resist forcibly the operation of the state courts." Thad W. Tate, "The Social Contract in America, 1774-1787: Revolutionary Theory as a Conservative Instrument," in *William and Mary Quarterly*, 3rd. ser., XXII (1965), 387.

10. Shaw noted that "strictly speaking, 'ritual' implies the formal enactment of a prescribed ceremony or routine, whereas American crowds added routines of their own to the traditional practices that they adopted." Peter Shaw, *American Patriots and the Ritual of Revolution* (Cambridge, Mass., 1981), 9.

cruel. . . ." Shays wrote Lincoln, who soon defeated him, that his men were "patiently waiting and hoping for constitutional relief from the burdens they now labour under."[11]

But the first step toward this effort was to reinstate Hancock and elect representatives to mend their crooked framework of government. The Regulators shared the opinion of the people of Middleborough (Plymouth County): "That the said frame of government is fairly agreed upon by Two thirds of The people or inhabitants of this State we Deny and say it is not so; when more than three Quarters of the Voters in This State have Never acted or Voted on the Same at all; as appeared by the returns from the severall Towns. . . . Use your uttmost on your Neighbouring Towns To Join you and us with all Their Might in overthrowing the said Constitution or frame of government as a huge monster whose uncouth and unhallowed Strides may Crush the people to a State of abject Slavery. . . ."[12]

With these violent sentiments in mind, the Regulation can be recognized as a commendably placid reaction. Indeed, to the extent that the Regulation was Shays's Rebellion, it was determinedly peaceable. But by November, when Bowdoin responded with force instead of meaningful conciliation by issuing warrants, suspending *habeas corpus*, and running Job Shattuck to ground, the non-violent preponderance of Daniel Shays within the protesters' leadership was progressively diminished, and the restraint that he had imposed upon his followers was in danger of being overcome.[13] Thereafter, small

---

11. "An examination of the Convention's methods of tabulating the popular vote raises the suspicion that the two-thirds majority was manufactured." Morison, "The Struggle over the Constitution," *AHA Proceedings* (1917), 354. Minot, *History*, 53; Grover letter, dated 7 Dec., 1786, *ibid.*, 85; Parsons quoted in *ibid.*, 146; Shays in Lienesch, *op. cit.*, n.p.

12. Petition of Middleboro, 1780, as quoted in Arthur Lord, "Some Objections Made to the Constitution," *American Historical Association Proceedings*, L (Boston, 1917), 58-59.

13. As Jonathan Smith put it, "when it was manifest to leaders and followers that the cause must fail, and that they were liable to indictment and punishment for grave offences, things were said and done for which no apology can be offered." Smith, "The Depression of 1785," *WMQ*, 3rd Ser. (1948), 77-94.

parties of men began to fulfill the worst that people expected of mobs.

The Regulation began on August 29th, 1786, in Northampton, Massachusetts, when four or five hundred men carrying guns, swords, and clubs prevented the sitting of the Court of Common Pleas and the General Sessions of the Justices of the Peace.[14] They were led by a number of veterans, including Captain Luke Day of West Springfield, who had served in the military throughout the six years of the Revolutionary War.[15] Although Daniel Shays is nowhere reported to have been present, this stopping of the court was entirely in character with the subsequent, eponymous commotions. This first event was apparently organized, not at a convention, but at a traditional town meeting: in his diary, Jonathan Judd, the son of Southampton's first Minister who ran a small store in his father's house, had noted that, at a town meeting in Southampton a week before, "the Design is to break up the Court next week."[16]

Despite this foreknowledge, no preparations were made to organize the militia. On August 29th, Judd summed up the first demonstration, as well as his own reactionary opinion. "Went to Northampton, this Afternoon Mob [illegible] this Court urged to adjourn without Day. All is again afloat. No Law nor Order. Full of criminals but none can be punished. Monarchy is better than the Tyranny of the Mob."[17] The "mob" of "criminals" sent a six-man delegation to the justices where they had opened court in a tavern — "a not altogether convincing vindication of the authority of government," as

---

14. As with all the episodes of the Regulation, estimates of the numbers of men involved vary widely; this number appears in the *Massachusetts Gazette*, 8 Sept., 1786, whereas Minot puts the number of Northampton "rebels" at 1500, which seems unlikely. Minot, *History*, 37. The protesters' demand was reprinted in the *Massachusetts Gazette*, 26 Sept., 1786.

15. Feer, *Shays's Rebellion*, 180-181, and "Luke Day" in *Massachusetts Soldiers and Sailors of the Revolutionary War*, 17 vols. (Boston, 1896-1908), IV, 579-580.

16. Jonathan Judd Diary, 21 Aug., 1786, Forbes Library.

17. *Ibid.*, 29 Aug., 1786.

Feer put it — and made their demand that the court adjourn.[18] Having succeeded, they dispersed peacefully.

Who were these earliest Regulators? The truth is that we shall never know their "identity" as a crowd, beyond the demands they expressed. Many of the first to arrive were following Captain Day from West Springfield and other Hampshire towns, but like so much about their planning and activities, there are strict limits on what can be said with certainty. By the end of the Regulation, almost a thousand names were compiled by pro-government witnesses, spies and accomplices, including those of protesters who had taken oaths of allegiance; doubtless many of these were participants. But the emergence of new towns (where dispossessed farmers often resettled) and the incompleteness of records makes it impossible to identify with any certainty the majority of these men, their military records, or the validity of accusations made against them. Generalizations about crowds of demonstrators are notoriously fallible, and always subject to deliberate as well as unintentional distortion.[19]

The best we can do is to identify crowds of people by their behavior, rather than their backgrounds. In that regard, the Regulators were certainly not "rioters," as Van Beck Hall described them.[20] Hall, whose useful demographic and statistical analysis set a shining example for the golden age of cliometrics in the 1970s, was weakest when it came to mat-

---

18. Feer, *Shays's Rebellion*, 182; "Aug 1786 Answer to Body of Insurgents — Court Adjourned," Shays' Rebellion Folder #98, Forbes Library.

19. Gilje wrote of "the ambiguous status of crowd politics. After years of public meetings, ad hoc committees, and the introduction of new groups into the political arena during the 1760s and 1770s, the exact role of these agents of popular will in the 1780s and early 1790s remained ill-defined." Paul Gilje, *The Road to Mobocracy: Popular Disorder in New York City, 1763-1834* (Chapel Hill, 1987), 99. Nonetheless, the crowd remained, in Hoerder's words, "an institution" in Massachusetts. Dirk Hoeider, *Crowd Action in Revolutionary Massachusetts 1765-1780* (New York, 1977), 40 *ff*. See also Richard D. Brown, *Revolutionary Politics in Massachusetts: The Boston Committee of Correspondence and the Towns, 1772-1774* (Cambridge, Mass., 1970), 29-30.

20. Hall, *Politics Without Parties*, 204, 208.

ters of ideology and personality. For that matter, so was Noah Webster, who described the Regulators as "the yeomanry of the country."[21] Doubtless many, perhaps even a majority, were yeomen; an even greater majority were almost certainly right-handed, but neither description explains their consistent, disciplined deportment, under a shifting leadership, as long as they were embodied and commanded by Revolutionary veterans. Even after pay was assured to Regulator recruits (no doubt attracting many who would otherwise have stayed home), the orderly restraint of this "mob" remained their most salient feature.[22]

Were the Shaysites agrarian revolutionists, aiming to tear down the constitutional government, or disaffected veterans, seeking their "just right?" William Pencak has argued that "Shays's Rebellion was a revolution against the Revolution . . .," conducted by a "large number of insurgents with no traceable military history...," who "sought to supplant a social order based on republicanism and a communitarian vision of civic virtue with a minimal government. . . ."[23]

This description does not conform to the Regulators' sole demand, that the court sessions be postponed. And it ignores the *character* of the demonstrations which, like its leadership, was unquestionably military. Neither the crowds collected by the Regulators nor their leaders were a monolithic body, and as events progressed, the unexpected hard-line response from

---

21. Webster to Bowdoin, Philadelphia, 15 Mar., 1787, *Bowdoin-Temple Papers*, II, 181.

22. The Regulators' Form of Enlistment read: "We do each of us acknowledge to be inlisted into a company . . . in Col. Hazleton's Regiment of Regulators, in order for the suppressing of tyrannical government in the Massachusetts State. And we do Ingage to obey such orders as we shall receive from our Superior officers, and to faithfully serve for the term of three months from the Date in Witness hereof we have set our names. The conditions of Service Will Be for a Sargt. Sixty Shillings, per month, Corpl. Fifty Shillings a Month, Privet Forty Shillings a Month and if [we win] the Day their Will be a Considerable Bounty — Ither Forty or Sixty Pounds." 189 M.A. 429.

23. William Pencak, "'The Fine Theoretic Government of Massachusetts is Prostrated to the Earth:' The Response to Shays' Rebellion," in Allis and Gross, eds., *In Debt to Shays* (forthcoming), n.p.

Bowdoin's government radicalized some leaders beyond their original purposes. As Pencak noted, many of the Regulators were "boys, raw, ragged, and undisciplined," and certainly it is true that "the rebels' conduct under fire" in the final confrontation of the Regulation lacked any semblance of valor.[24] But the reason for this is that, even at the end, they were not conducting a military expedition, but a ritual demonstration. In fact, the Regulators were always surprised that they were charged with treason, seized, and shot. It is plausible that they had received assurances that they would never be fired upon, and therefore they never returned fire.

The second episode of the Regulation came one week later in Worcester, after Bowdoin had sought legal advice on the power of county sheriffs, and released his first proclamation urging the people to "value the blessings of freedom and Independence, which at the expence of so much blood and treasure they have purchased;" the Boston establishment clearly dreaded "a state of anarchy, confusion and slavery."[25] As one historian observed, "the ancient cycle for the decay of republics seemed close to completion almost as soon as it had begun."[26]

Just how close to completion that cycle must have seemed can be gauged from the experience of Artemas Ward, a powerful symbolic figure, who led the pro-government response to the second court-closing. As early as 1762, Ward had served as a judge of the Court of Common Pleas. On September 6, 1774, he had marched at the head of 6,000 patriots from the home of Timothy Bigelow to the Worcester County courthouse and, setting himself in opposition to his fellow judges,

---

24. Lemuel Taylor, quoted by Pencak, *op. cit.*, n.p. For more on this final confrontation, see below, 96-98.
25. Advice on "The Powers of the Sheriff" by Theophilus Parsons, *Bowdoin-Temple Papers*, II, 108-111; Bowdoin's Proclamation (printed broadside), 190 M.A. 226.
26. Charles Royster, *Light-Horse Harry Lee and the Legacy of the American Revolution* (New York, 1981), 93.

resolved that *"the court should not sit on any terms."*[27] Over the next dozen years Ward led an extraordinarily prestigious public career, as first Commander-in-Chief of the Continental Army (replaced by Washington, to promote continental unity with the South), Chief Justice of Massachusetts, the head of the Council of Massachusetts, and twice Speaker of its House of Representatives (twice declining election to its Senate).

Now, on September 5, 1786, twelve years later almost to the day, Ward strode to the same court-house, this time determined that the court *should* sit. But now Bigelow lay confined for debt in the county jail, and Ward's path to the Worcester court-house was blocked by three or four hundred men, many of whom had served under him during the war, but who now obeyed the apparent command of Captain Adam Wheeler. Most sported sprigs of evergreen in their hats, just as Washington's men had worn at Brandywine. And this impromptu "army" was as determined as Ward himself had been a dozen years before that the court should *not* sit.[28] Now it was plain for all to see that this was the world turned upside-down.

Bowdoin himself had been President of the Watertown Convention in 1774; now, the very men who had raised troops against the British standing army — like Bowdoin and Ward — felt a pressing need for one of their own, to uphold the principle of contract against the supposed threat of a general redistribution of all private property. This threat, however spurious, "made the movement seem more far-reaching than it really was," wrote historian J. P. Warren in 1897. "Many conservative and influential persons believed that the insurgents desired to overthrow the state government, and to establish some purely democratic or even communistic system in its place."[29] But according to Adam Wheeler, nothing could

---

27. This incident is described melodramatically in Charles Martyn, *The Life of Artemas Ward: The First Commander-in-Chief of the American Revolution* (New York, 1921), 64-65.
28. Martyn, *Artemas Ward*, 283.
29. For Bowdoin at Watertown, see William Alexander Robinson, "James Bowdoin," in *Dictionary of American Biography*, Dumas Malone, ed., 20 vols. (New York, 1928-1936) II, 498. J. P. Warren, "The Confederation and the

have been further from the Regulators' minds. In an open letter printed in the *Worcester Magazine*, Wheeler insisted he
had "no Intentions to Destroy the Publick Government but to
have the . . . Courts . . . suspended, to prevent Such abuses
as have of late taken place by the sitting of these Courts." He
was "moved with the distress of the People," as he watched
"Valuable and Industrious members of Society dragged from
their families to prison, to the great damage not only of their
families but to the Community at large." His only motive was
to postpone the courts' sessions until they could redress their
"grievances in a constitutional way. . . . As Liberty is the prize
that I so early stepped forth in defence of the country to gain,
and so cheerfully fought for, so Liberty is the prize I still have
in view. . . ."[30] Once again, as in Northampton, the judges adjourned to a tavern, consulted with Regulator delegates, and
agreed to postpone the court's sessions; unable to successfully call out the militia, they had no choice.[31]

One week later, court sessions were scheduled for Concord (Middlesex County), Taunton (Bristol), and Great Barrington (Berkshire). At this time the General Court was not
in session, and many of the Governor's Council were out of
Boston, so for several days Bowdoin consulted with a number of gentlemen, including Samuel Adams, Benjamin Austin,
William Cushing and other members of the Supreme Court,
and Attorney-General Robert Treat Paine, to decide whether
or not to call out troops to support the courts; whether dis-
patching troops from one county to another was constitutional; and above all, how they could be paid from Massachusetts'
empty treasury.[32] Though members of this informal Council
reinforced their shared commitment to law and order, a few
recommended lenient measures. But all agreed that the militia should be sent to Concord — the court session closest to

---

Shays Rebellion," in *American Historical Review*, II (New York, 1897), 42.
30. Folder 1, Shays' Rebellion, AAS, and quoted in *Worcester Magazine*,
fourth week of November, 1786; see also Feer, *Shays's Rebellion*, 187.
31. Jonathan Warner to James Bowdoin, 5 Sept., 1786, 190 M. A. 231-233;
Joseph Henshaw to Bowdoin, 7 Sept., 1786, 190 M.A. 237.
32. 189 M. A. 9, 190 M. A. 242.

Boston — and elsewhere be prepared to march at a moment's notice. Then they heard that the Concord town meeting had called a county convention, to placate the Regulators and to prevent government troops from being sent in; Bowdoin decided to let them deal with the situation there themselves. In both Taunton and Berkshire, the sheriff was given the authority (and responsibility) of calling for troops, while being counseled to avoid bloodshed.

On September 12th, Concord filled with county delegates from twenty-three towns, with justices of the peace, and with some one hundred Regulators. These were led by Captain Job Shattuck, former constable and tax collector of Groton; they were soon reinforced by Adam Wheeler from Worcester, with another hundred men.[33] Prudently, the justices again adjourned. The same occurred that day thirty miles south, at Taunton, despite military preparations there to guard the court.[34] And that afternoon at Great Barrington, sixty miles west, a significant number of the militia-men, under General John Patterson, deserted their posts and joined the (apparently) leaderless Regulators.[35] Patterson asked those of his troops who would support the law to muster on one side of the court-house, and some two hundred men obeyed; those who would not numbered eight hundred. Perhaps more than any other moment, this portended the most devastating implications for Bowdoin's government. The protesters then drafted a proclamation for the justices to sign, agreeing that the Court of Common Pleas would not meet until the Constitution had been revised. They then broke open the jail to free the prisoners held there, whom they presumed were being held for debt. This was easily the most provocative action of the early protests.

Thus, in the first fortnight of the Regulation, four courts had been prevented from sitting by some five hundred divers

33. Feer, *Shays's Rebellion*, 205.
34. For a more thorough account of the two Taunton episodes, see Richard R. Mros, "Shays' Rebellion in Taunton," *Shays' Rebellion: Selected Essays*, Martin Kaufman, ed., (Westfield, Mass., 1987), 26-33.
35. I owe much of this account to Feer, *Shays's Rebellion*, 206-211.

men *acting* in a military manner, without bloodshed, rioting, or looting. Bowdoin had no response to the situation: determined not to acknowledge the Regulators' grievances, he could not afford troops to defend the courts. This was the history of the "insurrection" at the moment when its two key figures entered the fray: Captain Shays and General Knox. The next episode centered around the Springfield Arsenal, the most valuable property belonging to the threadbare United States government, and the very ομφαλοσ of Shays' Rebellion.

Daniel Shays was an honorable man at the end of his tether. Approaching forty years of age, he had been born in Hopkinton and settled with his Presbyterian wife, Abigail Gilbert, in North Brookfield (Shutesbury), before moving to Pelham.[36] Shays had served five years in the Revolutionary war, beginning on April 19, 1775, when he responded to the conch by enlisting in Captain Reuben Dickinson's Regiment, before being promoted in 1777 to Captain in Colonel Rufus Putnam's Fifth Regiment of the Massachusetts Line.[37]

Shays, in his own words, had served "in battles at Bunker Hill, and was at the taking of General Burgoyne, assisted in storming Stoney Point under General Wayne, served under the Marquis de La Fayette, and was also in many other battles and skirmishes . . ." in the course of which he suffered a serious wound that later prevented him from working.[38] During the war, Shays and his brother-in-law, Benjamin Gilbert,

---

36. Gregory Nobles wrote that "Pelham had a long history of civil violence against the country élite, rioting against a sheriff in 1762, marching on Hatfield in February 1775 to smoke justice Israel Williams into submission. . . . Action against the courts in 1786 was thus part of a continuous tradition of direct action among a people for whom the provincial public culture manifested in placeholding and representation had been alien and inaccessible." Quoted in Brooke, "To the Quiet of the People . . .," *WMQ*, 3rd Ser., XLVI (1989), 456.

37. For biographical data and the military career of Shays, see Elmer S. Smail, "The Daniel Shays Family," *New England Historical and Genealogical Register*, CXL (Oct 1986), 291-302; *Massachusetts Soldiers and Sailors . . .*, XIV, 76; James Russell Trumbull, *History of Northampton*, 2 vols. (Northampton, Mass., 1902), II,491-492.

38. Daniel Shays's "Declaration for Pension" quoted in *NEHGR* (1986), 295.

frequently socialized with Putnam, sometimes at a Masonic Lodge; in 1778, he joined the Freemasons.[39] Wounded early in the war, Shays wrote in a pension petition, "for the three last years of said service. . . he received no compensation Except what was made in a depreciated Currency. . . . he hath never recieved the five years Pay, which hath usually been allowed to other officers who continued in the service."[40] Before the war was over, Shays was obliged to sell a sword awarded to him for valor by Lafayette himself, after which "the officers refused to associate with him and talked about trying to Court Martial him for his base conduct;" he returned home from the war a wounded, penniless, bitter man.[41] From then on, Shays failed to stay ahead of his debts, even while he remained a creditor of the United States for his unremunerated war service. He sold off part of his land in 1783, but was sued for debt later that year, and again in August, 1786.[42]

Shays was an unlikely rabble rouser. "It is manifest that Shays is very thoughtfull," wrote one government informer, "and appears like a man crouded with embarrassments."[43] Even as Knox raised the alarm to Congress over the Spring-

39. Masters Lodge, No. 2, Albany, New York, according to Mabel Cook Coolidge, *History of Petersham, Massachusetts* (Hudson, Mass., 1948), 132-133. For evidence that Putnam and Shays socialized during the war, see 22 Feb., 1780, in Benjamin Gilbert, *A Citizen-Soldier in the American Revolution: The Diary of Benjamin Gilbert in Massachusetts and New York*, Rebecca D. Symmes, ed. (Cooperstown, New York, 1980), 65.

40. Daniel Shays of Pelham . . ., "Petition to the Senate and House of Representatives of the United States in Congress assembled," n.d., Caleb Strong Papers, Forbes Library. Soldiers and non-commissioned officers were promised one hundred acres, twenty dollars, and a suit of clothes; ensigns would receive one hundred fifty acres; lieutenants, two hundred; and captains, three hundred acres. In January, 1777, Captain Shays became eligible to receive three hundred acres upon completion of his service, which he was never granted; *Massachusetts Soldiers and Sailors*, XIV, 76; 16 and 18 Sept., 1776, *JCC*, II, 357-358, 361, 404.

41. Trumbull, *History of Northampton*, II, 492, and *NEHGR* (1986), 295. See also Robert A. Gross, "Daniel Shays and Lafayette's Sword," *OAH Newsletter*, 15 (Nov. 1987), 8-9.

42. *NEHGR* (1986), 296-297.

43. Levi Shephard to James Bowdoin, Northampton, 28 Dec., 1786, *Bowdoin-Temple Papers*, II, 125.

field Arsenal, he noted Shays's role in regulating the Regulators. "They were headed by a Captain Shays of the militia, and formerly in the continental army . . ., embodied in a military manner, and exceedingly eager to be led to action," wrote the Secretary of War," "but the prudence of their leader prevented an attack on Government troops. . . ."[44] Nowhere is Shays known to have expressed any anti-aristocratic sentiments, nor even to have evinced the widespread feeling that the postwar period was producing economic injustice.[45] While there is no doubt that Shays was indeed one of the leaders of the Regulation, he was not "insolent & imperious," as the others were described.[46] Nor were his words or his deeds those of an ambitious, political demagogue. As he told one friend, he "knew no more what government to set up, than he knew of the *dimensions of eternity*."[47]

On Saturday, September 23rd, 1786, two days before the first confrontation at the Arsenal (and a week before Knox's second visit to Boston and Springfield), a demonstration in New Hampshire provided the Secretary of War and other nationalists with useful evidence that the New England demonstrators were driven by the most radical ambitions; for those who dreaded levelling, this was one of the most ominous events, and among the most widely reported. It was certainly no less threatening for having occured in Exeter, New Hampshire, forty miles north of Boston — no further than Worcester.

---

44. Henry Knox to the President of Congress, Springfield, Oct. 3, 1786, *Papers of the Continental Congress* 150, 1, 587; also in *JCC*, XXXI, 751-753 (read on 6 Oct., 1786).

45. It was the opinion of Nathaniel Ames that one cause for Shays' Rebellion was 'all property accumulating with greater rapidity than ever known into a few people's hands.' Nathaniel Ames Diary, 21 Jan., 1787, as quoted in Jackson Turner Main, *The Social Structure of Revolutionary America* (Princeton, 1965), 225.

46. Shephard to Bowdoin, Northampton, 28 Dec., 1786, *Bowdoin-Temple Papers*, II, 125.

47. Webb Testimony in Isaac Chenery Case, Insurgents Tried Folder, Shays' Rebellion Box, AAS.

Three factors made the Exeter demonstration especially frightening: first, this "body of armed men," estimated at four hundred, with some on horse-back, were "marching under the orders of the Rockingham convention."[48] This gave them significantly more weight than a mere mob, and contributed to the widespread conviction that *all* the demonstrations that autumn were "under orders" from town and county conventions. Thereafter, throughout the fall, the public imagination linked each court-closing to the most sensational petition demands. Second, the Exeter dissidents were under the command of a half-dozen militia officers, so this demonstration had both a political and a military base. They "affected military parade," though "they made a miserable appearance — dirty, ragged, fellows — many of the were young and most of them ignorant." Nonetheless, they "surrounded the Meeting House in which the Legislature were sitting, and placed centinels at the door and windows, with bayonets fixed," forbidding "any person from going in or coming out." This was a much more disciplined action than anyone expected from "an armed mob," as President Sullivan called them. Finally, from one or two widely reprinted reports, the aims of this rag-tag army of the convention appeared to include the most radical demands. As William Plumer recounted, "I went up to the mob. . . . Some demanded paper money; others, an equal distribution of property. Some the annihilation of debts, freedom from taxes, the abolition of lawyers, the destruction of the Inferior Courts, the reduction of salaries, and all of them exclaimed against law and government."[49] The next day, President Sullivan dissolved the commotions with a volunteer force of some 4000 men, half of whom were armed.[50]

48. *New Hampshire Gazette* (Portsmouth), 28 Sept., 1786, reprinted in *Boston Magazine* (Sept./Oct. 1786), III, 401-404, and in Richard B. Morris, ed., *Basic Documents on the Confederation and Constitution* (New York, 1970), 148-152; William Plumer to John Hale, 20 Sept., 1786, *Colonial Society of Massachusetts, Transactions,* 11 (1906-1907), 392-393. See also Main, *The Antifederalists*, p. 67.
49. William Plumer to John Hale, 20 Sept., 1786, *Colonial Society of Massachusetts, Transactions,* 11 (1906-1907), 392-393.
50. *Ibid.*, 393.

On Monday, two days later, Daniel Stebbins witnessed the first arrivals of Shays and some one thousand men in Springfield — more than General William Shepard of the militia could muster. According to Stebbins, their motives were varied. "Some perhaps were unable and others unwilling to pay even their honest debts — some in hopes that it might become the strongest party, others with the hope that of obtaining spoils, the oblivion of all indebtedness and an equalisation of property between the Rich and poor. This had been told the writer by Luke's members. As all men were born equal, so ought they to share equal in property, such was the creed of many of the party."[51]

"It had been resolved by the Insurgents," wrote Stebbins, "that . . . the Continental Stores of arms and ammunition at Springfield should be obtained, 'peaceably if they could.' A large party of Insurgents, under Captain Shays, were assembled in Springfield Street, at the North End, extending near one mile above the Court House. Their main encampment was in the shed above ferry Street - the numbers daily increasing. . . ."[52] While Stebbins imputed the most radical motives to the demonstrators, his description of the events that Tuesday afternoon sounds more like pageantry than rebellion.

> As a matter of Show, Captain Joseph Williams of Springfield, who had known Shays during the Revolutionary War as a brave soldier, took command of a company of Volunteers hastely collected. . . . Capt. Shays was permitted to march his men through Main

---

51. Daniel Stebbins's Notebook — Reminiscences (1845), Forbes Library, Northampton, I, 43. I am indebted to Prof. William Pencak and Forbes Librarian Elise Feeley for directing me to this little-known eyewitness account, which has not been cited by Feer, Szatmary, Hall, Gross, or any other leading study of the Regulation; only Pencak, *op. cit.*, made a brief allusion to Stebbins' account. This quotation is perhaps the best evidence that Jefferson's democratic clarion in the Declaration of Independence was as operative in the Regulation as it was in the Massachusetts Constitution, in which the First words of Article I were "All men are born free and equal." Taylor, ed., *Massachusetts Documents*, 128.
52. Stebbins Notebook, I, 45.

Street with full display of military parade and thence on to Continental Hill — along and around the arsenal — public stores and buildings — unmolested with music, colors flying, nominally to take possession of the Public Grounds — but to do no injury — and in like peaceable manner to return again to their encampment — and thence to disperse his men to their respective towns. It might have been the wish of Capt. Shays to let his men see the Ground which, at some other day, he hoped to possess with all the military Stores thereon standing — and that his men, from this eminence, might see the goodly town of Springfield spread out before and beneath them — a pleasant sight to behold — but which, no doubt, some of the beholders had already adjudged, would become a heap of ruins.

Capt Shays made all the display he could in passing the Court House — and the men under Capt. Williams and the principle men of the town. . . . Between the Court House and old Meeting House was a large open space, now filled with a dense crowd of spectators ready to join the strongest party. Captain Shays marched in front of his men, with Flags flying, a large band of music with Drums and fifes — While passing Capt. Williams Company; with arms present complimenting each other in military Style. . . . Shays and Williams exchanged the Wink of the Eyes. . . .

When Shays troops had passed, many of the spectators cast about them what to do, whether to stand their ground or join Shays, whose party numerically appeared the Strongest, when compared with the small number under arms with Capt. Williams. Then, like a flock of sheep, one & another sprang forward, then a general rash of idle fellows, [illegible] upon Shays rear with shouldered stocks & Clubs, and thus marched on to the Continental Hill and returned with the party. . . [53]

---

53. *Ibid.* For a description of the Arsenal, see below, 107.

"A very sorrow full day," wrote Jonathan Judd. "Brother against Brother. Together against Son. This Mob threaten Lives of all that oppose them."[54] But while threats and bluster filled the air, hot lead did not. What was most significant about this symbolic demonstration was that, having been able "nominally to take possession" of the Continental Arsenal, the Regulators then dispersed peacefully, without seizing its field pieces, rifles, or ammunition. In all, the Regulators paraded through Springfield for four days.[55]

On September 27th, Bowdoin convened the General Court a month early to address the situation. The government combined carrot and stick: a pardon was extended to any who stepped forward to take an oath of allegiance before January 1st, 1787, and partial, temporary debt relief was enacted, as well as a limited Tender Act, allowing payment of taxes due for more than two years in pot ash and some manufactured goods.[56] Bounties were also offered to those who helped to develop local industry, and an excise tax levied on several imports, to stimulate domestic sales.[57] And, prudently, all but the Supreme Court Sessions were postponed in Hampshire, Berkshire, Bristol, and Plymouth counties.[58]

But at the same time the General Court passed a new riot act, providing for the arrest of any who failed to disperse when so ordered, and allowing for their imprisonment (with periodic whippings) for six months and confiscation of all their property. As well, a general search warrant was authorized, along with the right to try an individual outside any county where the courts were not sitting; this meant that anyone could be transported to Boston for trial.[59] Finally, and most ominously, *habeas corpus* was suspended for eight months, for any whom

---

54. Jonathan Judd Diary, Tuesday, 26 Sept., 1786, Forbes Library.
55. *Ibid.*
56. *1786 Acts*, Chaps. 39, 43, 44, and 45 (15 Nov., 1786).
57. *Ibid.*, Chaps. 83 and 108 (8 and 17 Nov., 1786).
58. *Ibid.*, Chaps. 86, 99, and 137 (9, 14, and 17 Nov., 1786).
59. *Ibid.*, Chap. 38 (28 Oct., 1786).

the Governor considered a threat to the Commonwealth.[60]

Having just returned to Congress in New York from his first trip to Springfield and Boston, Knox expressed his alarm in a letter to Congress, already elevating the demonstrations to a problem of continental dimensions, and linking them to his two favorite hobby-horses: a nationalist vision of the United States, and a permanent standing army.

Enough of a lawless and desperate spirit had been manifested to alarm the well affected to Government for the safety of the stores. The mal-contents openly avowed the idea. . . . Their conduct had already evinced that they were capable of perpetrating this crime. . . . *A feeble attempt to raise a guard would probably precipitate [the arsenal's] loss, as the mal-contents might regard it as the first step towards their destruction. . .* . Were there a respectable body of troops in the service of the United States . . . the propriety of the measure could not be doubted. . . . For it may be observed that if one of the Arsenals . . . is suddenly endangered from strange circumstances, the others are liable to the same evil, and in an instant the nation be deprived of its invaluable apparatus of war, which may be converted to the subversion of all government. *But it would be an evil of the most dangerous tendency to raise an additional body of troops and station them at the Arsenals without the absolute certainty of paying them much better than those now in service on the frontiers.*[61]

On September 29th, the Secretary of War received secret authorization from Congress "to repair to Springfield . . . to take such measures as may be necessary for the protection and safety of the federal magazine. . . ,"[62] Three days later Knox

---

60. *Ibid.*, Chap. 41 (10 Nov., 1786).
61. Knox to Congress, War Office (New York), 28 Sept., 1786, *JCC*, XXXI, 698-700. [Knox's underlining.]
62. 29 Sept., 1786, *Secret Journals of the Congress of the Confederation*, 2

arrived there, and reported that payment of the supplementary fund to Congress appeared to have been the immediate cause for the Regulation, again relating the commotions directly to the weakness of national government rather than the enormous accumulation of private and public debt (to which most of his ilk attributed the protests).[63] From Springfield, Knox proceeded to Boston to consult with Bowdoin and "the most respectable characters in the state for their political knowledge" on the touchy questions of who was responsible for the safety of the Arsenal and — touchier still, given the empty treasuries of Massachusetts and the United States — who would pay for the additional troops necessary to defend it.[64]

In October three Regulations ensued, at court-houses in Great Barrington, Taunton, and Cambridge.[65] None was attended by the most prominent Regulators: Shays, Day, Wheeler, Parsons, or Shattuck. The Supreme Court was scheduled to meet in Great Barrington on October 3rd, but already the day before some two hundred men from Egremont, Sheffield, and northern Berkshire had surrounded the court-house. The justices themselves never appeared, so the insurgents vented their frustration upon Theodore Sedgwick; without the leadership of Daniel Shays (or any other officer, apparently), the demonstrators felt no qualms about shouting threats at the most prominent lawyer of Stockbridge, who happened to be riding through town, but who passed unharmed. Sedgwick fled to Sheffield, and the Regulators dispersed, after committing some minor vandalism upon the court-house.[66]

---

vols. (Boston, 1821) I, 174. This was only the ninth entry in the *Secret Journal* since the Treaty of Paris.

63. Knox to Congress, Springfield, 3 Oct., 1786, *JCC*, XXXI, 751-3. For much more on Knox's perception and use of the Regulation, see below, Chapter Four. Interestingly, Knox himself was suffering from financial problems which he attributed to taxes: four months later he admitted to a friend that "I am in great debt on account of some public debts." Knox to Wadsworth, New York, 28 Feb., 1787, Knox Papers, XX, 6.

64. Knox to Congress, War Office, 18 Oct., 1786, *JCC*, XXXI, 886.

65. These minor episodes are thoroughly described in Feer, *Shays's Rebellion*, 236-248.

66. For a full account of this and Sedgwick's later travails with Perez Ham-

At Taunton, on October 25th, 200 men came within yards of the court-house where the Supreme Court was in session, only to find that the commander of the militia had posted 375 militiamen around the building after receiving intelligence from the Governor. The protesters presented a petition to the judges, requesting that they adjourn, and then dispersed peacefully, but the Court continued its session, uninterrupted.

Less than a week later the Supreme Court was scheduled to sit at Cambridge, just across the Charles River from the seat of Massachusetts government. Bowdoin took this opportunity to mobilize the Suffolk and Middlesex militia. Had any imprudent Regulators appeared, they would have been greeted by some two thousand government troops: but none did, and the Court completed its business there without incident. Bowdoin made a personal appearance, together with the President of Harvard College, to thank the militiamen for their loyal service. Bowdoin also issued a lengthy *Address to the People of Massachusetts*, widely reprinted in the press, which blended a conciliatory attitude with threats of reprisal, and blamed the present economic hardships upon the people's lack of economy and their fondness for "foreign gewgaws."[67] The state and federal debt would be discharged through the sale of public lands, Bowdoin asserted, and the state Constitution, if not perfect, was better than risking alterations urged by a minority; if the majority wanted modifications, they could have their way through the elective process. This, of course, was what the Regulators had in mind, though the elections were still six months away.

By the time the *Address* was printed in newspapers across the state, the Regulators had already been stunned by the General Court's threats of punishment for the Regulators, and the suspension of *habeas corpus*.[68] Shays, or someone using his

---

lin, see Richard E. Welch, *Theodore Sedgwick, Federalist* (Middletown, Ct., 1965), 48-53.

67. The *Address* is in *Acts and Resolves 1786 and 1787* (Boston, 1893), 142-164; the quotation is in *ibid.*, 160.

68. "[The *Address*] hath not come to minister or selectmen of this town. . . ."

name, sent a circular letter to the towns that supported the Regulation of the judiciary, warning the men there that danger was imminent, and that they should be "well armed and equipped . . . and be ready to turn out at a minute's warning."[69] Meanwhile, Shays was routinely drilling his men, instilling a sense of discipline that he had practiced during the war as a drill-master.

On Tuesday, November 21st, 1786, when justices of the Court of Common Pleas and the Court of General Sessions arrived in Worcester, they were greeted by some sixty Regulators, led by Abraham Gale; the next day a further contingent of some one hundred reinforcements blocked the court-house, and once again submitted a petition, asking only that the courts' sessions be postponed until after the spring elections. The sheriff who accompanied the justices replied by reading them the newly-minted riot act, providing a legal basis for subsequent prosecution, and then the judges adjourned.[70]

A week later, on November 28th, when the county courts were due to meet at Cambridge, Bowdoin again made preparations to send in the militia from Suffolk, Middlesex, and Essex counties; once again, the Regulators caught wind of the government's activities, and abstained from any action, allowing the court to sit without interference. The next day some of these militiamen were sent directly to Groton, together with a cavalry detachment of prominent gentlemen — including Stephen Higginson — led by General Hichbom, to apprehend a number of well-known Middlesex Regulators, including Job Shattuck, Oliver Parker, and Benjamin Page [Paige].[71] These three were apprehended and transported to

---

Ward to Bowdoin, Shrewsbury, 16 Dec., 1786, *Bowdoin-Temple Papers*, II, 119.

69. Shays said it was "a cursed falsehood" that he had sent out this circular himself, and that "some body else who I dont know put my name to the coppy." Rufus Putnam to Governor Bowdoin, Rutland (Mass.), 8 Jan., 1787, typescript of letter in Shays' Rebellion Box, AAS; for more on this see below, 91-94. *Hampshire Gazette*, 15 Nov., 1786.

70. *Worcester Magazine*, fourth week of November, 1786.

71. *Ibid.*, first week in December, 1786; *Independent Chronicle*, 7 Dec., 1786. For more on this episode, see below, Chapter Five.

Boston, clearly demonstrating for the first time Bowdoin's resolve to set aside *habeas corpus* and provide stem justice for those who instigated popular disobedience. This incident, more than any other, provoked enormous alarm among the Regulators, who realized that they were now condemned to treatment as criminals, unless they were prepared to renounce their ways and take the oath of allegiance.

Shortly before the Court of Common Pleas and General Sessions was to sit in Worcester on December 5th, Bowdoin received intelligence that Shaysites were planning to disrupt the session.[72] The vacillations with which he reacted speak volumes about his indecisive leadership. First, he ordered Sheriff William Greenleaf to organize the defense of the courts; then he wrote the militia commander, Major General Jonathan Warner, ordering him to obey Greenleaf. Bowdoin rewrote that letter, putting Warner in charge, and the next day he halfway countermanded the order, insisting that Warner not bring in troops unless he was sure he had sufficient numbers. That same day Bowdoin wrote to the justices, explaining that there had not been sufficient time to organize a defense of the court-house, and asked that they meet wherever they could safely gather in Worcester in order to *formally* adjourn until January 23rd, 1787. When Warner encountered some four or five hundred Regulators on the day of the sessions, he withheld his men, and the justices announced their adjournment at the United States Arms Tavern. When Sheriff Greenleaf asked the Regulators what their grievances were, one leader replied that the Sheriff's fee for executing criminal prosecutions was one of the most intolerable hardships. Greenleaf replied, "I will hang you all, Gentlemen, for nothing with the greatest pleasure."[73]

---

72. In the week before this Regulation, wrote General Rufus Putnam, "I spent many hours with Shay and his officers, endeavoring to dissuade them from their measures." Rufus Putnam to Governor Bowdoin, Rutland (Mass.), 8 Jan., 1787; typescript of letter in Shays' Rebellion Box, AAS. For more on this see below, 91-94.

73. *Massachusetts Centinel*, 13 Dec., 1786. Anecdote in William Lincoln, *His-*

The next day Daniel Shays himself marched into Worcester at the head of hundreds of Regulators whom he had been drilling at an abandoned Revolutionary barracks in Rutland. For the next few days, the largest group of Regulators yet — about one thousand Shaysites, according to Feer — filled the city; one anxious report in Boston put the number as high as 13,000.[74] But again, the discipline shown by the men throughout one of the most brutal winters in living memory was both notable and exceptional. On their march home from Worcester, wrote Jonathan Smith, "so severe was the weather that a number were frozen to death, and almost every one frost bitten."[75] Still, no homes or provisions were invaded or comandeered, nor rowdy deeds committed.

A fortnight later, Shays called for his men to assemble at Springfield again on December 26th, as did Luke Day and Thomas Grover, and a large body of Regulators appeared by surprise just hours before the Courts of Common Pleas and General Sessions was to assemble. As Eleazer Porter informed Bowdoin, "a committee from the insurgents (who were more than three hundred in number) waited on the Court and requested (with intimations of disagreeable consequences on failure of a speedy compliance) that the . . . 'Honble. Judges of this Court not . . . open said Court of this Term, nor do any kind of business whatever, but all kind of business to remain as tho no such Court had been appointed. Luke Day. Daniel Shays. Thomas Grover.'"[76]

Throughout December and January, emotions on both sides of the Regulation intensified, as government dithered, and the population remonstrated — especially against the imprison-

---

tory of Worcester, as quoted in Charles A. Chase's opening remarks to John Noble, "A Few Notes on The Shays Rebellion," *American Antiquarian Society, Proceedings*, New Series, XV (Worcester, 1904), 112-113.

74. *Worcester Magazine*, second week of December, 1786; see also Feer, *Shays's Rebellion*, 327n.

75. Jonathan Smith, "The Depression of 1785," *WMQ*, 3rd. Ser. (1948), 91.

76. Eleazar Porter To James Bowdoin, Springfield, 26 Dec., 1786, *Bowdoin-Temple Papers*, II, 121.

ment without bail of Shattuck, Page, and Parker in Boston.[77] While Bowdoin vacillated, and grappled with the economic quandaries of responding to the Regulation, and Knox was maneuvering to elevate the protests to an issue of dire national concern, Shays himself was wrestling with the decision of how to proceed, now that he was, apparently, beyond pardon. And, as he had been all along, he was also in a power struggle within the Regulation's leadership, urging the movement's more aggressive fringe — hot-heads and loose cannons — to act with caution, restraint, and non-violence.

We know all this from the single most revealing document about the character of Daniel Shays, and the diverse intentions of the Regulation's leadership. Two weeks after the December Regulation at Springfield, and less than three before the final debacle at the Arsenal, General Putnam met with Shays in his home town of Pelham, ostensibly by chance. This conversation between two old friends and comrades-in-arms, reported sympathetically to Bowdoin by Putnam in writing, has been quoted in snippets by many historians; it has usually been interpreted cynically, as Shays's last attempt to save his own neck.[78] But the document does not support that view, for during the conversation, Shays acknowledged writing "to a few towns in the County of Worcester and Hampshire," and insisted that "by God, I'll never run my country."[79] Such defiance would hardly have brought the Captain a pardon.

In their conversation, Shays indeed appears like a man "crouded with embarrassments," betrayed by his confrères, and resigned to everlasting infamy, since the Act of Indemnity had just expired. At Worcester he had produced his own petition which, apparently, his fellow leaders had failed to forward to Bowdoin. "It was very wrong that they did not,"

---

77. See, for example, the petition from "several towns in the County of Worcester," *Worcester Magazine*, second week in December, 1786. For a lengthy list of petitions relating to the three captured Regulators, see Feer, *Shays's Rebellion*, 343.

78. Rufus Putnam to Governor Bowdoin, Rutland (Mass.), 8 Jan., 1787, typescript of letter in Shays' Rebellion Box, AAS.

79. *Ibid.*, 2.

Shays said wistfully, "but I dont know that it will alter the case for I don't suppose that the Governor and Councill will take any notice of it."[80]

Putnam advised him that it was more honourable to flee "than to fight in a bad cause and be the means of involving your country in a civil war, and that it is a bad cause you have always owned to me: that is you owned to me at Holden the week before you stoped Worcester court that it was wrong in the people to take up arms as they had." Shays replied, "I told you then, and I tell you now that the sole motive with me in taking the command at Springfield was to prevent the sheding of blood . . . and I am so far from confessing of it as a crime that I look upon it that government are indebted to me for what I did there." But thereafter "it was noised about that warrants were out after me and I was determined not to be taken. . . . I never ordered a man to march to Shrewsbury nor nowhere else except when I lay at Rutland I wrote to a few towns . . . You are deceived — I never had half so much to do with the matter as you think for, and the people did not know of the Act of Indemnity before they collected."[81]

When Putnam asked him why he had not sent his petition before closing the court at Worcester, Shays acknowledged that "it would have been better, but I cannot see why stoping that court is such a crime that if I might have ben pardoned before I should not be exempted now." Putnam answered that, "as you are at the head of the Insurgents and the person who directs all their movements, I cannot see you have any chance to escape."[82]

"I at their head I am not," Shays retorted. Not much of a Cromwell, this Daniel Shays. "But," said Putnam, "I saw your name to the request presented to the Justices . . ." at Springfield. "I know it was their (*sic*) and Grover put it their without my knowledge . . . I was sent to and refused and told them I would have nothing to do in the matter . . . I told them it was inconsistent, after we had agreed to petition as we did

80. *Ibid.*, 1.
81. *Ibid.*, 2-3.
82. *Ibid.*, 3-4.

at Worcester and promised to remain quiet, to medle with the Courts any more till we knew whether we could git a pardon or not. . . . Upon my refuseing to act they have chose a Committee who have ordered the men to march . . . I tell them that I never will have anything more to do with stoping courts or anything else but to defend my self, till I know whether a pardon can be obtained." If not, "I will collect all the force I can and fight it out, and I sware so would you or anybody else, rather than be hanged."[83] The transcribed conversation ends with Putnam's declaration that "I fully beleve he may be brought off, and no doubt he is able to inform government more of the Bottom of this plott then they know at present."[84]

Three conclusions must be drawn from this unusual encounter between old friends. First, Shays did not believe he had violated constitutional law in stopping the courts, even though he had grave misgivings about other schemes of the Regulation's leadership. Whether or not he had studied the Massachusetts Constitution, Shays clearly believed in certain of its guarantees, that had been abrogated: "All power residing originally in the people," magistrates are "at all times accountable to them." (Part One, Article V); "Government is instituted for the common good. . . and not for the profit, honour, or private interest of any one man, family or class of men: . . . Therefore the people alone have the incontestable . . . right to . . . reform, alter, or totally change . . . [Government]" (Part One, Article VII); "No subject ought, in any case, or in any time, to be declared guilty of treason or felony by the legislature" (Part One, Article XXV); and "In criminal prosecutions, the verification of facts in the vicinity where they happen, is one of the greatest securities of the life, liberty, and property of the citizen" (Part One, Article XIII).[85] This last guarantee had clearly been violated in the seizure and removal to Boston of Shattuck, Parker and Page.

Second, one must conclude that, for his part, Shays was prepared to end the Regulation, in which he had acted as a

---

83. *Ibid.*, 4-5.
84. *Ibid.*, 6.
85. Taylor, ed., *Massachusetts Documents*, 128-131.

moderating force, and no longer planned to participate at all, except to defend himself. This clearly was what Putnam believed, although it is unlikely that Shays would have betrayed the other Regulators, as Putnam's final note implies. Had Shays been offered a pardon at this juncture (as his undelivered petition apparently sought), the final confrontation at the Arsenal might not have transpired, given Shays's importance in the Regulation.

Lastly, it is clear Shays felt that, without the possibility of a fair trial, his position was hopeless, and that by now his choice was, in Stebbins' words, either "Neck or Nothing."[86] His only hope was that he might be able to bargain from a position of strength if they first took the continental stores at the Springfield Arsenal.

In early January, Bowdoin announced the formation of a special body of 4,400 troops under the command of Major General Benjamin Lincoln.[87] This volunteer force was recruit-

---

86. Putnam suggested that Shays submit to the mercy of the General Court, "and if your submission is refused I will venture to be hanged in your room." Shays replied, "In the first place I dont want you hanged and in the second they would not accept of you." Rufus Putnam to Governor Bowdoin, Rutland (Mass.), 8 Jan., 1787, typescript of letter in Shays' Rebellion Box, AAS, 6. Daniel Stebbins's Notebook, Forbes Library, Northampton, 1, 45. For a comparison of Shays' moderation with the Regulators who were more radical and more desperate, especially after the Springfield, see Eli Parsons's letter to "Friends and Fellow Sufferers," 15 Feb., 1788, quoted in Minot, *History*, 146-147; Parsons recommended that they "destroy Shepard's army . . . with a determination to carry our point, if fire, blood and carnage will effect it. . . . Help us to *Burgoyne* Lincoln and his army." *Ibid*. However, by this time the few remaining parties of Regulators had fled to New Lebanon, New York, and Pownal, Vermont; the letter is nothing but desperate bluster.

87. Less than a year and a half after General Benjamin Lincoln had surrendered Charleston, "the greatest single military disaster suffered by the Americans during the war," it was he whom Washington sent to receive Cornwallis's surrender. A month later, in October 1781, Congress chose him over Knox as the first Secretary at War, even though, as Page Smith wrote, "Lincoln's weaknesses as a general were . . . painfully evident;" though Knox's artillery had, in Washington's words, with "the resources of his genius supplied the deficit of means." John Gregory Rossie, *The Politics of Command in the American Revolution* (Syracuse, 1975), 207; Oct. 30, 1781, *JCC*, VII, 216. Page Smith,

ed from the militias of Suffolk, Essex, and Middlesex counties.[88] Supplying these troops was a touchy problem: the state
treasury was empty, and new taxes could not be levied as long
as the legislature was adjourned. So Bowdoin began a subscription among the wealthiest to raise a loan of £6,000, starting with his own £250, as well as contributions from Stephen
Higginson and several directors of the Massachusetts Bank.[89]
But the loan was not raised until Lincoln himself visited a
"club of the first characters of Boston," recommending that
they part with a small portion of their wealth in order to secure the remainder; thus, the explicit purpose of the force was
to protect these gentlemen's fortunes.[90] With the Governor's
assurance that the loan would be repaid, and Lincoln himself
passing the hat, the money to supply the gentry's army was
quickly collected.[91]

The final confrontation in Springfield was all thud and
blunder, it was both a mirthless comedy of errors and a pe-
tit-mal tragedy, producing the first fatalities of the convulsion. This was not, strictly speaking, a Regulation. It did not
take place at the Massachusetts court-house, but at the United States Arsenal, and it did not aim to prevent the seizure
of property: one cannot guess the results had the Regulators
seized the military stores. Shays was one of the leaders of this
siege, and his men never fired a single shot; it is pointless to
speculate how events might have proceeded if the Arsenal had

A New Age Now Begins, 2 vols. (New York, 1976), II, 1382; Washington to
President of Congress, 31 Oct., 1781, *Writings of Washington*, XXIII, 308.
88. 189 M. A. 60, 61, 68.
89. Initial subscription list, 189 M. A. 64.
90. Lincoln to Washington, 4 Jan., 1786, *Washington Papers*.
91. Ultimately, this loan superseded the failed attempt by Colonel Henry Jackson (with Knox's help), to raise and pay for federal troops. See *JCC*, XXXI,
895-6: "in the present embarrassments of the federal finance Congress would
not hazard the perilous step of putting arms into the hands of men whose fi-
delity must in some degree depend on the faithful payment of their wages had
they not the fullest confidence from authentic and respectable information of
the most liberal exertions of the money holders in the State of Massachusetts
and the other States in filling the loan authorised by the resolve of Congress
of this date."

been unguarded, as it was when the Regulators surrounded its buildings four months earlier.

Modern historians have described these events before, but Daniel Stebbins's eyewitness account has not been cited in any published study of Shays' Rebellion. On January 24th, 1787, in four feet of snow, Luke Day and some 800 Regulators to the west, Eli Parsons, with several hundred to the north, and Daniel Shays with more than a thousand to the east, converged on the Arsenal, defended by General Shepard and 1,200 militiamen.[92] Lincoln, with 3,000 men, was still on his way from Worcester. "Capt. Shays and his Council," Stebbins wrote, "were to meet and take the premises by surprise. . . . Arangements were made that intelligence should to and from the Tripple Alliance.... An express from Shays headquarters to Capt. Parsons & Day, designating the day and hour to concentrate and unite their forces on Continental Hill . . . was intercepted developing the whole plan of Shays — this gave ample time to prepare for the defence of the public Property."[93]

> General Shephard had caused a line of demarcation to be made & sent a message to Capt. Shays, that if he attempted to pass that Line he (Genl Shephard) would feel justified in repelling the violation of his orders....
>
> Most of General Shephard's troops were secreted within and behind the Public Buildings and out of sight — scouting parties were hovering in the Bushes. . . . the Cavalry also in readiness with mounted Continentals constantly passing and repassing in front of the Insurgents but knew when to come in — the passing of the Line....
>
> [The insurgents] advanced guard of about 400 Old Soldiers, who had seen service, began march toward

---

92. A number of incidents occurred, just before the Arsenal was threatened, in which nearby shopkeepers were held prisoner; it is unlikely, however, that any of the Regulation leadership condoned such actions. See Szatmary, *Shays' Rebellion*, 101.

93. Daniel Stebbins's Notebook, Forbes Library, Northampton, I, 47.

the Public Buildings — Eight deep, Shoulder to Shoulder, in plain sight of the writer, commanded with one Capt. White, with whom the writer became personally acquainted in afteryears — Captain was a brave soldier of the Revolution — General Shephard's Aids and Cavalry being called in, were drawn up on the left of the field pieces. . . . The Insurgents called them 'Government puppies' — but they dare not open their mouths and 'bark' or evin dare bark at them. . . . The field pieces were elevated so that the Balls might pass over the heads of the Insurgents or far on either side, in hopes that the discharge might check them. . . . But it only hastened them onward, the Balls falling far in the rear among the pine shrubbery and within the hearing of Shays mounted Volunteers, who were so frightened or astonished it was said that no less than 20 fell from their horse through sheer fright.

The firing of the pieces accelerated the step of the advance Guard into a trot — at every flash of the Cannons, the old soldiers in range of the Guns dropped prostrate — but instantly in place again as soon as the Balls had passed.

After the first two discharges I heard General Shephard's directions to lower the Pieces waistband high. At this time the advance were passing a curve in the Road — so that a shot to take affect would reach them about midway of the line.

One of the Artillery men . . . stepped forward to sponge his gun, thrust it into the muzzle while the Fuzee was applied. The ball took off both of the arms of poor Challender, killed two of the Insurgents and mortally wounded a third.

The rear of Shays Party began to run and so rapid in flight that Capt. White the Commander was left entirely alone — he halted a moment, casting a look of scorn behind and before, brought the breech of his gun to his fist, and with contemptuous look upon the Government

Party and turning towards the party that had deserted him sprang into the bushes at the top of his speed.[94]

Such was the debacle at the Springfield Arsenal, according to Stebbins, as confirmed by other narrative accounts.[95] The next day Lincoln's army arrived and followed the Regulators to Amherst and Petersham, where Shays's men had regrouped. After a night-long march through a blizzard, Lincoln caught the Shaysites by surprise, and again they were routed. Many leaders, including Shays and some 2,000 Regulators, fled to Vermont, receiving sanctuary and support from both the Governor and — more importantly — Ethan Allen. From there, and from New York state, raiding parties made forays into Stockbridge and other Massachusetts towns, for plunder and reprisal.[96]

In the days, weeks, and months that followed, parties of fleeing Regulators committed crimes against the persons and property of shopkeepers and homeowners which had nothing to do with the Regulation itself. These felonies continued sporadically even beyond the April election of Hancock, in which Bowdoin was soundly defeated, along with many pro-government members of the House. Some of these crimes led to long prison sentences, and before the end of 1787, two Regulators — John Bly and Charles Rose — were hanged for burglary.[97]

The principal conclusions that must be drawn from any examination of the Regulation itself — discounting the secondary and peripheral acts of violence which had nothing to do with the movement's purpose — are, first of all, that this was intended as a traditional exercise of communitarian disobedi-

---

94. *Ibid.*, I, 47, 48.
95. For Shepard's account of the episode, see "Documents Relating to Shays' Rebellion," *American Historical Review*, 2 (July 1897), 694. See also Szatmary, *Shays' Rebellion*, 102-103.
96. All of this has been meticulously chronicled by Feer, *Shays's Rebellion*, 370-381, and Szatmary, *Shays' Rebellion*, 105-114. For a glorified account of Perez Hamlin's activities, see Edward Bellamy, *The Duke of Stockbridge* (Boston, 1879).
97. See Feer, *Shays's Rebellion*, 420.

ence, on behalf of westerners oppressed by eastern authority: the fact that that authority was now American did not make the oppression any more palatable. From the first court closing in August to the last in December, 1786, the Regulators expressed one consistent demand: that the seizure of property be postponed until after the next election.

Second, the Regulators were stunned, disillusioned, and confused by the untraditional, hard-line response of Bowdoin's government. Clearly, it was the "patriarchs" rather than their "dependents" who violated the protection covenant. After independence, *noblesse oblige* was as obsolescent as blue-blooded nobility. While some, like Adams and Jefferson, recognized that the westerners were responding to the accelerated amortization of the war-debt, Bowdoin's men continued pursuing policies which benefited their ilk over the interests of the community as a whole. It is not too much to say, then, that the Regulators' primary goal was not only understandable, but justified, particularly in light of the tradition of court-closings that had persisted in the state as late as 1780.[98]

The Regulation reached an unprecedented and perilous plateau after the November suspension of *habeas corpus* and the imprisonment of Job Shattuck in Boston.[99] This abrogation of constitutional guarantees by the General Court was not

---

98. For an account of the Massachusetts court-closings between 1774 and 1780, see Taylor, *Western Massachusetts*, 75, 84, 87, 98.

99. Immediately after Shattuck and his comrades were seized, one of the indicted Regulators wrote: "To the good people of boylston as this is perelous times and blood Shed and prisoners made by tirants who are a fighting for promotion and to advance their Intrest wich will Destroy the good people of this Land — we that Stile ourselves Rigelators think it is our Duty to Stand for our lives and for our familys and for our Intrest wich will be taken from us if we Dont Defend them therefore we would have you take it into Consideration and fly to our assistance and Soon as possible in this Just and Rightous Cause as there must be Seperation made, this Request from Daniel Shays and Adam Wheeler who are Chief Commanders of the army as I am greatly Requested by these gentlemen to notify you I think it my Duty to Do so." Letter to people of Boyleston, from (indicted) Sylvanus Billings, 2 Dec., 1786, in Suffolk Court Files, *Worcester*, Sept. 1787, No. 155325, as quoted in John Noble, "A Few Notes on Shays Rebellion," in *Proceedings of the American Antiquarian Society* XV (1902-3), 212-213.

warranted by the demonstrations, but was inspired, apparently, by the fearful realization that the state had neither an effective military force, nor the means to pay for it. (It is also fair to wonder how the Regulators planned to pay the troops they recruited, but the historical record provides no answer.)[100]

According to Stebbins, in the last moments of the siege of the Arsenal, Shays crossed the line — literally — into rebellion. But it is clear from his statements, as well as the conduct of his men, that this was at best a half-baked plan, half-heartedly executed, for the Regulators to avoid prosecution: the demonstrators showed no interest in seizing Boston, or Worcester, or even Springfield. Even their march on the military stores seems to have been, in their minds, a symbolic act of defiance: the Regulators were stunned when they were fired upon — as if the rules of the game had suddenly been broken. If they had planned to overwhelm the Arsenal, surely some of the hotheaded veterans would have fired a few rounds before retreating with the others; but even when the cannonfire was leveled at them, not a single shot was fired in return.

Few of the Regulators would have supported the Philadelphia Convention, and a majority of them opposed its ratification: they were seeking more direct political control of their lives, not a greater central government. Nonetheless, as a result of the Regulation — albeit an indirect result — conservatives seized the long-awaited moment, and threw all their force into what seemed to them a last-ditch effort to save the United States. But to accomplish that greater goal, they would first have to recruit a well-paid, new army to suppress the unpaid, old army.

---

100. For promise of pay to Regulators, see above, 74 n.22.

PART TWO
THE NATIONALISTS' RESPONSE

CHAPTER FOUR

General Knox and the Springfield Arsenal

"The Union is older than any of the States and, in fact, it created them as States."

— Abraham Lincoln[1]

In the spring of the leaf, 1770, late of a Monday evening, a large youth named Henry Knox, twenty years old, was returning home down Cornhill, near the bookstore where he worked and studied military science, when he heard the bell of the Brick Meeting House. As Boston townfolk flooded the streets, he realized that it was not a building that had caught fire, but the mood of the crowd. Some two hundred citizens had collected to taunt the Twenty-Ninth Regiment — the standing army which His Majesty had billeted in Boston. When Captain Preston joined his regiment, Knox "took him by the coat," according to one biographer, "and told him for God's sake to take his men back again, for if they fired his life must answer for the consequence."[2] Then, without warning and without orders, one of the regiment fired into the crowd, killing five and wounding six more. The crowd fled, dropping hats and coats across the blood-dappled snow.

So it was that the young Henry Knox stepped out from

---

1. Special Session Message, 4 July, 1861, James D. Richardson, ed., *A Compilation of the Messages and Papers of the Presidents, 1789-1897* (Washington, D. C., 1897), VI, 27.
2. Francis S. Drake, *Life and Correspondence of Henry Knox, Major-General in the American Revolutionary War* (Boston, 1873), 11.

an aimless, angry mob and took command of the situation —
just as Daniel Shays would do sixteen years later. "From that
moment" wrote Daniel Webster, "we may date the severence
of the British Empire."[3] And, from that moment, as the leader
of this impromptu rebellion, Knox became the patriot-hero
of the Boston Massacre. Two years later, having opened his
own bookstore among the fashionable merchants of Cornhill,
and succeeded (despite his reputation as a rebel), in marrying
the daughter of an aristocratic Tory, Knox joined the Boston
Grenadiers.[4] On the fateful date of April 19, 1775, the same
day Shays and many others enlisted, Knox fled Boston and
reported for duty to General Artemas Ward, then commander
of the Patriot troops. Two months later, Ward's supreme rank
was passed to General Washington.[5]

A fortnight after he was appointed commander-in-chief,
Washington visited Cambridge to inspect the defensive works
erected by Knox, who wrote to his wife that Washington and
General Charles Lee "expressed the greatest pleasure and surprise at their situation and apparent utility, to say nothing of
the plan, which did not escape their praise."[6] That was the
beginning of the extraordinary friendship and trust between
Washington and Knox, who became a regular dinner-guest of
his General's, and was soon put in charge of artillery.[7]

---

3. Daniel Webster quoted in North Callahan, *Henry Knox: General Washington's General* (New York, 1958), 11.
4. Among the volumes which Knox advertised were histories of England by
Rapin, Goldsmith, and Mrs. Macauley — mostly re-workings of David Hume's
History. Knox also advertised Montesquieu, *Cato's Letters*, and *Life of Cromwell*; see *A Catalogue of Books, imported and to be Sold by Henry Knox, at the
London Book Store, a little Southward of the Townhouse, in Cornhill, Boston*,
MDCCLXXIII. Shays' Rebellion Box, Folder 7, AAS.
5. According to John Adams "the greatest number" in Congress wanted Ward
to remain in command, but political considerations recommended Washington;
Charles. F. Adams, ed., *The Works of John Adams*, 10 vols. (Boston, 1850-
1856), II, 415-418, X, 162-165. Ward's "title to first place," wrote Martyn,
"was sacrificed by the New England statesmen to meet the overwhelming necessity of uniting the colonies." Martyn, *Artemas Ward*, 148.
6. Henry Knox to Lucy Knox, Roxbury, 6 July, 1775, as quoted in Drake, *Correspondence of Knox*, 18.
7. Freeman wrote that "from the time Washington met Knox on the road be-

It was also the beginning of Knox's ardent nationalism. To understand what an important opportunity Shays' Rebellion was to Knox's ambitions for himself and his country, one must chart the tangled trail of the nationalists' agenda during the intervening years, and recognize how, repeatedly, those sentiments were thwarted by the military structure, by Congress, and by the several states. Throughout that decade, all his efforts — for promotion, for higher pay, for pensions, for the impost to pay for the pensions, for the Cincinnati, for a permanent military establishment, and for a revised Constitution — all had fallen far short of his aspirations, and all had contributed to the polarization between continental and particularist interests. By 1786, Knox felt that, if he could not use the commotions in his home-state to their best purpose, no further opportunity might ever arise.

It should become clear in the following chapters that a number of important issues inspired the nationalists to strive for a fundamental restructuring of the United States government: foreign trade agreements, foreign loans, and the redemption of securities would benefit most of these men personally. Still, though, nationalist sentiment was born, not in Congress, but in Washington's army, created well before the Declaration of Independence and long before the Articles of Confederation. Washington's second general orders, issued two days before he met Knox, declared that all the soldiers raised "are now the troops of the UNITED PROVINCES of North America, and it is hoped that all distinctions of Colonies will be laid aside."[8] It is arguable that in this moment, rather than in the

---

tween Cambridge and Roxbury, the commander in chief had constant and highly proficient service from the bulky young Bostonian," then twenty-five years old. Douglas Southall Freeman, *George Washington, A Biography*, 7 vols. (New York, 1948-1957), IV, 131. "Knox won the affection of Washington as no other man. . . ever did;" Noah Brooks, *Henry Knox, A Soldier of the Revolution* (New York, 1900), 37; see also Flexner, *Washington*, II, 43, 70; Drake, *Correspondence of Knox*, 18. Knox also had the trust of Massachusetts leaders: in October John Adams wrote to Knox, whom he had known when Adams was "a man of business in Boston," "requesting his sentiments upon a plan for the establishment of a military academy." Drake, *Correspondence of Knox*, 19.

8. *Writings of Washington*, III, 309. This was a blow to the particularists' inter-

first meeting of the Continental Congress, or the separation from England, the American nation was conceived. From the start, Washington reminded the soldiers that "all distinction of colonies will be laid aside, so that one and the same spirit may animate the whole, and the only contest be, who shall render on this great and trying occasion the most essential service."[9] Years later, Washington wrote that "a century in the ordinary intercourse" could not have done for nationalist sentiment "what seven years' association in arms did."[10]

It was with this same spirit of nationalism that Knox was imbued, from the beginning of the Revolution to the ratification of the Constitution; but, despite his humble origins, he was not inspired by any democratic idealism. Alan Taylor described Knox precisely, emphasizing that he "believed in a Revolution that preserved a governing élite based on demonstrated 'morality and virtue' rather than simply on inheritance. Knox had not engaged in the Revolution to promote an egalitarian society without social distinctions. Such a society would have debased what he had achieved. Having risen from modest origins through military service . . . he wanted to preserve and enhance the social distinctions traditionally enjoyed by the colonial élite. . . . He understood the importance of a natural aristocracy."[11]

In the next three months, Knox justified all the confidence placed in him by reaching the fort captured by Ethan Allen at Ticonderoga. Summoning up all his boldness and ingenuity to transport the heavy artillery across snow, ice, and the Hudson River, the young Knox returned to Boston with "55 pieces of iron and brass ordnance, 1 barrel of flints, and 23 boxes of

---

ests, since "those who favored a strong central government naturally wished to increase the dependence of the army on Congress. . . . by the beginning of the new year [1776] Congress had gone a long way toward creating a truly 'Continental' army." Rossie, *Politics of Command*, 61, 74.

9. Quoted in Page Smith, *A New Age Now Begins*, 2 vols. (New York, 1976), I, 568.

10. *Writings of Washington*, XXXV, 199-200.

11. Alan Taylor, *Liberty Men and Great Proprietors* (Chapel Hill, N.C., 1990), 38.

lead."[12] This "noble train of artillery" completely altered the balance of power, and ensured the swift departure of the British from Boston and environs.[13]

Congress, meeting in Philadelphia, recommended that Massachusetts form a government, but took no prompt action to adopt the state's nascent military force; as a result, the Massachusetts army never considered itself a creature of Congress.[14] Thus, because the deployed troops were not a constituted body, the appointment of other officers was a knotty problem.[15] Despite all the praise that Colonel Knox received, over the next several years the intense quarrels over military rank made it difficult for Washington to elevate him formally to 'General Washington's General.' Promotion was very important to Knox, both socially and financially; but John Adams told James Hawley that Knox was "so far down on the seniority list that he regarded it as dangerous to promote" him over others.[16]

Frustrated, and unable to achieve a promotion, Knox conceived a scheme to elevate his position socially, at least. In September, 1776, John Adams later recalled to Jefferson, Knox wanted some distinction — if only a ribbon in his hat — that he could leave to his children, to prove their descent from a true Patriot.[17] Seven years later, that ribbon had evolved into Knox's constitution for the hereditary Cincinnati.[18]

---

12. Brooks, *Knox*, 38.

13. *Ibid.*, 44.

14. *JCC*, I, 115.

15. "The several colonies," wrote Louis Clinton Hatch, "wished not only to furnish officers for their troops, but also to make appointments for all ranks below that of brigadier-general. The army around Boston was formed before the meeting of Congress; and its officers were necessarily appointed by local authority. When Congress adopted the army, they appointed generals; but made few if any changes in the lower grades." Louis Clinton Hatch, *The Administration of the American Revolutionary Army* (New York, 1904), 39.

16. Callahan, *Knox*, 67.

17. Jefferson Diary, 16 Mar., 1788, *Jefferson Papers*, XIII, 11. See above, Chapter Two, 45 n.24.

18. Minor Myers, Jr., *A History of the Society of the Cincinnati* (Charlottesville, 1983), 17-19. The manuscript of "The Institution" appears in Francis S. Drake, *Memorials of the Society of the Cincinnati of Massachusetts* (Boston,

Knox was also frustrated by the low pay that he and other officers were receiving, and wrote to Adams that Americans received only half as much as British officers. "They are not vastly riveted to the honor of starving their families for the sake of being in the army;" loyal as they were, they would not suffer "the ruin of themselves and families."[19] By 1777, the officers were demanding the same stipend that retired British officers received: half-pay for life. Washington finally capitulated to this idea in April, 1778, writing to Congress that "I do most religiously believe the salvation of the cause depends upon it."[20]

But Henry Laurens, then President of Congress, argued that, with such pensions, the retired officers would be the "drones and incumbrances of society, pointed at by boys and girls — there goes a man who every year robs me of a part of my pittance. . . . This will be the language of republicans; how pungent, when applied to gentlemen who shall have stepped from the army into the good remaining estate; how much deeper to some, who, in idleness and by speculation, have amassed estates in the war!"[21] This is a near-perfect description of popular sentiment in Massachusetts. But despite Laurens' emotionalism, Congress reluctantly passed a modified measure that was increased to half-pay for life in 1780. Soldiers and non-commissioned officers, on the other hand, were to receive a bounty of only eighty dollars at the end of the war — equal to just one year's pay for a private.[22] Ultimately, they received that bounty in Continental certificates, whose value plummeted immediately.

That Knox was aware of the soldiers' dire plight is clear from his correspondence, in which he ignored the distinctions between the lot of privates and the more comfortable circumstances provided for officers. Knox wrote to his brother, "we

---

1873).

19. Henry Knox to John Adams, 21 Aug., 1776, Knox Papers, III, 23.

20. Washington, *Writings* (Ford), VI, 301-304.

21. Laurens to Washington, 5 May, 1778, as quoted in Hatch, *Administration*, 82.

22. Hatch, *Administration*, 84.

depend upon the great Author of Nature to provide subsistence and clothing . . . for the people, whose business, according to the common course of things, it was to provide the materials necessary, have either been unable or neglected to do it."[23] The effects of this tension between the soldiers, Congress and 'the people' who failed to support the troops, would last for years to come.

In February, 1777, Knox visited Springfield, where he wrote to Washington that "it was the best place in all the four New England States for a laboratory, cannon foundry, etc., and I hope your Excellency will order it there."[24] Washington followed Knox's advice, and construction began on what would soon be the Continental Army's largest store of weapons north of Harper's Ferry, Virginia. Ten years later, writing to Congress after the siege of the arsenal, Knox described it "as one of their important deposits of Ordnance and Stores. A lease of 10 acres of ground in an eligible situation was purchased of the town for 99 years, on which were erected a variety of large wooden buildings for the reception of the Stores, and accomodation of the troops and artificers, a laboratory, a foundery for casting of brass cannon, and a spacious and well constructed brick Magazine."[25] Chosen and championed by the young Massachusetts colonel, the Springfield Arsenal was, if you will, the original Fort Knox.

With the defeat of Cornwallis, the states began re-asserting their sovereignty, and Congress abolished its maladroit Board of War in October, 1781. By this time Congress had begun considering the impost as a means of paying the army, but that raised the most highly-charged political issue of all:

---

23. Henry Knox to William Knox, 2 Dec., 1780, Drake, *Correspondence of Knox*, 64.
24. Brooks, *Knox*, 87. He also noted that he was "surprised at the very extraordinary bounty offered by the State ($86 1/2) for recruits. . . . Enlistments in this town have been exceedingly rapid. . . ." Naturally, that bounty was to be paid by taxing the same citizenry that produced the recruits.
25. 13 Mar., 1787, *JCC*, XXXII, 109-114.

that of giving Congress the power to tax. So it was upon this question of the impost that the first expressions of anti-Federal sentiment were heard.[26] Since the states looked upon this 5 percent tax on most imports as an amendment to the Articles, the issue would require unanimous assent, but in November, 1782, Rhode Island formally rejected the impost.[27] Rhode Island's veto was proof apparent to the Army that the Articles of Confederation were structurally inadequate to fulfill the obligations of Congress. Indeed, the constitutional implications were inescapable: under the Articles of Confederation, a slim majority within any single state could always thwart the will of the vast majority in the United States.[28] Effectively, this meant that representative government in the states could always outweigh their representation in the Continental Congress.

In 1783, Congress submitted a modified plan, limiting the duration of the impost to twenty-five years, and involving the states in the collection of taxes.[29] But even merchant Stephen Higginson, generally a firm supporter of the impost, called this draft an "artful plan of finance, in which are combined a heterogeneous mixture of imperceptible and visible, constitutional and unconstitutional taxes . . . no part of it to be binding unless the whole is adopted by all the states. The cessions are to serve as sweeteners to those who oppose the impost,"[30] It did not work; a simple majority might have been obtained this way, but not a unanimous vote.

---

26. "The immediate effect of the impost would have been to confer a limited power of taxation upon Congress," wrote Main. "Antifederalism originated as a political force during and after the Revolution when a decisive crystallization of opinion occured," beginning with the debate over the impost. Jackson Turner Main, *The Antifederalists: Critics of the Constitution, 1781-1788* (Chapel Hill, 1961), 72.

27. *JCC*, XIX, 112-112.

28. Similarly, in June 1992, the Danish referendum on European union was defeated by 50,000 "Anti-Federal" votes, casting into doubt the economic future of 350,000,000 Europeans.

29. *JCC*, XXIV, 257-261.

30. Stephen Higginson to Theophilius Parsons, Sr., Apr. 1783, Burnett, *Letters*, VII, 123-124, 171-172.

There was widespread concern that if Congress did not respond to the army's demands, the officers would turn to the state governments. Alexander Hamilton, in a letter to Washington, explained why he, like Knox, favored funding by continental securities: first, officers from states that opposed half-pay would come out poorly; second, there would be inequality of half-pay between the states, causing greater discontent; and third, "such a reference was a continuance of the old wretched state system, by which the ties between Congress and the army have been nearly dissolved."[31] If Congress failed to deliver on its promise, however, even the most ardent nationalists would have to turn to the states.[32]

Massachusetts was divided on the impost. At first, surprisingly, westerners favored passage, probably because, as Main suggested, they did not depend upon imports as much as easterners.[33] But the impost bill lost the vote, because, while it would have won in the Senate, the House was four-to-one against it.[34] Samuel Osgood, one of Massachusetts' delegates in Congress, wrote Knox that half-pay was excessive, arguing that length of service should be a factor; but, for Knox, this "did not touch the crucial point; the faith of Congress was already pledged to grant half-pay to the officers."[35] By then, the world had spent years watching Congress wrangle over whether or not to keep its pledges to the army that had liberated them.

31. Alexander Hamilton, *The Papers of Alexander Hamilton*, Harold C. Syrett, ed., 15 vols. (New York, 1961-1969), III, 320.
32. Hatch, *Administration*, 144. Knox himself, together with General Rufus Putnam, had been chosen to deliver a memorial in 1782, asking Massachusetts to assume their half-pay, or offer commutation. Finally, Knox did not attend in Boston, because Washington was unable to spare him. In Massachusetts, Hancock first offered the officers his full support, then promptly neglected their demands, pushing the officers further into Bowdoin's political camp, where they remained until 1787.
33. "The impost may have seemed an easier way of paying the federal debt than a system of state taxes which might be levied not only on imports but on land and polls," which is what eventually happened. Main, *The Antifederalists*, 86.
34. Hatch, *Administration*, 145.
35. *Ibid.*, 146.

The encamped and unpaid army, awaiting the formalities of peace, had to act. The officers in particular could foresee a dismal post-war future, many having spent their personal fortunes on the war, and lost out on the privateering opportunities which others of their class had seized upon.[36] Something would have to be done, while they still had strength in numbers, to assure their future security. It was among the officers of Massachusetts that agitations first began.[37]

After Rhode Island rejected the impost, Knox drafted a fervent Address to Congress and, compiling remonstrances he had received from the regiments, he recruited officers of other states to plead with him.[38] Together with Secretary of War Benjamin Lincoln, Knox also primed Congress to respond positively.[39] In light of the 1786 petitions that Knox would

---

36. "Most officers were apprehensive about returning to civilian life," wrote Richard H. Kohn, perfectly describing Knox's cast of mind. "Many had been impoverished by the war while friends at home had grown fat on the opportunities provided by the war." Richard H. Kohn, *Eagle and Sword: The Federalists and the Creation of the Military Establishment in America, 1783-1802* (New York, 1975), 19.

37. Hatch noted that "Massachusetts had given her troops interest-bearing certificates of indebtedness, to make good the loss caused by the depreciation of the Continental money; but these certificates had themselves depreciated, and on some the State had refused to pay the interest unless the time for which the notes ran were extended." Hatch, *Administration*, 147. "Many officers were driven by necessity," wrote William H. Glasson, "to part with their certificates for what they could obtain, and their cash value in the market soon fell to twelve and a half cents on the dollar." William H. Glasson, *History of Military Pension Legislation in the United States* (New York, 1900), 22.

38. *Ibid.*, 149. On 24 Nov., according to Knox's aide, Samuel Shaw, "it was unanimously agreed that Major-General Knox. . . [and four others]. . . draft an address and petition to Congress, in behalf of the army." Samuel Shaw, *The Journals of Major Samuel Shaw: the First American Consul at Canton* (Boston, 1847), 102. "Probably under [Knox's] guidance," wrote Minor Myers, Jr., "three delegates from each regiment of the Massachusetts line" met with other military representatives, to seek written grievances. Myers, *Liberty Without Anarchy*, 6-7. For the Address, see Knox Papers, X, 101-115; draft of Address, *ibid.*, 118.

39. Kohn, *Eagle and Sword*, 19; Knox to Lincoln, Nov. 25, 1782, Lincoln to Knox, 3 and 20 Dec., 1782, Knox Papers.

interpret so radically, it is worth noting some of its features, including its blend of pleas and threats.

"Our distresses are now brought to a point. We have borne all that men can bear. . . . We therefore most seriously and earnestly beg that a supply of money be forwarded to the army as soon as possible. The uneasiness of the soldiers for want of pay, is great and dangerous; any further experiments upon their patience may have fatal effects. . . . We shall all be like asses of burden who, after having drudged through the heat of the day, are turned out to graze the streets for support . . . at the close of the sixth year of the contract we have not received more than one-sixth part of our pay."[40]

Knox's Address and Petition, when delivered to Congress, made three demands: an immediate payment of some of the arrears, security for the remainder, provisions for half-pay, and the eighty-dollar bounty for the soldiers. This last was almost an afterthought: they were primarily representing the officers, who threatened dire measures.[41] In Hatch's words, "the most intelligent and thoughtful part of the army were affected by the weakness of the central government, for they feared that, should it dissolve. . . in the dissensions which might follow disunion the officers would be arrayed against each other."[42] This was just what happened three years later, in Shays' Rebellion.

The greatest threat was that the army would simply re-fuse to muster out until Congress had settled with them; this was, in Jensen's apt phrase, the politics of demobilization.[43] On March 3, 1783, Knox wrote to Lincoln, "I most earnestly conjure you to urge that every thing respecting the army be decided upon before peace takes place. Let the public only

---

40. Henry Knox *et al.*, "Address and Petition of the Officers of the Army of the United States," Dec. 1782, *JCC*, XXIV, 291-293.

41. Hatch, *Administration*, 151.

42. *Ibid.*, 154.

43. Jensen, *New Nation*, 54-87. "The nationalist failure to keep the army in be-ing," wrote Jensen, "was part of their failure to establish a peacetime military establishment." *Ibid.*, 82.

comply with their promises, and the army will return to their respective homes, the Lambs and Bees of the community. But if they should be disbanded previous to a settlement without knowing whom to look to for an adjustment of accounts and a responsibility of payments, they will be so deeply stung by the injustice and ingratitude of the country as to become Tigers and Wolves."[44] Even those who had been mustered out were a threat, according to Knox: they too were "bad off, destitute and odious in the eyes of their neighbors."[45]

For all intent and purpose, the politics of demobilization were the politics of nationalism. Early in 1783, Knox wrote to Gouvemeur Morris that "it is a favorite toast in the army, 'A hoop to the barrel,' or 'Cement to the Union.' America will have fought and bled to little purpose if the powers of government shall be insufficient to preserve the peace, and this must be the case without general funds. As the present Constitution is so defective, why do not you great men call the people together and tell them so: that is, to have a convention of the States to form a better Constitution?"[46] At about the same time, in Congress, Hamilton, Madison, and Higginson were also discussing such a convention.

There were many reasons why Knox, contemplating the end of the war, was anxious to see a new Constitution drafted. To begin with, it would mean the best chance for the army to be paid. That was the crucial first step for his long-range goal: the creation of a standing army, which he now referred to euphemistically as the 'Peace Establishment.' To consider this eventuality, a committee chaired by Hamilton asked Washington's advice regarding a "military department . . . for the interior defence of these states" which would "conciliate security with œconomy and with the principles of our government."[47] Washington requested the opinions of several

---

44. Knox to Lincoln, West Point, 3 Mar., 1783, Drake, *Correspondence of Knox*, 79-80.
45. Quoted in Callahan, *Knox*, 196.
46. Knox to Gouverneur Morris, 21 Feb., 1783, Drake, *Correspondence of Knox*, 77-78.
47. *Hamilton Papers*, Syrett, ed., III, 322. James Madison, April 3-6, 1783, in

confidants, in and out of the army, including Steuben, Knox, Lincoln, Pickering, and Clinton, who unanimously called for the creation of a permanent, national army.[48] Washington synthesized these views in his own "Sentiments on a Peace Establishment," proposing a regular force of more than 2,600 men and officers, guarding the United States from New England to the Great Lakes, down the Ohio River and then to the Georgia frontier.[49]

Hamilton, in turn, on behalf of his committee with Madison and Ellsworth, drafted extensive recommendations from Washington's report, dated June 18, 1783, proposing an army of more than 3,000. "The Committee, are of opinion," he wrote, "if there is constitutional power in the United States . . . there are conclusive reasons in favour of federal in preference to state establishments," even for recruitment and supplies.[50] Acknowledging restrictions in the Articles of Confederation, Hamilton argued that precautionary measures were crucial for general security. "When the forces of the Union should become necessary . . . the United States would be obliged to *begin to create* at the very moment they would have occasion *to employ* a fleet and army."[51] Three years later, Shays' Rebellion fulfilled that prophesy perfectly.

But four days after Hamilton read his report to Congress in Philadelphia, "Mutinous soldiers presented themselves," in Madison's words, "drawn up in the street before the statehouse, where Congress had assembled. . . . President Dickinson . . . thought that . . . the militia could not be relied on. . . . It was observed that spirituous drink from the tippling-houses began to be liberally served out to the soldiers."[52] Since the

Elliott, ed., *Debates*, V, 82: "A Come., consisting of Mr. Hamilton, Mr. Madison & Mr. Ellsworth was appointed to . . . provide a system for foreign affairs, for Indian affairs, for military and naval peace establishments."

48. For a list of these separate letters, see Kohn, *Eagle and Sword*, 320 n.8.

49. For Washington's "Sentiments. . .," see John McAuley Palmer, *Washington, Lincoln, Wilson: Three War Statesmen* (Garden City, 1930), 10-27, 55-71.

50. *Hamilton Papers*, Syrett, ed., III, 381. Hamilton's "Report on a Military Peace Establishment" is in *ibid.*, 378-397.

51. *Ibid.*, 380.

52. Elliott, ed., *Debates*, V, 93.

Continental Congress had no means of defending its members even from this small, drunken mutiny by soldiers of the Pennsylvania line, they adjourned to Princeton. But Robert Morris remained at the Pennsylvania state-house, to block Hamilton's recommendations. Even Stephen Higginson, one of the most ardent nationalists then in Congress, was more ardent in his dislike of Morris than he was fond of Hamilton, and glad to see any scheme fail that was suspected of originating with the "great man."[53]

Washington visited Princeton in August to add his influence to the nationalist cause, and perhaps bolster the respectability of Congress, where attendance was dwindling monthly. But opposition to Hamilton's plan was so intense that even Washington's participation did not help the cause, and Congress could not even agree to consider "the question of a Peace Establishment."[54] Hamilton's report, amended by Washington, was not presented to Congress until October 23rd, and there it died. States like Rhode Island, Delaware, and New Jersey could not see why they should pay for frontier posts. Besides, by then, anti-militarist sentiment was being widely fueled by the issues of commutation and the Cincinnati; as Kohn put it, "Never again would they [the nationalists] attempt to realize their program within the framework of the Articles of Confederation. . . . The peacetime military establishment went underground in 1783, awaiting a constitutional structure which would make its legality unquestionable. . . ."[55]

But to accomplish this, Knox would have to use all his influence to produce a profound revision of the frame of government. The single most powerful reason Knox had for desiring a new Constitution was that the Articles of Confederation *specifically* forbade that "vessels of war shall be kept up in time of peace by any state . . . nor shall any body of forces be kept up in any state, in time of peace. . . ."[56] Anti-nationalists

53. See Stephen Higginson to Nathaniel Gorham, Princeton, 5 Aug., 1783, in Burnett, *Letters*, VII, 252.
54. *JCC*, XXIV, 524-526.
55. Kohn, *Eagle and Sword*, 53.
56. Articles of Confederation, Article VI, Para. 4, in Commager, ed., *Docu-*

construed this clause as forbidding even the establishment of the military academy that John Adams had proposed to Knox eight years earlier.

Recognition of the need for a stronger constitutional government had begun long before the Articles were ratified, and was universal among those who were part of General Washington's staff and circle of friends, including, first and foremost Knox, Lafayette, Hamilton, and Lincoln. Both Morrises were of the same persuasion, but from somewhat different motives. Washington explained his special point of view in a letter to Hamilton, that sums up his eight years' experience with Congress.

> My wish to see the Union of these States established upon liberal & permanent principles & inclination to contribute my mite in pointing out the defects of the present Constitution, are equally great. All my private letters have teemed with these sentiments. . . . No man in the United States is or can be more deeply impressed with the necessity of a reform in our present Confederation than myself. No man perhaps has felt the bad efects of it more sensibly; for to the defects thereof, & want of Powers in Congress may justly be ascribed the prolongation of the War. . . . More than half the perplexities I have experienced in the course of my command, and almost the whole of the difficulties & distress of the Army, have there origin here.[57]

Washington insisted that he had done all that he could. In a passage foreshadowing his reaction to Shays' Rebellion, Washington added "how far any further essay, by me, might be productive of the wished for end, or appear to arrogate more than belongs to me, depends so much upon popular opinion, & the temper & disposition of People, that it is not

---

ments of American History, I, 112.
57. Washington to Alexander Hamilton, Newburgh, 31 Mar., 1783, *Hamilton Papers*, Syrett, ed., III, 310.

easy to decide."[58] With good reason, Washington was concerned about the public perception of his motives. Clearly, in the absence of any sort of mandate or national crisis, Washington felt there was nothing more he could do to substantiate the need for constitutional reform, without appearing hungry for personal power, a perception that was always anathema to him.

The political movement for a revision of the Articles had begun before their ratification, and years in advance of the military agitation. In 1776 Tom Paine had first equated freedom from Britain with continental unity. "Nothing but independance, i.e., a continental form of government, can keep the peace of the continent and preserve it inviolate from civil wars."[59] "It might be difficult to form the Continent into one government half a century hence," wrote Paine, and proceeded to prescribe a Continental Charter, an outline for representative participation, even insisting that "no nation ought to be without a debt. A national debt is a national bond."[60] He also equated George III with Charles I, "wherefore, the principle itself leads you to approve of every thing which ever happened... to kings as being his work, Oliver Cromwell thanks you."[61]

In December, 1780, Paine published the pamphlet *Public Good*, provoking heated discussion of the eventual fate of the western lands: Paine disputed the claims of Virginia and argued that the west did not belong to any state, but rather belonged *collectively* to the United States, as "the fund by which the debt of America would in the course of years be redeemed."[62] "The United States now standing on the line of sovereignty, the vacant territory is their property collectively. . . . The several states will, sooner or later, see the convenience, if not the necessity of . . . electing a Continental

58. *Ibid.*
59. Paine, *Common Sense*, 94.
60. *Ibid.*, 108, 102.
61. *Ibid.*, 126.
62. Thomas Paine, "Public Good," *The Complete Writings of Thomas Paine*, Philip S. Foner, ed., 2 vols. (New York, 1945), II, 305.

convention, for the purpose of forming a Continental consti-tution."[63] Later that year, conventions in Boston and Hartford argued for enhanced powers for the "general government of the continent," but these meetings, intended to help with re-cruitment, produced little or no substantive resolutions, apart from "expressing our earnest wishes for a Reform."[64]

Three years after the date originally set by Congress for ratification, on March 1, 1781 (after Maryland finally con-curred), Congress declared the Articles in force. But just five days later Congress appointed the twenty-nine year-old Con-gressman from Virginia, James Madison, to a committee with James Duane of New York and James M. Varnum of Rhode Island — whom Jensen characterized as "an out-and-out be-liever in dictatorship" — to find a means of granting coercive powers to Congress, without which, as Madison wrote to Jef-ferson, "the whole confederacy may be insulted, and the most salutary measures frustrated, by the most inconsiderable State in the Union."[65]

The collapse of the Newburgh Conspiracy in 1783 dis-credited the nationalists' goals for the next three years — un-til Shays' Rebellion. While the machinations of the Morrises, Hamilton, and Gates in the conspiracy do not require scrutiny in relation to the Massachusetts insurrection, there are two very relevant lessons to be drawn from the military debâcle and the political designs which preceded it. First of all, with-

---

63. *Ibid.*, 332. Eric Foner has explained that, as Paine's interests "returned from state to national affairs, it was perhaps inevitable that he drew closer to men like Robert Morris, who possessed the continental breadth of vision, the capital and the organizational ability which the army and Congress so sorely needed." Foner, *Tom Paine. . .,*188.

64. George Bancroft, ed., "Proceedings at a Convention . . . holden at Hartford . . . the eighth day of [November] . . . 1780," *Magazine of American History*, VIII (1882), 698. See also Franklin B. Hough, ed., *Proceedings of a Convention of Delegates From Several of the New England States, Held at Boston, August 3-9, 1780 . . .* (Albany, 1867), 35-52.

65. Jensen, *New Nation*, 52; *JCC*, XIX, 236; Gaillard Hunt, ed., *The Writings of James Madison*, 9 vols. (New York, 1900-1910), I, 130. At that moment, Delaware was the principle obstructionist.

out the participation of Knox, all the scheming of Brooks, McDougall, and Armstrong was for naught. As Kohn put it, "Knox was the pivot in the nationalist scheme. As the leader in all the agitation at Newburgh since mid-1782, as a friend of the most important officers, and as a respected member of Washington's military family, Knox could best influence the corps to cooperate."[66]

Knox flirted with the Newburgh conspiracy, but in February he wrote to McDougall at Congress that "much has been said about the influence of the army: . . . it can only exist in one point, that to be sure is a sharp point, which I hope in God will never be directed but against enemies of the liberties of America. . . . I consider the reputation of the American army as one of the most immaculate things on earth, and that we should even suffer wrongs and injuries to the utmost verge of toleration rather than sully it. . . . But there is a point beyond which there is no sufferance. I pray sincerely we may not pass it."[67] With Knox's rejection of the scheme, the plot appeared as merely an attempt by Gates to topple the one unswerving Continental leader. For seven years the toast, "God bless Washington and God damn the king!" rang out from every tavern in the land, if not from every home; the attempt to sully Washington so soon after the war was useless.

The second lesson that Knox and other nationalists drew from the Newburgh incident came from Washington's speech in reply to the conspirators, purposefully delivered to the assembled officers on the Ides of March, at a time when coy references to Washington as Caesar were commonplace. Knox and Rufus Putnam were present, and Gates presided uncomfortably over the proceedings. The "Officers' Address," began Washington, was "calculated to impress the Mind, with an idea of premeditated injustice in the Sovereign power of the United States."[68]

---

66. Kohn, *Eagle and Sword*, 27.
67. Drake, *Correspondence of Knox*, 78.
68. Morris, ed., *Basic Documents*, 47. His greatest objection to the mutinous plot, apart from its impropriety and ineffectuality, was its intention of "sowing the seeds of discord and separation between the Civil and Military powers of

Had he meant Congress, Washington probably would have said so, but Congress obviously did not have sovereignty. Referring to "the United States" when he was commissioned, in 1775, Washington was appealing to a greater ideal than that embodied in the Articles: what he meant was "our common Country." To Washington there was nothing exceptional about this phrase, but for those whose allegiance was to their states, this was an uncommon notion. What Washington clearly intended by this was a country that was presupposed by the first two Continental Congresses. In fact, he was using the word "country" much as Tom Paine had in *Common Sense*: "by a just parity of reasoning, all Europeans meeting in America . . . are *countrymen*," simply by rising above "distinctions too limited for continental minds."[69]

Taken together, Washington's statements make it clear that, to his way of thinking, Congress and the Army of the Continent had shared an inseparable mandate from "our common Country" long before the Articles of Confederation were ratified, and a "Sovereign power of the United States" before the "Civil powers" had a constitutional basis. That is simply how it had taken place, according to Washington's experience.

What was also clear from this "Appeal" was that Washington would never participate in any seditious plot against the same authority, however maladroit, ill-defined and badly constructed, which had commissioned him. He ended his speech with a Jeffersonian vision — a teleological perspective of America. "You will . . . afford occasion for Posterity to say . . . 'had this day been wanting, the World had never seen the last stage of perfection to which human nature is capable of attaining.'"[70]

---

the Continent." *Ibid.*

69. Paine, *Common Sense*, 85.

70. Morris, *Basic Documents*, 50. General Shuyler later wrote, "Never, through all the war did his Excellency achieve a greater victory. . . . The whole assembly were in tears at the conclusion of his address. I rode with General Knox to his quarters in absolute silence, because of the solemn impression on our minds." Schuyler to Van Rensselaer, 17 Mar., 1783, John Benson Lossing, *The*

Less than a week later, Congress overcame the reluctance of Massachusetts and Connecticut, and commuted the officers' half-pay for life to full-pay for five years. One swift result was that the Massachusetts General Court replaced its representatives in Congress and remonstrated against both the commutation and the impost, though eventually the Bay state joined eight others in passing the commutation.[71]

In his "Notes on Debates in the Congress of the Confederation," Madison wrote with prescience that, at this point, while "the dissipation of the cloud which seemed to have been gathering afforded great pleasure . . . the part which the gen[l] [Washington] had found it necessary . . . to take, would give birth to events much more serious, if they s[d.] not be obviated by the establishment of such funds as the gen[l], as well as the army, had declared to be necessary."[72] By this Madison must be taken to mean that, absent Washington, if Congress failed to meet its obligations, civil government could not assure its authority over the military.

Probably the greatest effect of the Newburgh Conspiracy was to taint the causes of both nationalism and militarism for years to come. Less than a fortnight later, on April 1, 1783, "the Eastern States at the invitation of the Legislature of Mass[ts.] were with N.Y. about to form a convention for regulating matters of common concern."[73] But Madison noted that "Mr. Madison and Mr. Hamilton disapproved of these partial conventions, not as absolute violations of the Confederacy, but as ultimately leading to them & in the mean time exciting pernicious jealousies; the latter observing that he wished . . . to see a General Convention take place . . . to strengthen the federal Constitution." Stephen Higginson, near the end of

Life and Times of Philip Schuyler, 2 vols. (New York, 1872-1873) II, 427n. Doubtless, one thought on Knox's mind was whether Washington's Appeal would help or hinder the Peace Establishment.

71. William H. Glasson, Federal Military Pensions in the United States (New York, 1918), 43, 48.

72. 22 Mar., 1783, Writings of James Madison, Gaillard Hunt, ed. (New York, 1900), I, 421.

73. 1 Apr., 1783, Madison's "Notes on the Debates in the Congress of the Confederation," Writings of Madison, Hunt, ed., I, p.438.

his one year in Congress, opined that "no Gentleman need be alarmed at any rate for it was pretty certain that the Convention would not take place. He [Higginson] wished with Mr. Hamilton to see a General Convention for the purpose of revising and amending the federal Government."[74] So, while nationalists like Hamilton and Higginson saw eye to eye, in 1783 they also agreed that such a convention was premature; but they did not necessarily agree on the future of the army. From Congress, Higginson reported to Samuel Adams that "there are those also among us who wish to keep up a large force, to have large Garrisons, to increase the navy. . . . Their professed view is to strengthen the hands of Government. . . . I believe they might add to divide among Themselves and their Freinds, every place of honour and of proffit. . . . Congress I think is not yet prepared for such Systems."[75]

When his General retired in 1783, Knox was faced with a terrible loss, not only of his closest military friendship, but also of his own authority; for although Washington was to leave Knox in general command of the Continental Army, his only responsibility was its dissolution. When the formal cessation of hostilities with Britain were announced on April 19, the army would soon be disbanded, and Knox faced the prospect of regressing from General to bookseller. Right away he began working on the establishment of the military society he had mentioned to John Adams seven years earlier, so that each retired officer might at least have "some ribbon to wear in his hat." Within weeks Knox had instituted the Society of the Cincinnati, explicitly "to promote . . . between the states that union and national honor . . . and the future dignity of the American empire."[76]

---

74. *Ibid.*, 438-439.
75. Higginson to Samuel Adams, 20 May, 1783, Burnett, *Letters*, VII, 167.
76. The "Institution" appears in William S. Thomas, *The Society of the Cincinnati, 1783-1935* (New York, 1935), 24-32. Knox wrote to Lincoln that same week that "The sole objects are the union of the states as far as the humble influence of the officers may intend." Knox to Lincoln, 21 May, 1783, Knox Papers. As Forrest McDonald pointed out, apart from Congress itself, the So-

At about the same time, in Washington's well-known "Circular Letter to the States," Knox's mentor stated as forcefully as he could the nationalists' position, and coupled the question of pay for the army with his most ardent demand yet for constitutional revision. "It appears to me there is an option still left to the United States of America, that it is in their choice . . . whether they will be respectable and prosperous, or contemptible and miserable, as a nation. . . . This is the time of our political probation, this is the moment when the eyes of the whole World are turned upon them, this is the moment to establish or min their national Character forever, this is the favorable moment to give such a tone to our Federal Government, as will enable it to answer the ends of its institution, or this may be the ill-fated moment for relaxing the powers of the Union, annihilating the cement of the Confederation, and exposing us to become the sport of European politics, which may play one State against another to prevent their growing importance. . . ."[77]

Washington then emphasized his conviction that, with the Articles of Confederation, the States had not yet arrived at their constitution; and if his speech employed rhetorical devices of the age, it was no less resonant and forceful for doing so. "For according to the system of Policy the States shall adopt at this moment, they will stand or fall; and by their confirmation or lapse it is yet to be decided, whether the revolution must ultimately be considered as a blessing or a curse . . . not to the present age alone, for with our fate will the destiny of unborn millions be involved."[78] Throughout this emotional plea, Washington made it clear that the political character of the Revolution was still to be determined and, *pace* Jensen, that Fiske's phrase "the Critical Period" was perfectly justified.

On March 8, 1785, Knox was appointed Secretary at War

---

ciety of the Cincinnati was virtually the only national organization in America. Forrest McDonald, *E Pluribus Unum* (Boston, 1965), 33.

77. Washington, Circular Letter, 8 June, 1783, *Writings of Washington*, X, 254-265; 256.

78. *Ibid.*, 257.

by Congress, succeeding Lincoln — albeit to command an army that no longer existed.[79] Obviously, without the establishment of an authorized force, Knox's military career was over. Congress, ever loathe to pay the troops anyway, was not empowered to create a national militia, without a major alteration of the Articles of Confederation, and any such revision could be thwarted by a slim majority in a single state. The only circumstance which might reasonably improve the prospects for constitutional revision would be some urgent and persuasive threat. But it was more than a year before Knox found the opportunity which would demonstrate the need for a such a force, and override the powerful, ingrained antipathy toward a standing army. That opportunity, of course, was Shays' Rebellion.

A fortnight after the first court-closing at Northampton, Knox paid the first of two hasty visits to the Springfield Arsenal, and "minutely inspected the ordnance. . . . Learning from a variety of information that some lawless people . . . had intimated their intention under certain circumstances, of seizing the arsenal, and converting the ordnance and stores therein to their own rebellious purposes," Knox asked Governor Bowdoin to take "measures for the security of the store. . . ."[80]

But he knew it would not be so simple, given the condition of the state's finances, as well as the Confederation's. So Knox began a series of efforts to raise a federal force, under the subterfuge of preparing troops to fight Indians in the western regions. He explained his covert actions to Congress by

79. "By January of 1784," wrote Kohn, "all that remained of the army that had consummated the Revolution and established American independence was a small corps of artillery and one regiment of infantry, about 600 rank and file under Henry Knox's command, guarding leftover stores at West Point and Springfield, Massachusetts . . ." Kohn, *Eagle and Sword*, 41.

80. Knox to Congress, 20 Sept., 1786, *JCC*, XXXI, 675-6. Knox's inventory of the Arsenal included "new arms and bayonets about seven thousand in number . . . the powder amounting to upwards of thirteen hundred barrels of excellent quality . . . about two hundred tons of shot and shells. . . ." Just the month before, he had been unable even to move a store of weapons to Springfield from Rhode Island, because of the expense. 1 Aug., 1786, *ibid.*, 457.

saying that, if plans for such a defense became known, "the mal-contents might regard it as the first step towards their destruction."[81] Congress concurred, giving the Secretary of War virtual *carte blanche* to operate in a clandestine manner; he swiftly recruited the services of a Captain William North, former aide to General von Steuben, to drum up alarm in the west about the dangers of an Indian war.[82]

Did Knox sincerely believe, at this early date, that the Regulators would be so bold as to attack the Arsenal? Possibly, for it was not out of the question, as Shays demonstrated two weeks later. But throughout every one of his letters on the subject, the defense of the Arsenal was always closely tied to larger political questions; specifically, the anti-authoritarian tendencies of the people, and the need for a well-endowed central government.

In a long and revealing letter to Lafayette a few months later, recapping the events of the Regulation, Knox began with a brief disquisition on "the nature of man," *à la* Montesquieu. "Place him nearly on the same latitudes; impress him with the same manners and habits; govern him by the same laws and political constitution, and his conduct will be nearly the same, whether he followed and supported the Grachii of the new Roman republic, or a demagogue in a Town meeting of Massachusetts,"[83] This classical reference provides a remarkable and telling comparison: the brothers Gracchus, sons of prætor Tiberius, had set up a people's tribune in 133 B.C., which proposed agrarian laws limiting the amount of public land that a citizen could occupy, and redistributing the remainder in small parcels. The result was to dispossess wealthy, Roman aristocrats of their enormous land-claims, and raise their ire to murderous fury.[84] At no point during

---

81. Knox to Congress, War Office [New York], 28 Sept., 1786, *ibid.*, 698-700. [Knox's underlining.]

82. I have deliberately omitted from this account the spurious rumors that British agents were instigating or assisting the Regulation.

83. Knox to Lafayette, 13 Feb., 1787, Knox Papers, XIX, 164.

84. For more on the Gracchii, see the Oxford Companion to Classical Literature, Paul Harvey, ed. (Oxford, 1955), 190.

the Regulation of the courts was anything like this proposed; yet Knox persisted with this radical interpretation, even after Shays had fled Massachusetts. Indeed, Knox's perception of Shays' Rebellion seems to have owed as much to Tiberius and the Gracchi as to Winstanley and the Diggers, judging from his consistent references to the "agrarian law" that Shaysites supposedly desired.

His letter to Lafayette continued: "Opinions which perhaps were excessively dissimulated previous to and during the late revolution seem to produce effects materially different from which they were intended. For instance, the maxim that all power is derived from the people and that all government is influenced [by them is] perverted to a certain proportion of the people, easily the minority, to [mean] an annihilation of debts, and a division of property [and that the government of the people means that the people shall participate in the prosperity of the wealthy] [illegible]. . . . The object and ultimate end of republican government being thus delusively established in their minds they have no hesitation of embracing any means for the accomplishment of their purposes."[85]

This same interpretation appears throughout Knox's letters about the Regulation, from October through February.[86] But did he really believe the Shaysites were such extremists? Knox's later letters are remarkably consistent in this view, and we have no other window into his soul. But at first Knox described the Regulators' motives as defensive, at best: "I cannot find that the stores are an immediate object with the malcontents although they certainly have an eye upon them. . . ." To Congress, he wrote only that, "should the government attempt to punish [the Regulators] . . . they easily could obtain the means of defence from the Arsenal."[87] This was a more

85. Knox to Lafayette, 13 Feb., 1787, Knox Papers, XIX, 164. Knox has crossed out the bracketed portion in his letterbook.
86. See his letter to Washington, below Appendix B; also Knox to Congress, 18 Oct., 1786, *JCC*, XXXI, 886-888.
87. Knox to Wadsworth, Springfield, 3 Oct. [letterbook draft], Knox Papers XIX, 20. He began this rough draft elevating the protests into rebellion: "The commotion or The insurrection here has certainly been of an alarming nature.

accurate assessment than his assertion, just three weeks later, that the Shaysites sought the annihilation of all debts and an agrarian law.

The proximity of the Arsenal raised the stakes dramatically beyond the previous demonstrations. But also, these disturbances appeared to have found an experienced leader in the person of Captain Daniel Shays, lending the protest a distinctly military character and, thanks to Knox himself, a name.[88] The commotions came to be known as "Shays' Rebellion" when Knox returned to Springfield in early October, just after the Arsenal was surrounded by men commanded by Shays; Knox reported to Congress that Shays was responsible for all the commotions.[89]

During this second trip to Massachusetts, Knox proceeded from Springfield to Boston for a series of meeting with the Governor and "Gentlemen . . . of the most respectable characters in the state for their political knowledge."[90] From Knox's first letter to Higginson on October 22nd, it is evident that they had conferred during this visit, and discussed the situation in considerable detail. "My conjectures about an indian war were right," Knox wrote Higginson, whom he had known for years. "Congress were so impressed with the apprehension that they have with near unanimity resolved to augment the

---

It must have extensive consequences. . . ." [Knox's strike-through]. See also Knox to Parsons, Springfield, 3 Oct., *ibid.*, XIX, 21: "It is possible the malcontents may not have any designs on the Stores here, but if they should, the United States must depend on their good friends the late Officers. . . .;" "they easily could obtain the means of defence . . .," Knox to Congress, War Office [New York], 28 Sept., 1786, *JCC*, XXXI, 698-700.

88. "Interview With Daniel Shays," Rufus Putnam to Governor Bowdoin, 8 Jan., 1787, Shays' Rebellion Box, AAS.

89. Knox to Congress, Springfield, 3 Oct., 1786: "They were headed by a Captain Shays of the militia" *JCC*, XXXI, 752. Though the names of Shattuck, Parsons, and Day were more often cited in Boston, Knox still referred to Shays as the principal leader four months later, see Knox to Lafayette, 13 Feb., 1787, Knox Papers, XIX, 164. It was also Knox who coined the phrase "Shays' Rebellion" in a letter to Lincoln, 14 Feb., 1787: "Shays' Rebellion is not a field in which you could gather fresh laurels. . . ." Knox Papers, XIX, 166.

90. Knox to Congress, Boston, 18 Oct., 1786, *JCC*, XXXI, 886.

troops . . . but exertions must be made & something must be hazarded by the rich."[91]

It was with this letter, secretly conveyed by William North, that Knox and Higginson began their consequential correspondence. Utter secrecy was important to them both; as long as they were discussing "a radical reform" of the Confederation, they felt their exchanges were too sensitive to entrust to the post. At the same time, Bowdoin was already consulting confidentially with "gentlemen, connected in the affairs of Government" regarding the Arsenal, and these certainly included his long time ally and banking associate, Stephen Higginson.[92]

Higginson replied to Knox on November 12th that funds, "upon the view of a War with the *Indians* and the consequent requisition of Congress, [were] obtained with more ease than I expected . . . the money wanted for the men will, I trust, be soon raised. The Treasurer has just opened his Loan. . . ."[93] Higginson also echoed Knox's very thoughts on the matter: that "the present moment is very favorable to the forming further and necessary Arrangements, for increasing the dignity and energy of Government. . . . the public mind is now in a fit State, and will shortly I think become more so. . . ."[94] Herewith the two began shaping the scheme that would produce the Philadelphia Convention and, ultimately, the ratification of the Constitution.

---

91. "Congress were so impressed with the apprehension" of an Indian war, Knox wrote Higginson, "that they have . . . unanimously resolved to augment the troops. . . . Recourse must be had for the immediate exigencies to the monied men. . . . exertions might be made & something might be hazarded, by the rich." Knox to Higginson, 22 Oct., 1786, Knox Papers, XIX, 31. This was written the day before the first draft of his letter to Washington, in Appendix A; it was delivered personally to Higginson by Capt. William North, who was responsible for supplying testimony of "indian wars."
92. Knox to Congress, Boston, 8 Oct., 1786, *JCC*, XXXI, 875, 886.
93. Higginson to Knox, 12 Nov., J. Franklin Jameson, ed., "The Letters of Stephen Higginson," in the *American Historical Association*, Annual Report, (1896) I, 741-742.[Higginson's italics.]
94. Higginson to Knox, 25 Nov., 1786, Knox Papers, XIX, 58. Regarding North, Higginson adds "I saw Capt. North but a moment, I intend a private moment with him. . . ."

In Boston, "Billy" North was successful enough in stirring up concern about Indians that the General Court promised to reimburse Higginson and other investors in Lincoln's campaign; Knox instituted the same ploy with a committee of Congress, which also noted the "threat."[95] Thus the "Indian war" conspiracy, cooked up in Boston between Knox, Higginson, Bowdoin, and others, was now a national ruse. Charles Pettit wrote to Benjamin Franklin, then President of Pennsylvania, "Some Resolutions will probably issue for an Augmentation of Troops, the Reasons assigned for which may be our Intelligence respecting the Western Indians; but in Fact this Augmentation seems to be necessary to the preservation of interior Government."[96] Under this pretense, funds were solicited from other states to pay for the troops in Massachusetts, though the voters in those states were never told the truth.

But those in the know made little pretense with each other. A week later James Swan wrote Knox that he hoped "in this declaration, 'Indians' is meant all who oppose the Dignity, Honour, and happiness of the United States." Swan had short-term personal gain in mind, along with his nationalist goals: in the same letter, he beseeched Knox "to give me your advice as to . . . buying or selling into the Continental funds. . . ."[97] And members of both factions in Massachusetts recognized the transparent ruse; as Elbridge Gerry wrote to Rufus King, "Some . . . of the country members laugh and say the Indi-

---

95. It was Nathaniel Gorham who sent a message introducing North to Bowdoin: "Justice to the character of Major North who is going to Boston induces me to mention him to your Excellency as a Gent'n who supports the fairest reputation, and is spoken of by all the military Men as an excellent Officer." Nathaniel Gorham to Governor James Bowdoin, New York, 22 Oct., 1786. Burnett, *Letters*, VIII, 490. The Committee [consisting of Charles Pettit, Henry Lee, Charles Pinckney, John Henry and Melancton Smith] were referred "a letter from the War Office . . . containing intelligence of the hostile movements of the Indians in the Western Country. . . ." 20 Oct., 1786, *JCC*, XXXI, 895-6.
96. Charles Pettit to Franklin, New York, 18 Oct, 1786, Burnett, *Letters*, VIII, 487.
97. James Swan to Henry Knox, 26 Oct., 1786, Knox Papers, XIX. For more on this see East, "Massachusetts Conservatives . . .," *American Revolution*, Morris, ed., 38.

an War is only a political one to obtain a standing Army."[98] By this time, though, North was not particularly concerned whether their ruse was being uncovered. "The people here smell a rat," he wrote Knox from Boston, "that the Troops about to be raised are more for the Insurgents than the Indians, however this makes no odds, every body seems to wish a strong Government, & to believe that the Government can only be strengthened by an army."[99]

The ploy of an Indian war to mask the suppression of Shays' Rebellion had by then largely served its purpose as an alarum with which to raise a military force. It had also brought together two of the key nationalist collaborators who would secretly plan, persuade, and prepare for the next three months, in thousands of written words, how to effect a dramatic change in the fundamental law of the Confederation, and then assure its ratification. "Perhaps . . . [the Philadelphia] convention originated, and has been imbued with ideas, far short of a radical reform," Knox wrote to Higginson at one point. "May it notwithstanding be turned to an excellent purpose?"[100]

Recruiting George Washington to an active role in the Constitutional movement was key to achieving that purpose. Not only his victory over the British, but even more, his retirement from power thereafter, had bestowed upon Washington an unparalleled position in the firmament of historical leaders. Even King George III had purportedly predicted that Washington would be "the greatest man in all the world" if he renounced all military and political ambitions.[101] Changing

---

98. Gerry to King, 29 Nov., 1786, King, ed., *Life of King*, I, 197. See also King to Gerry, 19 Oct., 1786, Burnett, *Letters*, VIII, 488, and Nathan Dane to the Massachusetts House of Representatives, 9 Nov., 1786, in *Boston Magazine* (November and December, 1786), quoted in *ibid.*, 503.

99. William North to Knox, Boston, Sunday, 29 Oct., 1786, Knox Papers, XIX, 36.

100. Knox to Higginson, New York, 28 Jan., 1787, Drake, *Correspondence of Knox*, 94.

101. Wood, *The Radicalism of the American Revolution*, 206. "The greatest act of [Washington's] life," wrote Wood, "the one that gave him his greatest

141

Washington's mind, and compelling him to abandon the life he loved at Mount Vernon as well as his reputation for disinterested virtue, would require a threat to the public welfare of enormous proportions. It would also take all of Knox's cunning, together with Madison's respectful suasion, to nudge Washington out of his entrenched position as a private citizen.

So, for several days in late October, 1786, Knox, the bookseller become general, facing professional and financial ruin, carefully composed a letter to Washington that drew the most appalling conclusions and forecast the most dire eventualities of Shays' Rebellion, including the swift demise of the moribund Confederation government.[102] As in all his letters on the subject, Knox tightly interwove his account of the Regulation with the fate of the United States. Exaggeration is an understated word for the way Knox elevated this popular disobedience — which to date had been perfectly peaceful — into an American Götterdämmerung.

Knox began his letter on Shays' Rebellion with a critique of government under the Articles of Confederation. "Our political machine constituted of thirteen independent sovereignties, have been constantly operating against each other, and against the federal head. . . . The powers of Congress are utterly inadequate to preserve the balance between the respective States. . . . The machine works inversely to the public good in all its parts. Not only is State against State, and all against the federal head, but the States within themselves possess the

---

fame, was his resignation as commander in chief of the American forces. . . . In order to enhance the disinterestedness of the political advice he offered . . . he promised not to take 'any share in public business hereafter.' He even resigned from his local vestry. . . . This self-conscious and unconditional withdrawal from power and politics was a great moral action, full of significance for an enlightened and republicanized world, and the results were monumental." *Ibid.*, 205-206.

102. Knox's entire letter of 28 Oct., 1786, appears in Appendix B, from the Washington Papers. Note that in his own copy (in the Knox Papers), Knox dated the letter October 23rd, and many historians, including Drake, in *Life and Correspondence of Henry Knox*, have perpetuated the mistake. "I am in great debt on account of some public debts;" Knox to Wadsworth, New York, 28 Feb., 1787, Knox Papers, XX, 6.

name only, without the essential concomitant of government, the power of preserving the peace. . . ."[103]

"The fine theoretic government of Massachusetts has given way, and its laws arrested and trampled under foot," continued Knox, "high taxes are the ostensible cause of the commotions, but that they are the real cause is as far remote from truth as light from darkness. The people who are the insurgents have never paid any, or but very little taxes — But they see the weakness of government; They feel at once their own poverty, compared with the opulent, and their own force, and they are determined to make up the latter, in order to remedy the former."[104] Leaving aside the inaccuracy of Knox's assertions, his views were obviously inspired and reinforced by the Boston gentlemen with whom he had consulted.

Unlike many of those gentlemen, though, Knox did not describe the Shaysites merely as "lawless banditti." Instead, he ascribed to them a precise ideology that could only horrify Washington, and every member of the propertied classes — an ideology so clearly communistic as to seem like an anachronism. "Their creed is," wrote Knox, appearing to offer a verbatim quotation, "'That the property of the United States has been protected from confiscation of Britain by the joint exertions of all, and therefore ought to be the common property of all. and he that attempts opposition to this creed is an enemy to equity and justice, and ought to be swept from off the face of the earth. . . .' In a word, they are determined to annihilate all debts, public and private and have agrarian Laws which are easily effected by the means of unfunded paper money, which shall be a tender in all cases whatever."[105]

Knox offered Washington a wild estimate of Shaysite forces throughout New England: "a body of 12 or 15000 desperate and unprincipled men . . . chiefly of the young and active part

---

103. *Ibid.*

104. *Ibid.*

105. *Ibid.* A day or two after he received this letter, Washington copied this entire passage for Madison; see below, 202. For a comparison with Winstanley's language, see above, 23-24.

of the community."[106] He also predicted how this bloodless mutiny would evolve into a revolution. "They will probably commit overt acts of treason which will compell them to embody for their own safety — once embodied, they will be constrained to submit to discipline for the same reason. Having proceeded to this length, for which they are now ripe, we shall have a formidable rebellion against reason."[107]

Fusing Shays' Rebellion with the need for a Constitutional Convention, Knox approached the point of this lengthy letter. "What is to afford us security against the violence of lawless men? Our government must be braced, changed or altered to secure our lives and property. . . . we find that we are men, actual men, possessing all the turbulent passions belonging to that animal, and that we must have a government proper and adequate for him. . . . Something must be done, or we shall be involved in all the horror of faction and civil war without a prospect of its termination."[108]

And what was the practical purpose of Knox's letter? He appeared to be simply informing Washington of the state of affairs — as well as preaching nationalism to its first convert. But finally he arrived at his point: "Every tried friend to the liberty of his country is bound to reflect, and to step forward to prevent the dreadful consequences which will result from a government of events."[109] By an unwritten syllogism, Knox was challenging Washington's patriotism in a manner that no one else could. "I mention the idea of strengthening government confidentially...," he added cautiously.

Knox's letter achieved its purpose: less than two weeks

---

106. During the Revolutionary War, the size of the Continental Army under Washington had fluctuated between five and fifty thousand men; see Charles H. Lesser, *The Sinews of Independence: Monthly Strength Reports of the Continental Army* (Chicago, 1976), *passim*.

107. Knox to Washington, New York, 28 Oct., 1786, Washington Papers.

108. *Ibid*. This foreshadows Madison's declaration, in *Federalist*, No. 51: "If men were angels, no government would be necessary."

109. *Ibid*. This "government of events" is later echoed in Hamilton's *Federalist* No. 1, which asks whether or not men "are forever destined to depend, for their political constitutions, on accident and force."

later, Washington tentatively admitted to Madison that, under the circumstances, he might foresake his retirement from public life to lend his reputation to the Convention proposed in Philadelphia. Washington's reaction will be discussed below, but for the present it is important to note that he trusted Knox's impressions of the situation implicitly, even though the accounts that he read of the Regulation in the *Pennsylvania Packet* were nowhere near so extreme.

Knox continued his correspondence with Higginson and, of course, with Washington through the winter. He also oversaw the collection of funds for federal troops that was soon eclipsed by General Lincoln's fund.[110] But he had completed his most important effort in the nationalist movement with his October letter to Washington, throwing his considerable weight against his mentor's determined inertia. There is no evidence that Knox had fomented, frequented, or financed the Regulators; but as a Massachusetts citizen, and Washington's trusted aide, he saw an opportunity to accomplish what Higginson, Madison, and Hamilton could not do: to persuade Washington that Shays' Rebellion and similar commotions would only multiply unless "every tried Mend to the liberty of his country" stepped forward to prevent "a government of events."

---

110. "If Mr. Phillips, T. Russell, S. Higginson & Mr. Breck was to take this business into their hands . . .," wrote Knox's frustrated friend and aide, Henry Jackson, "I am sure something of consequence may be procured. But... nobody appears to father it" Jackson to Knox, Boston, 11 Dec., 1786, Knox Papers, XIX, 84. In the meantime, those gentlemen were raising funds for Lincoln's expedition.

CHAPTER FIVE

Stephen Higginson and the Mercantile Cabal

"The present moment is very favorable . . . for increasing the dignity and energy of Government. What has been done, must be used as a stock upon which the best Fruits are to be ingrafted."

— Stephen Higginson to Henry Knox[1]

T he response to Shays' Rebellion by the nationalist-minded leadership of Massachusetts concealed a curious backgame: even as these concerned gentlemen raised the money and troops to defeat the protesters, they recognized that a credible threat of civil war would provide, as Stephen Higginson wrote to Knox, "a Stock upon which the best Fruits are to be ingrafted" — meaning a fundamental revision of the American government by a Constitutional Convention.[2] Minot hinted at this backgame in his *History*, but omitted any details. Referring to the earliest members of the "Essex Junto," he wrote that these men, "though few in number, and but the seeds of a party, consisted of persons respectable for their literature and their wealth," who "had been so long expecting measures, for vindicating the dignity of government" that they were "almost ready to assent to a revolution, in hopes of erecting a political system, more braced than the present . . .

---

1. Stephen Higginson to Henry Knox, 12 Nov., 1786, Jameson, ed., "Letters of Higginson," *AHA Annual Report* (1896), I, 742.
2. *Ibid.*

The insurgents themselves at length brought about, what their opposers, perhaps, could not have effected without them."[3] In effect, armed insurrection and the inability of Congress to contain it might finally persuade the public of the need for a vigorous central government, at the very moment the states were deciding whether or not to send delegates to the Constitutional Convention. This notion of demonstrating the need for revising the Articles echoed the opinion Hamilton had expressed in 1783, while Higginson was working with him in Congress to advance the nationalists' agenda. "There is a fatal opposition to Continental views," Hamilton wrote to Washington. "Necessity alone can work a reform. But how apply it and how keep it within salutary bounds?"[4] Three years later, Higginson recognized that Shays' Rebellion was perfectly suited to demonstrate that necessity for reform, and went about personally shaping the outcome of the uprising.

Though the use to which the conservatives put the rebellion has been examined, the extensive role Higginson played has gone largely uncharted, as has the continuity which his involvement provided between the early nationalist movement, Shays' Rebellion, the Constitutional Convention, and even the procedure which ultimately made ratification possible.[5] Higginson's correspondence clearly demonstrates the evolution of his thinking as he waited for just such an opportunity as Shays' Rebellion to produce "the best Fruits," and by forging a convergence between the political polarization in

---

3. Minot, *History*, 61-2. He also wrote that "Among the great body of the disaffected . . . [were] many who wished to carry popular measures to such extremes, as to shew their absurdity, and demonstrate the necessity of lessening the democratick principles of the constitution." *Ibid.*, 105. See also below, 156 n.86.

4. Hamilton to Washington, Philadelphia, 17 Mar., 1783 Burnett, *Letters*, VII, 86.

5. The historians to whom I am most indebted for some of the pieces of this puzzle include the late Richard B. Morris, both from conversation, and from his article "Insurrection in Massachusetts," in Daniel Aaron, ed., *America in Crisis* (New York, 1952); East, "The Massachusetts Conservatives," Morris, ed., *Era of the American Revolution*, 349-391; Main, *The Antifederalists*, and Szatmary, *Shays'Rebellion*, esp. 70-90.

Massachusetts and the nationalists' ambition of writing a new constitution. To accomplish this goal, Higginson and Knox embarked upon their secret, impromptu collusion replete with intrigue, influence, and the deliberate fabrication of an Indian war by Congress.

By the time the Shaysite court closings began in 1786, the progressive polarization between eastern and western Massachusetts had been exacerbated by such a wide variety of issues that the problem no longer seemed to be one of specific political and economic disagreements, but a more fundamental question of sectional ideology. The heat generated by these issues — the Constitutions of 1778 and 1780; the impost; half-pay and commutation; the Cincinnati; paper money and tender laws; the supplementary payment to Congress; judicial procedures and costs; and the very existence of the Senate — sparked a powerful conviction in the west that the General Court should be relocated out of Boston, to diminish the undue influence of men like Stephen Higginson.

The contending opinions in each of these controversies were informed by the different expectations the two regions had for the post-war world. Even before the Declaration of Independence, the Berkshire Constitutionalists had indicated their intention of restructuring the new Massachusetts government from the ground up, challenging Congress's recommendation that the State should proceed according to the framework of government prescribed by its royal charter. "We have calmly viewed the nature of our ancient mode of government," wrote Rev. Thomas Allen. "We can discern no present necessity of adopting that mode. . . ."[6] By 1778 much

---

6. Rev. Thomas Allen, "The Petition, Remonstrance and Address of the Town of Pittsfield . . .," 26 Dec., 1775, in J. E. A. Smith, *The History of Pittsfield, (Berkshire County), Massachusetts, From the Year 1734 to the Year 1800* (Boston, 1869), 344. Allen and the other Constitutionalists were seeking exactly what Congress had recommended to New Hampshire and South Carolina: that "a full and free representation of the people" should "establish such a form of government, as in their judgment will best produce the happiness of the people." John Adams, *Works* (Boston, 1851), III, 16.

of the Berkshire population was in revolt against the legislature, forbidding the courts of justice from sitting, and even
threatening to secede from the state, if the people were not
allowed to determine the basis of their new government.[7] In
fact, it was sometimes assumed in the west that Independence
had restored society to a state of nature, a political and possibly economic *tabula rasa*, to be written afresh by all.[8]

In the east, of course, there remained widespread determination to sustain the received social and economic orders.
Rather than dismantle the hierarchies of colonial society and
politics, the conservative element had moved swiftly during
the War to fill the commercial, political, and social vacu-
ums left behind by Loyalists.[9] Nowhere was this resolve to
conserve the old order more hardened than in Essex County, which sustained the legacy of an especially conservative
brand of Puritanism, with traditions dating back to Calvinist
precepts of determinism established in Salem by Rev. Francis
Higginson five generations earlier. "The men of Essex," Henry Cabot Lodge wrote of his ancestors, "were the oldest Puritan stock. . . . Their intellectual vigor and clear perceptions
were in many instances combined with great mental narrow-
ness and rigidity," unable to adapt, or to "bend sufficiently to
the new political forces" of county conventions, petitions, and
remonstrances.[10]

The "Essex Junto" first received their moniker in the 1780s
from John Hancock and his party; for, from the first, they were

---

7. See Taylor, *Western Massachusetts*, 79, and Morison, "The Struggle over the
. . . Constitution," *AHA Proceedings, L* (1917), 367.
8. In February, 1776, during the first court closing by the Berkshire Constitutionalists, after Allen read the newly published *Common Sense* from the pulpit,
the Pittsfield Convention declared that government had been returned to "a
state of nature." Smith, *History of Pittsfield*, I, 347.
9. A vivid example of this process came when General James Warren settled
into the former Milton home of Governor Thomas Hutchinson. See Arthur Lee
to James Warren, Philadelphia, 8 Apr., 1782, "Warren-Adams Letters," *MHS
Collections 73* (1925) II, 171.
10. Henry Cabot Lodge, *Life and Letters of George Cabot* (New York, 1974
[orig. publ. Boston, 1878]), 17.

"the party opposed to Hancock."[11] Hancock's premature departure from state government in 1785 created a long-awaited opportunity for these ardent foes to coalesce around the respected but unpopular figure of James Bowdoin, forming the nucleus of what would become the Federalist Party in Massachusetts. The men who made up that nucleus — including Theophilus Parsons, George Cabot, Jonathan Jackson, Edward Payne, John Lowell, Nathaniel Tracy, Fisher Ames and, most actively, Stephen Higginson — were closely connected by business and family ties. Not only were Higginson's two sisters married to John Lowell and George Cabot; as David H. Fischer pointed out, "Cabots were wed to Lowells, Lowells to Jacksons, Jacksons to Tracys."[12] They had long been disenchanted with the Articles of Confederation when they marshalled support for Bowdoin in the bitter election of 1785. With Hancock's departure, Higginson first saw a chance to activate a chain of events that would produce radical alterations of the Confederation.

A good deal of attention has been paid by historians to the later activities of the "Essex Junto": how they opposed Hancock in 1789, John Adams in 1796, Jefferson in 1800 and how, at the Hartford Convention of 1814, they seriously

---

11. "*The Essex Result . . .* was one of the grounds — perhaps the chief one — for that nickname of 'The Essex Junto,' which Mr. Hancock afterwards fastened upon my father and his companions." *Memoir of Theophilus Parsons, Chief Justice of the Supreme Judicial Court of Massachusetts, with Notices of Some of His Contemporaries, by his son Theophilus Parsons* (Boston, 1859), 48. George Cabot, Stephen Higginson, and Theophilus Parsons were later identified by both John Adams and Thomas Jefferson as the leaders of the clique; see Thomas Wentworth Higginson, *Life and Times of Stephen Higginson* (Boston, 1907), 42. See also entry in Jefferson's diary, 25 Dec., 1800, in J. J. Randolph, ed., *Memoirs, Correspondence, and Miscellanies from the Papers of Thomas Jefferson*, 4 vols., (Charlottesville, 1829), IV, 515. The first use of the 'junto' label in print, seems to be in a letter to the *Massachusetts Centinel*, 11 Aug., 1787, from "Plain Truth": "S. H. is the *Guy Faux*. Kill him. . . . If there was a junto preparing amidst Shays's rebellion . . . I wish to see them dragged forth to public infamy." See also "Cato" in *Massachusetts Centinel*, 15 and 22 Aug., 1787.

12. David H. Fischer, "The Myth of the Essex Junto," in *William and Mary Quarterly*, 3rd Ser., XXI, No. 2 (April 1964), 197.

contemplated a separate peace for New England with Britain. But the origins of their ideological cohesion can be found in *The Essex Result* of 1778, drafted by Theophilus Parsons, rejecting the Constitution proposed that year, and offering his view of the dichotomy natural to all human society.[13] Parsons unabashedly supported an aristocracy, insisting "that among gentlemen of education, fortune and leisure, we shall find the largest number of men, possessed of wisdom, learning, and a firmness and consistency of character. That among the bulk of the people, we shall find the greatest share of political honesty, probity, and a regard to the interest of the whole. . . . The former are called the excellencies that result from an aristocracy; the latter, those that result from a democracy."[14] There was no need for Parsons to add that the majority of these gentlemen in Massachusetts lived within a day's ride of Boston. Such gentlemen could be identified easily enough in the street, as Higginson's grandson observed, what with "the gentry wearing wigs, silk stockings, and silver shoe buckles, and the lower classes wearing corduroy coats and leather knee britches, and going largely barefoot in summer."[15]

The Harringtonian belief in a home-grown aristocracy as an indispensable component to a mixed republican constitution was the distinguishing characteristic of the Essex conservatives.[16] "I sometimes almost lament that the Aristocracy

13. Theophilius Parsons, *Result of The Convention of Delegates Holden at Ipswich* (orig. publ. Newburyport, 1778), in Taylor, *Massachusetts Documents*, 73-93. Rossiter describes *The Essex Result* as "one of the three or four most profound pieces of general speculation in the entire Revolutionary period." Clinton Rossiter, *The Political Thought of the American Revolution* (New York, 1963 [orig. publ. 1953]), 14.

14. Parsons, "Essex Result," in Taylor, *Western Massachusetts*, 77-8. It was hardly necessary to convince Knox of this point, who despised both Monarchy and "a mad democracy." Still, Knox insisted in 1785 that "When I consider the inestimable value of liberty, I cannot hesitate to prefer a democracy to every other form of government. . . ." but "a species of Aristocracy . . . could be made use of as the means of creating and preserving those Sentiments and manners which are so essential to our existence." Knox to General Samuel Parsons, 4 Apr., 1785, Knox Papers.

15. Higginson, *Life of Stephen Higginson*, 87.

16. "The central Harringtonian idea is that property confers independence, and

in 1783 was surpressed," wrote Higginson at the height of Shays' Rebellion, in this instance referring to the Cincinnati.[17] Higginson's business partner, Jonathan Jackson, wrote that "Much has been lately said of aristocratical men and principles," but that the greatest risk to the people is "their proneness to a highly democratical government; a government in which they would be directed by no rule but their own will and caprice, or the interested wishes of a very few persons, who *affect* to speak the sentiments of the people."[18] Jackson went further: "The people in any numbers cannot even be trusted to appoint those who shall manage for them, they are so liable when together in large numbers, to be acted upon and cajoled by those, who in every community are upon the watch to deceive, and active to gain authority to themselves for sinister views."[19] For him, the separate orders of society were natural features of "a social compact . . . reciting the reciprocal duties of rulers and ruled."[20] This interpretation of 'social compact' is not very far removed from the notion expressed in 1645 by John Winthrop: "This covenant between you and us is . . . that we shall govern you and judge your causes by the rules of Gods laws and our own."[21] Almost a century and a half later, Higginson insisted that "the bulk of the people know but little of the government under which they live."[22]

The most consequential principle that Parsons set forth in *The Essex Result* was embodied in the Massachusetts Consti-

---

the central idea of the Harringtonian balance is that power must not be so distributed that it encroaches on the independence of property." Pocock, "Machiavelli, Harrington . . .," *WMQ*, 3rd Ser., XXII (1965), 570.

17. Higginson to Samuel Osgood, 7 Feb., 1787, Osgood Papers, NYHS, as quoted in Main, *The Anitfederalists*, 104.

18. [Jonathan Jackson] *Thoughts upon the Political Situation of the United States of America, in which that of Massachusetts is more particularly considered... By a native of Boston* (Worcester, 1788), 55.

19. *Ibid.*, 154.

20. *Ibid.*

21. John Winthrop, "Oration of 1645," quoted in Perry Miller, *The New England Mind: The Seventeeth Century* (Cambridge, Mass., 1939), 426.

22. [Stephen Higginson], *Ten Chapters in the Life of John Hancock* (Boston, 1857, [orig. publ. as *The Writings of Laco*, 1789]), 25.

tution two years later: that "the legislative body should be so constructed, that every law affecting property, should have the consent of those who hold a majority of the property."[23] This highly unpopular notion was codified in the new constitution, ostensibly by none other than the President of the Convention of 1780, James Bowdoin.[24] In practical terms, it meant that the 40 Senate seats were now to be chosen, not by the town representatives in General Court, but rather by the county districts; and the seats were now appropriated, not according to their populations, but rather "by the proportion of the public taxes paid by the said districts."[25] This principle was at the heart of western antagonism toward the Senate, and provoked the demands for its abolition.[26]

While the "Essex Junto" supported Bowdoin throughout his political career, Stephen Higginson was perhaps his most ardent booster, as well as the most clandestine, for he preferred to remain hidden by "the curtain, behind which Art can be exercised," as one critic observed.[27] Born in 1743

23. Taylor, *Massachusetts Documents*, 82.
24. The only other members of the committee which drafted the document were "the brace of Adamses," John and Samuel; it is presumed that they actually contributed most of the writing. See "The Constitution of 1780" in Taylor, *Massachusetts Documents*, 125. Bowdoin was on a committee with John and Samuel Adams to draft this Constitution and the accompanying "Address," but according to Morison, the conservatives principles "were imposed on the Convention by John Adams and the future Essex Junto (Parsons, Lowell, Jackson, and Cabot) with some difficulty; but the Convention seems to have been thoroughly converted." Morison, "The Struggle over the . . . Constitution," *AHA Proceedings, L* (1917), 384.
25. The Constitution of 1780, Chapter I, Section II, Taylor, *Documents*, 133. The Constitution also raised property qualifications for Senators to a freehold valued at £300 or a personal estate of £600, well beyond the means of most western voters, suggesting that their *de facto* disenfranchisement might never be reversed, especially given the power demonstrated by the Senate of overriding the House — as in the case of Bowdoin's election.
26. See, for example, Abigail Adams to Thomas Jefferson, 2 Jan., 1787, *Jefferson Papers*, XI, 86-7. "it is true that some Persons have proposed in County Conventions to annihilate the Senate." James Warren to John Adams, Milton, 18 May, 1787. "Warren-Adams Letters," II, *MHS Collections 73*, 291-3.
27. See below, 147 n.50.

and raised in Salem, Higginson had traveled abroad before the War of Independence, cultivating business relations and a distinctly transatlantic perspective of American affairs. At the age of twenty-eight, his standing among British merchants was such that, while visiting London, Higginson was called to Parliament to be questioned by Edmund Burke on the state of American commerce. This interview, along with Higginson's extensive business dealings with England, contributed to the post-war accusations that he was a British agent.[28]

During the war Higginson is said to have earned more than $70,000 by profiteering, and eventually amassed a fortune of more than $400,000.[29] Like other successful merchants who filled the vacuum of departing Loyalists, Higginson moved to Boston during the war, where he formed a commercial partnership with his kinsman Jonathan Jackson, and underwrote marine insurance through the office of Edward Payne. After having served as a representative from Boston in the General Court and as a Justice of the Peace, Higginson himself went to Congress in 1783, where he sat for just part of a year.[30] "My taste for public life was always very inadequate," he later wrote a friend.[31]

Higginson was among the earliest and most committed nationalists outside of the army. Just six weeks after Higginson arrived in Congress, James Madison noted that the Salem

28. For this "interview," see Higginson, *Life of Stephen Higginson*, 21-33. While there is no evidence that Higginson was involved in British intrigue, neither is there any doubt that he and his family maintained close ties with fleeing Loyalists. See, for example letter from Timothy Pickering to Mrs. Mehitible Higginson, Newburgh, June 15, 1783, Pickering Papers, MHS, suggesting that the country would be better off exchanging patriots for Loyalists.
29. Ms., Probate Records of Suffolk County, CXXVI, 585; CXXVII, 1-4. The estimate of $70,000 came from his nephew and friend, John Lowell; see T. W. Higginson, *Life and Times of Stephen Higginson* (Boston and New York, 1907), 43. For detailed records of Higginson's role in shipping and bonding see numerous entries in Gardner Weld Allen, *Massachusetts Privateers of the Revolution, Massachusetts Historical Society, Collections,* LXXVII (Boston, 1927).
30. *JCC*, XXIV, 153.
31. Higginson to Theodorick Bland, Boston, 31 Mar., 1785, in *The Bland Papers*, 2 vols. (Petersburg, 1840), I, 117.

merchant, along with Hamilton, desired a Constitutional Convention, but noted Higginson's conviction that, for the time being, "it was pretty certain that the Convention" proposed by Nathaniel Gorham would not take place.[32] Higginson was largely skeptical of militarists like Knox who claimed they wanted to fortify the army to enhance the government, and he was positively hostile to the economic policies and the regime of Robert Morris, including the Impost, which Hamilton championed.[33] According to Higginson, France, not Britain, represented the greatest external threat to American interests. In the spring of 1784 he blamed French interests for the "Jealousies and Animosities" excited between the states over both the commutation and the Society of the Cincinnati, warning that France was conniving to produce "general confusion and convulsions."[34]

As early as April, 1784 Higginson foresaw a potential connection between social disorder and reform of the Articles, suggesting that "we shall fall into general Confusion, and perhaps undergo another Revolution. . . . If anything can prevent [this], it must be a revision of our Constitution and the establishment of an effective government." What was required to demonstrate this need for constitutional revision, wrote Higginson, was a credible threat of armed warfare. In the same letter, he was already casting about for just such an opportunity: referring to the border disagreement between New York and Vermont, Higginson made the remarkable speculation that "this paltry dispute may be the means of involving the

32. James Madison, 1 Apr., 1783, *Writings of James Madison*, Hunt, ed., I, 439. This was just two weeks after Hamilton's letter to Washington mentioned above, 135 n.4. Six months later, Hamilton, Madison, and Higginson, formed a committee together to draft a treaty with Sweden; see *JCC*, XXIV, 477, n.1.
33. Stephen Higginson to Samuel Adams, 20 May, 1783, Burnett, *Letters*, VII, 167; Stephen Higginson to Arthur Lee, October, 1783, Jameson, ed., "Letters of Higginson," *AHA Annual Report* (1896) I, 711-712.
34. Higginson to —, Apr. 1784, "Letters of Higginson," *AHA* (1896) I, 715-16. At the same time, Higginson was negotiating personally with Lafayette to sell whale oil from Essex County fisheries for lighting Paris and other cities. For more of his Francophobia, see Stephen Higginson to Theophilus Parsons, April [7?], 1783, in Burnett, *Letters*, VII, 122-124.

States in a civil War."[35]

In such an event, despite his ambivalence toward the retired officers, Higginson could envisage a valuable role for the Cincinnati. Writing to Elbridge Gerry, also in April, 1784, Higginson mentioned that "I have had much conversation with Gen¹· Knox on the subject," leading him to further meditations about the link between anarchy and constitutional revision that, one concludes, he also discussed with Knox. This letter deserves to be cited at some length because of the remarkable precision with which, after "much conversation with Gen¹· Knox," Higginson predicted to Gerry the scenario that would be played out in Massachusetts almost three years later.

> there is but one reason that can with any weight be urged in favour of [the Cincinnati] — it is said, & I wish it may not prove true, that Our present federal Constitution can not last long & is incompetent to the purposes for which it was intended, the disposition and habits of the People require one of a firmer instance and higher toned, with Our manners & Ideas such a Government can not be sufficiently energetic.[36]

Higginson then forecast a succession of *coups* that reads like a page from Vico's *Scienza Nuova*.

> now if this be true, which will not readily be granted, & general confusion & convulsions should be the result, a distressing scene of Anarchy must be endured for a time, which will then issue in Despotism under some form or other; & unless there shall then be formed a united & determined Interest, either by the associating of the best informed and most virtuous Citizens for the purpose, or the existence of such a Society as the Cincinnati, who have no other Int^t· but that of the public to determine the period of anarchy & the

---

35. *Ibid.*
36. Stephen Higginson to Elbridge Gerry, Boston, 28 Apr., 1784, Elbridge Gerry Papers, New-York Historical Society.

principles of a new Government by their combined Efforts, you may depend & probably will altogether upon the Contingencies of the day for your future political situation.[37]

It should be noted how closely linked in Higginson's mind were the notions of "the best informed and most virtuous" aristocrats, whose duties are "to determine the period of anarchy" and also "the principles of a new Government." In the absence of an established aristocracy, Higginson felt that the best existing defense against tyranny and anarchy was:

a Body as the Cincinnati directed by reason & anxious only for the public Good. But this Supposition asks more of us than can be granted. Our Government it is true is as yet feeble, but will not the good Sense of the States lead them to revise the Constitution & provide such amendments as may be found necessary before such general confusion can take place, should such a scene arise, associations will be necessary to collect the force of independent men to a point, but can no association be formed that will be as effective and disinterested as the Cincinnati.[38]

After he left Congress, Higginson joined William Phillips and four other insurance underwriters in petitioning the General Court for the right to establish the Massachusetts Bank, where Higginson remained a founding director from 1784 to 1786.[39] Phillips appointed James Bowdoin, the Governor's

---

37. *Ibid.*
38. *Ibid.*
39. According to Gras, Phillips was "the merchant [who] was also becoming a capitalist;" he had owned a shop in Cornhill Street in 1771, near the London Bookstore owned by Henry Knox. The other petitioners for the Bank were Thomas Russell, Jonathan Mason, Isaac Smith, and Higginson's nephew, John Lowell. "Probably all of the petitioners had been accustomed to underwrite marine insurance," wrote Gras. "We might find that the nucleus of supporters for the Massachusetts Bank really came from Edward Payne's insurance office." Though a director, along with his loyal nephew, John Lowell, Higginson

chief political opponent, as the bank's first President — *after* the bank's charter had been approved by the Hancock government.[40] Bowdoin was still President of the Bank when Higginson and most of the other Directors helped to elect him Governor.[41]

Bowdoin epitomized pre-Revolutionary aristocracy. He was immensely wealthy, heir to what one biographer called unequivocally "the largest estate in New England," with strong ties to Britain through his son-in-law John Temple, and an ideological commitment to the right wing of Massachusetts politics proven during twenty-seven years in the General Court. Having served as President of the Watertown Convention of 1774, Bowdoin's Patriot credentials were respectable enough to allow for his election as President of the Constitutional Convention of 1780. But, outside Boston, his popularity paled next to Hancock's: for five years in a row, he had lost to Hancock by factors of ten and even twenty to one.[42] But when Hancock resigned suddenly in January 1785, the conservatives felt confident at last that their candidate could defeat Thomas Cushing, Hancock's Lieutenant-Governor, especially given the dire economic straits the state had reached during Hancock's administration. By the day Hancock relin-

owned only a little stock. See N. S. B. Gras, *The Massachusetts First National Bank* (Cambridge, Mass., 1937), 19-21.

40. "The director on whom chief reliance was placed," wrote Gras, "was Edward Payne. . . . On two occasions Payne presided . . . in the absence of Governor Bowdoin." *Ibid.*, 27.

41. Bowdoin participated very little in the affairs of the bank; he resigned in Dec. 1785, possibly in anticipation of the spring election. It is interesting to note that Bowdoin's father, together with other merchants, had formed a bank to emit notes as early as 1740. *Ibid.*, 9.

42. William Alexander Robinson, "James Bowdoin," in *Dictionary of American Biography*, Dumas Malone, ed., 20 vols. (New York, 1928-1936) II, 498. Election returns: in 1780, John Hancock, 11,451, to Bowdoin 1,141; in 1781, Hancock, 7,996 to Bowdoin, 304; in 1782, Hancock, 5,855 to Bowdoin, 1,155; from Anson E. Morse, *The Federalist Party in Massachusetts to the Year 1800* (Princeton, 1909), 19n., 26n., and 27-31; or see M. A. MS., "Votes for Governor and Lieutenant-Governor," except for 1783 and 1784: for these, see *Journal of the House of Representatives*, M. A. IV, 14, V, 9.

quished his office, the Assembly was divided by such rancor that "his enemies discovered marks of indecent joy," according to Charles Gore, "while his admirers chose to display their sorrow by unmanly blubbering. . . ."[43]

In fact, though, Hancock's popularity had only masked the extent of Bowdoin's unpopularity outside of Essex and Suffolk counties, which owed much to his close personal identification with the Constitution. Bowdoin seemed to embody all that was most disliked about that document. The two aspects of the Constitution which produced the most controversy were its formal establishment of Congregationalism, and its increased property qualifications for voters. Article III required "the several towns, parishes, precincts . . . to make suitable provision, at their own expense, for the institution of public worship."[44] This inevitably favored the orthodox Congregational (i.e., Calvinist) Church, over Baptists and Unitarians, who argued that they were hereby being taxed without representation, and whose opposition to the Constitution, led by Rev. Isaac Backus, was fierce, widespread, and lasting.[45]

Second was the increase in property qualifications, raised fifty percent higher than under the provincial charter, creating further western apprehension about the class of men responsible for its drafting, as well as for their own franchise. This apprehension is well expressed in "The Return of Northampton, 1780," which demands to know why so many citizens had lost their vote for "one branch of the two branches which are to consitutute our legislative, when they are willing that your men of property should enjoy the exclusive right of chusing the first branch?"[46] "The People accepted the Report of the

43. Charles Gore to Rufus King, 20 Mar., 1785 in C. R. King, *Life and Correspondence of Rufus King*, I, 81.

44. Taylor, *Massachusetts Documents*, 128.

45. "Article III was reactionary," wrote Morison. "It not only continued the religious system of the province, but exalted it to fundamental law." Morison, "Struggle over the . . . Constitution," *AHA Proceedings, L* (1917), 370. For a typical example of western reactions to Article III, see "The Return of Ashby (Middlesex County), 1780," in Taylor, *Massachusetts Documents*, 151.

46. Morison, "Struggle over . . . the Constitution," *AHA Proceedings, L* (1917), 408. Regarding concerns about the new property qualifications, and represen-

Convention without the alteration of an iota," gloated Theophilus Parsons, "though objections were made to every article."[47] The people could not help but notice that all their
objections were for nought since, as Morison has shown, the
Convention applied "such principles of counting that a two-
third majority for every article was assured in advance. . . ."[48]
Because Bowdoin was so closely identified with this Constitution, it certainly appears to have been a factor in his four
defeats by Hancock.

Bowdoin's popularity was hardly enhanced by the circumstances whereby he became Governor in 1785, after failing
to win a majority of the popular vote.[49] When the election
was thrown into the legislature, Higginson campaigned for
Bowdoin with a series of letters signed "Civis," printed in the
Continental Journal and the *Massachusetts Centinel*; he was
promptly denounced as the 'Salem Wizzard,' a title by which
he was identified in the press for years to come.[50] As a result,

---

tation in general, Morison wrote that "The return of Worcester . . . gives the
deliberate voice of western Massachusetts on this question of representation.
Failure of the Convention to heed their demands was one cause of Shays' Rebellion." *Ibid.*, 388.

47. Theophilus Parsons to Francis Dana, 3 Aug., 1780, Dana Papers, MHS,
also in Taylor, *Massachusetts Documents*, 159.

48. Morison, "Struggle over the. .. Constitution," *AHA Proceedings, L* (1917),
397, 400. See above, 29 n.57. While Morison added that he was unaware of
any contemporary "charges of dishonesty," the citizenry remained acutely
aware that their objections had not been met.

49. Bowdoin recieved 3,519 votes (to Cushing's 3,005), out of 9,065 votes
cast. See M. A. MS., "Votes for Governor and Lieutenant-Governor, 1785;"
also, Anson E. Morse, *The Federalist Party in Massachusetts to the Year 1800*
(Princeton, 1909), 29.

50. See *The Continental Journal*, 19, 26 May, 2 June, 1785. For identity of
"Civis," see Morse, *The Federalist Party*, 29, n. 10. The first attack on 'The
Salem Wizzard' seems to have been from "A Shopkeeper," in the *America
Herald*, 11 Apr., 1785: "Drop the curtain, behind which Art can be exercised
toward *sinister views*, and no *Wizzard* ever escaped from Salem can be more
assiduous in promoting his own interest." See also the *Massachusetts Centinel*,
7 May, 1785, encouraging citizens to "strenuously oppose all British agents or
their connections, and should the Salem Wizzard or any of his Faction have
the effrontery (again) to offer himself a candidate he ought to be treated with
neglect. . . ." Four years later Higginson's better-known "Laco" attacks on

Higginson may have done the political climate more harm than good, since his activities generated as much suspicion and personal animosity as Bowdoin himself.[51]

Largely because of this suspicion of the conservatives' motives, the Essexmen were unable to push Bowdoin through the House of Representatives, where he was resoundingly defeated by Cushing, 134 votes to 89. It was probably just at this moment that most of Massachusetts discovered that the Constitution specified the House could only "make return to the Senate of the two persons so elected; on which, the Senate shall proceed, by ballot, to elect one."[52] The Senate voted for Bowdoin 18 to 10, and the House, faced with a constitutionally stacked deck, acquiesced. William Sullivan noted that "this is the only instance of the failure of an election, by the people, from 1785 to 1833."[53]

It is worthwhile then, to review the new Governor's reputation through western eyes at the start of his administration, just a year before Shays' Rebellion. Bowdoin, possibly the wealthiest man in New England as well as the President of its only Bank, had British grandchildren, and was surround-

---

Hancock appeared in the Centinel, also published in the pamphlet *Writings of Laco* (Boston, 1789). Historians who suspected that Higginson was more opposed to Hancock than he was in favor of Bowdoin have overlooked the letters of 1785, when Hancock was not a candidate.

51. "The gentleman who has the majority of votes for governor possesses a character that is amiable: but who are the men who cloak themselves in his influence? . . . Are they not agents for British merchants?" *Massachusetts Centinel*, 18 May, 1785. But Bowdoin's record during the Revolution was at least suspect: "A True Whig" observed that "The only instances where [Bowdoin] was to be found was as President of the Provincial Congress at Watertown. . . . President of the Convention, President of the Arts and Sciences, and now President of the Bank. . . . But on any great and trying occasion, where was he?" The same writer alludes to Bowdoin's son-in-law, John Temple, "a British officer, a newly appointed Consul-General, who during the war was also spy General. . . ." *Massachusetts Centinel*, 25 May, 1785 Temple's return to America in Nov. 1785 further agitated sentiments regarding the problem of Loyalist refugees.

52. Taylor, *Massachusetts Documents*, 137.

53. William Sullivan, *The Public Men of the Revolution* (Philadelphia, 1847), 41.

ed by a *de facto* party of merchants and financiers.[54] He was only Massachusetts' second Governor, and Hancock's hard-earned popularity was at best a tough act to follow, especially in those western regions where it was "our Opinnion that we Do not want any Goviner but the Goviner of the universe."[55] Bowdoin was closely identified with the unpopular Constitution, including the increase of property qualifications, and dramatically larger poll taxes. The majority of the state had declined to vote Bowdoin into office, and the House of Representatives had unequivocally rejected him. Bowdoin was made Governor only by the Senate, that branch of government that represented property, according to the Constitutional Address to the Constituents — signed only by Bowdoin.[56]

The significance of Bowdoin's election to the nationalists' ambitions can hardly be overestimated, and after a five-year contest to become Governor, he did not hesitate to pursue them. In his very first action as Governor, on May 31, 1785, Bowdoin became the only head of state to call for a Constitutional Convention, and on July 1st, the new legislature asked the Massachusetts delegates to Congress to recommend a Convention "to revise the Confederation and report to Congress how far . . . to alter or enlarge [its powers] to secure the primary objects of the Union."[57]

54. Immediately following Bowdoin's election, the "Merchants and Traders in the Town of Boston" applauded him. "It is a peculiar felicity that in the present alarming state of our commerce, we have for our Governor a gentleman who cannot fail to sympathize with us at the gloomy prospect of our declining trade." See the *Continental Journal*, 9 June, 1785; These "Merchants and Traders" included Higginson, Jonathan Jackson, Edward Payne, William Phillips and other proto-Federalists who formed the new Governor's Council; see *Bowdoin-Temple Papers*, II, 50-52.
55. "Return of Ashfields (Hampshire County), 4 Oct., 1776," in Taylor, *Massachusetts Documents*, 43.
56. *Ibid.*, 125. It is fitting to note, in this context, Main's remark that "The Antifederalists, like most Americans, believed that if the government were truly to represent the people, the principal power should rest in the popular branch." Main, *Antifederalists*, 13.
57. *Acts and Laws of the Commonwealth of Massachusetts* (Boston, 1890-98), 1784-1785, 666-668, 706-711.

The recommendation was, however, promptly quashed by the state's delegates to Congress.[58] In a lengthy, stinging rebuke to the Bowdoin government, Elbridge Gerry, Rufus King, and Samuel Holton collectively refused to forward the recommendation to Congress, dreading "artfully laid" plots, which, "had they been successful, We think would inevitably have changed our republican Governments, into baleful Aristocracies. . . . The Cincinnati . . . we fear, if not totally abolished, will have the same fatal tendency." The delegates declared that they were, apprehensive "that such a Measure would produce thro'out the Union, an Exertion of the Friends of an Aristocracy, to send Members who would promote a Change of Government." The revised government would surely be "an Aristocracy, which would require a standing Army, and a numerous train of pensioners and placemen. . . ."[59] Given the "Junto's" ideological commitment to aristocracy, the delegates' concern is not surprising.[60]

After Bowdoin took office, Higginson's letters continued to reflect his unwavering conviction that, while the federal constitution required fundamental alterations, the crisis was not yet ripe enough to persuade the people. As a merchant, banker, and insurance underwriter, Higginson had powerful personal interests in establishing a stronger central government, especially for settling foreign treaties. But the usual lack of a quorum in Congress, "nine States being necessary," meant that, whenever attendance was sufficient, more pressing matters were always addressed.[61] In August 1785, Higginson began an extensive correspondence with John Adams in Europe by deploring the fact the "Congress are not *yet* impowered to regulate Trade, nor have they any Funds given them. . . . So great is the Jealousy of the States and so exces-

---

58. As Burnett put it, "the Massachusetts delegates deemed themselves wiser than the governor and the General Court." Burnett, Preface, *Letters*, VIII, xxxv.
59. The Massachusetts Delegates to James Bowdoin, New York, 3 Sept., 1785, in Burnett, *Letters*, VIII, 208-209.
60. See above, 139-140.
61. Stephen Higginson to — , Apr. 1784, "Letters of Higginson," *AHA* (1896) I, 718.

sive their attachment to local and partial interests, that there is no probability of their giving *very soon* to Congress the necessary powers. . . ."[62]

Six months before the first Regulation, Higginson offered Adams a shrewd analysis of the circumstances that might enable "the best informed and most virtuous citizens" to restructure the continental government. "Perhaps nothing less than an apprehension of common danger will induce the States to attend less to their separate and more to the general Interest in such Cases; but, however plain it may appear to the real politician, it is not easy in the moment of peace to impress upon the public mind an apprehension of danger . . . or to show that the individual Interests of the states can not be permanently secured, till those of the Union shall first be established on a firm and equitable Basis."[63] With this letter Higginson proudly included a state financial report, demonstrating that "the character of Massachusetts stands high:" the report projected a state budget that would serve "not only to provide amply for the Interest on the States Debt, but to reduce the principal" and "give Massachusetts additional weight in Europe and America."[64] This accelerated repayment, which Bowdoin had previewed in his first address as Governor, provided one of the major grievances in the western counties.[65]

---

62. Stephen Higginson to John Adams, 8 Aug., 1785, *ibid.*, 724. [My italics]. He requested Adams' strict confidence, acknowledging that since some his views might "be considered piratical, if not savouring of Toryism, I wish to be kept out of sight. . . . Mr. [Jonathan] Jackson has told me that you intimated a Wish to have such communications."

63. *Ibid.*, 729. He also expressed to Adams his thoughts on why the Southern States, which could never be "the Carriers of their own produce" would perpetually oppose empowering Congress. "The southern and northern States are not only very dissimular, but in many instances directly opposed. . . . If their was a greater coincidence of Sentiment and Interest . . . then might we expect those national arrangements soon to take place." *Ibid.*, 728.

64. *Ibid.*, 732.

65. For Bowdoin's first address, see *Continental Journal*, 9 June, 1786. After Shays' Rebellion had begun, Adams wrote to Jefferson that "to get the better of their debt," the Massachusetts Assembly had "laid on a tax rather heavier than the people could bear." Adams to Jefferson, 30 Nov., 1786, as quoted in Dumas Malone, *Jefferson and His Time*, 6 vols. (Boston, 1951), II, 157. See

In June, 1786, Higginson observed to Adams that, given the narrow trade policy of Britain, "the Commerce of Massachusetts will sink to almost nothing. there is no State in the Union which suffers in any degree equal to this from restrictions," owing to their impact upon the cod fisheries. But the Act for regulating foreign trade had been "met with much Opposition from Country Gentlemen."[66] He then informed Adams of "a commercial Convention which is to be held in September" in Annapolis, the ostensible object of which "is the regulation of commerce. . . . But when I consider the men who are deputed . . . I am strongly inclined to think political Objects are intended to be combined . . . The Men who I have mentioned are all of them esteemed great Aristocrats."[67] In fact, Higginson was himself appointed a delegate to Annapolis, despite his preferred method of working behind the scenes.[68] For a while, then, it seemed that the "Junto" might have its way at Annapolis. But lack of support in the General Court scotched their mission, and ultimately no delegate from Massachusetts attended.[69]

As reports concerning town conventions appeared in the summer of 1786, Higginson recognized the imminent arrival of his long awaited "confusions and convulsions." Less than a year after insisting there was "no probability" the States would grant Congress the necessary powers "very soon," he told Adams in July, 1786 that "we appear to be fast verging to a Crisis. . . . It is a serious and important Question, whether our Government may not get unhinged, and a revolution take place, before the Cure can be effected, and the people at large discover, that to secure their liberties and the great bulk of

---

also below, 157 n.91.

66. Stephen Higginson to John Adams, July 1786, "Letters of Higginson," *AHA* (1896) I, 734.

67. *Ibid.*, 734-735.

68. With the other delegates initially appointed, (Dana, Gerry, Parsons, Cabot, Lowell, and James Sullivan) the "Junto" members would have constituted a majority. See Burnett, *Letters*, VIII, 469 n. 5.

69. See Burnett, *Letters*, VIII, 469 n.5.

their property a certain portion of the latter must be parted with."[70] Higginson added that "A change of Ideas and measures must soon happen, either from conviction or from necessity. . . . It will then behove every man of property and influence to aim at giving the Tide a right direction."[71] A month later the crowds at Northampton closed the court, defying the law for the first time.[72] In September, courts were prevented from sitting at Concord, Taunton, and Great Barrington, unmistakably suggesting the existence of some statewide organization.

If Higginson's tone suggests he was pleased that a curative convulsion had begun, he was not alone. Different observers chose different metaphors, but the presumption shared by many was that a period of therapeutic turbulence was necessary. In May, 1786, Charles Pettit wrote that "Such Disorders both within and without cannot fail to bring on a Crisis. . . . However we may dread the Event, it seems to be the only chance we have of restoration to political health, and therefore a Convulsion of some kind seems to be desirable."[73]

Washington shared a similar view. In 1785 he wrote to the President of Congress "it is unfortunate for us, that evils which might have been averted, must be first felt."[74] By April,

---

70. Stephen Higginson to John Adams, July, 1786, in "Letters of Higginson," *AHA* (1896) I, 741. By this time most other close observers of the situation in Massachusetts had already come to the opinion that anarchy was now at hand. Rufus King, for example, had written to Adams three months before Higginson that "The people generally throughout the confederacy, remark that we are at a crisis." Rufus King to John Adams, New York, 5 May, 1786, in Burnett, *Letters*, 355.

71. Stephen Higginson to John Adams, July 1786, in "Letters of Higginson," *AHA* (1896) I, 741.

72. All the previous demonstrations had arguably been protected by the Constitution of 1780, Article I, XIX: "The people shall have a right, in an orderly and peaceable manner, to assemble to consult upon the common good. . . ." Taylor, *Massachusetts Documents*, 130.

73. Charles Pettit to Jeremiah Wadsworth, Burnett, *Letters*, VIII, 371. New York, 27 May, 1786.

74. Washington to Nathaniel Gorham, Mount Vernon, 22 June, 1785, *Writings of Washington*, XXVIII, 174. He repeated exactly this sentiment two years later "It is one of the evils — perhaps not the least, of democratickal govern-

1786, his thinking along this line had advanced further — "I have little hope of amendment without another convulsion."[75] A month later Washington still did not feel that the moment had arrived, for he wrote to Jay that "my fear is that the people are not yet sufficiently *misled* to retract from error."[76]

Washington was expressing the same fear most nationalists shared that May: that another untimely attempt at constitutional revision would produce inadequate results. No one expressed this concern better than William Grayson, in a letter to Madison that same month:

> I am of opinion our affairs are not arrived at such a crisis as to ensure success to a reformation on proper principles; a partial reformation will be fatal; things had better remain as they are than not to probe them to the bottom, if particular states gain their own particular objects, it will place other grievances perhaps of equal importance at a greater distance, if all are brought forward at the same time one object will facilitate the passage of another, and by a general compromise perhaps a good government may be procured. Under these impressions I cannot say I think it will be for the advantage of the Union that the Convention at Annapolis produce anything decisive: as in this event nothing more is to be expected from Massachusetts, etc.[77]

Thomas Jefferson, in Paris, was told by John Adams that "All will be well, and this commotion will terminate in addi-

ments, that the people must *feel* before they will *see* or *act.*" Washington to Humphreys, 8 Mar., 1787, *Writings of Washington*, XXIX, 173.

75. Washington to Henry Lee, 5 Apr., 1786, *ibid.*, XXVIII, 402.

76. Washington to John Jay, 18 May, 1786, *Writings of Washington*, XXVIII, 431. Jay responded that "Our affairs seem to lead to some crisis, some revolution, something that I cannot foresee or conjecture." *Correspondence and Public Papers of John Jay*, J. Franklin Jameson, ed., 4 vols. (Washington, 1897), III, 204.

77. William Grayson to James Madison, 28 May, 1786, in Burnett, *Letters*, VIII, 374.

tional strength to government."[78] Abigail Adams wrote Jefferson that "I cannot help flattering myself that [the 'ignorant, restless desperadoes'] will prove salutary to the state at large, by leading to an investigation of the causes which have produced these commotions,"[79] Jefferson's oft-quoted reply was even more sanguine: "the spirit of resistance . . . will often be exercised when wrong, but better so than not to be exercised at all. I like a little rebellion now and then. It is like a storm in the atmosphere."[80] Jefferson used the same meteorological metaphor to Madison: "I hold it that a little rebellion now and then is a good thing, and as necessary in the political world as storms in the physical."[81] Like other nationalists, Jefferson fully expected positive results to flow from the defeat of the uprising: "Unsuccessful rebellions, indeed, generally establish the encroachments on the rights of the people which have produced them. . . . It is a medicine necessary for the sound health of government."[82] Later Jefferson reached beyond this curative metaphor to the botanical: "God forbid that we should ever be 20 years without such a rebellion. . . . The tree of liberty must be refreshed from time to time with the blood of patriots and tyrants. It is its natural manure."[83]

It may seem unusual at first glance that such ideological adversaries as Jefferson and Higginson could share the same views regarding civil mutiny; but of course they reached this juncture from opposite directions. Higginson had no enthusiasm for the expression of popular will other than to flaunt it as

---

78. John Adams to Thomas Jefferson, 30 Nov., 1786, cited in Dumas Malone, *Jefferson and His Time*, 6 vols. (Boston, 1951), II, 157.

79. Abigail Adams to Thomas Jefferson, 2 Jan., 1787 *Jefferson Papers*, XI, 86-7.

80. Thomas Jefferson to Abigail Adams, 22 Feb., 1787, cited in Malone, *Jefferson* (1951), II, 158.

81. Thomas Jefferson to Madison, 30 Jan., 1787, cited in William Benton, ed., *The Annals of America* (Chicago, 1968), III, 81.

82. Jefferson to Madison, cited in Malone, *Jefferson*, II, 160. See also Robbins, "Algernon Sidney's . . . Textbook of Revolution," *WMQ*, 3rd. Ser., IV (1947), 292.

83. Thomas Jefferson to William Smith, 13 Nov., 1787, *Jefferson Papers*, XII, 356-357.

a threat to the Confederation and then crush it decisively. Jefferson, on the other hand, was drawing directly from Sidney's *Discourses*: "I mention Seditions, Tumults, and Wars upon just occasion; but I can find no reason to retract the term. . . . If the laws of God and Men are therefore of no effect . . . those Seditions, Tumults and Wars are justified by the Laws of God and Man."[84]

Some of Knox's friends in the Cincinnati reacted to the protests with the undisguised hope that "something important will be the event;" but there is no evidence to support Mercy Warren's assertion that the "discontents [were] artificially wrought up, by men who wished for a more strong and splendid government."[85] Mrs. Warren was the leading source of the suggestion that nationalists were employing *agents provocateurs*. At the end of 1786, she wrote to John Adams that "Time will make curious disclosures, and you, Sir, may be astonished to find the incendiaries who have fomented the discontents among the miserable insurgents of Massachusetts, in a class of men least suspected."[86] Minot, too, was suspicious: after the Springfield rout, he wrote privately to Nathan Dane that "this was almost too decisive a victory for the friends of government to gain, as it was likely to shut the door against opposition in future, a circumstance which I believe many specious patriots wish not to take place until their favorite plans are properly in train."[87] George Bryan suggested an even more sinister plot, just before the Philadelphia Convention, insisting that Cincinnati members had expressed their desire for a

84. Sidney, *Discourses* . . ., cited in Robbins, "Algernon Sidney's . . . Textbook of Revolution," *WMQ*, 3rd. Ser., IV (1947), 292.
85. Henry Jackson to Henry Knox, 28 Sept., 1786, who added "you will observe a meeting of the Cincin is called on the 11th October . . .," Knox Papers XIX, 19; Mercy Otis Warren, *History of the American Revolution*, 3 vols. (Boston, 1805), III, 346.
86. Mercy Otis Warren to John Adams, Dec. 1786, cited in Charles Warren, "Elbridge Gerry, James Warren, Mercy Warren, and the Ratification of the Federal Constitution in Massachusetts," *Massachusetts Historical Society, Proceedings, LXIV* (1930-1932), 160.
87. "George Richards Minot to Nathan Dane," Boston, 3 Mar., 1787, *MHS Proceedings, XLVIII* (June 1915), 430.

monarchy, and "that the people of Massachusetts were driven into Rebellion for the very purpose of smoothing the way to this step by their Suppression."[88] Indeed, General Brooks of theCincinnati hoped that atrocities by the protesters would provide propaganda for the government cause. "Should the insurgents begin to plunder," he wrote, "I think it will have a good effect."[89] Similar allegations appeared in the press, from a writer who accurately identified the distinguishing moral precept of those who sought a more powerful central government, that "a number of men who have pretended to be disgusted at the late unhappy commotions secretly rejoice at the opportunity of establishing, under pretence of necessity, a tyrannical rule. . . . A certain mark by which these are distinguished, is their repeated declarations, that the people have not virtue enough to bear a free government, when in fact nothing has taken place here, but what has happened in every form of government yet established in the world."[90]

If Higginson or any others of his class supported the western demonstrations, the proof is still wanting; the opinion of the Warrens and other Massachusetts particularists can be explained by their aversion to the nationalists' ambitions. If, by "fomenting the discontents," Mrs. Warren meant that "men least suspected" gave direct aid to the malcontents, her hypothesis strains credulity. Possibly she meant that the insurgents were "artificially wrought up" and "driven into rebellion" by the preceding repressive measures, including the supplementary payment to Congress.[91] But it is difficult to imagine that the conservatives had such prophetic powers when supporting

---

88. MS in Bryan Papers, Historical Society of Pennsylvania, quoted in Main, *Antifederalists*, 64, n. 76.
89. Brooks to Oliver Prescott, 25 Nov., 1786, cited in Feer, *Shays' Rebellion*, 328, n. 2.
90. See "David," 4 Oct., 1787, *Independent Chronicle*.
91. This is not entirely farfetched: during his tour of the region in October, Knox wrote to Congress that "the granting of the supplementary funds to the United States appears to have been the immediate cause of its bursting forth in such a violent manner." Knox to Congress, Springfield, 3 Oct., 1786, *JCC*, XXXI, 752. Two weeks later Knox offered Congress a more radical assessment of the protesters' motives. *Ibid.*, 887.

the legislation which rapidly redeemed the state's debt. It is true though that, once the protests began, many agreed with Higginson: "The sooner and more rapidly disorder overtakes us, the shorter will its duration be. . . ."[92]

One cannot wholly discount the possibility that someone may have given the rebels secret assurances of limited indemnity, for example, or some financial support, perhaps anonymously; neither Higginson, nor the General Court, nor Congress were beyond subterfuge in achieving their aims during the rebellion. Indeed, there were numerous occasions when such an exchange might have occurred, including the implausibly 'accidental' encounter between Captain Daniel Shays and General Rufus Putnam, his former commander, in Pelham three weeks before the Springfield confrontation.[93] But any speculation on actual complicity between the conservatives and their foes is only that.

The reaction of the government was swift, but at best indecisive. With the first court closing in Northampton on August 29th, Bowdoin turned to his unpopular political intimates for advice and support. First he asked Theophilus Parsons for a legal opinion on the circumstances and method whereby he might use the county militia to prevent incidents of unlawful assembly. Parsons wrote an outline of the possible eventualities, and advised that if he crowd "fill the Court-House, or the avenues to it, so that the Justices cannot enter, having met for the purpose of preventing the sitting of the Court, this is more than an unlawful assembly, it is a rout. . . . If they refuse to

---

92. East called the amortization "an unfortunate plan for the abrupt and early redemption of an extraordinary debt." East, "Massachusetts Conservatives," *Era of . . . Revolution*, 357. This essay, along with Richard Morris's, makes the argument for *agents provocateurs* most forcefully — but with only the evidence cited here. For a lengthy but unconvincing refutation of this notion, see Feer, *Shays' Rebellion*, 299-314. Stephen Higginson to Nathan Dane, 3 Mar., 1787, "Letters of Higginson," Jameson, ed., *AHA Annual Report* (1896), I, 753.

93. "Shays' Rebellion Letter," General Rufus Putnam to Governor Bowdoin, Rutland, 8 Jan., 1787, Shays' Rebellion Box, American Antiquarian Society.

move out of the way . . . it is a riot."[94]

His constitutional powers clarified, Bowdoin swiftly issued his first proclamation on the subject.[95] The proclamation was sent to the Sheriffs and militia leaders of the five counties which had thus far evidenced unrest.[96] But three days later the court at Worcester was disrupted, led by veteran Adam Wheeler, who also avowed his constancy with Revolutionary principles.[97] Wheeler insisted that the crowds had no wish to overthrow the government: they sought merely to postpone property seizures by the court until just grievances could be addressed constitutionally.

The two-day confrontation in Worcester caused enormous alarm in Boston, and on September 7th Bowdoin sought the advice of an informal council of Boston financiers, merchants, and state office-holders, including his successor as President of the Massachusetts Bank, William Phillips. Together, the gentlemen tried to determine the best course of action for government to take on September 12th, when the courts at Concord, Taunton, and Great Barrington were scheduled to meet. At the end of four days in which much was discussed and little decided, this council gathered a crowd of well-affected and well-heeled supporters at Faneuil Hall to express "their disapprobation of the measures lately adopted in several parts of the country," and show their support for the Constitution. Samuel Adams was moderator of the drafting committee, which included Higginson, his partner Jonathan Jackson, and insurance underwriter Edward Payne.[98] This display of solidarity for the Governor may have encouraged some like-minded citizens, but to the west it represented further proof that the "great men" of Boston were circling their wagons to defend

---

94. [Theophilus Parsons], "Some Brief Observations on the Power of Sheriff," *Bowdoin-Temple Papers*, II, 110.
95. Proclamation from Governor Bowdoin, 2 Sept., 1786, Broadside in 190 M.A., 226.
96. Berkshire, Hampshire, Worcester, Middlesex and Bristol.
97. Adam Wheeler, Hubbardston, 7 Nov., 1786, in *Worcester Magazine*, last November issue.
98. *Independent Ledger*, 11 Sept., 1786; *Boston Gazette*, 18 Sept., 1786.

the perceived injustices produced by the Constitution.

A few weeks later, in a similar public address, the Massachusetts Society of the Cincinnati also deprecated the commotions insisting that "if grievances are suffered by any particular citizens, surely the yet unpaid army may be said to be aggrieved." Since the officers of the Cincinnati had received their commutation, the malcontents included more unpaid veterans than their adversaries. The officers' resolves also threatened military counter-action, declaring that "this society will never tamely suffer those inestimable blessings to be wrested from their hands by foreign force, or domestick faction."[99] Taken together with Bowdoin's Address, it was clear that government, commerce, and the military élite were united to defend the status quo.[100]

On September 12th, the courts at Taunton, Concord, and Great Barrington were prevented from transacting business, despite the presence of some government troops; but in Great Barrington, the militia lined up four-to-one in favor of the insurgents.[101] The implications were baleful for government, which lacked any other means for supporting law and order. Alarmed for the military supplies at Springfield, Knox made a hasty trip to Springfield on September 16th, and reported to Congress four days later on the safety and condition of the 7,000 arms and thirteen hundred barrels of powder stored there. Having learned that "some lawless people . . . had intimated their intention . . . of seizing the arsenal," he asked Governor Bowdoin to secure the stores.[102] Bowdoin returned the problem to Congress, ordering Major General Shepard of the Hampshire militia to obey any orders he received from Knox — aiming to spare Massachusetts the responsibility (and cost) for defending the Continental Arsenal. But, it should be noted that, had the demonstrators ever intended to use the weapons,

---

99. *Massachusetts Centinel*, 18 Oct., 1786.
100. A few months later, "Brutus" wrote that "The consequences to be feared from a union of the Military and Monied interest is truly alarming." *Boston Gazette*, 2 Apr., 1787.
101. See 190 M.A. 241, 263 and 318 M.A. 12, 17.
102. Knox to Congress, 20 Sept., 1786, *JCC*, XXXI, 675-6.

it would have been against officials of the state.

The Governor and the General Court reacted to the commotion at Springfield with fresh alarm, owing to the two factors which distinguished this event from previous protests: first and foremost, the proximity of the Arsenal raised the stakes dramatically beyond the previous demonstrations. Second, the disturbances appeared to have found an experienced leader, in the person of Captain Daniel Shays, lending the protest a distinctly military character — and a name. Although Shays insisted that his aim was to prevent bloodshed, his name was forever thereafter joined to the protests, by Knox himself.[103] Knox returned to Springfield in early October, just after the Arsenal was surrounded by Shays and his men appeared to be in command; Knox reported to Congress that Shays was responsible for all the commotions.[104]

After a few days of investigation in Springfield, Knox proceeded to Boston for a series of meetings with the Governor and "Gentlemen . . . of the most respectable characters in the state for their political knowledge."[105] From Knox's first letter to Higginson on October 22nd, it is evident that these two men had conferred during this visit, and discussed the situation in considerable detail, including the ruse of an Indian war, and raising private funds.[106] It was with this letter, secretly conveyed by William North, that the two men began their consequential correspondence — and North began his campaign of persuading Massachusetts that an Indian war was imminent. Bowdoin had already "consulted confidentially" with "gentlemen, connected in the affairs of Government" regarding the

---

103. Knox to Congress, Springfield, 3 Oct., 1786: "They were headed by a Captain Shays of the militia. . . ." *JCC*, XXXI, 752.

104. Though the names of Shattuck, Parsons, and Day were more often cited in Boston, Knox still referred to Shays as the principal leader four months later; see Knox to Lafayette, 13 Feb., 1787, Knox Papers, XIX, 164.

105. Knox to Congress, Boston, 18 Oct., 1786, *JCC*, XXXI, 886.

106. Knox to Higginson, 22 Oct., 1786, Knox Papers, XIX, 31. This was written the day before the first draft of his letter to Washington, in Appendix B; it was delivered personally to Higginson by Capt. William North, who was responsible for supplying testimony of "indian wars."

protection of the United States' Arsenal at Springfield, and this certainly included his long time ally and banking associate, Stephen Higginson.[107]

Higginson replied on November 12th that "upon the view of a War with the *Indians* and the consequent requisition of Congress, [were] obtained with more ease than I expected . . . the money wanted for the men will, I trust, be soon raised. The Treasurer has just opened his Loan. . . ."[108] And, at this critical moment, after biding his time for three well-documented years, Higginson declared that at last "the present moment is very favorable to the forming further and necessary Arrangements, for increasing the dignity and energy of Government. what has been done, must be used as a stock upon which the best Fruits are to be ingrafted. the public mind is now in a fit State, and will shortly I think become more so, to come forward with a System competent to the great purpose . . . of promoting and securing the happiness of society." This exchange represented a critical nexus, then, between Shays' Rebellion and the alteration of the federal government. Emphasizing the conspiratorial nature of their collaboration with Major William North, Higginson added "I love to know what passes in the World, but I had at this moment rather not appear to know it."[109]

A fortnight later Higginson wrote to Knox that, thanks to "some alarming reports of Shays being on the march in force . . . we shall, I think, in a few days have the money wanted for enlisting the men." Rebuking the General Court its placative measures, he told Knox that "you will feel not a little mortified, I presume, to find, that They have so much contributed to increase the infection prevailing in Our Back Counties."[110]

107. Knox to Congress, Boston, 8 Oct., 1786, *JCC*, XXXI, 875, 886.
108. Higginson to Knox, 12 Nov., 1786, Jameson, ed., "Letters of Higginson," *AHA* (1896), I, 741-742. [Higginson's italics.]
109. Higginson to Knox, 25 Nov., 1786, Knox Papers, XIX, 58. Regarding Capt. North, Higginson adds "I saw Capt. Worth [*sic*] but a moment, I intend a private moment with him. . . ."
110. *Ibid.* Higginson is presumably referring to the act pardoning any who had participated in "obstructing the sitting of the Courts of Law," provided only that they would swear to an oath of allegiance before the last day of 1786. *Acts*

Higginson almost gloated that this generous conduct of the General Court "will tend much to prepare the public mind, for transferring power from the individual Governments to the federal, and may facilitate those measures which we esteem essential to Our public happiness."[111] For the first time since he left Congress in 1783, Higginson evinced some optimism, even as he blamed the government for the situation, instead of the mob. "I am often disposed to think that We shall, in spite of Our folly and timidity, become a respectable people, when from the Vices and Follies of Our Rulers We seem to be in danger of Anarchy, some new Event turns up to avert the Evil, and show us the necessity of abridging the power of the states to controul or impede the measures of the Union." His optimism arose from the popular reaction to the insurrection. "I never saw so great a change in the public mind, on any occasion, as has lately appeared in this State as to the expediency of increasing the powers of Congress. . . . By the next Summer I expect We shall be prepared for anything that is wise and fitting." Prodding Knox, at the War Office in New York, Higginson suggested that "Congress should be making the necessary Arrangements for improving this disposition. . . . They must be prepared not only to support a proper force in the field, but to consolidate the Several Governments into One, general and efficiant. But I am going too fast."[112]

Four days after writing this letter, Higginson made his involvement in the counter-revolution even more personal, by joining the *posse comitatus* of General Benjamin Hichborn which captured three of its leaders. Having said that it behooved every gentleman "to aim at giving the Tide a right direction," Higginson, forty-three years old and without military experience, apparently rode as second-in-command of the

---

and Laws of the Commonwealth of Massachusetts (Boston, 1890-98), 1786, ch. 44, Nov. 15, 1786. As well, court sessions in the affected areas were postponed, suggesting that the protesters had succeeded in their aims. *Ibid.*, ch. 86 (Nov. 9), ch. 99 (Nov. 14), ch. 137 (Nov. 17).
111. Higginson to Knox, 25 Nov., 1786, Knox Papers, XIX, 58.
112. *Ibid.*

force of 300 "lawyers, physicians, and merchants," according to Mary Cranch, "joined by a number of Gentlemen" under General Benjamin Hichborn, which set out from Cambridge on November 28 to capture Shattuck, Parker, and Page.[113] This was accomplished so effortlessly that Hichborn was concerned: "I am afraid," he wrote to Knox, "that the Insurgents will be conquered too soon."[114]

Not until January could Higginson report real success to Knox in wringing coin from the purses of his wealthy confrères, by shrewdly posting the subscription papers in various marine insurance offices; and his success owed to reports that Shays' intended to lay seige to the Springfield Arsenal.[115] "A new Event has again roused [the insurgents]," Higginson reported to the Secretary of War, "and by seising on the lucky moment I hope enough has been subscribed to provide for Gen¹ Lincolns expedition and to compleat the other Object" — meaning the funds for the federal expedition under the command of Knox's friend, Col. Henry Jackson.[116]

Since Lincoln's last military expedition had been his dismal defeat by Clinton at Charles Town in 1780, where he had

---

113. "giving the tide . . .," Higginson to John Adams, July 1786, "Letters of Higginson," Jameson, ed., *AHA* (1896), I, 741. For Higginson's role in this raid see Abigail Adams to Thomas Jefferson, 2 Jan., 1787, in *Jefferson Papers*, XI, 87; for the assertion that Higginson was second-in-command on this raid see William Sullivan, *The Public Men of the Revolution* (Philadelphia, 1847), 391, where Sullivan imagined Jefferson addressing Colonel Hichborn:"Did you not go out with Stephen Higginson as your second in command?" See also Higginson, *Life of Stephen Higginson*, 90-95, as well as note signed "TWH," Higginson Family Papers, Box 2, Folder marked "Genealogical Papers," MHS. Mary Cranch to Abigail Adams, 26-30 Nov., 1786, Adams Family Papers, MHS, as quoted in Szatmary, *Shays' Rebellion*, 92-93; and the *Independent Chronicle*, 6 Dec., 1786. This arrest, following the suspension of *habeas corpus* on 15 Nov., was the first military reprisal of the rebellion, which Minot described as "a very important event" whereby "the sword of government was unsheathed." Minot, *History*, 77-78.

114. Hichborn to Knox, Dec. 14, 1786, Knox Papers, XIX, 92.

115. This was reported to Bowdoin by Rufus Putnam in a letter from Rutland, 17 Jan., 1787, in the Wetmore Family Collection, Yale University Library.

116. Higginson to Knox, Boston, 20 Jan., 1787, Knox Papers, XIX, 130.

surrendered 5,400 troops, it is reasonable to suppose that Lincoln's foremost qualifications for this command were his position as President of the Massachusetts Cincinnati, and his ability, demonstrated in December, to raise the money necessary to feed the 4,400 men he was chosen to lead to protect the court scheduled to sit in Springfield in late January.[117] But he was also known, even in the west, for being fairminded and evenhanded, a reputation borne out by his conciliatory disposition toward the protesters after they had been routed.[118]

In the same letter to Knox, on January 20, Higginson reported the departure of Lincoln and his troops the day before, and again connected the subject of Shays' Rebellion to that of the federal constitution, observing that "the friends of Government in the most seditious Towns now venture to talk with firmness and in a manly tone. Should this Spirit pervade the other States, it will give rise to Sentiments favorable to the Union. The moment must be seised by Congress &c. We must make the most of it whilst the fire burns, it will not be durable perhaps."[119]

A week later, just as Lincoln chased the remnants of Shays' troops, Knox replied to Higginson that "Massachusetts, by an exertion in the present instance, may even acquire a temporary vigor; but the poor, poor federal government is sick almost unto death. . . . A convention is proposed . . . imbued with ideas far short of a radical reform. . . . may it notwithstanding be turned to an excellent purpose?"[120] Knox then went further, turning their correspondence into a detailed analysis of the consequences of the Constitutional Convention, suggest-

---

117. Lincoln had also been appointed by Washington to supervise Cornwallis' surrender at Yorktown, thus making him a symbolic figure of revolutionary valor — if not exactly a paragon of military competence. For a thorough portrait of Lincoln, see David B. Mattern, *A Moderate Revolutionary: The Life of Benjamin Lincoln*, [unpublished Ph.D. dissertation, Columbia University, 1990]. Note that the money Lincoln raised was specifically for provisions, leaving to Higginson's machinations the problem of paying the officers and soldiers.

118. See esp. Lincoln to Knox, 14 Mar., 1787, Knox Papers.

119. Higginson to Knox, 20 Jan., 1787, Knox Papers, XIX.

120. Knox to Higginson, 28 Jan., 1787, Knox Papers, XIX.

ing that State conventions could choose delegates to a *second* continental convention to decide finally on a Constitution. "Would not this, to all intents and purposes, be a government derived from the people, and assented to by them . . .? If it be not the best mode, is it not the best which is practicable?"[121]

Higginson, "pleased to find that your Sentiments and my own are so exactly coincident," replied with two letters totaling 4,000 words, in which at last he unburdened himself to Knox of his overall view of the rebellion and its crucial connection to amending the Confederation, noting that "As early as '83, while I was at Congress, I pressed upon Mr. Maddison and others the Idea of a special Convention" for that purpose.[122] Because they demonstrate the nexus between the rebellion and the convention, and because he had no interest in deceiving Knox, these two letters deserve to be quoted at some length.

Higginson began by pointing out to Knox the crucial failure of the Articles: the self-defeating conflict of sovereignty between the states and the central government — a conflict which, of course, has continued to reverberate throughout American history:

> to delegate rights to Congress, and at the same time to withhold from them the means of exercising those rights, is trifling and absurd, the powers of the Union must be increased, and those of the States individually must be abridged; they cannot both be perfectly sovereign and independent at the same time. . . . By an early adoption of a liberal and extensive system of Government . . . we may avert these public Calamities, which now threaten the dissolution of the Governments of the several States, and which may eventually involve them in all the horrors of a civil War.[123]

But how could a new Constitution be achieved without

---

121. *Ibid.*
122. Higginson to Knox, 8 Feb., 1787, Knox Papers, XIX, 157.
123. *Ibid.*

violating the stringent demands of the Articles, which had, for example, allowed a majority in the Rhode Island legislature alone to overrule the impost approved by the twelve other states? Not by the Congress:

> no representation from Congress to the States will ever have the same weight, as from a well appointed and special Convention. When a man who is to exercise them, asks for additional powers, especially of the legislative and executive kind, we naturally suppose that a lust of domination may have led him to ask for more than absolutely necessary. . . .
> This State entered into the measure of appointing a general Convention the last year with much readiness; but the Sentiments delivered to the two houses by Mr King and Mr. Dane have produced a great change in the disposition of the members. Those Gentlemen, I fancy, have now different Ideas of the matter, and will not now think there is so great a resemblance between our County Conventions, in their views and principles, and that proposed to be held at Philadelphia in May. . . .[124]

He then turned to the problem of finding a sure means of ratifying the Constitution he hoped would emerge from Philadelphia. And here Higginson — who did not even attend the Philadelphia Convention — proposed the system which would indeed be adopted, and which would, from the outset, prevent three or four states from impeding ratification.

> To refer the doings of the Convention to the several Legislatures for adoption, would be to hazard the object, as much perhaps, as to recur to the people at large. . . . If the referrence should be made to the people at large throughout the Union what can be expected, considering their discordant views and interests, but a

---

124. *Ibid.*

diversity and opposition of Sentiment, that cannot be done away and which must in all probability prevent their agreeing upon any general system of Government. The most probable way in my mind, of meeting with Success, would be to have special State Conventions appointed, to whom the report of the general Convention should be referred, and they be directed to report to Congress their dissent or approbation therefor, and if nine of those State Conventions shall report in favour of the system, Congress shall be authorized thereupon, to declare it to be the federal Constitution of Government; and the States shall be compellable to conform to and govern themselves by it.[125]

Higginson ended this letter by appealing for Knox's confidentiality in these matters. Then, five days later, he resumed his discourse with the important point that the States could be led gradually to consent to ratification — *even against their will*:

> If then the States will make the appointments for the purposes proposed, will they not have all consented to the alteration, tho' nine only of the State Conventions should report in favour of it to Congress? . . . the consent of the States, or some of them, may possibly be obtained in this way when they may not intend it, and perhaps without their knowing it at the time; but having in any way gained it, and the Constitution reported being ratified by Congress, a small minority may then clamour or complain in vain.[126]

Higginson then returned directly to the subject of the rebellion and Lincoln's recent success at defeating his opposition, but he cautioned Knox against undue confidence, since "the disaffection is evidently much more deeply rooted, and

125. *Ibid.*
126. Higginson to Knox, 13 Feb., 1787, Knox Papers, XIX, 165.

extensive, than was apprehended."

> You will endeavor no doubt to draw strong Arguments from the insurrection in this State in favour of an efficient General Government for the Union. As all the States are at least equally exposed with this to such Commotions, and none of them are capable of the exertions we have made, they will have reason to fear the worst consequences to themselves, unless the Union shall have force enough to give the same effectual aid in a like case. — Those who now have the administration of Government in the several States and for the Union, must seize every opportunity to increase its energy and stability; or Insurgents will soon rise up and take the reins from them.[127]

He concluded his discourse with a further caution that, for the success of their conspiracy (rather than out of personal concern), they must still maintain absolute discretion. "These are Sentiments too free and bold to be, as yet, very freely and generally held forth; but the time is coming, and every man in his sphere should contribute to accelerate its arrival, when they will be very popular and generally practiced upon. But as it is yet at some distance, you will, I am persuaded, not too openly hand them out, even as those of another."[128]

Thus Knox, the Secretary of War and founder of the Cincinnati, conferred with the merchant and bank director on how the rebellion could lead to the ratification of a new constitution, even as the latter raised money (including a loan from the Massachusetts Bank), to pay Cincinnati officers to defend the arsenal of the continental government.[129]

---

127. *Ibid.*

128. *Ibid.*

129. "February 20th, 1787. At a special meeting of the Directors. . . . Passed upon a Note of Thos. Ivers Esqr. State Treasurer for a Discount of 1,666 2/3ds dollars, dated this day — Voted that the Subscription paper, which by a Resolve of ye. General Court of this date is to be lodged in the hands of the President & Directors the Mass. Bank, be now lodged in the hands of Mr. Payne & Mr.

Had this been known, it would have been proof that there was a "Union of the Military and Monied interests," combining and conspiring to force a Federal Constitution out of class warfare.[130] And that argument would have been complete had there been proof that Higginson and his associates were giving orders to Lincoln directly, without even a nod to the elected officials of Massachusetts.

In fact, Higginson did instruct Lincoln directly during the rout of the insurgents. Because this did not come to light for many months, and then only through curious channels, this communication has never been noted in relation to Shays' Rebellion.[131] A letter, addressed to Lincoln from "S. H.," was found in July, 1787, and printed in the *Boston Gazette*, well before any outcome in Philadelphia was known.[132] The letter was reprinted in the *Massachusetts Centinel*, and internal evidence suggests that it was indeed written by Higginson to Lincoln. Both its style and substance are entirely in keeping with the rest of Higginson's correspondence, most notably in the way it closely links the rebellion with larger intentions.

You will have seen by the letters you received by the same post with my last, that I was mistaken as to the execution of your orders; the *means used* to procure the *new orders* were found more efficacious than

---

Russell 'till further orders. Voted, that a sitting Director, be impowered to Discount for the Treasurer of this Commonwealth, a sum not exceeding £1,500. — including the £500 — now discounted, without calling the Directors together." N. S. B. Gras, *The Massachusetts First National Bank* (Cambridge, Mass., 1937), 296. See also *Acts and Laws of the Commonwealth of Massachusetts* (Boston, 1893), 1786-1787, chap. XL, 445-446.

130. This was exactly the accusation that appeared in the press: "Rapidly are you dividing into two classes — extreme Rich and extreme Poor"; the alliance of Bowdoin and Lincoln represented a "Union of the Military and Monied interests"; and Bowdoin's supporters were "Men of Property and Fortunes, who expect one Day to lord it over, impoverish and enslave, YOU." See "Brutus" in *Boston Gazette*, 2 Apr., 1787.

131. Parts of this letter were quoted in a footnote by Anson Morse, *The Federalist Party*, 41-42, n.3.

132. *Boston Gazette*, 30 July, 1787. This issue is missing from the MHS and the AAS, including the microfilm edition of Early American Newspapers.

I expected; they were *obtained by surprize*, and the manner in which it was done will afford good matter for *derision* at a future day. You now have your hands *at liberty*, and must use them to purpose; and *effect* if possible. From our last advices I have some hope you may get Shays, this would *finish the business to our wishes*. We are here preparing matters more HARD TO MANAGE and MORE DANGEROUS than Shays and his party. But if you can give a *decisive stroke* to the latter, we can more easily obtain the former. We are not here much less active in pursuing the GREAT OBJECT than you are above. Our party is small and our operations not seen it is true. But I hope we shall co-operate most forcibly with you — I have the means of contributing to the supression of the Rebels — But all this must be 'inter nos' at least for the present. Adieu, Yours, S. H.[133]

The best speculation is that this letter was written on Sunday, February 4th, for on that same day the General Court adopted an official declaration of *"a horrid and unnatural* Rebellion *and* War," which gave Bowdoin and Lincoln almost unlimited constitutional authority to deal with the insurgents, and may well have been the *"means used* to procure the *new orders."*[134]

When this letter was reprinted six months later, a fulgent loathing for Higginson erupted in the press. The attacks came primarily from those most firmly attached to the Massachusetts Constitution, some of whom would soon ignite the bonfires of Antifederalism. "S. H. is the *Guy Faux*. Kill him. — Kill him. . . . If there was a junto preparing amidst Shays's

---

133. Exactly as reprinted in the Massachusetts Centinel, 1 Aug., 1787. The letter was dated merely "Boston, Sunday Noon."

134. *Acts and Resolves, 1787*, ch. 5, 4 Feb., 1787. For Shepard's and Lincoln's hope that a rebellion would be declared "to remove all occasion of scruple in the most nice," see Shepard to Bowdoin, 30 Dec., 1786, *Bowdoin-Temple Papers*, II, 127; also, Lincoln to Washington, Hingham, 4 Dec., 1786, Sparks MSS., LVII, Houghton Library, Harvard University.

rebellion to subvert our present republican government and introduce in its stead a monarchy or an aristocracy . . . I wish to see them dragged forth to public infamy."[135] "Stephen, you are . . . a junto infinitely more infamous than those under Bernard and Hutchinson. . . . I saw Stephen at a certain office . . . grinning ghastly a horrible smile; his eyes darting at once, triumph, terror and treachery. . . . [He] ought to be burnt for sedition, treason stratagem and spoils. . . ."[136] "The 'authenticity' [of the letter] can no longer be doubted, as the *silence* of the person justly suspected must be considered as full proof of its reality. . . ." [Its author] "was in the cabinet, and was informed as a favourite, of every transaction as soon as the General [Lincoln] himself. . . . A person who was tampering with the Executive; using an undue influence to obtain measures agreeable to himself and his party. . . . What authority has any individual to obtrude his sentiments, and to dictate to the General in such language. . . . Were the operations of government to be the result of the deliberations of S. H. and his party? It is true the supposed author generally exercises an air of mystery and importance; but this is no argument why he should be suffered to write in this extraordinary manner to a general officer while under the immediate orders of the executive, and at an alarming crisis, without being called upon to explain his mysteries."[137] ["The decided friends to the Constitution"] "express their indignation against the rebellion, its secret and open abettors, and execrate the pusillanimity and treachery of a junto. . . ."[138]

One consequence of the discovery of this letter was to eliminate Higginson from the Massachusetts ratification convention. For though he wrote Knox that he had "neither the qualities nor the leisure for the business," Higginson's name was tendered for the Boston convention, only to be defeated.[139]

135. "Plain Truth" in the *Massachusetts Centinel*, 11 Aug., 1787.
136. *Massachusetts Centinel*, 15 Aug., 1787.
137. "Lucius" *Massachusetts Centinel*, 18 Aug., 1787.
138. "Cato" in the *Massachusetts Centinel*, 22 Aug., 1787.
139. Higginson to Knox, 8 Feb., 1787, Knox Papers, XIX, 157. Knox wrote to

On January 20th, 1787, Higginson wrote to Knox that Lincoln had set out after the Regulators with 5,000 men and that his orders were "very extensive, his powers great. . . ." Although neither he nor Knox had been elected to any office, they were clearly trying to control the state legislature with regard to the Philadelphia Convention, at least.

> If we can manage the Gen[l] Court and bring them to right measures, massachusetts may recover her former and proper station among the States of the Union. But I fear that may prove more difficult to manage than the Insurgents without Doors, to affect it however must be Our great Object, every one must contribute his mite. . . . men in the Country have taken their Sides, and the friends of the Government in the most seditious Towns now venture to talk with firmness and in a manly tone. Should this Spirit pervade the other States, it will give rise to Sentiments favorable to the Union, the moment must be seised by Congress &c. We must make the most of it while the fire bums, it will not be durable perhaps.[140]

Higginson received Knox's reply within days of writing his impolitic "S. H." letter to Lincoln. Knox agreed, of course, that suppressing the Regulation was not enough by now the Continental Congress was breaking down completely. "Massachusetts," wrote Knox, "by an exertion in the present instance, may even acquire a temporary vigor; but the poor, poor federal government is sick almost to death. But one feeble sign of life for upwards of two, almost three months past.

Lincoln that "I hope. . . that Massachusetts will choose, and that you, Mr. King, and Mr. Higginson should be three of the delegates." Knox to Lincoln, 14 Feb., 1787, *ibid.* For Higginson's nomination to the Boston Convention, see Samuel B. Harding, *The Contest Over the Ratification of the Federal Constitution in Massachusetts* (New York, 1896), 55-56, n.3.
140. Higginson to Knox, 20 Jan., 1787, "Letters of Higginson," Jameson, ed., *AHA* (1896), I, 744.

No Congress but for part of one day."[141] A quorum had long been a rare event in Congress, and when it occurred, only the most pressing business was addressed.[142]

Knox went on to propose to Higginson that, once a new Constitution was proposed in Philadelphia, "State conventions might be assembled" to choose delegates to consider this general government. "Would not this, to all intents and purposes, be a government derived from the people . . .? If it be not the best mode, is it not the best which is practicable?"[143] The most practicable purpose of this plan was to avoid ratifying conventions within the several states; Knox clearly felt less confident of the nationalists' ability to control such conventions. In fact he was not even sure that Massachusetts and other New England states would send delegates to Philadelphia; if not, "it will operate in a duplicate ratio to injure us by annihilating the rising desire in the Southern States of effecting a better national system. . . ."[144] The importance of Massachusetts' decision, and the danger of this domino effect scotching the federalists' agenda was already appreciable; it would become even more so during the process of ratification.[145]

It was to that subject that Higginson turned his attention in his next two letters to Knox, on February 8th and 13th, 1787, totalling almost three thousand words. Higginson offered his most explicit reaffirmation yet of the political perspective they shared: that "the Confederation is incompetent to the purposes for which it was established. . . . The Union . . . must have

---

141. Knox to Higginson, New York, 28 Jan., 1787, reprinted in Drake, *Correspondence of Knox*, 93.

142. In 1787, there was no quorum until Jan 27th, nor after October 27th. In the intervening 112 days on which Congress assembled, there were only two days when a delegate was present from each of the thirteen states; 11 states were there on 4 days; 10 states on 6 days, 9 states on 39; 8 states on 35. On 102 days, 6 or less states attended. See *JCC*, XXXII, vii-x.

143. Knox to Higginson, New York, 28 Jan., 1787, reprinted in Drake, *Correspondence of Knox*, 94.

144. *Ibid.*

145. Soon after this letter, Knox wrote to Lincoln that "none of the New England States have yet chosen, and it appears quite problematical whether any will choose unless Massachusetts." *Ibid.*, 95.

the power of compelling obedience . . . otherwise our federal Constitution will be a mere dead letter. . . . The powers of the Union must be increased, and those of the States individually must be abridged. . . . Unless the States shall soon consent to part with some of their rights as Sovereign States, they will very soon be involved in one general scene of disorders and distress."[146]

Since Knox was well-placed at Congress to influence delegates from across the continent, Higginson offered all the intellectual ammunition he could to the former chief of ordnance. Higginson methodically spelled out his views on the connection between Shays' Rebellion, the urgent need for a new Constitution, and the best way to guarantee ratification by the states, "perhaps without their knowing it at the time." Though he failed to see that the cause lay in the national government's failure to compensate the retired soldiery it had recruited, Higginson did see that these local protests were symptoms of a continental malady, of the Revolution.

[By] concentrating our Views to the Union, we may avert these public Calamities, which now threaten the dissolution of the Governments of the several States, and which may eventually involve them in all the horrors of a civil War.[147]

He rehearsed for Knox the reasons why a special Convention was more appropriate than Congress to effect constitutional revisions, perhaps recalling conversations he had had with Hamilton and Madison four years earlier. The most important reason for this was the credibility of the final document.

When a man who is to exercise them, asks for additional powers, especially of the legislative and executive kind, we naturally suppose that a lust of

146. Higginson to Knox, 8 Feb., 1786, "Letters of Higginson," Jameson, ed., *AHA* (1896), I, 745-746.
147. *Ibid.*

domination may have led him to ask for more than is absolutely necessary. . . . from this Jealousy, so natural to Man, we may expect an opposition to the most clear and judicicious recommendations. . . . From these observations you will easily perceive, that I am quite of your Sentiment, and in favour of the proposed Convention. . . .[148]

Higginson made it equally clear that only "a radical Cure" in Philadelphia would be sufficient to save the Union, in his eyes, and suggested that Massachusetts should send as its delegates "King, Lowell, Dana, Parsons and Gerry," of whom three were actually chosen (King, Dana and Gerry). He then addressed the best method for ratification, rightly assuming that the Philadelphia Convention itself would not be so empowered. "To refer the doings of the Convention to the several Legislatures for adoption would be to hazard the object, as much perhaps, as to recur to the people at large."[149] In Massachusetts, at least, either of these possibilities would have probably meant victory for the Anti-Federalists, given the success of "Shaysite" candidates in the previous election, who were generally opposed to central government.

The most probable way, in my mind, of meeting with Success, would be to have special State Conventions appointed, to whom the report of the General Convention should be referred, and they be directed to report to Congress their dissent or approbation therefor, and if nine of those State Conventions shall report in favour of the system,, Congress shall be authorised thereupon to declare it to be the federal Constitution of Government; and the States shall be compellable to conform to and govern themselves by it.[150]

To insure that "the whole Business might soon be in train

148. *Ibid.*, 746.
149. *Ibid.*, 748.
150. *Ibid.*, 149.

for a speedy and happy issue, Higginson wanted Congress to urge the States to *appoint* delegates to Philadelphia, and to *appoint* delegates to the States' ratification conventions. But Higginson's most consequential recommendation was to establish from the start that fully five states would be needed to repudiate the new Constitution. This was hardly a blueprint for popular sovereignty; little wonder, then, that Higginson cautioned Knox that his letters were "fitted only for your private inspection," since the avowed purpose of his proposal was to foist a potentially unpopular form of government upon the unwilling population of four states![151]

Higginson turned directly from the matter of ratification to that of Shays' Rebellion. "You will endeavour no doubt to draw strong Arguments from the insurrection in this State in favour of an efficient General Government for the Union. As all the States are at least equally exposed with this to such Commotions, and none of them are capable of the exertions we have made, they will have reason to fear the worst consequences to themselves, unless the Union shall have force enough to give the same effectual aid in a like case." Those currently in power "must seize every opportunity to increase its energy and stability, or Insurgents will soon rise up, and take the reins from them."[152] Did Higginson really believe that? Evidently, since he added, "This consideration, which I take to be founded in truth, and the nature of things, should guard those in office and power from an undue and ill-timed modesty, as to the means to be used for increasing the powers of Government, and the manner of exercising them when acquired." Clearly the ends, in Higginson's mind, justified any means whatsoever. Once again he acknowledged that his sentiments were "too free and bold" to be shared with strangers, "but the time is coming . . . when they will be very popular and generally practiced upon. But as it is yet at some distance, you will, I am persuaded, not too openly hand them out, even as those of another."[153]

---

151. Higginson to Knox, 13 Feb., 1787, *ibid.*, 750, 749.
152. *Ibid.*, 751.
153. *Ibid.*, 752.

Higginson's extensive involvement in raising the alarm (and the money) to defeat Shays' Rebellion was important; for while the Regulation was not exactly the anarchy he had been anticipating for years, it was certainly close enough. But his most critical role lay in relating the commotions in Massachusetts to the stalemate of governance under the Articles of Confederation. His patronage of General Lincoln connected him directly to the suppression of the protests; his early alliance with Hamilton and Madison gave him a direct link to the call for the Philadelphia Convention; and his partnership with Knox gave him a direct, open channel to Washington and to Congress.

Higginson and other nationalists were not certain that the Philadelphia Convention was the right venue for finding "a radical Cure" until early 1787. By then Higginson could write that "while we have any hope of warding off the evil by means of a convention, we shall not patiently submit to a temporary anarchy, nor propose to claim any advantage from a state of convulsion; but having tried the experiment and found that our National Government must arise out of necessity alone, and be the effect of confusion, we shall then give way to dire necessity, and with vigilance turn every event to good purpose."[154] This notion that government must be the *effect* of confusion — that order could only arise out of necessity, demonstrated by disorder — was at the core of the nationalist and conservative agenda, from the time the Newburgh conspiracy collapsed in 1783 until the new framework of government was ratified in 1788.

---

154. *Ibid.*, 753.

CHAPTER SIX

General Washington and Shays' Rebellion

"I could not resist the call to a convention of the States which is to determine whether we are to have a Government of respectability under which life, liberty, and property will be secured to us, or are to submit to one which may be the result of chance or the moment, springing perhaps from anarchy and Confusion, and dictated perhaps by some aspiring demagogue.

— Washington to Lafayette[1]

A few weeks after Washington resigned his command, he described retirement to Knox in elegiac tones. "I feel now . . .," he wrote, "as I conceive a wearied traveller must do, who, after treading many a painful step with a heavy burthen on his shoulders, is eased of the latter, having reached the haven to which all the former were directed."[2]

---

1. Washington to Lafayette, Philadelphia, 6 June, 1787, *Writings of Washington*, XXIX, 229-230.
2. Washington to Knox, 20 Feb., 1784, *Writings of Washington*, XXVII, 340-341. One must understand just how avidly Washington relished the "tranquil enjoyments" of Mount Vernon, to appreciate how loath he was to give them up In a passage to Lafayette that nearly presages Thoreau, Washington revealed much about his character and perspective, and also proclaimed the permanence of his retirement. "I am become a private citizen on the banks of the Potomac," he wrote, "and under the shadow of my own vine and my own fig tree. Free from the bustle of a camp and the busy scenes of public life, I am solacing myself with those tranquil enjoyments of which the soldier who is forever in pursuit of fame; the statesman whose watchful days and sleepless nights are

Knox already knew that Washington would not care to contemplate any return to public life, especially in the political arena. For Washington to exchange pastoral bliss for political business would require the most strenuous moral and intellectual persuasion from all his closest confidants. Knox was determined to do his part in this persuasion (along with Madison, Hamilton, Jay and others), by contending that Shays' Rebellion posed a communistic peril that would eventually threaten even the tranquility of Mount Vernon — unless Washington actively championed the nationalists' cause.

Not only Washington's serenity made his rustication seem irreversible: his reputation seemed to demand that he remain above the political fray — though here he was faced with a very public dilemma. Washington had long been preoccupied with his "reputation," by which he meant not just prestige, but something akin to the immortal stature of his soul.[3] For this reason, the public perception of his motives was often

---

spent in devising schemes to promote the welfare of his own, perhaps the ruin of other countries (as if this globe was insufficient for us all); and the courtier who is always watching the countenance of his prince, in hopes of catching a gracious smile, can have very little conception. I am not only retired from all public employments, but I am retiring within myself, and shall be able to view the solitary walk and tread the paths of private life with heartfelt satisfaction. Envious of none, I am determined to be pleased with all, and this, my dear friend, being the order for my march, I will move gently down the stream of life until I sleep with my fathers." Washington to Lafayette, 1 Feb., 1784, *Writings of Washington*, XXVII, 317; and later to Knox, "to see this Country happy whilst I am gliding down the stream of life in tranquil retirement is so much the wish of my Soul, that nothing on this side of Elysium can be placed in competition with it." Washington to Knox, 8 Mar., 1787, *ibid.*, XXIX, 170.
3. Minutes after receiving his commission in 1775, Washington turned to Patrick Henry and said, "Remember, Mr. Henry, what I now tell you. From the day I enter upon the command of the American armies, I date my fall and the ruin of my reputation." Quoted in Flexner, *Washington*, II, 9. Perhaps the best expression of his metaphysical perspective of reputation came a few years later, when he wrote: "It should be the highest ambition of every American to extend his views beyond himself, and to bear in mind that his conduct will not only affect himself, his country, and his immediate posterity; but that its influence may be co-extensive with the world, and stamp political happiness or misery on ages yet unborn." Washington to Pennsylvania Legislature, September 1789, *Writings of Washington*, XXX, 395n.

more compelling to him than personal considerations. Washington's well-deserved and well-tended reputation had been enhanced even more by his forfeiture of power than it had been by his victory over the British Empire. Wood observed that "his retirement had a profound effect everywhere in the Western world. . . . Washington was a living embodiment of all that classical republican virtue the age was eagerly striving to recover. . . ." As John Trumbull wrote from London, his resignation "excites the astonishment and admiration of this part of the world. 'Tis a Conduct so novel, so unconceivable to People, who, far from giving up powers they possess, are willing to convulse the empire to acquire more."[4]

Washington's desire for a stronger federal government was universally known: he had hoped his retirement would prove that his belief in the need for a more powerful central government was thoroughly disinterested; he had even resigned as vestryman of Truro Parish, Virginia, in order to separate himself absolutely from public life.[5] What would the world think of him if he returned to power three years later? But, then, what would the world think if he *failed* to come to the aid of his country in its hour of peril? Knowing full well

---

4. Wood, *The Radicalism of the American Revolution*, 206. Wood went on: "It was extraordinary, unprecedented in modem times — a victorious general surrendering his arms and returning to his farm. Cromwell, William of Orange, Marlborough — all had sought political rewards commensurate with their military achievements. . . . Though it was widely thought that Washington could have become king or dictator, he wanted nothing of the kind. He was sincere in his desire for all the soldiers 'to return to our Private Stations in the bosom of a free, peaceful and happy Country,' and everyone recognized his sincerity. It filled them with awe. King George III supposedly predicted that if Washington retired from public life, and returned to his farm, 'he will be the greatest man in the world. . . .'" *Ibid.* Trumbull quoted by Wood, *ibid.* See also Garry Wills, *Cincinnalus: George Washington and the Enlightenment* (New York, 1984), 13.

5. In his Circular Letter to the States, he wrote that "the determination I have formed, of not taking any share in public business hereafter . . . will, I flatter myself, sooner or later convince my Countrymen, that I have no sinister views" in calling for a more energetic central government. Washington, 8 June, 1783, in Ford, ed., *Washington Writings* X, 254. Washington to Capt. Daniel McCarty, *Writings of Washington*, XXVII, 341-342.

the symbolic impact of his decision, Washington fretted with this moral dilemma — as Knox and Madison knew he would — from the involuntary beginning of his involvement in the Philadelphia Convention.[6]

From the start of his military career, Washington's impact had often owed much to his symbolic resonance. Twenty years before the Second Continental Congress, Colonel Washington's troops had shot ambassadors from France carrying diplomatic credentials and thus triggered the Seven Years' War. In 1775, he was still known best outside Virginia for having ordered the first gunshots in a conflict that took more than a million lives.[7] That year, his selection over Massachusetts men was intended as a symbol of the united provinces — a living image of national unity.[8] And it was not lost on contemporaries that, in that moment, he became not only the Commander-in-Chief: until money was raised for the first recruitments, Washington was also the *only* soldier in the American army.[9]

6. Washington explained his concerns two years later, when faced with his imminent election as President this was an office he would not accept he wrote to Benjamin Lincoln, "unless it be a *conviction* that the partiality of my Countrymen had made my services absolutely necessary, joined to a *fear* that my refusal might induce a belief that I preferred the conservation of my own reputation and private ease, to the good of my Country." Washington to Lincoln, 26 Oct., 1788, *Writings of Washington*, XXX, 119.

7. "Washington had, indeed, shed the first blood in the Seven Years' War, a conflict which, according to Frederick of Prussia, cost the lives of about 853,000 soldiers plus civilians by the hundreds of thousands." Flexner, *Washington*, I, 9.

8. According to John Adams, the principal reason Washington was made Commander in Chief over Artemas Ward was that his leadership *represented* the participation of the southern states. See above, 102, n.5.

9 Flexner wrote that "in all history no general had been more strangely commissioned. Far from stepping to the head of a constituted force, the commander in chief was the only man (no riflemen having yet been enlisted) actually to be enrolled in the Continental Army. Not by any direct vote or broad decision had Congress brought the thirteem colonies into the war then being waged in New England, but by the act of elevating Washington. There was no nation to fight for the Declaration of Independence lay more than a year in the future. There was, except for intangibles — grievances and resented atrocities

While swift decisiveness in command was not always Washington's to offer, as a symbol of personal fearlessness he was an awesome inspiration to his men, from Trenton in 1776 to Yorktown in 1781, where a young Virginia private "witnessed a deed of personal daring and coolness in General Washington which he never saw equalled. During a tremendous cannonade from the British . . . Washington visited that part of the fortifications . . . he took his glass and mounted the highest, most prominent, and most exposed point of our fortifications, and there stood exposed to the enemy's fire, where shot seemed flying almost as thick as hail and were instantly demolishing portions of the embankment around him, for ten or fifteen minutes, until he had completely satisfied himself of the purposes of the enemy."[10]

Still, by 1786, the most impressive act of his life was not in exercising his power, but in renouncing it.[11] It was thanks to this that the concern he had expressed to Patrick Henry, that his reputation would be ruined by his accepting command, was for naught. By 1786 his metaphysical reputation had grown greater than anyone could have foreseen, even in New England. That year, for example, on his birthday, the *Massachusetts Centinel* reported that the people of Boston cele-

---

— only Washington." Flexner, *Washington*, I, 339. It was not long after that Washington demonstrated his careful attention to the symbols of protocol by refusing a message from General Howe that failed to recognize his rank in the Continental Army, and was addressed to "George Washington, Esq." And at Yorktown, Washington had refused to personally accept Cornwallis's sword from the British General's aide, and appointed his own aide, General Benjamin Lincoln, to receive it.

10. It cannot be charged that Washington took such a risk for show; but neither can he have been unmindful of his appearance to his men. "During this time his aides, etc., were remonstrating with him with all their earnestness against this exposure of his person and once or twice drew him down. He severely reprimanded them and resumed his position." From the personal account of Private John Suddarth, in John C. Dann, ed., *The Revolution Remembered: Eyewitness Accounts of the War for Independence* (Chicago, 1980), 239-240.

11. Even in this, he took great care in the protocol: Washington and Thomas Mifflin, then President of Congress, meticulously choreographed the surrender of his military commission to Mifflin personally, rather than to his Secretary. Schwartz, *George Washington*, 140-141.

brated "by a discharge of cannon, &c. A circumstance which then occured, being singular, may deserve notice. About 10 o'clock, the scholars of the several publick schools in town, to the number of two or three hundred, proceeded into State Street, where they testified their respect for the day, on which was born the Deliverer of their Country. . . . [All this in] the remembrance of the virtues of the illustrious American Cincinnatus."[12]

Thus Washington's *participation* — not just his endorsement — had enormous potential for moving the states toward union, precisely because his emergence from retirement would provide such a dramatic reaffirmation of the nationalist cause. Nothing else could foreseeably do so much to avert a fiasco in Philadelphia as the impact of Washington's presence: in attracting a quorum of the states, in the drafting of a new constitution, and in its ratification. Not only was he the greatest symbol of authority in America: he was, in fact, the only national figurehead to whom Americans could look with pride and confidence. The President of Congress certainly was no competition; after all, no one could serve in that office for more than one year out of three.

Neither was Congress itself. By 1786, Congress's reputation, and that of many of its members, was as bankrupt as its treasury, having suffered irreparable damage by its assorted failings: the dwindling attendance of its delegates, the continual bickering between small and large states, and its inability to meet obligations — even interest payments — to creditors, civil and foreign. Meanwhile, other problems both critical and urgent accumulated in the states and in Congress, only to be put off again and again: payments due to the veterans, the impost, pre-war debts to British merchants, the issue of the Loyalists, boundary disputes, the sale of western lands, commercial treaties, problems of the national economy, and the question of paper money which, to the alarm and dismay of the élite, was being issued in more than half the states by

---

12. *Massachusetts Centinel*, 15 Feb., 1786.

1786.[13]

The nomadic national assembly did not even have a permanent address: its unscheduled wanderings every six to twelve months further diminished any pretence that this was a capital forum, much less a central government.[14] All this, together with the dismal failure of the Annapolis Convention to attract delegates from even half the states, made it abundantly clear that the Confederation could not be sustained. Without some basis for renewed trust between the states, it seemed that nothing could arrest the progressive collapse of continental government, except perhaps "the Deliverer of the Country." If America's foremost hero would not rise to the occasion, why then should anyone else? If, on the other hand, Washington renounced his cherished retirement to rebuild the framework of American government, how many could fail to support him?

In a brief and unconvincing essay meant to refute any causal connection between the Regulation and the Constitution, Feer allowed that "if it can be shown that without Shays's Rebellion Washington would not have attended the Convention or have lent his name to the Federalists on behalf of ratification, then the Rebellion did help produce the Constitution."[15] It does not take a logical positivist to see that

---

13. These issues and others that faced Congress are examined in Merrill Jensen, *The New Nation*, 194-335.

14. An article in the *Worcester Gazette* (quoting the *Philadelphia Gazette*) during the first week in September, 1787, described most of the country's feelings toward Congress by then. "It is to be hoped that the name of Congress will be laid aside in the new federal government . . . who can hear of the word Congress without associating with it the ideas of *weakness — instability — slender power* — in some instances of *faction — of continental money — of the forty for one measure — of tender laws* — and lastly, of a *pendulum*, vibrating for near two years between Annapolis and New-york . . . The word *Congress* should be retained in our language only to signify an hasty representation of the people for the purpose of redressing grievances, as the term *Convention*, by general use, is applied to a deliberate representation of the people, for the purpose of making or altering a government."

15. Feer, "Rebellion and Constitution," *NEQ* (1969), 395." Although people talked about Shays's Rebellion and some were momentarily frightened by it," argued Feer, "there is no evidence that it changed in any significant way the

any such double-negative, counterfactual hypothesis cannot be argued, much less proved. What can be shown, however, is that as late as August 1st, 1786, Washington still emphatically eschewed any public business; but by November 18th, less than two weeks after receiving Knox's alarming letter about Shays' Rebellion (and many others in the same vein), Washington began to prepare himself, albeit with much reluctance and equivocation, for a return to public life. His correspondence makes it clear that Shays' Rebellion was the determinative factor.[16] After being alarmed by exaggerated reports about the Regulation, Washington did not merely lend his name to the nationalists, as he always had done: he rescinded his unqualified retirement from public life. Washington might have attended the Convention 'in any case,' but we will never know. His presence in Philadelphia was in fact linked to the Regulation; they occurred together.[17]

The nationalists were not motivated only by their ideological precepts or personal finances: the progressive entropy of continental government from a variety of inherent defects was not just the fabrication of an interested few. Congress's authority had actually declined after its ratification in 1781;

thinking of the people who drew up and ratified the Constitution. The movement for Constitutional revision . . . was well under way prior to Shays's Rebellion." *Ibid.*, 410. But that movement had no assurance of success before there was evidence of armed insurrection; preparations for America's entry into World War Two were well under way before Pearl Harbor, but the Japanese attack was the determinative factor.

16. *Pace* Feer. The effect of Shays' Rebellion upon Washington has generally been overlooked, but it is not an original idea: Jensen wrote that Washington was already optimistic about economic recovery "before Shays's Rebellion frightened him out of retirement and into politics." Jensen, *New Nation*, 250. Szatmary as well wrote that "Shays' Rebellion played an integral part in the genesis and formation of the United States Constitution adopted at Philadelphia," citing Washington's participation as one of its effects. Szatmary, *Shays' Rebellion*, 120, 127. See also Flexner, *George Washington*, 111, 102-109.

17. Washington himself wrote that Shays' Rebellion and the series of events following the war formed "a link of no ordinary magnitude in the chain of the American Annals." Washington to Minot, 28 Aug., 1788, *Writings of Washington*, XXX, 65.

till then, owing to the exigencies of war, questions about its ill-defined powers were generally postponed. Thereafter, a number of the states' legislatures and their Congressional delegates doubted whether there was any further need for Congress at all.

Endeavoring perhaps to remain even-handed in the debate over Federalism, many historians have reserved judgement about government under the Articles, and written about the Confederation as if it might have served as a viable constitutional premise.[18] But one need not necessarily believe that the Federalists had the solution just to see that the Articles were the problem, or to agree with Hamilton that "the principal defects of the confederation . . . do not proceed from minute or partial imperfections, but from fundamental errors in the structure of the building." The Confederation was a loose war-time alliance between sovereign states, built upon a fundamental contradiction that could never be overcome: the Articles burdened Congress with responsibilities for which the states did not grant commensurate authority.[19]

Of the Confederation's many weaknesses, the most fatal lay in the second Article, introduced after John Dickinson's draft for the very purpose of hobbling the powers of Congress. This key Article, whose significance still reverberates through American political life, was largely a result of the anti-conservative strategy of Dr. Thomas Burke. Burke, an Irish-born delegate from North Carolina, had, like John Trenchard, attended Trinity College, Dublin, and fostered the

---

18. For a brief review of this historiography, and a useful evaluation of the Articles, see Merrill Jensen, *The Articles of Confederation: An Interpretation of the Social-Constitutional History of the American Revolution, 1774-1781* (Madison, Wis., 1963), 3-15 *et passim*. In this work, as in *The New Nation*, Jensen gives considerable credit to the Articles, arguing that they were well-suited to the political purpose for which they were intended, c. 1778; i.e., the restriction of central authority.

19. Hamilton, *The Federalist*, No. 15, in Jacob E. Cooke, ed., *The Federalist* (Middletown, Ct., 1961), 93. Hatch observed that the states "allowed Congress a temporary and indefinite authority for the purposes of the war, and left their permanent relations to be determined by future agreement." Hatch, *Administration*, 74.

same intense suspicion of unchecked authority. Pitted against nationalist James Wilson of Pennsylvania, born and educated in Scotland, it was Burke who proposed the amendment to Dickinson's draft which, in 1778, became Article II: "Each state retains its sovereignty, freedom and independence, and Every Power . . . which is not by this confederation express- ly delegated to the United States in Congress assembled."[20] Since the powers expressly delegated to Congress were so slight, the impact of this Article was to virtually negate any pretense this "august assembly" had of being a government.

This fundamental defect was especially apparent to those foreign governments which had done the most to support the nascent states — and which had the most to lose, as creditors, if the "perpetual Confederation" collapsed. Louis-Guillaume Otto, the French chargé d'affaires at Philadelphia, summed up the basic problem perfectly in a letter to the Comte de Vergennes. "The inconsistency of the idea of a sovereign body which has no right but to deliberate and recommend . . . cannot be concealed. . . ." Otto went on to observe that "the low condition into which congress had fallen since the peace begins to excite the attention of true patriots. . . . The feder- al government cannot remain in its present inaction without endangering the reputation of the United States. . . . The de- partment of finances has never been so destitute as at this moment. . . . It will require much time and negotiations to correct these defects, and it is impossible to foresee the end of the present embarrassments."[21]

20. The Articles of Confederation, Article II, in Commager, ed., *Documents of American History*, I, 111. For the substance of the important Burke-Wilson debates, see Abstract of Debates, Burnett, *Letters*, II, 275-284. For a close ex- amination of the problems of sovereignty under the Confederation, see Jensen, *The Articles of Confederation*, 161-176, 239-245.
21. Otto to Vergennes, June 17, 1786, in *Correspondence Politique: États- Unis, Ministére des Affaires Etrangéres, Paris*; translated in George Bancroft, *History of . . . the Constitution . . .*, I, 511-512. At about the same time, accord- ing to Jonathan Smith, "the French minister wrote to his master that there was now no general government in the United States, neither Congress, president, nor head of any administrative department Practically this was chaos, and the next step was anarchy." Smith, "The Depression of 1785," *WMQ*, 3rd. Ser.

The first permanent minister from the Netherlands discovered much the same on the day he arrived in Philadelphia, late in 1783: although he was accompanied by a respectable fleet, there was no official reception for Mynheer van Berckel, nor anyone from Congress to greet him. In fact, that errant assembly was not even in Philadelphia anymore: it was temporarily seated in Princeton, with half-baked plans to oscillate irregularly between Annapolis and Trenton. And the Confederation had not had a Minister of Foreign Affairs since Robert R. Livingston had resigned in June (because of the slim congressional salary). "Who will succeed," wrote Stephen Higginson at the time, "or whether any Successor will soon be appointed is uncertain at present;" in late September, Madison wrote to Jefferson that "the election of a Sec^y. has been an order of the day for many months without a vote being taken."[22] The office remained vacant until John Jay assumed the post more than eighteen months later. There was not even a gracious accommodation to offer the Dutch Minister in the village of Princeton, where, Madison wrote, "We are exceedingly crowded in this place; . . . Mr. [Joseph] Jones and my self are in one room scarcely ten feet square & in one bed."[23]

No wonder that maintaining a quorum proved an impossibility under such trying circumstances. Historians have duly noted the incessant, insoluble problem of achieving the minimum number of delegations: nine to vote, and seven even to deliberate. But some have treated this as if it were an irritating technicality, rather than the neutralization of Congress's negligible powers. Those powers did not even include the right to compel its members to attend, a crucial point that was demonstrated as early as 1778, by the selfsame Dr. Burke.[24]

(1948), 79.

22. Stephen Higginson, 10 June, 1783, in Edmund C. Burnett, *The Continental Congress* (New York, 1941), 583. Madison, 20 Sept., 1783, *ibid.* I owe much of this account of Congress's deterioration to Burnett.

23. James Madison, Jr., to James Madison, Sr., Princeton, 30 Aug., 1783, *Madison Papers*, VII, 294-295.

24. In 1778, trying to produce a quorum, Congress had ordered Burke to at-

From that time on the quandary of the quorum became progressively worse; after March 1st, 1781, the problem was greatly aggravated. Because one of the few changes instituted upon ratification of the Articles (neither the President, nor the members being replaced at that time), was to raise the minimum number of delegates from each state to two (with a maximum of seven): for a state to vote in favor of a measure, a majority of its delegates had to concur — otherwise, the state's vote was not counted at all. This change effectively doubled the inefficiency of Congress.

It is not necessary to accept the Federalists' agenda to see that the Confederation, as constituted in the Articles, simply did not work. Year after year, the little authority Congress had retained was ceaselessly eroded by its members' absences, and by 1786 the weakness of Congress was seen as a terminal malady that would, in and of itself, lead to the disintegration of this fledgling civilization. In January, the Chairman of Congress, David Ramsay (elected to replace no-show President John Hancock), wrote to all of the state legislatures that "three months of the federal year are now compleated, and in that whole period no more than seven states have at any one time been represented. . . . The most essential interests of the United States suffer from the same cause. The languishing State of the public credit is notorious both in Europe and America." Ramsay went on to note the insulting nature of the delegates' truancy. "Even in private life where two persons agree to meet at a given time and place . . . the one who attends has a right to complain that he is not treated with common politeness by the other who breaks the appointment. . . ." This produced an "unequal burden imposed on the states who are present: they incur a heavy expence to maintain their delegates . . .," even though the delinquent states might be absent for three months or more. According to Ramsay, the result of

---

tend a late evening session of Congress. "He said that he desired to know the authority of Congress over him; that he would attend at hours that he thought reasonable, unless compelled by force of his person . . . and that, if guilty of improper behavior, he would answer to his State." *Secret Journals of Congress*, (April 10, 11, 24, 25, 1778) I, 62-67, as quoted in Hatch, *Administration*, 22.

this delinquency "naturally tends to annihilate our Confederation. That once dissolved our State establishments would be of short duration. Anarchy, or intestine wars would follow till some future Caesar seized our liberties. . . ."[25] In the spring of 1786, this widely-held anxiety throughout Congress prepared all the states to expect the very worst from the Regulation that began six months later.[26]

The continuous pattern of arrivals and departures was the most frustrating aspect. In early March, even as the delegates continued to meet and adjourn from day to day, New Jersey defiantly rejected the latest requisition, prompting a fresh emergency — but still without a quorum. Finally, on March 24th, a missing delegate from Maryland arrived, producing nine states for the first time in almost five months. But days later a delegate from New Hampshire departed, leaving them once again crippled. Thus Congress stumbled on, acutely anticipating "the approach of some great crisis."[27]

If Congress was so patently ineffectual, one might well ask why *anyone* objected to constitutional revisions. Many of the anti-Federalist arguments will be addressed below, in Chapter Seven: but before the Philadelphia Convention, the answer lay largely in the distrust that had evolved between the states (especially between the large and the small), whose governments were the fonts of all power, and whose commercial interests, especially, were intrinsically at odds with one another. Confederationalists who supported the unrevised Articles distrusted the purposes behind, as well as the process of, any revisions. And, of course, many were state office holders, and did not want their own powers diminished by ardent nationalists who wished to see those governments stand, as Jay put it, "in the same light, in which counties stand to the State

---

25. Burnett, *Letters*, VIII, 291.
26. On 1 Mar., 1786, the Secretary of Congress, in still another plea to the states, noted that in the previous four months "there has not been for a single day a number of States assembled sufficient to proceed on the great business of the Union." Burnett, *Letters*, III, 312.
27. The Connecticut delegates to Governor Matthew Griswold, New York, 12 Apr., 1786, Burnett, *Letters*, VIII, 339; see also *ibid.*, xxiii.

. . . as districts to facilitate the purposes of domestic order and good government."[28] Such opposing views augured ill for the Confederation's survival, but even worse for its transformation.

Charles Pinckney of South Carolina put the problem thus: "Let us suppose . . . the present confederation dissolved, and an assembly of the states convened for the purpose of adopting a system calculated to render the general government firm and energetic . . . [will not] the large states . . . contend and insist upon a greater influence then they at present possess? Would they again consent to unite upon principles which should allow states not contributing a twelfth part of their quotas to public expences, an equal vote with themselves?"[29] So Congress trudged on, preferring the ills it knew, and tripping over all the stumbling-blocks built into the Articles. They were pushing their own vehicle, as it were: for this machine would not go of itself. Still, the states were not inclined to negotiate away their own powers, as shown at Annapolis.

Even as Washington dismissed appeals for his return to leadership, from his own backyard he set in motion the chain of events which resulted in the Philadelphia Convention. Within months of retiring, Washington turned back to his pet project of opening the Potomac to western trade — a vast scheme of canals that could provide a much more direct route to international shipping than the Ohio and Mississippi, and could provide Virginia with a vast increase in trade. He had an almost messianic vision of this project, as he described it to Lafayette: "I wish to see the sons and daughters of the world in peace . . . *increase and multiply*, as an encouragement to which we have opened the fertile plains of the Ohio to the

---

28. John Jay to John Adams, 4 May, 1786, Johnston, ed., *Correspondence of Jay*, III, 195.

29. Burnett, *Letters*, VIII, 327. Pinckney nonetheless recommends that New Jersey join in the call for "a general convention of the states, for the purpose of revising and amending the federal constitution. . . . I have long been of opinion, that it was the only true and radical remedy for our public defects." *Ibid.*, 324.

poor, the needy, and the oppressed of the earth."[30] Had Moses been a surveyor, he might have spoken thus of the Promised Land.

Washington's real motive in promoting the plan, he confided to Knox, was not petty profit, but political rapport. "I am now endeavoring to stimulate my Countrymen to the extension of the inland navigation . . . to connect the Western Territory by strong commercial bands with this. I hope I shall succeed, more on account of its political importance than the commercial advantages." It seemed that all of Washington's enterprises led him back to the problem of national government; his letter to Knox continued, "there is a kind of fatality attending all our public measures, inconceivable delays, particularly States counteracting the plans of the United States. . . . . Would to God our own countrymen, who are entrusted with the management of the political machine, could view things by that large and extensive scale upon which it is measured by foreigners, and by the Statesmen of Europe, who see what we might be, and predict what we shall come to. In fact, our federal Government is a name without a substance. . . . How then can we fail in a little time, becoming the sport of European politics, and the victims of our own folly."[31]

To overcome the resistance of Baltimore merchants whose trade would be circumvented by his canal scheme, Washington sought legislation from the Maryland government, where his personal participation insured cooperation.[32] In March, 1785, at what is now called the "Mount Vernon Conference" between Maryland and Virginia, an annual meeting was proposed to discuss commercial relations. Virginia went further, proposing that all the states be represented, and nine months later the House of Burgesses resolved that their delegates should meet with commissioners of other states "to consider trade and a uniform system in their commercial regulation. . . ."[33] In May, the Convention movement took on much greater

30. *Writings of Washington*, XXVII, 388-389.
31. Washington to Knox, 5 Dec., 1784, *Writings of Washington*, XXVIII, 4-5.
32. See Flexner, *Washington*, III, 74-75.
33. For the text of the resolution see Kate Mason Rowland, *Life of George*

political importance, when the New York Assembly appointed Hamilton as a delegate to Annapolis.[34] In some quarters,
hopes ran high: James Monroe considered the Convention "as
a most important era in our affairs."[35]

But the indifferent and even hostile response to the Annapolis Convention in the states' legislatures made it clear
that little would be achieved. To begin with, it was widely
presumed that the Convention *intended* to exceed its authority
to consider commercial cooperation, and to propose general
revisions. Otto noted that the convention had been called with
"deliberate obscurity . . . which the ordinary citizens could not
understand but which the powerful and enlightened portion
of the population would have no difficulty understanding."[36]
On the eve of the Annapolis Convention, Madison wrote to
Jefferson that, as far as constitutional revision, "I despair so
much of its accomplishment at the present crisis that I do not
extend my views beyond a Commercial Reform. To speak the
truth, *I almost despair even of this.*"[37] In the end only twelve
delegates attended (half of whom were from New York), representing just five states.[38] Worse still, Maryland was not
among them, for its legislature had decided that congressional
powers would be contravened at Annapolis. Since, according
to Congress's rules, there were not even enough delegates to
deliberate, the meeting was quickly adjourned, after Hamilton
called for yet another convention, this time in Philadelphia.

Mason, 2 vols. (New York, 1892), II, 93.
34. *Hamilton Papers*, Syrett, ed., III, 665-666. Thereafter, northern states seriously considered attending, because "we of New England ought not to let pass
unnoticed by any means if we can secure the carrying trade of the southern
states." J. Bowen to President Sullivan, 18 Aug., 1786, quoted in Jensen, *The
New Nation*, 406.
35. James Monroe to James Madison, 3 Sept., 1786, *Madison Papers*, IX, 114.
36. Quoted in Page Smith, *The Shaping of America* (New York, 1980), 51.
37. Madison to Jefferson, August 12, 1786 *Madison Papers*, IX, 96. [Madi-
son's underlining.]
38. New York, New Jersey, Delaware, Pennsylvania, and Virginia attended.
Delegates from Rhode Island and Massachusetts (minus Higginson, who had
been appointed), set out from home, but hastily turned back upon learning that
the Convention had adjourned.

"The convention . . . has terminated without credit . . .," Rufus King wrote to John Adams. "Whether the states will accede to the proposition of a convention at Philadelphia in May, is yet uncertain. . . ."[39]

So, the council which was to have laid the foundation for economic nationalism across the continent was reduced to calling for a single proposal: one more convention. During the fiasco at Annapolis, it should be noted, the first reports were being printed about court-closings in Massachusetts. It is tempting to speculate what might have happened if alarming reports of the Regulation had reached Washington three months earlier, and he had been persuaded to attend at Annapolis; tempting, but too hypothetical to be useful.[40]

Without some popular upheaval, Washington was not optimistic about the prospects of any convention. In April, 1786, four months before the first court-closing, he wrote to Henry Lee that "my sentiments with respect to the federal government, are well known . . . but my *opinion* is, that there is more wickedness than ignorance in the conduct of the States, or in other words, in the conduct of those who have too much influence in the government of them; and until the curtain is withdrawn, and the private views and selfish principles upon which these men act, are exposed to public notice, I have little hope of amendment without another convulsion."[41]

Until the situation had deteriorated further, Washington could not foresee any successful reformation of the Continental government — it was still too soon. He agreed with Jay's assessment of Annapolis, that it "may do some good, and would perhaps do more if it comprehended more objects. An opinion begins to prevail that a general Convention for revis-

---

39. Hamilton's call for a second Convention was signed by Dickinson; see *JCC*, XXXI, 678-680. Rufus King to John Adams, 2 Oct., 1786, Burnett, *Letters*, VIII, 475.

40. "No effort was made to persuade Washington to represent Virginia at the Annapolis Convention," noted Flexner. "He was too powerful a trump card to risk on so doubtful a venture." Flexner, *Washington*, III, 95.

41. Washington to Henry Lee, 5 Apr., 1786, *Writings of Washington*, XXVIII, 402.

ing the Articles of Confederation would be expedient Whether the people are yet ripe for such a measure, or whether the system proposed to be attained by it is only to be expected from calamity and commotion, is difficult to ascertain." Jay added that if the plan matured to take measures for forming a general convention, he fervently hoped that Washington would "favour your country with your counsels on such an important and signal occasion."[42]

Washington's reply, ninety days before Shays' Rebellion began, was clear. "I coincide perfectly in sentiment with you, my Dr. Sir, that there are errors in our national Government which call for correction, loudly, I would add; but I shall find myself happily mistaken if the remedies are at hand. We are certainly in a delicate situation, but my fear is that people are not yet sufficiently *misled* to retract from error. . . . I scarcely know what opinion to entertain of a general convention. That it is necessary to revise and amend the articles of confederation, I entertain *no* doubt; but what may be the consequences of such an attempt is doubtful. Yet something must be done, or the fabric must fall, for it is certainly tottering. . . . [This must lead to] a train of evils which oftentimes, in republican governments, must be felt before they can be removed. . . ."[43]

As for Jay's suggestion that Washington should favor his country with his counsel, the General replied on August 1st, 1786 that, "having happily assisted in bringing the Ship into Port, and having been fairly discharged; it is not my business to embark again on a sea of troubles."[44] In truth, though, Washington had never left the nationalists' boat. As he complained to his mother (who complained often enough to him), Mount Vernon "may be compared to a well-resorted tavern, as scarcely any strangers who are going from north to south,

---

42. Jay to Washington, New York, 16 Mar., 1786, Johnston, ed., *Correspondence of Jay*, III, 186-187.

43. Washington to Jay, 18 May, 1786, *Writings of Washington*, XXVIII, 431. Washington repeated these sentiments to Knox and Humphreys a year later, *ibid.*, XXIX, 171, 173.

44. Washington to Jay, 1 Aug., 1786, *Writings of Washington*, XXIX, 503-504.

or south to north, do not spend a day or two at it."[45]

He had also participated unceasingly in the nationalist cause with his voluminous correspondence, which is remarkable for a variety of reasons: notwithstanding the chilly and distant manner that Washington maintained in most of his personal encounters, his letters to close friends were blessed with the articulate *génie* of the eighteenth-century, while remaining emotionally florid, evoking courtly Romanticism. Political issues often appeared more cut and dried to him. For Madison, he framed the Federalist case neatly, in a manner echoed by Abraham Lincoln some seventy years later: "We are either a United people, or we are not. If the former, let us, in all matters of general concern, act as a nation, which have national objects to promote, and a national character to support. If we are not, let us no longer act a farce by pretending to it."[46] Few of his "countrymen" were so advanced in their thinking in the 1780s as to imagine that Americans would ever share a "national character." But there were no pollsters to ask Americans whether the United States was "thirteen nations or one."

There is a palpable sense of impending doom throughout the nationalists' correspondence in the months preceding Shays' Rebellion. Most of them dreaded an inevitable crisis, and some welcomed it — but soon enough, both groups found what they were waiting for in Shays' Rebellion.[47] In his next

---

45. Washington to Mary Washington, 15 Feb., 1787, *Writings of Washington*, XXIX, 160-161.

46. He went on: "In any case, it behoves us to provide good Military Laws, and look well to the execution of them, but, if we mean by our conduct that the States shall act independently of each other it becomes *indispensably* necessary, for therein will consist our strength and respectablility in the Union." Washington to Madison, 30 Nov., 1785, *ibid.*, XXVIII, 336.

47. A chronological sampling of that gloomy correspondence includes the following: "I fully expect we shall fall into general Confusion, and perhaps undergo another Revolution. . . ." Higginson (Apr. 1784), Franklin, ed., "Letters of Higginson," *AHA Annual Report* (1896), I, 716; "it is unfortunate for us, that evils which might have been averted must first be felt. . . ." Washington (June 1785), *Writings of Washington*, XXVIII, 174; "nothing short of severe

letter to Washington, Jay stressed that he was uneasy because "we are going and doing wrong, and therefore I look forward to evils and calamities. . . ."[48] Exactly four weeks before the first court-closing in Massachusetts, Washington replied that "our events are drawing rapidly to a crisis. . . . What the event will be, is also beyond the reach of my foresight. We have

---

sufferings and sad experience will teach them the necessity [of revisions]. . . ." Higginson (Aug. 1785), Franklin, ed., "Letters of Higginson," *AHA Annual Report* (1896), I, 724; "Perhaps nothing less than the apprehension of a common danger. . ." Higginson (Dec. 1785), Franklin, ed., "Letters of Higginson," *AHA Annual Report* (1896), I, 732; "Federal opinions grow, but it will be some time before they bear fruit. . . ." Jay (Feb. 1786), Johnston, ed., *Correspondence of Jay*, III, 183; "Whether the people are yet ripe for such a measure, or whether the system proposed. . . . is only to be expected from calamity and commotion is difficult to ascertain." Jay (Mar. 1786), *ibid.*, 186; "I have little hope of amendment without another convulsion." Washington (Apr. 1786), *Writings of Washington*, XXVIII, 402; "my fear is that the people are not yet sufficiently misled to retract from error. . . ." Washington (May 1786), *Writings of Washington*, XXVIII, 431; "a Convulsion of some kind seems to be desirable." Pettit (May 1786), Burnett, *Letters*, VIII, 371; "[I am] uneasy and apprehensive; more so than during the war. . . ." Jay (June 1786), Johnston, ed., *Correspondence of Jay*, III, 204; "An uneasiness prevails throughout the country, and may produce eventually the desired reformations, and it may also produce untoward events." Jay (July 1786), *ibid.*, 206; "whether our Government, may not get unhinged, and a revolution take place, before the Cure is effected. . . . We appear to be fast verging to a crisis. A change of Ideas and measures must soon happen, either from conviction or necessity." Higginson (July 1786), Franklin, ed., "Letters of Higginson," *AHA Annual Report* (1896), I, 740; "nothing but a good Providence can extricate us from our present difficulties & prevent some terrible convulsion." Humphreys (Nov. 1786), Frank L. Humphreys, *Life and Times of David Humphreys: Soldier, Statesman, Poet* (New York, 1917), I, 373; "By the next summer I expect We shall here be prepared for anything that is wise and fitting." Higginson (Nov.1786) Franklin, ed., "Letters of Higginson," *AHA Annual Report* (1896), I, 742-3; "this commotion will terminate in additional strength to government." Adams (Nov. 1786), quoted in Malone, *Jefferson*, II, 157; "Perhaps a few months more may produce a greater degree of decision." Jay (Jan. 1787), Johnston, ed., *Correspondence of Jay*, III, 222; "This moment must be seised by Congress, &c. We must make the most of it whilst the fire bums, it will not be durable perhaps." Higginson, (Jan. 1787), Franklin, ed., "Letters of Higginson," *AHA Annual Report* (1896), I, 744.

48. Jay to Washington, Philadelphia, 27 June, 1786, *Correspondence of Jay*, III, 204.

errors to correct; we have probably had too good an opinion of human nature in forming our confederation. Experience has taught us, that men will not adopt and carry into execution measures the best calculated for their own good, without the intervention of a coercive power. I do not conceive that we can exist long as a nation without having lodged some where a power, which will pervade the whole Union. . . ."[49]

Washington expounded further upon his perception of representative government "To be fearful of investing in Congress, constituted as that body is, with ample authority for national purposes, appears to me the very climax of popular absurdity and madness. Could Congress exert them for the detriment of the public, without injuring themselves . . . ? Are not their interests inseparably connected with those of their constituents? By the rotation of appointment, must they not mingle frequently with the mass of Citizens?"[50]

Washington again bemoaned the frailty of human virtue, though he was not as convinced as most Tories and Federalists that mankind was inherently evil.[51] He allowed, though, that "we must take human nature as we find it: perfection falls not to the share of mortals. . . . Things cannot go on in the same train forever. It is much to be feared, as you observe, that the better kind of people, being disgusted with the circumstances, will have their minds prepared for any revolution whatever. We are apt to run from one extreme to the other. . . . What astonishing changes a few years are capable of producing. I am told that even respectable characters speak of a monarchical form of government without horror. From thinking proceeds speaking, thence to acting is often but a single step."[52]

With the first forcible closing of a court, in Northampton on August 29th, events in New England seemed to fulfill the

---

49. Washington to Jay, 1 Aug., 1786, *Writings of Washington*, XXVIII, 502.
50. *Ibid.*
51. This was a perpetual theme in the nationalists' letters, echoed by Madison a year later in *The Federalist*, No. 51: "If men were angels, no government would be necessary." Hamilton *et al.*, *The Federalist*, 374.
52. Washington to Jay, 1 Aug., 1786, *Writings of Washington*, XXVIII, 503.

nationalists' grimmest premonitions, and the most dire interpretation came from Washington's personal correspondents. On September 8th, just before the few delegates gathered in Annapolis, three court-closings had been reported in the press, and Lee wrote to Washington that "the period seems to be fast approaching when the people of these U. States must determine to establish a permanent capable government or submit to the horrors of anarchy and licentiousness."[53] He included in his letter Bowdoin's proclamation of September 2nd, in which the governor implored the citizenry that they not "deprive themselves of the security derived from a well-regulated Society . . ., not devolve upon their children . . . a state of anarchy, confusion and slavery."[54]

Washington read a variety of news reports about Shays' Rebellion, primarily in the *Pennsylvania Packet*, but his best informants remained Knox and Lee, both then with Congress in New York.[55] On September 23rd the *Packet* reported that a drunken and disreputable mob of some four hundred had threatened a court in western Massachusetts, which had adjourned "to prevent any coercive measures,"[56] On October 13th a letter-writer in the *Packet* reported that among the causes for the commotion "one of the chief is the want of money . . . a Circulating Medium," adding, "I should suggest that you should pledge yourselves not to call upon the people for one farthing of the principle of our state debt," and recommending that Massachusetts "abolish . . . at a proper time, that real grievance, the Court of Common Pleas."[57] This certainly sounded radical to the Virginian, but it did not approach Knox's declaration, that "a body of 12 or 15000 desperate and unprincipled men," supported by twenty percent of New England, was prepared to take up arms against government, and redivide all American property equally.

---

53. Burnett, *Letters*, VIII, 463.
54. M.A. 190, 226. The proclamation was reprinted in the *New York Daily Advertiser* for the week ending September 9th.
55. See Flexner, *Washington*, III, 98.
56. As quoted in Flexner, *ibid.*
57. *Pennsylvania Packet and Daily Advertiser*, 13 Oct., 1786.

Lee wrote to Washington almost weekly throughout October, reinforcing the interpretation of events that, by mid-November, forced Washington to consider re-embarking upon "a sea of troubles." On October 1st, Lee reported that the commotions:

> which have for some time past distracted the two eastern states, have risen in Massachusetts to an alarming height. . . . After various insults to government, by stopping the courts of justice &c, the insurgents have in a very formidable shape States Arsenal one mile from Springfield. Congress have sent . . . General Knox, to take the best measures in his power in concert with Government for the safety of the Arsenal. This event produces much suggestion as to its causes. Some attribute it to the weight of taxes and the decay of commerce, which has produced universal idleness. Others, to British councils in the vicinity of Vermont and the fondness for Novelty. . . .[58]

On October 11th, Lee opined that "the sedition in Massachusetts is in some degree subsided;" but less than a week later he reported that "G. Knox has just returned from thence . . . with melancholy information . . . We are all in dire apprehension that a beginning of anarchy with all its calamitys has approached, and have no means to stop the dreadful work. Individuals suggest the propriety of inviting you from Congress to pay us a visit, knowing your unbounded influence and believing your appearance among the seditious might bring them back to peace and reconciliation. . . ."[59]

This appeal was, of course, just what Washington dreaded. Conscious that his advice to Lee would be passed on to Con-

---

58. Burnett omits most of this letter [Burnett, *Letters*, VIII, 474]; see *George Washington's Correspondence Concerning the Society of the Cincinnati*, Edgar Erskine Hume, ed. (Baltimore, 1941), 250-251. For Congress's concern about the Arsenal, see *JCC*, XXXI: 1 Aug., 20, 28, 29, Sept., 2, 4, 6, 13, 18, 19, and 21 Oct., 1786.

59. Burnett, *Letters*, VIII, 483, 486.

gress, Washington replied cautiously to his letters, as well as to Knox's. This was Washington's frame of mind in the days before receiving the Knox's inflammatory letter of October 28th:

> The picture which you have exhibited, and the accounts which are published . . . exhibit a melancholy proof of what our trans-Atlantic foe has predicted; and of another thing, perhaps, which is still more to be regretted, and yet is more unaccountable, that mankind when left to themselves are unfit for their own Government. I am mortified beyond expression when I view the clouds that have spread over the brightest morn that ever dawned upon any Country. In a word, I am lost in amazement. . . . You talk, my good Sir, of employing influence to appease the present tumults in Massachusetts. I know not where that taken possession of the town of Springfield, at which place the supreme court was sitting. The friends to government arrayed under the Militia General . . . but their exertions were not affectual. The court removed and broke up, the insurgents continued of the town & General Shepard has retired to the United influence is to be found; and, if attainable, that it would be a proper remedy for the disorders. Influence is no Government. Let us have one by which our lives, liberties and properties will be secured; or let us know the worst at once.[60]

Washington's "humble opinion" about how to deal with Shays' Rebellion was, first, "Know precisely what the insurgents aim at. If they have *real* grievances, redress them, if possible; or acknowledge the justice of them, and your inability to do it in the present moment. If they have not, employ the force of government against them at once."[61] He urged swift action, citing Newtonian mechanics: "like snow-balls, such

---

60. Washington to Lee, 31 Oct., 1786, *Writings of Washington*, XXIX, 33-34.
61. *Ibid.*, 34.

bodies increase by every movement, unless there is something in the way to obstruct or crumble them. . . ."[62]

But by October, the last façades of national government were pealing away, and delegates were fleeing the bankrupt Congress. "It has become a subject of admiration how Government existed," Rufus King reported to the Massachusetts legislature. "From foreign loans nothing was to be expected; the gleanings of these had hitherto kept things along. . . . So melancholly was the state of the federal treasury that all men seemed to turn away from it, as an evil which admitted of no remedy." Exaggerated reports of Regulators' intentions finally brought moderate particularists like King into the nationalist movement. By early 1787, many who had believed that Congress alone should amend the Articles painfully came to accept the notion of the Philadelphia Convention, which they had previously considered illegal. "If Massachusetts should send deputies," King wrote to Gerry reluctantly, "for God's sake be careful who are the men; the times are becoming critical."[63]

As further exaggerations of the crisis in Massachusetts arrived, Washington noted with near-disbelief the chimerical quality of the reports he received. "When I reflect on the present posture of our affairs, it seems to me to be like the vision of a dream. My mind does not know how to realize it, as a thing in actual existence, so strange, so wonderful does it

---

62. *Ibid.*

63. Rufus King, Address before the Massachusetts House of Representatives, 11 Oct., 1786 (as reported by *Boston Magazine*), in Burnett, *Letters*, VIII, 480. Although there had been just a handful of peaceable demonstrations, King went on to say that "that there was an evil in publick affairs, infinitely greater than any he had mentioned. . . . That he spoke of the commotions now existing in Massachusetts. This was viewed by Congress as the most important subject that ever came before that respectable assembly. Every member considered himself as personally interested in it. . . . Advantage might be taken of the divided state of people, to bring about measures which otherwise could never be effected by the enemies of our country;" Rufus King to Elbridge Gerry, 7 Jan., 1787, Burnett, *Letters*, VIII, 527. For King's earlier antipathy to the convention movement, see above, 149-150.

appear to me."[64] But through the fall of 1786 the reports grew worse: ostensible proof of the conservative credo that the people were too wicked govern themselves. "The mass of men," Jay wrote to Washington, "are neither wise nor good, and the virtue like the other resources of a country, can only be drawn to a point and exerted by strong circumstances ably managed, or a strong government ably administered."[65]

When Washington received Knox's letter of October 28th, he reacted with just the alarm that Knox, one of Washington's most trusted and treasured friends, had hoped for.[66] It was not, perhaps, the oft-quoted key phrases of Knox's letter that concerned him as much as the broad picture of rebelliousness that Knox painted of New England and, by implication, of the whole continent. Together with the more inflammatory news reports he probably read or heard, Knox's letter was credible. Knox had, after all, written a similar account to Congress ten days earlier, and, perhaps coincidentally, he had presented at the same time his *Plan for the General Arrangement of the Militia of the United States*.[67] Though Knox's letter was huge

---

64. Washington to Knox, 26 Dec., 1786, *Writings of Washington*, XXIX, 122. The same day he wrote to Humphreys: "The thing is so unaccountable, that I hardly know how to realize it, or to persuade myself that I am not under the illusion of a dream." *Ibid*, 126 See also quotation below, 209: "I should have thought him a bedlamite, a fit subject for a mad house." Washington to Knox, 3 Feb., 1787, *ibid*, XXIX, 153.

65. Jay to Washington, 27 June, 1786, Johnston, ed., *Correspondence of Jay*, III, 204-205.

66. For Knox's letter, see Appendix B. Note that the copy Washington received was dated October 28th, not the 23rd; "To corrispond with those I love," Washington wrote to Knox the year before, "is among my highest gratifications, and I perswade myself you will not doubt my sincerity when I assure you, I place you among the foremost of this class." Washington to Knox, 5 Jan., 1785, *Writings of Washington*, XXVIII, 23. "There is still a mystery in much of this," wrote East, "as regards the conduct of General Knox," who may have "recognized the possibilities of advancing Federal reforms as a result of the riots. . . ." East, "Massachusetts Conservatives in the Critical Period," *Era of American Revolution*, Morris, ed., 380.

67. *JCC*, XXXI, 886-888. Henry Knox, *Plan for the General Arrangement of the Militia of the United States* (New York, 1786 [Evans 20076]). This report, which called for universal military service of men between 18 and 60, would have created an army of 325,000 trained soldiers. Knox had his plan printed in

with hyperbole, Washington was no chump to suppose that many inland settlers, from New Hampshire to South Carolina, might agree with the belief attributed to Job Shattuck, that "it was time to abolish all debts and begin anew."[68]

Washington's immediate reaction was to transcribe key passages of Knox's letter to Madison who, along with Monroe, had visited him a fortnight earlier.[69] The passage which Madison surely appreciated most was Washington's clearest pronouncement yet on the fate of the Confederation; as well, it directly linked Knox's news of Shays' Rebellion to the need for constitutional revision. "Without some alteration in our political creed, the superstructure we have been seven years raising at the expence of much blood and treasure, must fall. We are fast verging to anarchy & confusion! A letter which I have just received from Gen¹ Knox, is replete with melancholy information of the temper, and designs of a considerable part of the people. . . ."[70] After citing Knox, Washington proceeded to express his anguish and, in effect, to challenge his own virtue, even as he found in Shays' Rebellion proof of the need for constitutional revisions.

How melancholy is the reflection, that in so short a space, we should have made such large strides towards fulfilling the prediction of our transatlantic foe! "leave them to themselves, and their government will soon dissolve." Will not the wise and good strive hard to avert this evil? . . . What stronger evidence can be given of the want of energy in our governments than these disorders? If there exists not a power to check them,

---

March, but chose this moment to present it to Congress. While Knox's military plan may have been disinterested, he was personally in a period of economic reversal; see Knox to Wadsworth, 28 Feb. 1787, Knox Papers, XX, 6: "as I am in great debt on account of some public debts."

68. *Independent Ledger*, 15 Sept., 1786. Washington wrote Knox on December 26th that the whole country was a tinder box. *Writings of Washington*, XXIX, 122.

69. See below, 204 n.76.

70. Washington to Madison, 5 Nov., 1786, *Writings of Washington*, XXIX, 51-52.

what security has a man for life, liberty, or property?
. . . Thirteen Sovereignties pulling against each other,
and all tugging at the federal head will soon bring ruin
on the whole; whereas a liberal, and energetic Constitution, well guarded and closely watched, to prevent
incroachments, might restore us. . . .[71]

Madison replied three days later from Richmond: "The intelligence from Gen[l.] Knox is gloomy indeed, but is less so
than the colours in which I have had it thro' another channel,"
referring, perhaps, to two letters from Henry Lee.[72] But Madison certainly saw the pedagogical value of the insurgency:
"If the lessons which it inculcates should not work the proper
impressions on the American Public, it will be a proof that our
case is desperate." Therefore, he took heart from the gloomy
intelligence. "I have some ground for leaning to the side of
Hope," because, he informed Washington, in the Virginia
Assembly "the Recomm[end]ation from Annapolis in favor
of a general revision of the federal System was *unanimously*
agreed to. . . ."[73]

It fell to Madison, in this same letter, to challenge Washington to sacrifice his tranquility, and return to public life.

---

71. *Ibid.* Of this passage, Rutland wrote: "After expressing these sentiments
Washington was vulnerable to the duty call made by the Virginia General Assembly. . . . [Madison] knew from this emotional letter that Washington was
obligated in the convention." *Madison Papers*, IX, 162 n2. "That signal was
all Madison needed to push ahead with his plan for a national convention to
follow on the heels of the aborted meeting at Annapolis. Working behind the
scenes Madison saw to it that a bill was passed and sent to all the states, urging
them to converge on Philadelphia in May." Robert Allen Rutland, *James Madison: The Founding Father* (New York, 1987), 5.
72. Madison to Washington, 8 Nov., 1786, *Madison Papers*, IX, 166. Lee
wrote to Madison about Shays' Rebellion on 19 and 25 Oct., 1786: "Massachusetts contains 75,000 men . . ., the five seditious countys possess 40,000
of this number. . . . I believe we may reckon that state divided for and against
government;" "The eastern gentlemen here . . . believe that the discontents will
never be settled but by the sword. . . . present appearances portend extensive
national calamity. The contagion will spread and may reach Virginia." *Madison Papers*, IX, 144, 145.
73. *Ibid.*, IX, 166.

The same day Washington received Knox's letter — Guy Fawkes' day — Madison had introduced his Bill Providing for Delegates to the Virginia legislature. Now he dropped the bomb. "It has been thought to give this subject a very solemn dress, and all the weight which could be derived from a single State," he wrote Washington. "This idea will also be pursued in the selection of characters to represent Virg[a.] in the Federal Convention. You will infer our earnestness on this point from the liberty which will be used of placing your name at the head of them."[74]

It was bold indeed, if not impertinent, for the young Madison to have volunteered the General's name, and then report it to him as a *fait accompli*; but then, he did have the full cooperation of Governor Randolph. This compelled Washington either to foreswear retirement for a venture of dubious prospects, or to damage those prospects from the outset by publicly refusing to participate — setting a poor example.[75] Nothing in then-correspondence suggests that Madison had prepared him for this choice, though he did have a chance to ascertain Washington's feelings on a visit a few weeks before. Having left the Annapolis Convention in discouragement on September 15th, Madison spent most of the month in Philadelphia. Then, he visited Mount Vernon, together with Monroe, whom Washington had never met, on October 23rd, and stayed for two days.[76] (At exactly this time Knox was writing Washington that one-fifth of New England aimed to make "the property of the United States . . . the common property of all.") No record was kept of the men's discussions, though Madison must surely have taken the opportunity to know Washington's opinions of the Massachusetts commotions and the planned Convention.

---

74. *Ibid.*
75. *Ibid.* In the next sentence, Madison did allow Washington an out: "How far this liberty may correspond with the ideas by which you ought to be governed will be best decided where it must ultimately be decided."
76. See "Madison Chronology," *Madison Papers*, IX, xxiv; "Col. Monroe . . . a delegate from Virginia . . . means to . . . pay his respects to Mount-Vernon." Lee to Washington, 11 Oct., 1786, Burnett, *Letters*, VIII, 483.

Now Washington was obliged to decide if he would return to public life, thereby violating the pledge he had taken so publicly, and with such resonance, three years earlier. He knew, as David Stuart wrote to him, that his presence in the Virginia delegation "appeared to be so much the wish of the House that Mr. Maddison conceived it might probably frustrate the whole scheme if it was not done." He also knew that if he attended the Convention he would be pressed hard to preside over the proceedings — and would be hard-pressed to refuse. And at that point, he knew, his eternal reputation would hinge on the success or failure of this perilous and uncertain endeavor.[77]

Washington replied to Madison's on November 18th and, with painful equivocation, opened the door to his participation, even as he seemed to decline the appointment. "Altho' I had bid adieu to the public walks of life in a public manner, and had resolved never more to tread that theatre; yet, if upon an occasion so interesting to the well-being of the Confederacy it should have been the wish of the Assembly that I should have been an associate in the business of revising the federal System; I should, from a sense of the obligation I am under for repeated proofs of confidence in me, more than from any opinion I should have entertained of my usefulness, have obeyed its call. . . ."[78]

There was, however, a problem. As his use of *four* subjunctives in a single sentence suggests, the problem was one of public perception, both of himself, and of the "aristocraticle" Society of the Cincinnati, to which Washington had been re-elected President. The Cincinnati was scheduled to hold its second triennial meeting in Philadelphia on the first Monday

---

77. Stuart to Washington, 19 Dec., 1786, as quoted in *Madison Papers*, IX, 171 n.2. Stuart went on to suggest that, to keep the movement's momentum going, Washington should at least accept the appointment for the time being, and excuse himself later, if he so chose. As for being elected president of the Convention, Knox need not have warned him that "however reluctantly you may acquiesce, that you will be constrained to accept of the president's chair." knox to Washington, 19 Mar., 1787, Drake, *Correspondence of Knox*, 148.
78. Washington to Madison, 18 Nov., 1786, *Writings of Washington*, XXIX, 70.

in May. But Washington was unhappy with the Society — notably, with the failure of several states to conform with the General Society by eliminating the same objectionable features — especially hereditary membership — that had caused such alarm two years earlier.[79] Washington had already sent out a circular letter on October 31st to all the presidents of the State Societies, declining to be chosen again as the president of the General Society, pleading "private concerns" and a "natural desire of tranquility and relaxation," as well as the "present imbecility of my health," including "fever & ague" and "rheumatick pains."[80] "Under these circumstances," he wrote Madison, "it will readily be perceived that I could not apper at the same time and place . . . without giving offence . . . to the late officers of the American Army."[81]

Washington's ambivalence notwithstanding, on December 4th, without further communication between the two men, the branches of the Virginia legislature met in response to a motion by Madison on November 30th, to elect George Washington, Patrick Henry, Edmund Randolph, John Blair, James Madison, George Mason and George Wythe as the commissioners to the Philadelphia Convention.[82] Two days later, Governor Randolph wrote to Washington to plead for his participation; "for the gloomy prospect still admits one ray of hope, that those who began, carried on & consummated the revolution, can yet rescue America from the impending ruin."[83]

---

79. See above, 47-48.

80. *Washington's Correspondence concerning the Cincinnati*, Hume, ed. (Baltimore, 1941), 264-265. Since Washington already knew that the Philadelphia Convention had been called for the same week, this makes it clear, that on 31 Oct. he had no intention of participating in the Convention. Washington was not malingering: he suffered terribly from rheumatism that spring, even wearing one arm in a sling. Flexner, *Washington*, III, 108.

81. Washington to Madison, 18 Nov., 1786, *Writings of Washington*, XXIX, 72.

82. *Madison Papers*, IX, 187.

83. Governor Randolph to Washington, 6 Dec., 1786, *Washington Papers*. See also *Madison Papers*, IX, 226 n2. According to Rutland, Madison and Randolph were "the principal agents in contriving to keep Washington at the head of the Virginia delegation against his will, however equivocal." *Madison Papers*, IX, 226, n.2.

Washington answered Randolph that "there exists *at this moment*, circumstances, which I am persuaded will render my acceptance. . . incompatible with other measures which I had previously adopted. . . ." He did not close the door entirely, but only recommended that the Governor appoint someone else, "the *probability* of my non-attendance being too great to continue my appointment."[84] But Madison urged Washington not to decline the appointment peremptorily, wishing "that at least a door could be kept open for your acceptance hereafter, in case the gathering clouds should become so dark and menacing as to supercede every consideration, but that of our national existence or safety."[85] And indeed, for the first time Washington did not merely repeat his oft-restated vow of retirement.

The reports Washington received about Massachusetts through December and January only reinforced the dire picture. From New Haven, his former aide David Humphreys offered some of the most alarming news. Humphreys advised Washington that the malcontents were animated by "a licentious spirit prevailing among the people; a levelling principle; a desire of change; & a wish to annihilate all debts public & private." As early as November 1st, Humphreys had warned Washington that "in case of civil discord . . . you could not remain neuter. . . . You would be obliged, in self defence, to take part on one side or the other: or withdraw from the continent. Your friends are of the same opinion. . . ."[86] Washington replied that he was well aware that "the Federal Government is nearly, if not quite, at a stand . . .," but worried that "if this second attempt to convene the States . . . should also prove abortive . . . there is an end of the Federal Government."[87]

For the next three months Washington wrestled with his

---

84. Washington to Randolph, 21 Dec., 1786, *Writings of Washington*, XXIX, 119-120. [My italics.]
85. *Madison Papers*, IX, 224.
86. Humphreys to Washington, 1 and 9 Nov., 1786, Humphreys, *Life and Times of David Humphreys*, I, 374, 378.
87. Washington to Humphreys, 26 Dec., 1786, *Writings of Washington*, XXIX, 128.

dilemma, suffering what Rutland called "a crisis of con-science."[88] Finally, on March 28th, 1787, Washington wrote to Governor Randolph that, "as my friends, with a degree of solicitude which is unusual, seem to wish for my attendance on this occasion, I have come to a resolution to go," health permitting.[89] But in the intervening months Washington went through a broad spectrum of opinions about the Convention's prospects for success, and the wisdom of his participation.[90] So, too, did most of his correspondents at one moment or an-other, when the states tarried in addressing the question of appointing delegates. Humphreys expounded at length upon "the inexpediency of your attending the Convention," and Madison, in a moment of doubt about how many states would attend, suggested it might be better to see first how the Con-vention made out without him; even Knox shared that opinion briefly.[91]

But once the majority of states had shown a serious in-terest in attending, and chosen "respectable" delegates, the majority of Washington's friends agreed that it was impera-tive that he attend. "I am persuaded," wrote Knox, "that your name has had already great influence to induce the States to come into the measure; that your attendance will be grate-ful and your non-attendance chagrining; that your presence would confer on the assembly a national complexion, and that it would more than any other circumstances induce a com-pliance to the propositions of the Convention."[92] By March,

---

88. *Madison Papers*, IX, 226 n.2.

89. Washington to Randolph, 28 Mar., 1787, *Writings of Washington*, XXIX, 187.

90. Freeman, a most sympathetic biographer, takes Washington to task for these months of vacillation. "In all the preliminaries of what may be regarded as a last effort to save the collapsing Union," wrote Freeman, "he had been too zealously attentive to his prestige, his reputation and his popularity — too much the self-conscious national hero and too little the daring patriot." Doug-las Southall Freeman, *George Washington*, 7 vols. (New York, 1954), VI, 86.

91. Humphreys to Washington, 28 Jan., 1787, *Life and Times of Humphreys*, I, 396-397; Madison cited in Flexner, *Washington*, III, 107; Knox, *ibid.*

92. Knox to Washington, 19 Mar., 1787, as quoted in Drake, *Correspondence of Knox*, 148.

Washington had concluded that the public would consider his failure to attend as a "dereliction of republicanism."[93] "Secure as he was in his fame," Knox wrote to Lafayette, "he has again committed it to the mercy of events. Nothing but the critical situation of his country would have induced him to so hazardous a conduct. But its happiness being in danger, he disregards all personal considerations."[94]

Those personal considerations included not only his own yearnings for privacy and repose, but also those of his wife Martha, who wrote that she could not have imagined that "any circumstances could possibly have happened" to lead Washington back "into public life again. I had anticipated that from this moment we should have been left to grow old in solitude and tranquility together."[95] She cannot have foreseen as clearly as her husband that a few months in Philadelphia could become almost a decade more of public service. Another personal consideration — the matter of the Cincinnati meeting — was resolved by news of his mother's sudden, critical illness, which detoured him on the way to Philadelphia, making his absence a moot point instead of a snub.

Did Washington believe that Shays' Rebellion represented a genuine threat to the whole nation? Apparently he did, for even after the Regulators' debacle at the Arsenal, he expected "that the political machine will yet be much tumbled and tossed, and possibly be wrecked altogether. . . . Anarchy and confusion must prevail, and everything will be turned topsy turvey in that State; where it is not probable the mischiefs will terminate. . . . I shall be surprized at nothing; for if three years since any person had told me that at this day, I should see such a formidable rebellion against the laws and constitutions of our own making as now appears I should have thought him a bedlamite, a fit subject for a mad house."[96]

Washington felt that "when this spirit first dawned, proba-

93. Washington to Knox, 8 Mar., 1787, *Writings of Washington*, XXIX, 171.
94. Knox to Lafayette, 25 July, 1787, *Knox Papers*.
95. Quoted in Flexner, *Washington*, III, 108.
96. Washington to Knox, 3 Feb., 1787, *Writings of Washington*, XXIX, 153.

bly it might easily have been checked; but it is scarcely within reach of the human ken, at this moment, to say when, where, or how it will end. There are combustibles in every State which a spark might set fire to."[97] He did not expect — and could hardly believe — that the vast, popular uprising he had been told to anticipate could vaporize with "so little bloodshed," as he wrote to Benjamin Lincoln, "an event as happy as it was unexpected."[98] Like other nationalists, in the wake of the commotions Washington hoped "that good may result from the clouds of evil which threatned, not only the hemisphere of Massachusetts, but by spreading its baneful influence, the tranquility of the Union."[99]

Also like other nationalists, Washington saw Shays' Rebellion as inextricably bound up with the inadequacies of the Articles of Confederation. Any such mutiny challenged, in his mind, the very premise of popular sovereignty. "What a triumph for the advocates of despotism," Washington wrote to Jay about the insurrection, "to find that we are incapable of governing ourselves, and that systems founded on the basis of equal liberty are merely ideal and fallacious!"[100] All his correspondence regarding the rebellion related it to the shortcomings of the Confederation. "Thus was Shays's Rebellion linked, in the logic of Washington's reasoning, with he appeal for a stronger Federal government," wrote Freeman. "Every development thereafter tightened the tie."[101]

Gradually, as a result of the alarm raised nationally by the commotions, Washington came to believe that the Philadelphia Convention presented the best opportunity to achieve constitutional corrections. So did Americans across the continent. "A realization of the need for self-discipline, for ef-

97. Washington to Knox, 26 Dec., 1787, *ibid.*, XXIX, 122.
98. Washington to Lincoln, 23 Mar., 1787, *ibid.*, XXIX, 182; also 24 Feb., 1787, *ibid.*, 168.
99. Washington to Knox, 25 Feb., 1787, *ibid.*, XXIX, 169. Likewise, the day before Washington wrote to Lincoln that "I hope some good may come out of so much evil, by giving energy and respectability to the Government." Washington to Lincoln, 24 Feb., 1787, *ibid.*, XXIX, 168.
100. Washington to Jay, 1 Aug., 1787, *Writings of Washington*, XXVIII.
101. Freeman, *Washington*, VI, 72.

fective government," wrote Flexner, "had been slowly augmenting, like water swelling subterranean streams. It had only been necessary to drill a hole to have the water rise, and that is what Shays's Rebellion had done."[102] After all the years of anticipated crisis, this opportunity, just as the call went out from Annapolis for a General Convention, seemed too serendipitous to pass up.

Was it the Regulation that caused Washington to return to public life — or at least the grossly exaggerated reports he received of "Shays' Rebellion?" According to Washington himself, it certainly was. In a letter written later which Feer and other skeptics must have overlooked, Washington told Lafayette that "I am again brought, contrary to my public declaration, and intention, on a public theatre. . . . I could not resist the call to a convention of the States which is to determine whether we are to have a Government of respectability under which life, liberty, and property will be secured to us, or are to submit to one which may be the result of chance or the moment, springing perhaps from anarchy and Confusion, and dictated perhaps by some aspiring demagogue who will not consult the interest of his Country so much as his own ambitious views."[103] Washington could hardly have said more, without crediting Daniel Shays for the new Constitution.

It was also *the public's* perception that Washington returned to public service because of the menace implicit in Shays' Rebellion. The *Philadelphia Gazette* effused that "in 1787 we behold him at the head of a chosen band of patriots and heroes, arresting the progress of American anarchy, and taking the lead in laying a deep foundation for preserving that liberty by a good government, which he had acquired for his country by his sword. Illustrious and highly favoured

---

102. For Washington's endorsement of the Convention, see Washington to Knox, 3 Feb., 1787, *Writings of Washington*, XXIX, 152; Flexner, *Washington*, III, 108.

103. Washington to Lafayette, Philadelphia, 6 June, 1787, *Writings of Washington*, XXIX, 229-230. For discussion of Feer, see above, 183, and below, 214.

instrument of the blessings of Heaven to America — live — live forever!"[104] Just as Shays' Rebellion suggested a national problem, Washington represented a national solution. The day he arrived in Philadelphia, the *Pennsylvania Herald* extolled this latest demonstration of his selflessness. "This great patriot will never think his duty performed, while anything remains to be done."[105]

The clear implication of the Regulation, to Washington, to the state legislatures, and to the delegates they chose, was that much remained to be done to achieve revolutionary settlement. There was already ample evidence of this in the impotence of Congress: still, it took an outbreak of violence — actual evidence of anarchy, however overblown — to turn the tide of American opinion. And, it took Washington's indispensable presence to forge the Constitution. While the Convention was still in progress, a correspondent in Philadelphia wrote: "General Washington presides in the Convention with his usual dignity. . . . From the characters of the gentlemen who compose this illustrious assembly — from the increase of our national difficulties — and above all, from the growing disposition our citizens every where discover, to improve our federal government, I have not a doubt but that American will in a few years realize all the happiness for which she has

---

104. *Worcester Gazette*, first week in September, 1787, quoting *Philadelphia Gazette*.

105. *Pennsylvania Herald*, 12 May, 1787, as quoted in Freeman, *George Washington*, VI, 87. Wood wrote that Washington's "presence and leadership undoubtedly gave the convention a prestige that they otherwise could not have had. His backing of the Constitution was essential to its eventual ratification." Wood, *The Radicalism of the American Revolution*, 209. According to the diary of John Quincy Adams, who was a student in the law office of Theophilus Parsons in the 1780s, the Constitution was "extorted from the grinding necessity of a reluctant nation." His grandson, Charles Francis Adams, wrote: "I believe it is generally conceded that Shays's 'Rebellion,' so-called, was one of the chief impelling and contributory causes to the framing and adoption of the constitution of 1788. A rude shock, it awakened the whole thirteen States to a realizing sense of the anarchical abysm on the edge of which they were then lingering. . . ." Adams, Preface to John Noble, "A Few Notes on Shays Rebellion," in *Proceedings of the American Antiquarian Society* XV (1902-3), 120.

contended."[106]

Although Washington's role during the Convention will
be discussed later, it should be noted here that nationalists
credited Washington (along with plausible evidence of possible civil war), with its success. "Be assured," Monroe insisted to Jefferson, shortly before ratification was achieved at
Poughkeepsie, "his influence carried the government."[107] As
Wood wrote, "Once committed to the Constitution, he worked
hard for its acceptance. He wrote letters to friends and let his
enthusiasm for the new federal government be known. Once
he had identified himself publicly with the new Constitution
he became very anxious to have it accepted. Its ratification
was a kind of ratification of himself."[108]

The arguments which Feer put forward to discount Shays'
Rebellion as the reason why Washington foresook retirement
were that: a). he had *always* been an ardent nationalist; b). he
had used similar, alarmist language about the Confederation
(e.g., as early as 1779 he had written "we seem to be verging
. . . fast to destruction"); and c). that "by the time he made
up his mind to go . . ., he had known for several weeks that
the Massachusetts government had suppressed Shays's Rebellion and that that particular threat to the United States had
passed."[109]

It is of course true that Washington had never wavered in
his belief that the Congress had to become a legitimate and
unchallenged government for the United States. But it is also
true that even three months before the Regulation, he had explicitly and determinedly refused to return to public affairs.[110]
Feer insisted that other issues changed Washington's mind,
including New York's rejection of the impost, which "finally
cut off any hope of governmental reform without a convention, and the possibility that the controversy over paper mon-

106. *Worcester Gazette*, first week in August, 1787.
107. Monroe to Jefferson, 12 July, 1788 in *Jefferson Papers*, XIII, 352.
108. Wood, *The Radicalism of the American Revolution*, 209.
109. Feer, "Rebellion and Constitution," *NEQ* (1969), 397.
110. See above, 194.

ey in neighboring Maryland might move from the legislature to the battle field."[111] Curiously, though Feer cited more than a dozen of Washington's letters as evidence (most of which have been cited above), none of those letters even mentions the impost or paper money. And Feer was apparently unaware of Washington's letter to Lafayette, declaring that he "could not resist the call to a convention . . . which is to determine" the security of Americans' "life, liberty, and property. . . ."[112] Only Shays' Rebellion had even appeared to threaten life, liberty, and property.

Feer was right that the General did not firmly decide to attend the Convention until after the Regulation appeared to have been quashed. But less than seven weeks before he formally accepted his appointment as a delegate, Washington believed that "the political machine will yet be much tumbled and tossed, and possibly be wrecked altogether. . . . anarchy and confusion must prevail, and everything will be turned topsey turvey" in Massachusetts. He had several times observed that the unrest had "spread its baneful influence" across the Union, and that one could not safely guess "when, where, or how it will end," since "in every State there were combustibles which a spark might ignite." In fact, from the time Madison had named him to the Virginia delegation in November, Washington had never once "closed the door" to his attendance — by citing, for example, his famous "retirement oath."

Why, then, did it take Washington so long to accede decisively to the Convention movement? Aside from his earnest personal wish to remain at Mount Vernon, and what Lafayette once called "his invincible repugnance to retract" (especially something as universally acclaimed as his avowal of retirement), neither he nor his friends wished to see the immortal

---

111. Feer, "Rebellion and Constitution," *NEQ* (1969), 397.
112. Of Shays' Rebellion he had written to Madison: "What stronger evidence can be given of the want of energy in our governments than these disorders? If there exists not a power to check them, what security has a man for life, liberty, or property?" Washington to Madison, 5 Nov., 1786, *Writings of Washington*, XXIX, 51-52.

stature of his soul — his "reputation" — gambled away on a dubious venture, if this was to be another abortive conference like Annapolis. This was not only vanity: pragmatically, his reputation was too valuable to the nationalist cause to be wasted, as Washington himself knew. By returning to any position of power, he was certain to be compared to Cromwell, instead of Cincinnatus: indeed, even as he was making up his mind about attending the Convention, he received as a gift a "piece of Antiquity" that had once belonged to Oliver Cromwell.[113]

But indecisiveness was also a character trait that had been noted and criticized throughout his conduct of the war. Flexner observed that "Washington's method of weighing evidence . . . took time, especially when the balance refused to tip one way or the other." At the battle of Fort Washington, this trait had almost catastrophic consequences.[114] Given that trait, and the variety of reasons he had for remaining at home, it is not at all surprising that he waited until a month before the Convention to make his decision firm.

The impact of Shays' Rebellion — as it was reported to him — had a synergetic impact upon Washington, influencing his judgment both directly and indirectly, by creating waves of alarm across the continent. News reports like those he read in the *Pennsylvania Packet* had a similar affect upon governors like Randolph and Bowdoin, congressmen like King and Lee, generals like Knox and Lincoln, protégés like Madison and Humphreys, and friends like Bland and Jay, who in return further amplified the alarm in their letters to Washington, the "Deliverer." The cumulative effect of these reports of the Regulation was to surround Washington with anxiety and gloom sufficient to dislodge him from civic repose; for at last he realized that Henry Lee might be right, and that "the contagion will spread and may reach Virginia."[115] In 1784, Wash-

---

113. Lafayette, *Memoirs . . . Published by his Family* (New York, 1837), I, 20, as quoted in Flexner, *Washington*, II, 538. Washington to John Henry, 23 Jan., 1787, *Writings of Washington*, XXIX, 148.
114. Flexner, *Washington*, II, 538; for battle of Fort Washington, see *ibid.*, 148-149.
115. Henry Lee to Madison, 25 Oct., 1787, *Madison Papers*, IX, 144, 145.

ington had deliberately launched the constitutional movement as a grassroots effort from the bank of the Potomac; in 1787, Shays' Rebellion convinced him that only by sacrificing his retirement could he preserve it.

PART THREE
THE CONSTITUTIONAL IMPACT
OF SHAYS' REBELLION

CHAPTER SEVEN

Shays' Rebellion, the Philadelphia Convention, and Ratification

"Should the alarming convulsions which have arisen, partly from the defects in our federal Constitution, prove to be the parents of one much preferable, as we cheerfully hope they will; we may rejoice in the Rock of our Salvation, and say to the distributers of our peace — ye meant these things for evil, but GOD meant them for good."

— "Observator," (Boston) *Independent Chronicle,* October 4th, 1787

During the formation and ratification of the Constitution, the exaggerated reports circulating about Shays' Rebellion continued to serve as illustrations of the violence that would attend a failure to rectify the self-defeating characteristics inherent in the Articles of Confederation: as Madison observed during the Convention, "symptoms of a leveling spirit . . . have sufficiently appeared in a certain quarters [*sic*] to give notice of the future danger."[1] Those exaggerated reports also provided the Federalists with powerful, rhetorical ammunition aimed at identifying anti-Federalists with insurgents in the public mind. Opponents of the Constitution were forced to disavow this identification from the start, and to defend the existing structure of governance across the continent,

---

1. "Madison: Notes on the Debates . . .," 26 June, 1787, Farrand, ed., *Records,* I, 422-423.

even though many anti-Federalists acknowledged that some revisions were necessary. Still, they could not convince the majority of citizens in the thirteen states that the Articles provided a satisfactory framework to guard against the "leveling spirit" that Shays' Rebellion was said to represent.

On Sunday, May 13th, 1787, the *Pennsylvania Packet* and other papers across the states reported the presence in Philadelphia of "His Excellency George Washington, one of the Delegates from the State of Virginia to the Fœderal Convention. His arrival was announced by a salute of the United States from the train of artillery and the ringing of bells. He was escorted from Chester by the Philadelphia light-dragoons. . . ."[2] Only Washington could have reflected so much glory upon the upcoming Convention, which was at best an unknown quantity.

No one would have attributed Washington's arrival in Philadelphia to anxiety, nor to the fear of ongoing anarchy. But concern and even alarm about Massachusetts was still widespread on the eve of the Convention since, as Jay wrote to Jefferson, "the Insurrection in Massachusetts is suppressed, but the Spirit of it exists and has operated powerfully in the late [Massachusetts] Election."[3] Even the day before the del-

---

2. *Pennsylvania Packet*, 14 May, 1787; similar, glowing reports of Washington's arrival were widely reprinted: in the *New York Daily Advertiser*, 18 May, 1787, for example, and the *Providence Gazette*, 26 May, 1787. Concern about "anarchy and confusion" was still alive when the convention began: the same issue of the *Packet* reported that, a few days earlier in Northampton, Massachusetts, "150 insurgents assembled with arms, beat drums and fired several guns at 11 at night."

3. Jay to Jefferson, 24 Apr., 1787, Johnston, ed., *Correspondence of Jay*, III, 244. In mid-February, Madison had warned Congress that "every State ought to bear in mind the consequences of popular commotions if not thoroughly subdued, on the tranquility of the Union & the possibility of it being itself the scene of them," and "M[r]. King . . . took notice of the possibility to which every State in the Union was exposed, of being visited with similar calamities. . . ." 19 Feb., 1787, *JCC*, XXXII, 722, 720. Likewise, in mid-March, Knox advised Congress that "all States in the Union, are liable in different degrees, to be agitated with similar commotions to those which have manifested themselves in Massachusetts, but that the issues may be dissimilar." "Report of Secretary at

egates actually began their work, the *New York Daily Advertiser* editorialized that "a convention of States, created from *fear* and *suffering*, are now to sit at Philadelphia. . . ." Characterizing the perceived connection between the Regulation and the Convention, the paper observed: "It is a recieved maxim that . . . oppression must necessarily precede awakening and enquiry. This cause and effect is borrowed from mechanical reasoning. The spring must be condensed before it can resist and expand. The operation of this principle must then always be violent."[4]

When misdiagnosed as "symptoms of a leveling spirit," the Massachusetts demonstrations of moral economy raised a specter of violent civil war as old as Cromwell and the Levellers; their movement, after all, had arisen during the only non-monarchical era of English history before the American Revolution. Since that epoch had ended in a bloodbath, it was easy to depict Shays' Rebellion as evidence of the imminent collapse of American civilization, and was also generally considered the "ripening incident," in Madison's phrase, that distinguished this well-attended assembly in Philadelphia from previous, abortive efforts to restructure the government of the United States.[5]

War on removal of military stores from Springfield," read 13 Mar., 1787, *ibid.*, XXXII, 109-114.

4. *New York Daily Advertiser*, 24 May, 1787. The editorial went on to assert that in reality the Convention contradicted this "recieved maxim."

5. "In the interval between . . . the meeting of . . . Commissioners at Annapolis . . .," Madison wrote near the end of his life,"and the meeting of Deputies at Philadelphia had continued to develop more & more the necessity & the extent of a Systematic provision for the preservation and Govt. of the Union. Among the ripening incidents was the Insurrection of Shays in Massachusetts against her Government; which was with difficulty suppressed, notwithstanding the influence on the insurgents of the apprehended interposition of the Fedl. troops. At the date of the Convention, the aspect & retrospect of the political condition of the U.S. could not but fill the public mind with a gloom which was relieved only by a hope that so select a Body would devise an adequate remedy for the existing and prospective evils so impressively demanding it. . . ." In an apparent allusion to former colleague Higginson and his cabal, Madison went on: "Those least partial to popular government or most distrustful of its efficacy were yielding to anticipations that from an increase of the confusion

While not easy to estimate, it would be difficult to exaggerate the importance of Washington's presence inside the State House, even though he rarely voiced an opinion. Perhaps his value as a figurehead can best be appreciated by considering his only plausible "competitor" as President of the Convention: at eighty-one, Ben Franklin may have been a well-loved figure nationally, but his health was so uncertain that he was even unable to personally nominate Washington at the first session. There, the General's election provided an auspicious beginning, for the vote was unanimous.[6]

While Washington said little during the Convention, no one else could at the same time have accomplished so much. His personal stature was brought to bear in one crucial particular throughout the proceedings: the rule of secrecy adopted on May 28th, without which, according to Madison, "no Constitution would ever have been adopted by the Convention. . . ."[7] Clinton Rossiter catalogued the many ways in which this confidentiality fostered collective confidence among the members. "The secrecy rule stirred the imaginations and loosened the tongues of the delegates on the floor, permitted them to take advanced positions and then to withdraw gracefully under fire, guarded them against both careless and willful misinterpretations of their gropings for constitutional solu-

---

a government might result more congenial with their taste or their opinions. . . ." "Madison: Preface to Debates . . .," Farrand, ed., *Records*, III, 547-549. [For clarity, I have altered some abbreviations and punctuation from Madison's notes.]

Annapolis delegates, wrote Rakove, had "had little reason to believe that the appearance of a handful of additional members would materially enhance the authority of the Convention. . . . They merely hoped that a further delay of nine months might bring the emergence of a climate more favorable to reform. . . ." The initial call for the Philadelphia Convention came from "the need to salvage something from the potentially harmful consequences of adjourning without reaching any decision at all." Jack N. Rakove, *The Beginnings of National Politics* (New York, 1979), 375.

6. "Docr. Franklin alone could have been thought of as a competitor." Madison, "Notes on the Debates . . .," Farrand, ed., *Records*, I, 4. In fact, Franklin's attendance thereafter was remarkably consistent.

7. As quoted in Clinton Rossiter, *1787: The Grand Convention* (New York, 1987), 167.

tions and political compromises, permitted one consensus after another to form out of a wealth of half-formed opinions and half-baked prejudices, encouraged them to express honest doubts about such sacred cows as the sovereignty of the states and the glories of the militia, and spared bravos like Randolph and Charles Pinckney the temptation of playing to any gallery save that of posterity, one that usually brings out the best in such men."[8]

Early in the Convention, after the adoption of the secrecy rule, Washington rose to address its members, according to delegate William Pierce. "'I am sorry to find,'" said the General, "'that some one Member of this Body has been so neglectful of the secrets of the Convention as to drop in the State House a copy of their proceedings . . . . I must entreat Gentlemen to be more careful, least our transactions get into the News Papers, and disturb the public repose by premature speculations. . . .' (throwing it down on the table), 'let him who owns it take it.'" Washington then "quitted the room with a dignity so severe that every Person seemed alarmed . . . . It is something remarkable that no Person ever owned the Paper."[9] Without Washington's commanding presence, it is not difficult to believe that the secrecy rule would have succumbed to the more gregarious and impetuous delegates, with incalculable adverse effect.

Doubtless, the Presidency of the United States was designed to a great degree for the person of George Washington, who, it was presumed even during the Convention, would accept the office.[10] Delegate Pierce Butler later lamented that

---

8. *Ibid.*, 167-168. "Under the watchful eye of the grand gentleman at their head," Rossiter added later, "they behaved for the most part in a manner that encouraged frankness, dampened suspicion, soothed hurt feelings, and made compromise a virtue rather then a sign of weakness." *Ibid.*, 180.

9. "William Pierce: Anecdote," Farrand, ed., *Records*, III, 86-87. "Like Gustavus Vasa," Pierce wrote of Washington, "he may be said to be the deliverer of his Country . . . and now only seeks for the approbation of his Country-men by being virtuous and useful." *Ibid.*, III, 94.

10. "George Washington it is said will be placed at the head of the new Government. . . ." Benjamin Rush to Timothy Pickering, 30 Aug., 1787, Farrand,

the executive office would not have been so powerful "had not many of the members cast their eyes towards General Washington as President; and shaped their Ideas of the Powers to be given to a President, by their opinions of his virtue."[11] One shining example of this virtue was his eight-year-long, unpaid service to the country — a point Madison felt compelled to mention during the Convention, as he discountenanced any fixed salary for the Executive.[12] A less obvious virtue that "the father of our country" was said to possess for the Presidency was his lack of off-spring: none could fear that Washington would establish an hereditary reign.[13]

Though his involvement was critical to the genesis of the Constitution, and his support for its ratification was unqualified, Washington did not pretend, as many others did and do, that this was a flawless charter for government During its invention he had moments of profound discouragement, especially in the weeks before "the Great Compromise." Halfway through the Convention, on the same day that Robert Yates and John Lansing, Jr. stood their ground by fleeing Philadel-

---

ed., *Records*, IV, 75. Shortly after the Convention, an unknown correspondent in Philadelphia wrote to Jefferson without hesitation that "Washington lives; & as he will be appointed President, jealousy on this head vanishes." _____ to Jefferson, Philadelphia, 11 Oct., 1787, in *ibid.*, III, 105.

11. Pierce Butler to Weedon Butler, 5 May, 1788, in *ibid.*, III, 302.

12. Madison reminded the delegates thus: "Have we not seen the great and most important of our officers [offices?] . . . executed for eight years together without the smallest salary, by a Patriot whom I will not now offend by any other praise. . . ." Madison asked if they should "doubt finding three or four men in all the U. States with public spirit enough" to bear similar sacrifices. Madison, "Notes on the Debates . . .," Farrand, ed., *Records*, I, 84. One can imagine Washington's discomfort as he presided over such praise from his protégé.

13. See *Pennsylvania Gazette*, 5 Mar., 1788. Wood wrote that "people even talked about the fact that he lacked an heir and therefore could not establish a dynasty." Wood, *The Radicalism of the American Revolution*, 404 n.52. This point was also made in Washington's undelivered inaugural address drafted for him, apparently, by David Humphreys; see Nathaniel E. Stein, "The Discarded Inaugural Address of George Washington," *Manuscripts* (Spring 1958), 7, and Ralph Ketcham and Nathaniel Stein, "Two New Letters Reveal Madison's Role, Unmask Ghost of Washington's Unused Inaugural," *Manuscripts* (Spring 1959), 54-60.

phia, Washington wrote to their confrère Hamilton: "I *almost* despair of seeing a favorable issue to the proceedings of the Convention, and do therefore repent having had any agency in the business."[14]

In a candid letter to Lafayette seven months later, during the Massachusetts ratification convention, Washington confessed that he was not yet "such an enthusiastic, partial or undiscriminating admirer of [the Constitution], as not to perceive it is tinctured with some real (though not radical) defects."[15] Still, he insisted, "it appears to me . . . little short of a miracle, that the Delegates from so many different States . . . should unite in forming a system of national Government, so little liable to well founded objections." Chief among its virtues, Washington felt, was the investment in that government of only those powers necessary unto it, and the distribution of those powers between its three branches. He wrote Lafayette that, while "I would not be understood . . . to speak of consequences which may be produced, in the revolution of ages, by corruption of morals, profligacy of manners, and listlessness for the preservation of the natural and inalienable rights of mankind . . . It will at least be a recommendation to the proposed Constitution that it is provided with more checks and barriers against the introduction of Tyranny . . . than any Government hitherto instituted among mortals. . . ." And, "should that which is now offered to the People of America, be found on experiment less perfect than it can be made, a Constitutional door is left open for its amelioration." Finally, Washington believed, "there is no alternative, no hope of alteration, no intermediate resting place, between the adoption of this, and a recurrence to an unqualified state of Anarchy, with all its deplorable circumstances."[16]

---

14. Washington to Hamilton, 10 July, 1787, *Writings of Washington*, XXIX, 245. With the departure of Yates and Lansing, only a muted if unchastened Hamilton rejoined the Convention to sign for New York.
15. Washington to Lafayette, 7 Feb., 1788, *Writings of Washington*, XXIX, 409-410.
16. *Ibid.*, 411.

"The insurrections in Massachusetts," Madison observed at the Convention, "admonished all the States of the danger to which they were exposed."[17] This danger, along with the risk of sullying Washington's reputation, furnished an abiding inducement to all the delegates to cooperate, to compromise, and to succeed in some measure by constructing a viable system of government. In mid-June, Theodore Sedgwick wrote to Rufus King at the Convention that, in Massachusetts, "a war is now actually levied on the virtue, property and distinctions in the community, and however there may be an appearance of temporary cessation of hostilities, yet the flame will again and again break out."[18] Even before the proposed Constitution had been made public, a letter to the *Pennsylvania Gazette* warned that, "Should the fœderal government be rejected (AWFUL WORDS)," Daniel Shays would seize control of the Bay state.[19] "When the commotions existed in Massachusetts . . ." as James Wilson declared later, during Pennsylvania's Ratification Convention, "I believe it is not generally known on what a perilous tenure we held our freedom and independence at that period. The flames of internal insurrection were ready to burst out in every quarter, they were formed by the correspondents of state officers . . ., and from one end to the other of the continent, we walked on ashes, concealing fire beneath our feet. . . ."[20]

Beyond the overall impact of Shays' Rebellion upon the Convention, there were also measures drafted into the framework to address similar insurrections. These were, specifically, Article I, Section 8, Clause 15, granting Congress the

17. James Madison, 19 June, 1787, "Madison: Notes on the Debates . . .," Farrand, ed., *Records*, I, 318. Madison had noted the "want of Guaranty to the States of their Constitutions & laws against internal violence" as one of the "Vices of the Political System of the United States." *Madison Papers*, IX, 350.
18. Theodore Sedgwick to Rufus King, 18 June, 1787, as quoted in Welch, *Theodore Sedgwick*, 57.
19. *Pennsylvania Gazette*, 12 Sept., 1787, as quoted in Merrill Jensen, John P. Kaminski, and Gasparé J. Saladino, eds., *The Documentary History of the Ratification of the Constitution* 16 vols. (Madison, 1976-1988), XIII, 192.
20. James Wilson, 11 Dec., 1787, Pennsylvania Ratifying Convention, in Elliott, ed., *Debates*, II, 521.

responsibility and the authority to call out the militia to "suppress Insurrections;" and Article IV, Section 4, which read: "The United States shall guarantee to every State in this Union a Republican Form of Government, and shall protect each of them against Invasion; and on Application of the Legislature, or of the Executive (when the Legislature cannot be convened) against domestic Violence."[21]

Both advocates and opponents of the nationalist cause supported the Federal guarantee to the states against domestic violence, since Shays' Rebellion had demonstrated that, as Oliver Ellsworth put it, "Massachusetts can not keep the peace one hundred miles from her capitol."[22] Even those delegates present at th conclusion who refused to sign the Constitution — Randolph, Mason, and Gerry — did not dissent from the federal provisions proposed to deal with insurrections and domestic violence.[23]

Shays' Rebellion had a profoundly negative effect on the logic of anti-Federalism both in the Convention, and throughout the process of ratification. Having mostly acknowledged the inadequacies of the Confederation, the anti-Federalists failed to propose an acceptable alternative to the emerging framework. Here it should be remembered once again how dire the situation of the Confederation had become by the summer of 1787. Under the Articles, the United States had

21. "The Constitution of the United States," in Commager, ed., *Documents of American History*, I, 141, 144. The issue was, of course, closely related to the question of an American standing army; *viz.* "Mr. Pinkney thought . . . There must be . . . a real military force. . . . The United States had been making an experiment without it, and we see the consequence in their rapid approaches toward anarchy." "Madison: Notes on the Debates . . .," Farrand, ed., *Records*, II, 332.

It is arguable that Article IV, section 10, Clause 15, denying the states the power to "make any Thing but gold and silver Coin a Tender in Payment of Debts," was also directly influenced by Shays' Rebellion, but evidence there is wanting.

22. "Madison: Notes on the Debates. . .," Farrand, ed., *Records*, I, 406. According to Yates's notes, Ellsworth said "Massachusetts cannot support a government at the distance of one hundred miles from her capital. . . ." *Ibid.*, I, 414.

23. "Madison: Notes on the Debates . . .," Farrand, ed., *Records*, II, 47, 317. Gerry was, as usual, ambivalent.

proven itself a helpless, pitiful giant, unable to defend its own arsenal, to pay even the interest on its debts abroad, or fulfill its obligations to its own soldiery; in fact, it could rarely even muster a quorum.[24] The best that the anti-Federalists appeared to offer was more of the same chaos, under an enhanced draft of the Articles. This gave the Federalists, who sought to supplant the Confederation with national sovereignty, some justification for calling themselves "the friends of order, of government and the constitution."[25]

The anti-Federalists' cause was also damaged more subtly by their perceived connection to the Massachusetts rebels. In a recent essay, Michael Lienesch has observed that, "in terms of strategy, Shays had placed the anti-Federalists in an untenable position: trapped, as it were, between rebellion and counter-revolution, supporting neither Shays nor his aristocratic enemies, they tried to hold a tenuous middle ground 'between these two parties.' But because supporters of the Constitution had already claimed the middle, its opponents were reduced to calling for caution, their radical concept of reform watered down almost beyond recognition into a desire for incremental changes within the existing Confederation."[26]

This strategic problem was illustrated by anti-Federalist Richard Henry Lee just a month after the Convention ended. In a pamphlet entitled "Letters of a Federal Farmer," Lee delineated "two very unprincipled parties in the United States. . . . One party is composed of little insurgents, men in debt, who want no law, and who want a share of the property of others; these are called levellers, Shaysites, &c. The other party

24. Burnett noted that, in 1787, Congress had "no quorum until January 27th, nor after October 27th. In the intervening 112 days on which Congress assembled, there were only two days when a delegate was present from each of the thirteen states; 11 states were there on 4 days; 10 states on 6 days, 9 states on 39; 8 states on 35. On 102 days, 6 or less states attended." Burnett, Prefatory Note, *JCC*, XXXII, vii–x.
25. Theodore Sedgwick to Henry Van Schaack, 10 Jan., 1788, as quoted in Welch, *Theodore Sedgwick*, 56.
26. Michael Lienesch, "Reinterpreting Rebellion: The Influence of Shays's Rebellion on American Political Thought," *In Debt to Shays*, Gross and Allis, eds., n.p.

is composed of a few, but more dangerous men, with their servile dependents; these avariciously grasp at all power and property; you may discover in all the actions of these men, an evident dislike to free and equal government. . . . Between these two parties is the weight of the community; the men of middling property, men not in debt on the one hand, and men, on the other, content with republican governments. . . ."[27]

Thus, at least outside the Pennsylvania State House, the Federalists kept then-opponents on the defensive, continuously identifying those who opposed them with the Massachusetts insurgency, and forcing a clear polarization between "principled Federalists" and "Shaysites." "Every state has its SHAYS," wrote a correspondent to the *Pennsylvania Gazette* before the end of the Convention, "who, either with their pens — or tongues — or offices — are endeavoring to effect what *Shays* attempted in vain with his sword. . . . The spirit of Shays," he insisted, inspired every objection to the Constitution, while it was being hammered out.[28] And shortly after the Convention another letter to the *Gazette*, widely reprinted across the country, asserted that Federalists "should be distinguished hereafter by the name of WASHINGTONIANS, and the ANTIFEDERALISTS, by the name SHAYITES, in every part of the United States."[29]

It was during the Convention, then, that anti-Federalism was first perceived as if it were closely associated with Shays'

---

27. Richard Henry Lee, "Observation leading to a fair examination of the system of government, proposed by the late Convention . . .," Letter No. V, in Paul Leicester Ford, ed., *Pamphlets on the Constitution of the United States* (New York, 1968 [orig. publ. 1888]), 321. Lee went on: "In 1786, the little insurgents, the levellers, came forth, invaded the rights of others, and attempted to establish governments according to their wills. Their movements evidently gave encouragement to the other party, which, in 1787, has taken the political field, and with its fashionable dependents, and the tongue and the pen, is endeavoring to establish in a great haste, a politer kind of government." *Ibid.*
28. Unidentified correspondent in the *Pennsylvania Gazette*, 5 Sept., 1787, as quoted in Steven R. Boyd, "Shays's Rebellion and the Campaign for the Constitution," *In Debt to Shays*, Gross and Allis, eds., n.p.
29. 26 Sept., 1787, as quoted in *ibid.*

Rebellion. But the reality was quite different: those who opposed the emerging Constitution within the State House were not the same as those who practiced politics "without doors;" indeed some, like Mason and Gerry, openly dreaded democracy.[30] As Main put it, "The Anti-Federalists who attended did not represent the rank and file of the party but the propertied minority."[31] What they shared with the lower-class and the dissidents was an intense mistrust of strong government and national consolidation, and the dread of "a *permanent* ARISTOCRACY."[32]

While one cannot equate anti-Federalism with "Shaysism," there are echoes of the Shaysite petitions of 1786 in the anti-Federalist objections to the Constitution: their most discernible common ground was a passionate allegiance to local government, especially in matters of taxation and military force. To anti-Federalists, the most objectionable specifics of the proposed framework were "the powers of the purse and the sword" granted therein to the federal government.[33] "What the Antifederalists feared . . . .," emphasized Main, "was that the power given to a national government would be wielded by an upper class."[34] Enslavement by a self-perpetuating ruling class appeared to all anti-Federalists the inevitable outcome of a monied, albeit elected, aristocracy and a standing army. In Main's words, "the two went together: taxes would be collected by the army which in turn would be supported by taxes."[35]

30. Farrand, ed., *Records*, I, 48. By the time the Convention had begun, Knox was more sanguine about democracy, as he wrote to delegate Rufus King. "The State systems are the accursed thing which will prevent our being a nation . . .," since "the democracy might be managed, nay, it would remedy itself after being sufficiently fermented" Knox to King, 15 July, 1787, in Drake, *Correspondence of Knox*, 94.

31. Main, *Antifederalists*, 116.

32. "Centinel," [Samuel Bryan], 5 Oct., 1787, Philadelphia *Independent Gazetteer*, as quoted in Cecilia M. Kenyon, *The Antifederalists* (Boston, 1985), 13.

33. Attributed by James Wilson to John Smilie, 11 Dec., 1787, Pennsylvania Ratification Convention, Elliot, ed., *Debates*, II, 522. Compare this to the Shaysite concern about a "Union of the Military and Monied interests" above, 169 n.130.

34. Main, *Antifederalists*, 132.

35. *Ibid.*, 147.

Since Congress determined the time and place of elections, anti-Federalists had no doubt that the deck could and would be stacked against them, to create "a monstruous aristocracy."[36] Similar concerns had been frequently expressed by the convention petitions of 1786 and the Regulators themselves, who wanted the seat of Massachusetts government moved west of Boston, to protect the people from "aristocraticle" intrigue. In 1787, one sarcastic Federalist commentator insisted that anti-Federalist writings were made from a predictable recipe of buzz-words: "WELL-BORN, nine times — *Aristocracy*, eighteen times . . . *Great Men*, six times. . . . These words will bear being served, after being used once, a dozen times to the same table and palate."[37]

Other objections made during and after the Convention reflected those raised by early, dissident Massachusetts conventions, mostly as objections to the Constitution of 1780: that the Senate was not sufficiently accountable to the people; that the Executive had too much power; and that the power of the judiciary could re-interpret the Constitution to extend federal jurisdiction.[38] But one can go too far, as Isaac Kramnick suggested, "in making the case for the anti-Federalists as antiliberal communitarians or Rousseauean republicans."[39] Equally, both Massachusetts anti-Federalist James Winthrop, librarian of Harvard College, and Luther Martin, a prominent Maryland lawyer, belie the assumption that anti-Federalists formed a plebian party; both illustrate, in Saul Cornell's words, "the existence of cosmopolitan localism among the Anti-Federalist

---

36. "Rusticus," 13 Sept., 1787 in the *New York Journal*. The point argued by Storing is that the anti-Federalists dreaded an aristocracy or oligarchy more than they feared democracy. Herbert J. Storing, *What the Anti-Federalists Were For* (Chicago, 1981).

37. Quoted in Saul Cornell, "Aristocracy Assailed: The Ideology of Backcountry Anti-Federalism," in *Journal of American History LXXVI*, No. 4 (1990), 1156. Cornell's statistical analysis of anti-Federalist writings shows this commentator was fairly accurate.

38. These objections are carefully studied in Main, *Antifederalists*, 119-167.

39. Isaac Kramnick, "The 'Great National Discussion': The Discourse of Politics in 1787," *William and Mary Quarterly*, 3rd Ser., XLV, No. 1 (Jan. 1988), 12.

élite."[40]

Anti-Federalists were composed of three basic groups: a small number supported the Confederation out of conviction, exactly as it was; more influential were the state office-holders and their dependents, who did not wish to see their authority diminished by the creation of a stronger superstructure; the largest group would have preferred some revisions of the Articles, but opposed a consolidated government that could dominate their lives. To over-simplify the anti-Federalists' critiques, perhaps, they believed that the fundamental law being proposed would not provide truly representative government such as they had experienced locally (in town meetings, for example), which actually mirrored the constituency. If structurally empowered, local representation could defeat any incipient, aristocratic junto, and insure republican rule. The Federalists' tenet that virtue and wisdom were not evenly distributed throughout society was taken as further evidence, if any were needed, that their Elitism was deeply rooted in a covert, anti-republican ideology, and antagonistic to the unassailable principle of popular sovereignty. Federalists like James Wilson, who asserted during the Convention that "Government ought to flow from the people at large," were considered disingenuous, at best.[41]

The question of how the Constitution should be ratified by the states — whether by their legislatures, by special conventions, or by the people directly — was an ongoing issue throughout the Convention, and recalled the travails of the Articles of Confederation to achieve acceptance. In Massachusetts, this question echoed the unconvincing ratification of the Constitution of 1780, which was a major grievance leading to Shays' Rebellion. Madison's proposal in the Virginia Plan at the outset of the Convention was that the draft Constitution "be submitted to an assembly or assemblies of Representatives, recommended by the several Legislatures

40. Cornell, "Ideology of Back-Country Anti-Federalism," *JAH LXXVI* (1990), 1166.
41. Farrand, ed., *Records*, I, 151.

to be expressly chosen by the people, to consider & decide thereon."[42] Higginson's recommendation to Knox regarding the method of ratification was eventually adopted. Though it cannot be proven that he was responsible, he may well have proposed this plan to Madison when they were both in Congress, and discussed their nationalist ambitions; and Knox, in Congress, certainly had the opportunity to relay the plan to other nationalists.[43] The decision was taken on August 30th that just nine states would be required to establish the Constitution, as Higginson had also proposed, so that "the consent of the States, or some of them, may possibly be obtained . . . when they may not intend it. . . ."[44] This formula was settled upon over the objections of Roger Sherman, who wanted ten states to ratify, and James Wilson, who felt that a bare majority — seven states — should suffice.[45] Madison, who wished for an incontrovertible ratification, observed that, if only the nine smallest states ratified, the Constitution might be instituted by a minority of the American people; and even some moderate nationalists, like Daniel Carroll, felt that ratification should be unanimous.[46]

But between August 30th and the final version to be ratified, the Machiavellian scheme that Higginson had suggested in confidence to Knox was defanged. The two Committees of Style charged with the final drafts in early September specified that "the ratification of the conventions of nine States, shall be sufficient for the establishment of this constitution *between the States so ratifying the same.*"[47] Thus Higginson's idea of the ratifying states imposing their constitution upon four states that "may not intend it" was scotched.[48]

---

42. "Madison: Notes on the Debates. . .," in Farrand, ed., *Records*, I, 22.
43. Higginson to Knox, 13 Feb., 1787, Knox Papers, XIX, 165. See above, 167. For Higginson and Madison in Congress, see above, 142.
44. *Ibid.* See above, 167.
45. "Madison: Notes on the Debates . . .," Farrand, ed., *Records*, II, 468-469.
46. *Ibid.*, II, 469.
47. Farrand, ed., *Records*, II, 603 [my italics]. An interim draft read "the ratification of the Conventions of nine States shall be sufficient for organising the Constitution *between the said States.*" *Ibid.*, 579.
48. As well, the preamble the Committee produced first, which included the

As preparations began for the signing of the Constitution, the anti-Federalists sensed that their position was too defensive to prevail against ratification; whereupon Mason and Gerry called for the inclusion in the document of a bill of rights.[49] This portentous issue, upon which would ultimately hinge Massachusetts' ratification and several other states' thereafter, was virtually ignored by the delegates, who voted it down ten to zero and, in Rossiter's words, turned "a blind eye to the Whig tradition and gave short shrift to the proposal of the author of the Virginia Declaration of 1776."[50] Five days later they signed their names to the final draft, and adjourned to the City Tavern.

Throughout the Convention, Shays' Rebellion had held the Framers' feet to the fire, to borrow Wilson's metaphor. The Massachusetts demonstrations, perceived as a violent insurrection, undercut the position of those who had faith in the Confederation, which had proven itself unable, militarily and economically, to protect its own store of weapons at Springfield. Even as the delegates hammered their empirical solutions and pragmatic compromises together into a framework of government, "the new constitution was viewed . . ., " wrote Pennsylvania's anti-Federal "Centinel" six months later, "through the medium of a SHAYS, the terrors of HIS insurrections had not subsided; a government that would have been execrated at another time was embraced by many as a refuge from anarchy, and thus liberty deformed by mad riot and dissention, lost her ablest advocates."[51]

---

names of the thirteen states *including* Rhode Island, was changed to read "We the people of the United States. . . ." Farrand, ed., *Records*, II, 565, 590.

49. Farrand, ed., *Records*, II, 587-588.

50. Rossiter, *1787*, 227. According to Wilson, the notion of a bill of rights — "neither an essential nor a necessary instrument" — "never struck the mind of any member in the late convention till, I believe, within three days of the dissolution of that body, and even then of so little account was the idea that it passed off in a short conversation, without introducing a formal debate or assuming the shape of a motion." "James Wilson at the Pennsylvania Convention," Farrand, ed., *Records*, III, 143.

51. [George Bryan], "Centinel," (Philadelphia) *Independent Gazetteer*, 5 Apr., 1788, in *The Complete Anti-Federalist*, Herbert J. Storing, ed., 7 vols. (Chi-

The campaign for ratification of the Constitution began once it had been signed, and just as quickly the anti-Federalists began their call for a bill of rights, which soon became the key to its acceptance. From the start the Federalists launched a pitched battle, with no holds barred and few insults left unpenned. It was also a dirty fight, first in Congress, then in Pennsylvania and Massachusetts. And, throughout the struggle, the shadow of anarchy and civil war darkened the battlefield.

The anti-Federalists failed to promote a coherent, alternative structure to the Constitution, and instead weakly defended the status quo with only minor alterations; so, to many, further rebellion seemed the inevitable result if ratification failed. Though some leading anti-Federalists in Massachusetts had been proven foes of the Regulators — James Winthrop, the Harvard librarian and author of the anti-Federalist "Agrippa" letters, had actually volunteered to fight the insurgents — they were soon all lumped together and identified in the press as advocates of disorder, an identification which came to define the nationalists' foes.[52] Had the Shaysites not disgraced their cause with incidents of violence and the specter of civil war, and had they not been tarred with the levellers' brush, they might easily have marshalled the political will to defeat ratification in Massachusetts, which most believed would have defeated the effort in subsequent states. In

---

cago, 1981), II, 204-205. "Centinel" was describing the view from Massachusetts during its Ratification Convention.

52. For James Winthrop, see Storing, ed., *Complete Anti-Federalist*, IV, 68. Some anti-Federalists tried to use the Regulation as an argument against ratification, including "Vox Populi": "Let the publick reflect but a moment on the immense expense of treasure, toil, fatigue, hardship and danger, as well as blood, with which we last winter defended our *invaluable constitution*, and consider whether they will now reduce it to *a mere skeleton*!" If a small majority only concurred in the Massachusetts constitutional revisions necessitated by the Federal Constitution, wrote "Vox Populi," "consider in what respect such a revolution would differ from the *bold* and *unprovoked* one which was attempted to be made last winter!" "Vox Populi," 9 Nov., 1787, *Massachusetts Gazette, ibid.*, IV, 50. See also "Candidus," 20 Dec., 1787, (Boston) *Independent Chronicle, ibid.*, IV, 135.

short, the Regulators' dissent "out of doors" contributed to the failure of the dissidents within the Massachusetts Ratification Convention, but also strengthened the cause of those who called for a Bill of Rights.

Speed was of the essence to the Federalists' strategy, and Congress — not known for its celerity — was the first arena in which their swiftness and overbearing tactics prevailed. Just ten days after the Constitution was signed, Richard Henry Lee tried and failed to attach amendments to the Constitution in Congress, before it was forwarded to the states for ratification. Most of his amendments would later be proposed at the Massachusetts Convention, where they overcame western "Shaysite" opposition and allowed for ratification; they were later the basis for the Bill of Rights. But in Congress, his recommendations were expunged and even erased from the official Journal, along with other anti-Federalist motions.[53] The Federalists also managed to give the unamended Constitution the appearance of Congress's unanimous approval, though in fact the representatives were only unanimous in agreeing to transmit the document to the state legislatures (over the objections of Lee and Grayson, who were outnumbered in the Virginia delegation).[54]

The need for a Bill of Rights was not only a fundamental tenet of the anti-Federalists: it was also a heresthetic gambit aimed at producing a second convention.[55] Even the most ar-

53. "Richard Henry Lee, Proposed Amendments to the Constitution," in Burnett, *Letters*, VIII, 648-649. For the fourteen amendments proposed at the Massachusetts Ratification Convention, see The nine amendments are in Elliott, ed., *Debates*, II, 177. See below, 248 n.101.

54. For Lee's account of these maneuvers, see Richard Henry Lee to Governor of Virginia [Edmund Randolph], New York, 16 Oct., 1787, Burnett, *Letters*, VIII, 658. See also "The Secretary of Congress to the Several States," *ibid.*, 650. Of this vote in Congress Washington wrote that, "as the multitude are often deceived by externals, the appearance of unanimity in that body on this occasion will be of great importance." Washington to Madison, 10 Oct., 1787, *Writings of Washington*, XXIX, 285. Washington added that the political tenets of Lee, rather than Mason, "gives the tone" for the opposition. *Ibid.* By this time, Rhode Island had abandoned Congress altogether.

55. "Heresthetic" is a term borrowed from political science that means political manipulation superseding rhetoric. William H. Riker, who has written exten-

dent Federalists could find little to dispute with the proposal of a Bill of Rights.[56] But since no mechanism had been established for amending the Constitution prior to ratification, such amendments appeared to necessitate another Federal Convention, which could foreseeably reduce the momentum toward ratification, and buy time for the anti-Federalists to develop an alternative framework for government.

The absence of a Bill of Rights was the most promising and positive argument that the anti-Federalists offered. Was this an inadvertent omission by the Federalists, or a more sinister abrogation of an ancient, basic principle of whiggish belief? If one judges by the reaction of Congress to Richard Henry Lee's amendments, one must believe the latter, this was certainly the opinion of Mason who, according to Robert A. Rutland, "promoted the idea that the failure to include a bill of rights was not an oversight, but a studied bit of Federalist deception."[57] This was perhaps the greatest miscalculation that the nationalists made during the years of their campaign, since, as William Pierce observed, "some of the greatest men I ever knew have objected to the government for no other reason but because it was not buttoned with a Bill of Rights."[58]

On September 28th, 1788, the Congressional resolution arrived at the Pennsylvania legislature, where sixteen anti-Federalist members fled, so that a quorum could not be achieved. The sergeant at arms, with the aid of a mob, returned two of them forcefully to the chamber, where a quorum was declared present, and the ratification convention was called for early

---

sively about the ratifying conventions, defines the term as the method whereby people win votes and elections "because they have set up the situation in such a way that other people will want to join them." See William H. Riker, *The Art of Political Manipulation* (New Haven, 1986), ix; see also his essay, "Gouverneur Morris in the Philadelphia Convention," *ibid.*, 34-51.

56. See, especially, Hamilton's unpersuasive sophistry in *Federalist* No. 84, where his best argument is that such a bill would be "dangerous. . . . For why declare that things shall not be done which there is no power to do?" Hamilton et al., *The Federalist*, (Franklin Center, Pa., 1977), 620.

57. Robert Allan Rutland, *The Ordeal of the Constitution: The Antifederalists and the Ratification Struggle of 1787-1788* (Boston, 1983), 33.

58. William Pierce to St. George Tucker, 28 Sept., 1787, quoted in *ibid.*, 33.

November.[59] From this time on, the anti-Federalists realized that they must try to stall the process: in Massachusetts, the new legislature elected with Hancock that contained many members sympathetic to the Regulators, postponed the convention until the new year.

The final vote in Pennsylvania, shortly after Wilson's theatrical speech about Shays' Rebellion, was 46 to 23 in favor of ratification. Two weeks later, in Carlisle, ritual demonstrations and counter-demonstrations erupted between the two parties, after which a large anti-Federalist crowd secured the freedom of twenty-one "rioters" through negotiation and a peaceful rally at the jail, much in the tradition of the moral economy.[60]

Delaware, where it was feared that "Shayites" dominated Sussex County in the South, ratified the Constitution unanimously even before Pennsylvania.[61] Here, the Whigs were no match for the dominant Tories, and again, anti-Federalist petitions were ignored. It was easy to argue that a small state like Delaware would benefit from equal representation in the Senate. So, the momentum toward ratification began there, and Delaware became "the first state in the Union;" before the end of the year, New Jersey joined its two neighbors, and soon after Georgia and Connecticut followed suit. So, at the start of the Massachusetts Convention, half the remaining states were needed to ratify.

Just as he had feared, Washington's name had been irrevocably politicized by his role at the Constitutional Convention.

---

59. This incident is mentioned in Rutland, *Ordeal* . . ., 20. For much of the narrative account of ratification, I am indebted to his work, along with Main, *The Antifederalists*, 187-248; Cecilia M. Kenyon, ed., *The Antifederalists* (Boston, 1985 [orig. publ. 1966]); and Cecilia M. Kenyon, "Men of Little Faith: The Anti-Federalists on the Nature of Representative Government," *William and Mary Quarterly*, 3rd Ser., XII (Jan. 1955), 3-43.

60. A close analysis of the western vote in Pennsylvania can be found in Cornell, "Aristocracy Assailed," *JAH* LXXVI (1990), 1148-1172. Cornell also describes the "rough music" that followed ratification in Carlisle, which compared unfavorably to the peaceable Regulation. The Carlisle riots were not reported in the *American Herald* until 23 Jan., 1788.

61. Rutland, *Ordeal* . . ., 59.

Having relinquished his retirement in the wake of Shays' Rebellion, he had placed himself at the center of a heated political battle — where the Federalists had determined he should be. "I have observed," wrote one of his correspondents, "that your name to the new Constitution has been of infinite service. Indeed, I am convinced that if you had not attended the Convention, and the same paper had been handed out to the world, it would have met with a colder reception, with fewer and weaker advocates, and with more and more strenuous opponents."[62]

Most of the anti-Federalist attacks upon Washington were relatively blameless assertions: that he was "fallible on a subject that must be in a great measure novel to him," and that the Federalists were "prostituting the name of a Washington to cloak then-designs upon your liberties."[63] But other attacks were less solicitous. "The *President-general*, who is to be our *king* after this government is established, is vested with powers exceeding those of the most *despotic monarch*. . . . Under the proposed [Constitution], composed of an *elective king* and a standing army, officered by his sycophants, the starvelings of the Cincinnati, and an aristocratical Congress of the *well-born*, an iota of happiness, freedom or national strength cannot exist."[64] And some of the attacks were even more brutal — however well-justified. "We cannot think the noble general, has the same ideas with ourselves, with regard to the rules of right and wrong. . . ." wrote "The Yeomanry of Massachusetts," "to this day, living upon the labours of several hundreds of miserable Africans, as free born as himself."[65]

It would be difficult to overestimate the importance of Massachusetts in the process toward ratification. Contempo-

---

62. Quoted in Rutland, *Ordeal . . .*, 17.
63. "Centinel" [Samuel Bryan?], Letter II (Philadelphia) *Freeman's Journal*, Oct. 1787, Storing, ed., *Complete Anti-Federalist*, II, 144, and Letter IV (Philadelphia) *Independent Gazetteer*, [Nov. ?] 1787, *ibid.*, II, 163.
64. "Philadelphiensis" [Benjamin Workman], Letter X (Philadelphia) *Independent Gazetteer*, Mar. 1788, Storing, ed., *Complete Anti-Federalist*, III, 131.
65. *Massachusetts Gazette*, 25 Jan., 1788, Storing, ed., *Complete Anti-Federalist*, IV, 224.

raries agreed with Main: "Here lay the decisive conflict; had the Constitution lost in Massachusetts, it would never have been ratified."[66] This was clear almost from the moment it was signed, when even Connecticut appeared to Federalists a possible defeat. Writing to Knox from Hartford less than a week after the Constitutional Convention ended, Jeremiah Wadsworth expressed concern: "There is a strong party forming against the Convention and much reason to fear the new Government will not go down. If the Massachusetts rebellion had continued, we might have —" [A page of the letter appears to be missing at this point]. "Their is many of our Leading men who dreaded the lessening of their own power & they will, joined with the little Polliticians, form a great Majority in this State — but if Massachusetts adopt it I shall still hope for its adoption here [in Connecticut] in time. . . ."[67]

In the wake of the Pennsylvania vote, all eyes were fixed upon the Bay State, where the Regulators of a year before were now a formidable political opposition. Knox wrote in one letter that it was "conceived that the decision of Massachusetts would most probably settle the fate of the proposition," and, in another, "everything depends on Massachusetts should she set the bright example. . . ."[68] Madison wrote Washington that "the intelligence from Massachusetts begins to be very ominous. . . . The antifederal party is reinforced by the insurgents, and by the province of Mayne. . . ." It seemed there was "very great reason to fear that the voice of that State would be in the negative. The operation of such an event on this State" [Virginia] "may easily be foreseen. . . . The decision of Massachusetts either way will involve the result in this State." The specter of a continental uprising was still very much alive in Madison's mind. "The minority in Penna. is very restless under their defeat. . . . If backed by Massts. they will probably

---

66. Main, *The Antifederalists*, 200.
67. Wadsworth to Knox, 23 Sept., 1787, Knox Papers, XXI, 13. My thanks to Patrick Flynn and Peter Drummie at the MHS for confirming that one page is apparently missing from the Knox Papers Collection.
68. Knox to — , 10 Feb., 1788, Drake, *Life and Correspondence of Knox*, 150; Knox to —, New York, 3 Jan., 1788, Knox Papers XXI, 125.

be emboldened to make some more rash experiment."[69] And shortly after the state's ratification, Edward Carrington wrote to Knox that "the decision of Massachusetts is perhaps the most important event that ever took place in America, as upon her in all probability depended the fate of the Constitution — had she rejected I am sure there would not have been the most remote chance for its adoption in Virginia."[70]

It is not too much to say, then, that the fate of the United States Constitution hinged upon the ability of the former Regulators and their supporters to channel their dissent into politics in-doors, and thereby reassert their popular sovereignty by achieving electoral and judicial equality for rural interests and the veteran soldiery. While they failed to defeat the proposed Constitution, they succeeded to a fair degree, by their amendments, in securing their rights at the national level.

From the Federalists' perspective, hostility in Massachusetts towards the new Constitution arose directly from "the principle of insurgency expanded," wrote Knox. "Opposed to it are the late insurgents and all those who abetted their designs, constituting four-fifths of the opposition."[71] There was no doubt in anyone's mind that anti-Federalists Field the majority at the beginning of the Convention; the anti-Federalists had already proven their strength by postponing the proposed convention until January. But even ten days before the vote was taken, Nathaniel Gorham wrote to Madison that "I am in doubt whether they will approve the Constitution."[72]

---

69. Madison to Washington, New York, 20 Jan., 1788, *Madison Papers*, X, 399. Washington, in turn, wrote to Lincoln that "the decision of other States will have great influence here; particularly of one as respectable as Massachusetts." 31 Jan., 1788, *Writings of Washington*, XXIX, 396.

70. Carrington to Knox, Richmond, 13 Mar., 178[8] (misdated 1787), Knox Papers, XXI, 167.

71. Knox to —, 10 Feb., 1788, Drake, *Life and Correspondence of Knox*, 150. Equally, a Pennsylvania article reprinted in the *Massachusetts Gazette*, 12 Sept., 1787, had equated Antifederalism with "Shaysism" and "Toryism." Cited in Steven R. Boyd, "Shays's Rebellion and the Campaign for the Constitution," in Allis and Gross, eds., *In Debt to Shays* (forthcoming), n.p.

72. Gorham to Madison, Charles Town, 27 Jan., 1788, in *Madison Papers*, X, 435.

The anti-Federalists in Massachusetts, perhaps more than in any other state, had an ideological basis for their opposition, rooted in the town-meeting politics which they had experienced, and the "medieval forms of attorneyship in representation," to use Bailyn's words, which they had come to trust.[73] This was the nature of the representation sought by the Regulators, as evidenced by their petitions, before and during their demonstrations. Accustomed by tradition to elect advocates from among their neighbors to address local issues in the General Court, they were suspicious of Edmund Burke's formula for Parliamentary government, in which "not local purposes, not local prejudices ought to guide, but the general good, resulting from the general reason of the whole."[74] Their suspicions were even more salient at the continental level: who would represent the local interests of Northampton, say, in the new Federal government? This was especially true, given the talents of eastern bankers and lawyers to control the electoral process; talents proven, most convincingly, in the dubious establishment of the Massachusetts Constitution.

The "inherent ideology" of popular sovereignty which propelled the Regulation had been kindled by a crisis of representation. Likewise, anti-Federalist ideology in Massachusetts was predominantly opposed to the structure of representation proposed in the Constitution which, from their point of view, lacked adequate checks to restrain aristocratic impulses. The further removed representative government sat from the localities that elected them, the greater that mistrust; if the General Court in Boston could not be relied upon to represent their interests, how could westerners accept the governance of a new federal capital in some distant, undetermined city? They could not, especially if the representatives were too few and their terms too long. To the anti-Federalists, the value of controlling their political representation outweighed the benefits they saw in a firm Union. This fact had enormous consequences for the new nation, because, as Wood wrote, "in these

---

73. Bailyn, *Ideological Origins*, 164.
74. Burke quoted by Bailyn, *ibid.*

populist Anti-Federalist calls for the most explicit form of representation possible, and not in Madison's *Federalist* No. 10, lay the real origins of American pluralism and American interest-group politics."[75]

By comparison, Federalists in Massachusetts and elsewhere envisioned the Republic "from the top down," and did not hide their scorn for a government composed of "plain, illiterate husbandmen whose views seldom extended farther than to the regulation of highways, the destruction of wolves, wildcats, and foxes, and the advancement of the other little interests of the particular counties which they were chosen to represent."[76] Instead, they sought a body politic composed of delegates with *"respectability, integrity, property, & ability,"* who would transcend the particular concerns of rural counties and neighborhoods.[77]

Simmering beneath these two distinct concepts of republicanism was the deeper question of whether, in Hamilton's words, "societies of men are really capable or not, of establishing good government from reflection and choice. . . ."[78]

---

75. Wood, *The Radicalism of the American Revolution*, 259. Wood also wrote that "the Anti-Federalists lost the battle over the Constitution. But they did not lose the war over the kind of national government the United States would have. . . ." *Ibid.*

76. Quoted in Bailyn, *Ideological Origins*, 165. The Federalist suspicion of localist representation has been examined in an essay by Martin Diamond, "Democracy and *The Federalist*," in *The Confederation and the Constitution: The Critical Issues*, Gordon S. Wood, ed. (New York, 1973), 137-156. In an introduction to the essay, Wood noted that "separation of powers, representation, and the extended sphere of government, were all devised to control the great evil of republican government, majoritarian factionalism, and to preserve popular government against its own excesses. . . . The new government would work because its extended structure would result" [in Diamond's words] "'in the substitution of representation whose enlightened views and virtuous sentiments render them superior to local prejudices and to schemes of injustice.'" *The Federalist Papers*, according to Diamond, present a consistent argument of that central theme. *Ibid.*, 137.

77. Henry Jackson, describing the Federalist delegates at the Massachusetts Ratifying Convention, to Henry Knox, 20 Jan., 1788, Knox Papers, XXI, 145.

78. See above, 6.

Anarchy, or "mad democracy," was the Federalists' greatest dread, while the anti-federalists feared tyranny above all other conditions, as had the Commonwealthmen before them. So had opponents of the Constitution of 1778, like the citizens of Lenox, who objected that steep property qualifications for voters "declares Honest Poverty a Crime for which a large Number . . . who have fought and bled in their Countrys Cause are deprived of the above mentioned Rights (which is Tyranny)." The clearest exposition of the anti-federalist tenet was penned by the unsteady hand of Elbridge Gerry, citing Helvitius.[79] "Even sedition is not the most indubitable enemy to the publick welfare ...; its most dreadful foe is despotism, which always changes the character of nations for the worse, and is productive of nothing but vice."[80]

Since the Massachusetts Federalists were clearly outnumbered by their opponents, in the convention they modified their strategy of swift resolution, and heeded Lee's advice, reiterated by Caleb Strong, that they "examine coolly every article, clause, and word in the system proposed."[81] They also employed unscrupulous maneuvers with considerable success, including withdrawing all advertising from the anti-federalist press, juggling themselves onto key committees, and apparently tampering with the public mail from Philadelphia. Even George Richards Minot, appointed Secretary of the Ratifying Convention, deplored the Federalists' use of "*bad* measures in a *good* cause." Among these, he noted that the Federal-

79. For the Lenox return to the Constitution of 1778, see Taylor, *Massachusetts Documents*, 59. The Confédération Hélvetique — Switzerland — predated French philosopher Claude Adrien Helvétius (1715-1771) by some four hundred years, but Gerry may have presumed some link between the two, as he was defending the American Confederation that had so much in common with the thirteen Swiss "independent Commonwealths in strict alliance," which Madison had analyzed in his "Notes on Ancient and Modern Confederacies," *Madison Papers*, IX, 8-11.
80. [Elbridge Gerry], "A Columbian Patriot," "Observations On the new Constitution, and on the Federal and State Conventions," Ford, ed. *Pamphlets on the Constitution*, 4.
81. Rutland, *Ordeal* . . . , 40-41. See Strong, 14 Jan., 1788, in Elliott, ed., *Debates*, II, 3.

ists had tried "to *pack* a Convention whose sense would be different from that of the people. . . ." One method came to light in Stockbridge, where it was falsely announced that the anti-Federalist candidate had thrown his support behind the Federalist candidate, Theodore Sedgwick. And Main noted that, shortly before the final vote, when western delegates inquired about travel money for their return home, a rumor was circulated that, if ratification failed, there would be no pay for the delegates. "Never was there a political system introduced by less worthy means," the Convention's Secretary wrote unequivocally in his diary, "than the new constitution for the United States."[82]

The press was, as usual, overwhelmingly Federalist, with the important exception of the *American Herald*, which called every citizen "a TRAITOR to himself and his posterity, who shall ratify it . . . without first endeavouring to understand it."[83] The first anti-Federalist salvo in the press came from Elbridge Gerry, in the form of a letter read in both houses of the General Court. Gerry noted, as his first objections, that "there is no adequate provision for a representation of the people — that they have no security for the right of election . . . — that the judicial department will be oppressive . . ." and, he deplored that "the system is without the security of a bill of

---

82. Regarding the public mail, see *ibid.*, 59, 128-134. Feer, "George Richards Minot's *History of the Insurrections,*" *NEQ*, XXXV (1962), 207, quoting the "Diary of Minot," 1788, Sedgwick Papers, MHS. The Sedgwick incident and ff. appear in Main, *The Antifederalists*, 202-204, where he also notes that Minot's appointment as secretary may itself have been inveigled. Such chicanery was rampant across the state, despite Washington's admonition to Lincoln (now a delegate from Hingham), regretting "so powerful an opposition to the adoption of the proposed plan of Government with you. . . . The business of the Convention should be conducted with moderation, candor, & fairness (which are not incompatible with firmness). . . . the friends of the new System . . . would never be able, by precipitate or violent measures, to soothe and reconcile their [opponents] minds to the exercise of Government, which is a matter that ought as much as possible to be kept in view, during the proceedings." Washington to Lincoln, 31 Jan., 1788, *Writings of Washington*, XXIX, 396].
83. Quoted in Rutland, *Ordeal . . .*, 23.

rights."[84] All these objections reflected features of the Shay-site petitions preceding the Regulation, but they were all the more convincing, coming from a known enemy of the dissent-ers. *"Damn him — damn him,"* Jackson fumed to Knox about Gerry. "Everything . . . had the most favorable appearance in this States [*sic*], previous to this — and now I have doubts."[85]

Leading the Federalist offensive was a secret caucus that directed the campaign for ratification, beginning with the elec-tion of delegates.[86] This was still largely the party of James Bowdoin, who was himself a Federalist delegate, along with Lincoln, who had fought the rebels, Parsons, who had leg-islated against them, and Sedgwick, who had been accosted by them; hardly a crowd-pleasing crew. Higginson, too, was nominated, but defeated, possibly because of the 'S. H. Let-ter.' The anti-Federalist delegates, by comparison, lacked their most eloquent spokesmen: as Steven R. Boyd has pointed out, "Elbridge Gerry, Benajmin Austin, and James Winthrop — all of whom had been attacked as Shaysites in the press — failed in their bids for seats in the Convention."[87] Like the Shaysites, the anti-Federalists proved to be largely the party of Hancock, also a delegate. Upon this contest of personalities — a central issue in Shays' Rebellion — the outcome of the Convention would ultimately depend. Of course, Sam Adams had yet to be converted to Federalism, and among his friends it was be-lieved that "if the new Government should take Place. . . the first Rebellion against it would break out in the Town of Bos-

---

84. "Hon. Mr. Gerry's objections to signing the National Constitution," New-York, 18 Oct., 1787, printed in the *Massachusetts Centinel*, 3 Nov., 1787, and the *American Herald* on 5 Nov.
85. Jackson to Knox, 5 Nov., 1787, quoted in Rutland, *Ordeal . . .*, 24.
86. T. Dalton to — , Boston, 3 Feb., 1788, quoted in Morse, *The Federal-ist Party*, 42 n.6. At the critical moment of the convention, Dalton wrote to M. Hodge that the unannounced support of Hancock and Adams "is scarcely known out of our caucus, wherein we work as hard as in the convention." 31 Jan., 1788, *Ibid.*
87. See Harding, *The Contest Over Ratification*, 56 n. For the 'S. H. Letter,' see above, 169-170. Steven R. Boyd, "Shays's Rebellion and the Campaign for the Constitution," in Allis and Gross, eds., *In Debt to Shays* (forthcoming), n.p.

ton."[88] But the only endorsement the Federalists really needed — and they *did* need it — was the big signature of the public's most popular pander, John Hancock.

Seeing the size of the opposition, the Federalists seemed prepared from the start to consider the prospect of amendments, though no such mechanism was allowed by the Constitution until after ratification. In the first day of business, staunch Federalist Theodore Sedgwick allowed for that possibility.[89] This calmed some of the alarm among anti-Federalists, who objected to the all-or-nothing nature of the decision before them. As Harding pointed out, in the preceeding decade the citizens of Massachusetts had been called upon six times to consider constitutional matters, in ratifying both the Articles of Confederation and the state Constitutions proposed in 1778 and 1780; each time they had been given the opportunity to propose revisions. Bitterness still remained from the disregard that their amendments to the state Constitution had received in 1780, and they were particularly incensed at the demand that they swallow whole this large Federal pill. The possibility of amending the federal charter also opened the door for a second Federal Convention; thus they were willing to participate peaceably in the clause-by-clause analysis that followed.[90]

The two parties found common ground in at least one instance: a sharp sectional antagonism toward Southern interests. Slavery, commerce, and the question of ceding the Mississippi to Spain were the issues on which both sides agreed. And, while the issue of direct Federal taxation was hotly disputed, there was surprisingly little discord over the Federalists' vision of economic nationalism. For on both sides, as Richard Buel, Jr. has written, "in the immediate wake of Shays's Rebellion, one thing only was clear: a radically new

---

88. Samuel Osgood to Samuel Adams, 5 Jan., 1788, quoted in Rutland, *Ordeal* . . ., 97.

89. Sedgwick, Elliott, ed., *Debates*, II, 4.

90. Harding, *The Contest Over Ratification*, 5-7. An alternative plan, to transmit any amendments to the other states for their direct concurrence, was first proposed by John Avery in a letter to George Thatcher on 19 Jan.; see *ibid.*, 84.

departure was necessary if public credit, the absolute prerequisite for the founding of an enduring republic, were ever to
be established on a national scale."[91] This was especially clear
to those who held or had held public securities, including the
continental certificates that the soldiery had received.

Some anti-Federalists even blamed the Federalist movement on die dereliction of the state governments: as one
wrote, "If the continental treasury had been so far assisted,
as to have enabled us to pay the interest on our foreign debt,
possibly we should have heard little, very little, about a new
system of government."[92] But a more typical anti-Federal attitude was expressed in the Boston Gazette: "I had rather be
a free citizen of the small republic of Massachusetts, than an
oppressed subject of the great American empire."[93] This con-
trasted with the provocative, Federalist sentiment of General
William Heath, who declared to the convention that he considered himself "not as an inhabitant of Massachusetts, but as
a citizen of the United States."[94]

The earliest debates in the Massachusetts Convention (January 15th — 21st) addressed the question of representation:
specifically, the proposed biennial elections for representatives (rather than annual), and the power of Congress to determine the time, place, and manner of elections. This was one of
only two occasions when Shays' Rebellion was referred to, by
anti-Federalist General Samuel Thompson, who insisted that,
"had the last" [Bowdoin] "administration continued one year
longer, our liberties would have been lost, and the country

91. Richard Buel, Jr., "The Public Creditor Interest in Massachusetts Politics,
1780-1786," in Allis and Gross, eds., In Debt to Shays (forthcoming), n.p.
92. "Alfred," Boston American Herald, 31 Dec., 1787, quoted in Rutland, Ordeal . . ., 39-40. Rutland maintained that the rejection of the impost by New
York and Rhode Island in 1785 had proved to be the fatal blow for the Continental Congress. "But for their stubborn localism, one shrewd observer later
noted, 'in all human probability the Federal Constitution would not have been
called into existence.'" Ibid., 6.
93. "A Federalist" [sic], November 26th, 1787, Boston Gazette, in Storing, ed.,
Complete Anti-Federalist, IV, 118.
94. Elliott, ed., Debates, II, 12.

involved in blood."[95] He was quickly silenced by both parties, for the anti-Federalists did not wish to defend the Regulation, and the Federalists did not wish to offend their large opposition.

Meanwhile, the Federalist caucus took full measure of the opposition and, reluctantly, began preparing a framework for amendments that might save the day. Rufus King warned Madison that the Federalists "were now thinking of amendments to be submitted not as a condition of our assent and Ratification, but as the opinion of the Convention subjoined to their Ratification."[96] But Federalists were still not convinced that amendments submitted "as the opinion of the Convention" would be sufficient to insure passage. Only then did they turn to Hancock, who had remained uncommitted.

Herein lay perhaps the "least worthy means," to quote Minot, whereby Massachusetts ratified the Constitution of the United States, as Harding has shown. Rufus King explained the transaction two days later to Knox: "Hancock will hereafter receive the universal support of Bowdoin's friends" [in his re-election for Governor]; "and we told him that, if Virginia does not unite, which is problematical, he is considered as the only fair candidate for President." Accordingly, on January 31st, a series of amendments drafted by Theophilus Parsons was proposed to the Convention by Governor Hancock, who had thus far been absent, but now took the chair to preside. A committee of two members from each county (carefully stacked in the Federalists' favor) was then selected to consider the amendments, on the explicit condition that these were not intended "as a concession that amendments were necessary" — whatever that meant.[97]

---

95. *Ibid.*, II, 15. See also the speech of Jonathan Smith, in *ibid.*, II, 102.

96. Rufus King to James Madison, January 23rd, 1788, in *Madison Papers*, X, 411.

97. Harding, *The Contest Over Ratification*, 86. The Federalists kept their word: in the next guernatorial election, as reported in the *Independent Chronicle* April 10th, 1788, Hancock received all but ten of the 1,437 vote cast in Boston. King to Knox, February 3rd, 1788, Knox Papers, XXI, 127. Obviously, if Virginia ratified, Washington would be elected. Hancock had already been proposed as Vice-President by southern politicians seeking accommoda-

On February 6th, the Constitution, with nine "recommend-ed" amendments, was submitted for the final vote, and was ratified by a majority of nineteen, 187 to 168. Had just ten delegates from the west adhered to the anti-Federalist senti-ments of the Shaysite towns they represented, the Constitu-tion would not have been ratified by Massachusetts and, in all probability, would have been rejected as the fundamental law of the United States. Instead, it would have been remembered only by historians as, in Richard D. Brown's words, "a failed reform — a well-intended, brilliantly conceived and crafted dead letter."[98]

To appreciate the full impact of Shays' Rebellion upon the genesis of the Constitution, one must understand all the fac-tors that accounted for ratification in Massachusetts, since, as Main wrote, "it seems clear that a majority, though not a large one, of the citizens of Massachusetts opposed the Constitution when it was ratified. . . ."[99] Some of those factors cannot be measured: for example, the fear inspired by the Regulation that anarchy would follow if ratification failed, or the general anti-establishment sentiments throughout the western coun-ties after the Regulators were apprehended and convicted. But other factors are more easily identified.

It is true that, in the aftermath of Shays' Rebellion, both the Federalist and anti-Federalist parties were politically en-ergized, as Brown has argued. "From the 190 representatives in the 1786 General Court," he wrote, "the number climbed to

---

tion with the North; see *Massachusetts Centinel*, January 9th, 1788. Elliott, ed., *Debates*, II, 123. For identification of Parsons, see Morse, The Federalist Party in Massachusetts, 51. Elliott, ed., *Debates*, II, 141. Parsons, and other Federalists, had also persuaded Sam Adams to join their ranks by organizing a meeting of the mechanics of Boston in support of the Constitution; see Eben F. Stone, "Parsons and the Constitutional Convention of 1788," *Essex Historical Institute Collections XXXV* (1899), 87, 90-91.

98. Richard D. Brown, "Shays's Rebellion and the Ratification of the Federal Constitution in Massachusetts," Richard Beeman, Stephen Botein, and Ed-ward C. Carter, II, eds., *Beyond Confederation: Origins of the Constitution and American National Identity* (Chapel Hill, 1987), 127.

99. Main, *The Antifederalists*, 209.

. . . 364 at the ratifying convention," and many of these were westerners. Brown rightly noted that "the heavy-handed repression of the rebellion created a nearly disastrous backlash against the Constitution," and that "the reaction against the Bowdoin government threatened to defeat the Constitution. . ."[100]

But Brown overlooked the three principal reasons why Shays' Rebellion prepared Massachusetts for ratification. The Federalists won their cause only because: 1). they had recruited Hancock in a corrupt deal, after he had reaffirmed his popularity in the west by pardoning the Regulators; 2). they had accepted amendments reaffirming the citizens' electoral, judicial, and constitutional rights, which reflected the local, political demands of the Shaysite petitions; and 3). they had already addressed some of the judicial reforms that Shaysites had demanded. Had any one of the three been wanting, the Constitution would almost certainly have been rejected.

Hancock, to begin with, had been utterly non-commital toward the fruits of Philadelphia. But it was well-remembered on both sides of the debate that the Regulators had consistently made one demand: that the sessions of the courts be postponed until after the next gubernatorial election, when they could replace Bowdoin with Hancock. Just as western antipathy toward Bowdoin personally has been overlooked, the extraordinary trust that Hancock inspired has been downplayed. Perhaps this is because, from the modern perspective, Hancock appears as a slightly ludicrous political whore; notwithstanding his peccadilloes, the influence he wielded was enormous. Had he kept his silence, the Constitution might have been ratified, with amendments; but if he had thrown his weight against the Federalists, that would have been unlikely, even with amendments. One can even surmise that, if his "arrangement" with the Federalists had become known through the press, it would not have diminished the effect of his endorsement on the swing-vote of western delegates. In fact, they would probably have been pleased to know in advance

100. Brown, "Shays's Rebellion . . .," 122-123, 127.

that he would be re-elected over Bowdoin, and even more pleased to see him as the first President or Vice-President of the United States.

Second, the amendments which placated the anti-Federalists — and served as the basis for the Bill of Rights — addressed issues nationally which, at the local level, had been at the heart of Shaysite discontent.[101] These included: limiting Congress's power to dictate the time, place, and manner of elections; guaranteeing adequate representation at the national level; limiting Congress's power to levy direct taxes; re-asserting an individual's right not to be tried for any serious crime without a prior grand jury indictment; limiting the Federal Courts' jurisdiction in interstate matters; and reserving to the states such powers not exclusively granted to the Union.

Granted, these amendments, as drafted by the committee stacked by Federalists, did not address all the Shaysites' demands; nor did they offer all the guarantees — freedom of the press and of religious conscience, for example — later contained in the Bill of Rights. But joined with the fact that it was John Hancock who presented them, and consequently gave his personal endorsement to the Constitution, they were sufficient to mollify western doubts. More than that, perhaps, the amendments gave the anti-Federalists a positive agenda to contend for, rather than merely defending "the good old way" of the Confederation. By proposing revisions that Federalists could not object to, they succeeded in impacting the fundamental law of the land with their reassertion of popular sovereignty — the lynch-pin of their traditional political ideology.[102]

---

101. The nine amendments are in Elliott, ed., *Debates*, II, 177. The fourteen amendments which erroneously appear in *Debates, Resolutions . . . of the Convention* (1808) are of a later date, proposed by the U. S. Senate, before they were reduced to twelve and sent to the state legislatures for ratification, where the first two amendments failed to pass.

102. After Massachusetts' ratification, Washington wrote that "there was not a member of the [Philadelphia] convention, I believe, who had the least objection to what is contended for by the Advocates of a *Bill of Rights* and *Tryal by Jury* . . .," but he felt that such measures were "nugatory." Washington to Lafayette, 28 Apr., 1788, *Writings of Washington*, XXIX, 478. Main identified

Finally, there was what John L. Brooke called "the interweaving of local circumstance and national revolutionary process."[103] In a recent essay, Brooke examined how, "to a startling degree, Massachusetts's ratification of the Constitution depended on the gradual progress of a revolutionary settlement of county institutions in these hinterland localities."[104] Brooke focused on the town of Chesterfield, in Hampshire County, where, in response to the dissenters' petitions, after the Regulation "the General Court established four registries of deeds and four sittings of the probate court at Deerfield, Northampton, Hadley, and Springfield. Ten months later, Benjamin Bonney and nine other delegates from small towns in the west Hampshire hills voted to ratify the Constitution. . . . If these [ten] towns had followed the example of their neighbors in Deerfield and Conway, of the east Hampshire hill towns, or of Worcester County, the Constitution might well never have been ratified in Massachusetts." Brooke concluded that "the selective settlement of county institutions in Hampshire County played a decisive role in the far grander national revolutionary settlement."[105]

---

fifteen delegates who shifted their votes after Hancock presented the amendments, though only a few of these had Shaysite sympathies. Main, *The Antifederalists*, 206. See also Michael Lienesch, "Reinterpreting Rebellion: The Influence of Shays's Rebellion on American Political Thought," in Allis and Gross, eds., *In Debt to Shays* (forthcoming), n.p.

103. John L. Brooke, "To the Quiet of the People: Revolutionary Settlements and Civil Unrest in Western Massachusetts, 1774-1789," *William and Mary Quarterly*, 3rd Ser., XLVI (July 1989), 460.

104. *Ibid.*, 459

105. *Ibid.* For a comparison between delegates' votes and the sympathies of their towns, see George Donald Melville, "Evidences of Economic and Social Influences at Work in the Massachusetts Convention Which Ratified the Constitution," [unpubl. Masters' Thesis, University of New Hampshire, 1920], copy at the Springfield Town Library, Massachusetts. Main noted that "a large number of towns (over fifty) did not send delegates to the convention, and of these, two-thirds would probably have been Antifederal. Their absence gave the Federalists a better chance to bring about the necessary shift of votes." Main, *The Antifederalists*, 209. In fact, if Main's estimates are accurate, those delegates alone would have defeated ratification. Unfortunately, there is no way to know why those towns were not represented.

It is impossible to know, but easy to guess, that without all three of these factors — Hancock's endorsement, the amendments, and the resolution of some local issues in the wake of the Regulation — ratification would not have received its slim margin. The outcome, then, of the Massachusetts Ratification Convention depended upon a series of concessions by Federalists which addressed some of the issues that had fueled the Regulation.

When Madison reported to Washington of the victory in Massachusetts, he added that "the Convention of N Hampshire is now sitting. There seems to be no question that the issue there will add a *seventh* pillar, as the phrase now is, to the fœderal Temple."[106] He spoke too soon: less than three weeks after Boston ratified, New Hampshire Federalists were forced to adjourn, after losing a preliminary, unrecorded vote of 54-51. Just weeks later, the people of Rhode Island, to whom the Constitution had been submitted directly as a referendum, overwhelmingly rejected the plan. Federalists had temporarily lost what today's politicians call "the big mo'," but it was soon recaptured in Maryland and South Carolina, leaving only the all-important assent of Virginia and New York still to be obtained.

The only explicit role that Shays' Rebellion played in the ratification debates after Massachusetts lay in *The Federalist Papers*. In the influential essay *No. 10*, published across the continent before the Boston Convention, Madison had argued that "a rage for paper money, for an abolition of debts, for an equal division of property, or for any other improper or wicked project, will be less apt to pervade the whole body of the Union, than a particular member of it. . ."[107] Hamilton rarely referred to "the actual insurrections and rebellions in Massachusetts Regulation," but he offered the observation that, "if SHAYS had not been a *desperate debtor*, it is much to

106. *Madison Papers*, X, 510.
107. Madison, *The Federalist, No. 10*, (Philadelphia, 1977, [orig. publ. 1787]), 70.

be doubted whether Massachusetts would have been plunged into a civil war."[108] These and other remarks make it clear that Hamilton was referring to Shays' Rebellion when he wrote, in *Federalist No. 1*, "the crisis, at which we are arrived. . ."[109]

In Virginia, as in Massachusetts, "the decision would be made in the west," according to Main, where, apart from the Shenandoah valley, sentiments were strongly anti-Federalist.[110] But on June 25th, 1788 the Constitution carried the day by eighty-nine votes to seventy-nine. Four days earlier, the second session of the New Hampshire convention had also finally ratified. News of ratification in these two states proved decisive to the contest in New York, where now the only prospect was to remain outside the union, and possibly see southern counties secede from the independent state, producing commotions that could lead to civil war.[111] So, on July 26th, 1788, the Convention at Poughkeepsie voted 30-27 to ratify unconditionally, while recommending a bill of rights, just as Massachusetts had done.

The impact of Shays' Rebellion on the ratification of the Constitution was greater than its effect during the Constitutional Convention — especially in Massachusetts. Again, of course, it was not the Regulation itself, but the shadow it cast of a possible civil war, that seemed to represent the inevitable outcome of a failure to ratify, and so held the nation's feet to the fire. Two full years after the first farmers gathered to prevent the courts from sitting, a national revolutionary settlement was achieved, in which even the most ardent anti-Federalists at last capitulated gracefully.

---

108. *Ibid.*, Hamilton, *The Federalist, No. 6*, 37-38, 33. It should be remembered that no shots were fired by the Regulators during this "civil war."
109. *Ibid., No. 1*, 3. Hamilton, of course, was especially concerned with "the amazing violence & turbulence of the democratic spirit." Hamilton at the Philadelphia Convention, June 18th, 1787, in Ferrand, I, 289.
110. Main, *The Antifederalists*, 225. See also the inestimable work of Orin Grant Libby, *The Geographical Distribution of the Vote of the Thirteen States on the Federalist Constitution* (New York, 1969 [orig. publ. 1894]), 34-37.
111. Main, *The Antifederalists*, 238.

CHAPTER EIGHT

Conclusion

The cost of war is blood and money: after the former has been freely spilt, the latter must still be squeezed from the citizenry. Such was the case with the War of Independence, which could only be paid for by a levy of taxes exceeding those which had provoked the imperial crisis. As early as 1779, Timothy Dwight wrote from Northampton that, "without a gift of prophecy, I will venture to foretell that the movement which forces small farmers to sell their real estate for the purpose of paying taxes will produce a revolution."[1]

In Massachusetts, as the war-debt grew in the early 1780s, Governor Hancock indulged the people with lenient tax measures, but his unpopular successor did not. Having fought a war for the better part of a decade motivated by the slogan "no taxation without representation," the citizens of western Massachusetts found themselves effectively disenfranchised by the machinery of the Constitution of 1780: what representation they had still did not protect their interests. As a result of this inadequate representation, the small farmers and former veteran soldiery rose up in a series of traditional demonstrations to postpone the seizure of their farms until after the next election, when they could reinstall Hancock. Although their movement was well within the bounds of customary protest, the former soldiers who were still owed backpay and land

---

1. Timothy Dwight to Samuel Parsons, 23 Apr., 1779, in Charles Hill, ed., *Life and Letters of Samuel Holden Parsons* . . . (Binghamton, N.Y., 1905), 237.

chose to act in a paramilitary fashion, marching with arms in rank and file across the western counties. They never fired a shot when assembled as a body; nonetheless, the widespread movement clearly represented a threat to the established government. By interfering with the judicial process, the Regulators exceeded their constitutional right to convene "for the common good." This might not have caused great alarm in the Royal Province of Massachusetts, but it posed an unprecedented challenge to the authority of the newly-established and untested Commonwealth.

The response to the Regulation was hindered by an empty treasury both in Congress, whose arsenal was surrounded, and in Massachusetts, whose harsh policies were being defied. This inability to react effectively was evidence in itself that the Confederation was not a viable revolutionary settlement, if it could not defend its store of weapons or provide the wherewithal to do so. Not even by misleading Americans with fabricated rumors of an imminent Indian war could Congress protect its own property. The only apparent solution was to raise money from the mercantile élite of the state, who had the most to benefit from the reimposition of law and order. Their money was used to recruit former officers of the Revolution to suppress the protests by the veteran soldiery. The result was to give this peaceable confrontation many of the aspects of class warfare.

The gentlemen and officers who united to crush the Regulation had a larger purpose in mind: by re-naming the demonstrations "Shays' Rebellion," and depicting the protests as the first stages of civil war, they found a long-awaited opportunity to alarm the thirteen independent states into national consolidation, and establish a federal government. Toward that end, their trump card was the unique figurehead of George Washington, who was persuaded to forswear his "oath of retirement" by distorted and inflated accounts of the Regulation. His participation in the formation of the new constitution provided the most effective propaganda the nationalists could engage to accomplish their objective.

The United States Constitution was the product of two dynamic social forces that had evolved together for more than a century, creating the rich, distinctive intellectual traditions — popular sovereignty and mercantile élitism — that collided in Shays' Rebellion. Popular sovereignty supposed that all power derived from the people, and returned to them as an electorate. Mercantile elitism assumed that an ever-expanding market was the supreme force — the "invisible hand" — that must govern political relations and, through new systems of capital formation, raise a few ambitious men above the many others.[2] Beginning in 1776, with the Declaration of Independence and *The Wealth of Nations*, these two republican strands of thought that had emerged from the Enlightenment fully spun, together provided the fabric of American fundamental law, to darn the gaping hole that remained after the colonies tore themselves free from regal authority. This fundamental law reflected not only the two strains of political economy across the continent, but also the personal convictions and aspirations of the individual Framers, whose opposition *mentalité* had ignited the Revolution, and whose economic ambitions had been reinforced by more than a century of free-market disciples and apologists, culminating with Adam Smith.

Only in the aftermath of Shays' Rebellion could the synthesis of these parallax views of civic humanism be achieved, not because of what the Regulators did, but because of what they evoked. During the first elimination of monarchy in British history, the Commonwealth of Oliver Cromwell had unleashed the powerful paradigm of self-governance by the

---

2. Appleby quoted Thomas Mun, the seventeenth-century economic theorist, asserting the autonomy of market relations: "'Let Princes oppress, Lawyers extort, Usurers bite, Prodigals wast,' treasure will follow trade . . .' and this must come to pass by a Necessity beyond all resistance.'" Thomas Mun, *England's Treasure by Foreign Trade* (London, 1664), 218-219, quoted in Joyce Appleby, "The Social Origins of American Revolutionary Ideology," *Journal of American History* LXIV (Mar. 1978), 941. Appleby also observed that "the development of the free market was one of the few true social novelties in history, changing the relation . . . of person to person and of people to government . . .;" this development could not be assimilated into classical theory, in which irreversible processes of change were "equated with degeneracy." *Ibid.*, 939-940.

people, or popular sovereignty. Loyalists, led by the aristocracy of Cavaliers, eventually restored themselves by restor-
ing their king, and thereby defined the dissenters as opposition. Now, after only the second occasion when a British
society had divested itself of monarchy, Shays' Rebellion
evinced that earlier trauma, raising the ghost of democratic
excess fueled by communistic fervor.[3] By sounding the alarm
that society might tear itself apart once again, as it had in
the 1640s, Shays' Rebellion provided an all-important *motive*
for reconciling these two views: the self-preservation of the
former colonies. This would entail a revolutionary transition
from traditional hierarchies of patriarchal dependence to a
new *Weltanschauung* based upon contract that featured the
notions of equal opportunity, capital formation, and meritoc-
racy. The result of Shays' Rebellion was not the defeat of the
lower classes by the upper, but the success of that transition,
setting the stage for the Industrial Revolution.

The subsistence farmer and the journeyman mechanic, just
a few generations removed from European peasantry, had not
yet understood the power of the producer over the consumer,
and so they sustained a traditional social order based upon
patronage and dependence.[4] But with the end of the Revolu-

---

3. Christopher Hill wrote about "the essential unity of the three great revolutions" [in the 1640s, 1680s, and 1770s], and the similarity of "the problems
set for the propertied classes in those revolutions when the overthrow of the
old order had led to the emergence of democratic movements." Christopher
Hill, *Puritanism and Revolution* (New York, 1986), 301. But the Regulation
represented *both* a democratic, political movement and a reactionary re-asser-
tion of traditional economic relations. In that respect, as Appleby wrote about
the English Country party, "nothing could have been more antithetical to the
goals of the Opposition" than the progressive developments of "the extension
of the market, the increase in the division of labor . . ., the commercialization
of agriculture, and the conversion of the English peasantry into a mobile, free
labor force." Appleby, *op. cit.*, 939.
4. Huntington noted that the potential for effective resistance by peasants
comes as "the barriers to communication and transportation are broken down.
. . . The peasant comes to realize not only that he is suffering but that something can be done about this suffering. Nothing is more revolutionary than
this awareness. . . ." Huntington went on to explain why "the tensions of the
countryside are potentially so much more revolutionary than those of the city,

tion and the departure of the hereditary aristocracy, the rising mercantile élite betrayed that traditional model of society to enforce a new economic order founded upon contractual commitment, an indispensable element of the emergent capitalism. Massachusetts farmers and wage-laborers who had risked their all in a war for self-government resisted that paradigm shift in a ritual, non-violent show of their numbers which, in a post-revolutionary English culture, evoked Levellers, the redistribution of property, and civil war.

In the Constitution, the two strains of thought (reflected, if imperfectly, in the motives behind the first settlements along the Chesapeake and Massachusetts Bays), merged in a single document intended to be accessible to all, that synthesized contractual dominion with popular sovereignty. In fact, the Constitution, whose principles were hammered out in a prolonged series of multi-faceted negotiations spanning a decade, was a social contract between a people and their government that asserted popular sovereignty but defended private interest. It served not only as a foundation for government, but also as a sort of warranty that every family could keep beside their Bible and read beside their hearth, to determine for themselves the legitimacy of the particular laws that governed their daily lives.

The synthesis of these two ideologies into a single doctrine, however it might be achieved, was intended by Madison to adapt the cyclical mechanism of history — the mainspring of human society — into a dynamic contest of interests that could, like a gyroscope, stand still on its own, because of its motion. Thereby the natural law of inevitable recurrence, which guaranteed that "what happen'd yesterday will come to pass again," might be co-opted into the political order and all its transactions, and be thereby transformed from a constant peril into a dynamic principle for governance.

The conflicting interests of local government, state authority, and federal jurisdiction were not resolved in Phila-

---

since 'the peasant has no choice but to attack the existing system of ownership and control.'" Samuel P. Huntington, *Social Change in a New Political Order* (New Haven, 1968), 299.

delphia in September, 1786, nor in the months of ratification that followed. What was produced by that process, however, was a framework whereby those authorities could be set in motion concentrically, along with the unconfirmed faith that, with proper management, their interaction would keep those interests in balance.

To the early Massachusetts nationalists — especially Knox, Higginson, Bowdoin, and the officers of the Cincinnati — Shays' Rebellion provided the critical occasion upon which to advance their cause. On the one hand, it was important to them that the malcontents be suppressed. Their greater goal, however, was not a Thermidorean coup, but the attainment of a stable, revolutionary settlement that would accommodate their global economic interests in a way that the Articles of Confederation could not. To do so, they played upon fears and memories that seemed to justify inherently whatever measures that they took.[5]

If the Regulation itself was not intended to threaten traditional economic relations, the fringe activities and declarations of a violent few sufficed to establish the potential for a war between the classes. An anonymous note sent to Governor Bowdoin during the Regulation is a good example:

> This is to lett the Gentellmen of Boston [know?] that wee Country men will not pay taxes, as the think. But Lett them send the Constabel to us and we'll nock him down for offering to come near us. If you Dont lower the taxes we'll pull down the town house about you ears. It shall not stand long then or else they shall be blood spilt. We Country men will not be imposed on. We fought of our Libery as well as you did. . . .[6]

---

5. In a very different context, David Brion Davis wrote that perhaps "the circumstances of the Revolution conditioned Americans to think of resistance to a dark, subversive force as the essential ingredient of their national identity. . . ." David Brion Davis, *Slave Power Conspiracy and the Paranoid Style* (Baton Rouge, 1969), 29.
6. An anonymous Regulator to Governor Bowdoin, n.d., *Bowdoin-Temple Papers*, quoted in James MacGregor Burns, *The Vineyard of Liberty* (New York,

While such threats did not represent the aims of the Regulation proper, they served to justify the nationalists' argument that civil war was possible if the established government lacked the wherewithal to enforce obedience to its laws.[7]

The causal connection between Shays' Rebellion and the drafting and ratification of the Constitution has often been assumed by historians, and occasionally challenged, but it has never been thoroughly examined. Early this century, for example, Charles Francis Adams quoted from the diary of his grandfather, John Quincy Adams (a student in the law office of Theophilus Parsons during the 1780s), asserting without much evidence or argument that the Constitution was "extorted from the grinding necessity of a reluctant nation," and added that "Shays's 'Rebellion' was the extorting agency."[8] A close examination of the evidence bears this out. While the patriotic antiquarian may prefer to envisage the Constitution as an embodiment of rational idealism, its formulation was, in fact, firmly rooted in practical exigencies and cautious empiricism. As John Dickinson put it during the Philadelphia Convention: "Experience must be our only guide. Reason may mislead us."[9] Without proof that the Confederation was bro-

---

1982), 14.

7. Even today, the Worcester Court House is engraved with the dubious doctrine: "Obedience to the Law is Liberty."

8. Charles Francis Adams, prefatory remarks to John Noble, "A Few Notes on Shays Rebellion," in *Proceedings of the American Antiquarian Society* XV (1902-3), 114-121, 200-232; quotation on 120. Adams also wrote: "I believe it is generally conceded that Shays's 'Rebellion,' so-called, was one of the chief impelling and contributory causes to the framing and adoption of the constitution of 1788. A rude shock, it awakened the whole thirteen States to a realizing sense of the anarchical abysm on the edge of which they were then lingering. In my belief poor old Shays, and his somewhat ragged, helter-skelter and tatterdemalion following have, at the hands of our so-called historians, received harsh and inconsiderate treatment. They have been pronounced guilty. . . . Undoubtedly law-breakers, they broke the law only under circumstances of almost intolerable hardship, not to say oppression. . . ." *Ibid.*, 114.

9. John Dickinson, quoted in Max Farrand, "The Federal Constitution and the Defects of the Confederation," in *The Formation and Ratification of the Constitution: Major Historical Interpretations*, Kermit L. Hall, ed. (New York, 1987), 155.

ken, it would not have been fixed.[10]

Nor would the constitutional remedy have been ratified — a point that has not been examined until very recently. The process of ratification presented the Federalists with a series of hurdles, among which any of the largest could have terminated the contest. This was especially true of Massachusetts, where local issues and personalities that had crystallized during Shays' Rebellion provided both obstacles to national union, and the means for surmounting them.

The consequences of Shays' Rebellion stretched well beyond its direct impact upon the constitutional process. Washington's use of federal troops during the Whiskey Rebellion six years later owed directly to the Regulation, and set the precedent for a number of instances in the twentieth century when federal intervention was a presidential option: in Birmingham, 1963, at Kent State, 1970, and in Los Angeles, 1992.

At the end of the turbulent 1960s, Supreme Court Justice William O. Douglas published a small book of essays entitled *Points of Rebellion*, in which he defended the right of citizens to peaceful protest, and traced the instances of political violence in American society back to Shays' Rebellion, comparing the "sense of futility which permeates the present series of protests and dissents" to that which had sparked the Regulation.[11] While Douglas's characterization of the rebellion may have been wanting, the comparison he drew nonetheless suggested both the importance and effectiveness of popular disobedience in influencing government policy and constitutional law. Interesting research remains to be done, for example,

---

10. Shortly after the Regulation was suppressed, Washington wrote to Lafayette that "these disorders are evident marks of a defective government; indeed the thinking part of the people of this Country are now so well satisfied of this fact that most of the Legislatures have appointed, and the rest it is said will appoint, delegates to meet at Philadelphia . . . to revise and correct the defects of the federal System." Washington to Lafayette, 25 Mar., 1787, in *Writings of Washington*, XXIX, 184.

11. William O. Douglas, *Points of Rebellion* (New York, 1970), 56-57.

on the impact of the Vietnam war and the anti-war movement on the Twenty-Sixth Amendment, adopted in 1971, which extended the franchise to citizens eighteen years of age or older.

Establishing the fact that Shays' Rebellion was a determinative factor in the constitutional movement of 1787-1788 may serve to place other less satisfactory historical interpretations in a more realistic light. Both the economic determinism of Beard and the localist perspective of Feer alike were flawed by their failure to recognize the importance of the ideological suppositions permeating eighteenth-century Anglo- American society. It was those suppositions that linked the demonstrations in western Massachusetts to the debates in Philadelphia.

Social historians may benefit from a closer examination of intellectual history, even in the study of unsophisticated and inarticulate crowd actions. The ideological precepts underlying riots, demonstrations, and other popular disobedience may often be obscure and elementary, but they may also provide the historian with the only means available for understanding mass movements. For, as Congresswoman Maxine Waters observed in the wake of the Los Angeles riots of 1992, such disturbances are often "the voice of those who are not heard."

HISTORIOGRAPHIC ESSAY

Minot and the Historiography of Shays' Rebellion

George Richards Minot, the first historian to address the Regulation, was concerned that Shays' Rebellion might have engendered "many misconceived ideas, tending to the discredit of the country."[1] So, less than a year after the unrest concluded, he published his *History of the Insurrections . . .*, acknowledging that "in some countries, strong reasons might operate, for leaving it to posterity to discover facts, under disadvantages of distance of time, and the false impressions, perhaps of imperfect tradition."[2] Regrettably, Minot did not avail himself of all those advantages that contemporaneity afforded him. Writing with a deadline more suited, perhaps, to a journalist than an historian, Minot initiated an imperfect tradition of his own, setting the tone for many scholars of the next hundred years.

Minot was the son of a successful Boston merchant who, like his father, graduated from Harvard, and soon after studied law in the cabinet of William Tudor. His law degree in 1781 prepared him, at the age of twenty-three, to become the first clerk of the House of Representatives under the new Massachusetts Constitution.[3] As a contemporary put it, "being clerk of the representatives at the time, when the causes which

---

1. Minot, *History*, iii.
2. *Ibid.*, iv.
3. "George Richards Minot," by Stewart Mitchell, in *Dictionary of American Biography*, Dumas Malone, ed., 20 vols. (New York, 1928-1936) VII, 31.

finally produced the insurrection were operating, [Minot] had an opportunity of being well acquainted with the debates and proceedings of the house."[4] From this vantage-point Minot knew all the views expressed in the House, but gained little understanding of the men who practiced politics "without doors." This phase of Minot's public career began with the Massachusetts Constitution and ended with the state's ratification of the Federal Constitution, for at the first meeting of the Massachusetts Ratification Convention Minot won the first vote, to become the secretary for the Convention.[5]

Less than six months later, Minot's *History of the Insurrections* . . . was published. He promptly sent a copy of the book to General Washington (as well as copies to John Adams, John Jay, and others), with a letter of introduction from General Benjamin Lincoln, "as a continuance of information upon the important subject of domestick history."[6] In three weeks Washington replied with just the sort of understated but enthusiastic endorsement Minot might have prayed for. "The intrinsick merit of the work (so far as I am able to form a judgement from its perspicuity and impartiality) carries a sufficient recommendation to ensure a favourable reception." Washington then related the Rebellion directly to the aftermath of the war, and characterized it as a major link in American, not just Massachusetts, history: "The series of events, which followed from the conclusion of the war, forms a link of no ordinary magnitude in the chain of the American Annals. That portion of domestic History . . . deserved to be discussed." He added that he "comprehended fully the difficulty of stating facts on the spot, amidst the living actors and recent animosities," and concluded by passing the torch unequivocally to Minot. "I always feel a singular satisfaction in discovering proofs of talents and patriotism in those who are soon to take the parts of the generation, which is now hastening to

---

4. James Freeman, "The Character of Judge Minot . . .," in *Massachusetts Historical Society Collections 8* (Boston, 1802), 91.
5. Elliot, ed., *Debates*, II, 1.
6. Minot to Washington, Boston, 7 Aug., 1788, as quoted in "Character of Minot . . .," *Coll. of Mass. Hist. Soc.* (1802), 99n.

leave the stage."[7]

With the publication of *The History of the Insurrections . . .*, Minot "became entitled to a high rank among the American authors," and three years later he was welcomed as one of the ten founding members of the Massachusetts Historical Society.[8] Although he wrote with a predictable bias, Miot's account merits special scrutiny because of its general accuracy, as well as its influence.[9] As Michael Kraus put it, "giving only one side of the controversy, [Minot] failed to explain why the debt-burdened farmers flouted authority. . . . His volume on Shays' Rebellion was, however, used by a number of historians and for a long time helped perpetuate the conservative interpretation of those troubled times."[10]

Considering his close ties to the General Court and his failure to seek out the views of any insurgents, the evenhandedness of Minot's narrative is remarkable. Perhaps its most valuable contribution lay in the fact that, unlike his more conservative acquaintances, Minot placed the unrest in the context of the state's war debt, which "when consolidated, amounted to upwards £1,300,000 besides £250,000 due to the officers and soldiers of their line of the army. Their proportion of the federal debt was not less, by a moderate computation, than one million and an half of the same money. . . . Upon the right management then, of the publick debt, the future tranquility of the Commonwealth greatly depended."[11]

By so framing the circumstances of the Regulation, Minot placed considerable responsibility for the unrest upon the members of the General Court; then, by depicting the division

7. *Writings of Washington*, XXX, 65.
8. "Character of Minot. . .," *Coll. of Mass. Hist. Soc.* (1802), 91-92.
9. Minot's opinions were even more one-sided while the Rebellion was in progress: during its final throes, he wrote that "Daniel Shays's decapitation would have dissolved a common tie, or prevented [the rebels] engrafting their several oppositions upon his." See Diary of Minot, 9 June, 1787, Sedgwick Papers, MHS, also quoted in David P. Szatmary, *Shays' Rebellion: The Making of an Agrarian Insurrection* (Amherst, 1980), xi.
10. Michael Kraus, *A History of American History* (New York, 1937), 140-141.
11. Minot, *History*, 5-6.

which appeared between the men of landed interests, who "began to speak plainly against trade," and the "commercial men," Minot stressed that this split "led to a division upon all questions of taxation, and even upon other subjects where it was supposed the strength of these parties could be tried."[12]

It is not surprising that a "government man" like Minot failed to note the heated division caused by the Constitution of 1780, and its role in the Regulation. He was not unaware of the connection, for he first noted that a petition from Worcester "prayed that the sense of all the towns in the Commonwealth might be taken, respecting the necessity of revising the constitution; and, in case two thirds of them should be in favour of that revision, that a state convention might be called for revising it."[13] Later he asserted that "the cry for revising the constitution was answered, by shewing the difficulties that were encountered in obtaining it; the little prospect there was of mending it; and the improbability of finding at this time, that unusual spirit and mutual condescension and domestick harmony" that would make revisions possible.[14] Thus Minot seemed to acknowledge that 'mending' was called for, but not that this issue had been a fundamental source of western discontent.

Minot also failed to recognize the cumulative impact of conservative fiscal policies upon the western population. Minot did cite the Hampshire county petition drawn up on August 22, 1786, in which one grievance specified was "the present mode of taxation as it operates unequally betweeen the polls and estates, and between landed and mercantile interests."[15] But he did not recognize how egregiously this operated in the cash-poor west. "The proportion of the state tax raised by poll taxes," wrote Morison, "rose from 30 per cent in 1778 to 40 per cent in 1786 — one of the many acts of injustice that helped bring on Shays' Rebellion."[16] Since the overall tax

---

12. *Ibid.*, 10.
13. *Ibid.*, 53.
14. *Ibid.*, 67-68.
15. Minot, *History*, 34.
16. Morison, "The Struggle over the Constitution," *AHA Proceedings* (1917),

burden grew dramatically in the postwar era, the combined effect of the various conservative policies showed a patent lack of concern for the people's ability to pay the taxes.[17] "When it is recalled that every male sixteen and over . . . had to pay a poll tax," emphasized Taylor, "one can see that a man with several grown sons was hard pressed by this tax if by their combined efforts he and his sons managed to run a farm only on subsistence level."[18]

The hardships brought about by these conservative policies were compounded by three other factors noted by Minot: "the scarcity of specie," the "loss of many markets to which Americans had formerly resorted with their produce," and "operative in the commotions . . ., if it may not be called their primary cause, was the accumulation of private debts."[19] This last cause, he blamed upon the "disposition of the people to indulge the use of luxuries. . . . An emulation prevailed among men of fortune, to exceed each other in the full display of their riches. This was imitated among the less opulent classes of citizens. . . ."[20] Still, Minot distanced himself somewhat from the harsher conservative attitudes of his contemporaries, whereby "the conduct of the insurgents was attributed to a wish to subvert all order and government."[21]

Minot noted that the desire for paper currency, which Feer called "the surest test of dissident 'radicalism,'" was "very strenuously made to the legislature" but added that "the proposition, however, was the less expedient, as great quantities of this currency in fact existed and were circulating in the Commonwealth at the very time it was made." He also ar-

---

353. Minot wrote that the poll tax "did not amount to sixteen pence upon a rateable poll," but the actual taxes demanded were much higher. Minot, *History*, 67.

17. "From 1774 to 1778, the most trying years of the Revolution, officials levied £408,976 in taxes. Tax assessments then jumped to £662,476 for the 1783-1786 period. . . ." Szatmary, *Shays' Rebellion*, 31. See also East, "Massachusetts Conservatives," in Morris, ed., *Era of the American Revolution*, 356.

18. Taylor, *Western Massachusetts*, 139.

19. Minot, *History*, 13.

20. *Ibid.*, 11.

21. *Ibid.*, 68.

gued that the schedule proposed by the dissidents for planned depreciation at fixed rates was "so wild a proposal [that it] served rather to retard than advance the views of the party."[22]

Minot's chronicle of the events of the insurrection is, for the most part, as thorough and even-handed as his enumeration of its causes. He recounted the obstruction of the various court sessions between August and November, in Northampton, Worcester, Concord, Taunton, Great Barrington, and Springfield, and the numbers of the disaffected which he cited coincides with other contemporary accounts. Still, his perception of the protesters is so colored as to skew his accounts, or render them inconsistent.

Writing about the attempt of Concord residents to prevent violence by holding a Middlesex convention when the protesters arrived, Minot opined that "no sooner was it known by the insurgents, who were contemptible in point of strength and character, that the government would not act with force, than they appeared in triumph on the spot." But no spokesmen for the disaffected had ever suggested they would not demonstrate in Concord; perhaps more importantly, they had neither a leader nor a spokesman — though it was on this occasion (before Captain Daniel Shays was even one of their number), that Job Shattuck began being mentioned as a leader.[23] And while Minot consistently attributed the commotions to a germ-like corps of instigators ("The contagion of this riotous disposition . . ."), he also acknowledged that "no recurrence was had to the militia; in Worcester, it was maturely concluded, that those in that vicinity, could not then be relied on. . . . When bodies of the militia were marched by order of their proper officers, numbers whose principles were concealed, would, at some critical juncture, openly change their sides in the field."[24]

This equivocal perspective of the Regulators permeates Minot's account, for he clearly sympathized with their griev-

---

22. Minot, *History*, 20, 22; Feer, *Shays's Rebellion*, 127.
23. Minot, *History*, 42; see Feer, *Shays' Rebellion*, 206.
24. *Ibid.*, 39-40.

ances while despising their actions, which he depicted with inflammatory language. "They could not realize that they had shed their blood in the field, to be worn out with burdensome taxes at home; or that they had contended, to secure their creditors, a right to drag them into courts and prisons." Yet he is convinced that "the opposition to the courts must have been unjustifiable even in the views of the insurgents themselves." And he admonishes "the rioters, on the madness of their conduct."[25]

Minot nonetheless berated them for their peaceful though threatening behavior: "the rage of the malcontents was not less violent in the county of Berkshire." "The counties of Worcester, Middlesex, Bristol and Berkshire," he wrote, "were set in a flame, and the tumult threatened to be general." In fact, it was only their rage, and not their protest, that was violent: at this point there had not been a single report of destruction, much less conflagration.[26]

As ardently as he disliked the actions of the protesters, Minot admired the reactions of the legislature and the eastern leadership generally, whom he painted as compassionate to the point of indulgence. "The General Court, in this dilemma, chose to consider the commotions of the populace, as evidence of their real distresses."[27] And, when a handful of Governor Bowdoin's inner circle assembled at Faneuil Hall, moderated by Samuel Adams, to express their opposition to western unrest, Minot extended their sentiments to the entire population of the city. "The . . . inhabitants of Boston . . . addressed the Governour, and in the most unequivocal manner, declared their determination to co-operate in support of constitutional government."[28]

In describing the carrot-and-stick measures with which Bowdoin and the legislature tried to quash the protests, Minot characterized the government as responding with benevolent

25. *Ibid.*, 16, 39, 38.
26. *Ibid.*, 43, 38.
27. *Ibid.*, 16.
28. *Ibid.*, 44. For an account of this gathering and the resulting 'address' see the *Boston Gazette*, 18 Sept., 1786.

firmness, while failing to appreciate with what repugnance the protesters viewed some of responses. He related how the General Court "agreed upon a plan for originating civil causes before Justices of the Peace, in order to lessen the business of the Courts of Common Pleas, and to render law processes less expensive;" for, as Barbara Karsky put it, "among the lower tribunals, the Court of Common Pleas was especially unpopular, for it was here that debt suits originated."[29] Minot failed to mention that the same plan increased both attendance fees and travel pay for the justices, and that it was in this court that legal fees had increased most significantly. The legislators also "industriously employed themselves in framing a tender act" which provided "for the payment of back taxes in specifick articles, at fixed rates, on account of the scarcity of money." Another bill allowed for the payment of private debts with such goods as beef, pork, butter, grains, wheat flour; and pearl ash could be submitted for taxes. Minot acknowledged, almost in passing, that "several cases were excepted from the tender law, and the operation of it was limited to eight months at the motion of the Senate."[30]

But to the west, these measures were widely perceived as minor remedies. In fact such tender laws, like the Pine Board Act of 1782, had been instituted almost routinely in several states during and after the war, most often in response to town and county conventions, when economic conditions warranted — as they did now.[31] Minot did not point out that, in the west, the preconditions for benefitting from these latest bills seemed unnecessarily demeaning: the debtor's whole estate had first to be appraised by three disinterested persons appointed by himself, the creditor, and the serving officer.[32] And while, in effect, these bills legalized certain forms of barter,

29. Minot, *History*, 59; Barbara Karsky, "Agrarian Radicalism in the Late Revolutionary Period (1780-1795)," in *New Wine in Old Skins*, Angermann *et al.*, eds., 92.

30. Minot, *History*, 59.

31. Taylor, *Western Massachusetts*, 110, 112, 117-118; Szatmary, *Shays' Rebellion*, 41.

32. *Acts and Resolves, 1786-1787, 113 ff.*

they also served the creditors, by delineating the procedures for seizing property, as well as determining its assigned value.

Minot recognized that the suspension of habeas corpus — a hard won treasure of the English Civil War — was an enormous concern among the westerners opposed to Bowdoin's General Court: they especially dreaded being taken to Boston to be tried for their 'mutiny.' He also linked that suspension to the first call to arms among the dissidents: a circular letter sent to the selectmen of towns in the west, above the name of Captain Daniel Shays, "requiring them immediately to assemble their inhabitants, to see that they were furnished with arms and ammunition. . . . another convention was also appointed to be held at Hadley."[33] Minot pointed out that at the same time that habeas corpus was suspended, a bill was passed pardoning all those who would take an oath of allegiance before January 1, 1787. "The conditions of this general act of indemnity, were mild and easy to be complied with, and the advocates for it were exceedingly sanguine as to its effects. They thought the insurrections arose from misapprehensions and ignorance of the evil consequence of violent measures, and they [members of the General Court] had too favourable an idea of their countrymen [the dissenters]. . . ."[34] This seems disingenuous, since the few actions taken by the General Court — minimal tender measures, slight reductions of court costs, and an address to the people chiding them for their 'excessive use of foreign luxuries' — were at best palliatives, and did not address the underlying structural grievance which had provoked western counties for years: the problem of adequate representation. Minot failed to see that the carrot offered was much smaller than the stick waved, for the oath of allegiance maintained the status quo, while the suspension of habeas corpus signified the abrogation of due process.

The failure of the dissidents' 'leaders' to accept the status quo — to seek pardon and take the oath of allegiance — is offered as justification "for suppressing the opposition

---

33. Minot, *History*, 62-63.
34. *Ibid.*, 65.

to government." Since the General Court had adjourned on November 18th, the Governor and his Council took it upon themselves to issue warrants for apprehending Job Shattuck and two other 'head men,' Oliver Parker and Benjamin Page. Colonel Benjamin Hichborn was ordered from Boston for that purpose on the morning of Novemeber 29th, 1786, with the merchant Stephen Higginson riding second in command.[35] Minot's account of this mild skirmish and the departure of Daniel Shays and other dissidents from Worcester in early December, in which "some were actually frozen to death," is marked mainly by its sympathy for all who had endured the famous winter of 1786-1787.[36]

Without comment, Minot quoted the moderate demands sent by the insurgents, over the name of Daniel Gray, to the *Hampshire Gazette* — a periodical created a few months earlier as a pro-government organ in the backcountry — as well as the more extensive additional reforms proposed in a subsequent letter to the *Hampshire Herald*, boldly signed by Thomas Grover, declaring first that the General Court must be removed from Boston, and second, that "a revision of the constitution is absolutely necessary."[37] Still, perhaps out of charity to the demonstrators, Minot declined to examine the significance of these changes proposed to the constitution.

Hereafter in his account, Minot's critical failing is its lack of thoughtful analysis. For example, in recounting General Shepard's suppression of the Springfield commotions in late January, he quickly glossed over one crucial, underlying fact: that neither the government of the Commonwealth nor that of the Confederation was able to raise the funds necessary to defend the Continental arsenal at Springfield. "Such was the

---

35. See above, 163.
36. "The quantity of snow is supposed to be greater now than has been seen in this country at any time since that which fell about 70 years ago, commonly termed the great snow. . . . The travelling is very difficult and in many places impracticable. . . ." *The Pennsylvania Packet and Daily Advertiser*, 26 Dec., 1786.
37. Minot, *History*, 85.

low state of the publick treasury, that perhaps not a single company could have been maintained from that source. . . . The legislature were not sitting, and had they been sitting, could not have laid a tax which would have raised the monies in season."[38] Surely this fact demonstrated both a greater inadequacy of the Constitution and a more desperate economic plight than the rest of Minot's narrative suggests; yet he ignored the implications of this situation for the future of Massachusetts or the Confederation. Neither did he find reason to examine closely the solution that was found. "In this situation a number of gentlemen, from a conviction of the necessity of maintaining good order, and from a consideration of the exigencies of government, voluntarily offered a loan to support the publick cause."[39] Minot did not recognize the larger implications of the predicament: members of one segment of society were the only apparent source of available funds for troops to suppress those who opposed their interests, and whose object, according to him, was "to annihilate the present happy constitution. . . ."[40]

Minot also failed to note the specific roles played by key individuals throughout the response to the rebellion — most notably Knox, Bowdoin, Higginson, Jackson, and Sedgwick, to name but a few. While this was in keeping with Minot's esteem for these gentlemen as well as a contemporary regard for their anonymity, it nonetheless rendered impossible a clear understanding of the motives of these pro-government figures. Clearly this was one disadvantage of Minot's position within the Boston social order and the Massachusetts government.

In characterizing the two opposing sides, Minot observed that the protesters were an ad hoc gathering of "the discontented of every class. . . . Many who only wished for an alteration in the Judicial Courts, were entangled with others who intended, if possible, to prevent the administration of justice in any way . . . who were for annihilating both publick and private debts, and who aimed to revise or extinguish the constitu-

38. *Ibid.*, 93.
39. *Ibid.*, 93.
40. *Ibid.*, 95.

tion. . . . Thus was formed a chequered, but numerous body, some have supposed a third part of the Commonwealth," including a "large proportion of old continental soldiers," many of whom were still owed back pay, but were threatened with emprisonment for their debts.[41] As for the supporters of the constitution, they were "a still more powerful body, of which the men of property formed a material part. The holders of publick securities, and private creditors must, from motives of safety, have inlisted on this side of the question" to collect on their debts, as well as to avoid "the horrors of a civil war."[42] Minot does not acknowledge that, from the protesters' point of view, these easterners seemed to be the ones threatening civil war.

Minot treated Perez Hamlin's supply raid as an important episode of Shays' Rebellion, its "severest engagement," and a century later, in his well-researched novel *The Duke of Stockbridge*, Edward Bellamy depicted it as the last, pivotal skirmish of the uprising. Many other writers have done the same, probably because the battle between Hamlin's followers and the eighty men commanded by Colonel John Ashley of the Berkshire militia produced four dead and more than thirty wounded — more casualties than any other event in the Rebellion. But there is scant documentation about the identity of these individual insurgents. And still, that information would not resolve definitively whether or not this was the tail end of the headless, multi-regional movement called Shays' Rebellion — or a new gang of outlaws, unconcerned with any issues greater than their personal survival.

The most one can say is that the band of raiders who obeyed Hamlin did not evidence the original purposes or the peaceable strategy of the Shaysites. Hamlin and his men raided homes, stole horses and provisions, and took as hostage some thirty wealthy citizens from Stockbridge and Great Barrington. Then, when confronted by Colonel Ashley just north of Sheffield, Hamlin used his hostages, "the first gentlemen of

41. *Ibid.*, 104.
42. *Ibid.*, 105, 96.

Stockbridge and of the county," as a human shield: he forced them "by point of bayonet, into the front of the battle, and kept them there for breastwork."[43] From the only personal interview with Daniel Shays extant, reported by General Rufus Putnam, and from petitions ostensibly from Shays himself, it is difficult to imagine that, even *in extremis*, he would ever have become so desperate for his own freedom that he would resort to such tactics.[44] The same assertion cannot be made about Eli Parsons, Luke Day, Adam Wheeler, Job Shattuck.

For Minot, the flight of the rebels to adjoining states transformed the whole Confederation into a veritable powder-keg; in fact, he asserts that the union was already close to combustion. "By their communication with the inhabitants, they diffused their principles, and created a partiality for their cause, which was said, in one state, to have reached the government itself. An inattention to authority, and a lurking disposition to enforce popular plans by insurrections, had appeared in several parts of the continent, and there was great room to fear, that a less operative cause than the emigration of so many incendiaries, might light up the passion, and throw the whole union into a flame."[45] This, of course, was exactly the perception promulgated by those who sought the framing and ratification of a federal constitution, as well as the language they used.

In April, Governor Bowdoin lost the election to the ever-popular John Hancock for the fifth time since the Constitution of 1780. Hancock had served as governor from October 1780 until his resignation by reason of illness in February 1785. Hancock won by a hearty 75.2% — roughly the majority he had had over Bowdoin in the elections of 1782-4.[46] On the subject of this election, Minot was at his most del-

43. Bellamy, *Duke of Stockbridge*, 323; John Ashley Jr. to Benjamin Lincoln, Sheffield, 27 Feb., 1787, Addendum I, Wetmore Family Collection, Yale University; Szatmary, *Shays' Rebellion*, 111; see also Feer, *Shays' Rebellion*, 403.
44. See General Rufus Putnam to Governor Bowdoin, Rutland, 8 Jan., 1787, typescript in Shays' Rebellion Box, AAS.
45. Minot, *History*, 151.
46. M. A. manuscript, "Votes for Governor and Lieutenant-Governor." For votes in 1783-4, see M. A. "Journal of the Massachusetts House of Representatives," IV, 14; V, 9.

icate, carefully overlooking years of political confrontation between these two antagonists and their factions. Indeed, he allowed Bowdoin his attempt at saving face. "The Governour took that opportunity . . . to express his wish for retirement . . . his happiness, that the voice of the people coincided with it. . . ."[47]

Minot acknowledged that across the state the various factions sought "constitutional means of effecting their wishes" in the election, and that "when the business was over, such alterations were made in the representations of towns; such divisions appeared in the votes for Senators; and the change in the chair was effected by so large a majority, as seemed to indicate a revolution in the publick mind. . . . When the returns of the representatives were published, it was in fact found, whatever may be the sentiments of the members, that about a quarter of them only had been in the late House. . . . Several persons who in the war had been thrown into prison as dangerous to the Commonwealth . . . were now to be seen on the seats of the legislature."[48]

Under Hancock, Minot noted, the new government acted swiftly to establish a conciliatory' atmosphere, moving to discontinue the troops still stationed in Hampshire and Berkshire, repealing the suspension of habeas corpus, and issuing a proclamation that extended the indemnification to anyone who would take the oath of allegiance, excepting only nine names, starting with Daniel Shays and Luke Day.[49] Hancock also swiftly volunteered to reduce his salary by £300. As well, many of the chief concerns of the Shaysites were at least given consideration: the tender act was continued, and a committee was appointed to consider moving the General Court out of Boston. As a measure of just how much the legislature had changed, "a motion was also made for appointing a committee to consider the expediency of issuing paper money; but this was lost, by the opinion of one hundred and three members

47. Minot, *History*, 173.
48. *Ibid.*, 176. Feer disputed Minot's view, arguing that "the turnover . . . was less revolutionary than generally claimed;" Feer, *Shays's Rebellion*, 462.
49. "A Proclamation," Shays' Rebellion Box, AAS.

out of one hundred fifty."[50] Minot did not mention that, in the next session, the poor law was revised, allowing that a debtor could be released by adjuring that he lacked the property to pay his debts or the cost of his keep in prison.[51] This was not actually a bankruptcy act but more importantly, in Taylor's words, "no longer could creditors keep a man in jail indefinitely by paying his board."[52]

But along with these items of inaugural amnesty, Hancock requested permission in advance to march Massachusetts troops into neighboring states, "for the purpose of destroying and conquering them."[53] As well, the legislature warned that no further clemency would be granted to those who failed to take the oath before September 12. So, Minot observed, the actions taken by the new legislature "were by no means so different from those of their predecessors, as appearances seemed to predict. . . . This uniformity of system, tended greatly to annihilate the expectations of the malcontents. . . ."[54]

Fifteen rebels had been sentenced to death during special hearings in April and May and, as directed by the General Court, most were actually marched to the gallows before the Sheriff unsealed the final orders, which announced their reprieve. However, Minot failed to mention that two of the Berkshire dissidents, Charles Rose and John Bly, were hanged; it is difficult to suppose that he was never aware of this fact.[55] Then, in early 1788 both Daniel Shays and Eli Parsons petitioned the legislature, "with a melancholy sense of their errours," for pardon; this was granted, upon condition they would never accept nor hold any civil or military office.

"Thus was a dangerous internal war finally suppressed,

---

50. Minot, *History*, 185.
51. *Acts and Resolves, 1786-1787*, 560, 590.
52. Taylor, *Western Massachusetts*, 166.
53. Minot, *History*, 183.
54. *Ibid.*, 185-186.
55. Samuel Green, "Groton during Shays' Rebellion," in *Proceedings of the Massachusetts Historical Society* I, no. 3 (July 1884), 311-312; *Worcester Magazine*, 2d week in December 1787; see also Szatmary, *Shays' Rebellion*, 115.

by the spirited use of constitutional powers," wrote Minot, overlooking the deaths at the Springfield arsenal and the executions, "without the shedding of blood by the hand of the civil magistrate." And in the last sentence, he concluded his narrative with a ringing endorsement of the Massachusetts Constitution, "which, from a happy principle of mediocrity, governs its subjects without oppression, and reclaims them without severity."[56]

Minot's diary made it clear that accommodating the principal actors and avoiding resentment were high priorities to him: he "showed the History to the principal actors in the suppression of the insurrections, in order that they might object to anything relative to their conduct, before it appeared in print. . . . Mr. _____ thinks I have extricated myself very well from the danger of incurring the resentment of the jarring administrations, which any improper comparison between them, or decisive eulogium of either, would have inevitably drawn upon me."[57]

In fact, in the opinion of Robert Feer, "from early manhood until his premature death at the age of forty-three, George Richards Minot was constantly concerned about what people thought of him."[58] In fact, he was even somewhat miffed at the praise he received. "The opinions respecting my History of the Insurrections have been favourable. If anything could lessen the pleasure arising from this circumstance, it is the surprise of many judicious persons at my performing it so well. . . . We do not love to think that we once stood in an inferiour light, however elevated we may now be, in the opinion of our friends."[59]

Feer pointed out that Minot "sympathized with the Massachusetts conservatives, but he frequently disapproved . . . of

---

56. Minot, *History*, 192.
57. Diary of Minot, 9 June, 1787, Theodore Sedgwick Papers, MHS, as quoted in "Character of Minot . . .," *Coll. of Mass. Hist . Soc.* (1802), 98.
58. Feer, "Minot's *History*," *NEQ* (1962), 204.
59. Diary of Minot, as quoted in "Character of Minot . . .," *Coll. of Mass. Hist. Soc.* (1802), 98.

their machinations. . . . But Minot never allowed these doubts about the virtues of Federalists to escape his diary." His greatest misgivings concerned the state's convention to consider the Federal Constitution, though he did not attribute either its drafting or its either its drafting or its ratification to Shays' Rebellion. "Never was there a political system introduced by less worthy means, than the new constitution for the United States."[60] Coming from the secretary for those proceedings, that is damning criticism indeed.

Minot's narrative was shaped by his concern for two sets of opinions: primarily, of course, he wanted to please the Boston conservatives among whom he lived and worked, by painting the disaffected as criminals. A measure of his success was that, as a result of this work, Minot was invited in 1791 to be one of the ten founding members of the Massachusetts Historical Society. But he also wanted to convince Europeans that American government was dignified and stable. This last preoccupation also inspired Franklin to publish a blatant bit of boosterism entitled *The Internal State of America* in 1786. But if Minot meant to write an objective history, he failed. Though Feer declared that "his *History of the Insurrections* can be read as history or propaganda or autobiography," in fact, it can only be read as a blend of all three.[61]

Perhaps the most enduring legacy of Minot's work is its failure to acknowledge the connection between the insurrection and the Constitutional Convention: in Minot's circles it simply would not do to credit the insurgents with the Federal Constitution. But also, it is not clear whether or not Minot was aware of Knox's exaggerated reports of the rebellion, whereby he intended to urge Washington out of retirement and lend his unique prestige to the federal Constitution.

There are many other significant oversights in Minot's account. The Society of the Cincinnati is not mentioned at all; either is the enormous personal involvement of Stephen Higginson, or the widespread western discontent with the Mas-

60. Feer, "Minot's *History*," *NEQ* (1962), 207; Diary of Minot, 1788, Sedgwick Papers, MHS.
61. Feer, "Minot's *History*," *NEQ* (1962), 228.

sachusetts Constitution. Some omissions arise naturally from the contemporaneity of his narrative: for example, it is understandable that Minot failed to question the policy of emprisonment for debt. But others seem deliberate: while many of the disaffected certainly were debtors, many of the same men were also creditors, awaiting military backpay from the very government that threatened them.

The Federalist interpretation initiated by Minot remained the staple of most nineteenth-century historiography of the Rebellion. Contemporaries Hannah Adams, Mercy Otis Warren (who had access to Benjamin Lincoln's papers), and John Marshall all accepted Minot's account at face-value.[62] Likewise, Timothy Pitkin toed the line of established government: "Fortunately, the state of Massachusetts by the firmness of its governor and legislature . . . was able to suppress the insurrection."[63] But Pitkin was also the first historian to firmly posit a connection between Shays' Rebellion and the call for a Constitutional Convention. "Many causes combined to convince Congress and the American people, of the necessity of this measure; none, perhaps, had greater influence, than the insurrection. . . . These scenes in Massachusetts were deeply felt throughout the union. By no one, however, more than by general Washington."[64] Later, conservative historians like Richard Hildreth followed suit.[65]

George Bancroft was eighty-two years old before he examined the Confederation Period, in his *History of the Formation*

---

62. Hannah Adams, *A Summary History of New England* . . . (Boston, 1799); Mercy Otis Warren, *History of the Rise, Progress and Termination of the American Revolution*. . . (Boston, 1805); John Marshall, *The Life of George Washington* . . ., 5 vols. (1804-1807). Benjamin Lincoln to Mercy Warren, Boston, 25 Mar., 1790, in *Coll. of Mass. Hist. Soc. LXXIII* (1925), 317-318.

63. Timothy Pitkin, *A Political and Civil History of the United States* . . ., 2 vols. (New Haven, 1828), II, 221-222.

64. *Ibid.*, 220, 222. For comparison see Marshall, *George Washington*, V, 94-95.

65. Richard Hildreth, *The History of the United States* . . ., 3 vols. (Boston, 1849), III, 535.

of the Constitution. . .[66] As Kraus wrote, "the uncritical nature of many of its pages and the complete neglect of economic factors have been noted by many students;" still, his work "at once became the standard history."[67] In fact, Bancroft offered a thorough examination of the Confederation, carefully chronicling the call for a more powerful federal government from the first days of the Articles.[68] Yet, in the five hundred pages of his first volume, he devoted just one paragraph to Shays' Rebellion. Interestingly, he sympathized with "the sufferings of the debtors," disparaged "the devices of attorneys to increase their own emoluments," and declared that "the real cause of the distress was, in part, the failure of the state of Massachusetts itself to meet its obligations; and still more, the bankruptcy of the general government, which owed large sums of money to inhabitants of almost every town for service in achieving the independence of their country."[69]

It was against this standard that, in 1888, John Fiske coined the phrase 'The Critical Period.'[70] Fiske related the insurrection specifically to the failure of the government, under the Articles, to address the war debt. More importantly, perhaps, he emphasized the post-war economic plight of debtors radicalized by the threat of emprisonment which, Fiske noted perceptively, "tended to make the debtor an outlaw, ready to entertain schemes for the subversion of society."[71]

66. George Bancroft, *History of the Formation of the Constitution of the United States of America*, 2 vols. (New York, 1882).

67. Kraus, *American History*, 236, 231.

68. Bancroft, *Formation of the Constitution*, I, 17.

69. *Ibid.*, 274-275.

70. John Fiske, *The Critical Period of American History, 1783-1789* (Boston, 1916). The section pertaining to Massachusetts was first published, absent some revisions, as "The Paper Money Craze of 1786 and the Shays' Rebellion," in *Atlantic Monthly* LVIII (Boston, 1886). Fiske insisted that, at the time of writing, he had not seen Trescot's use of the phrase 'critical period' in his *Diplomatic History. . . .*

71. *Ibid.*, 173. Fiske's general approach was followed by Joseph P. Warren, "The Confederation and Shays' Rebellion," *American Historical Review*, II (Oct. 1896), 42-67 and "The Shays Rebellion" (unpublished Harvard Ph.D. dissertation, 1900). The same is true of Smith, "The Depression of 1785," *WMQ*, 3rd. Ser. (1948), 77-94.

In an essay on the historiography of the Confederation, Richard Morris noted that "it has become the fashion of latter-day historians to criticize Fiske's scholarship. . . . the issue is not whether Fiske used first-hand sources, but whether he produced a valid synthesis."[72] Morris did not resolve that issue, though he acknowledged Fiske's "enormous impact" upon historians, and examined his influence upon the work of John McMaster and Andrew McLaughlin. Morris's essay aimed at contrasting their school of thought with "the Antifederalist or pro-democratic interpretation" of Charles Beard and Merrill Jensen. For Morris, the real difference between these two camps "springs from a deep divergence in interpreting the American Revolution and the issues for which it was fought. . . . In fact, this school of historiography depicts the American Revolution as essentially a civil war among Whigs."[73]

Beard, for whom Shays' Rebellion should naturally have seemed an important event, nonetheless took issue with Fiske. "It may be that 'the critical period' was not such a critical period after all; but a phantom of the imagination produced by some undoubted evils which could have been remedied without a political revolution. . . . Certainly, the inflamed declarations of the Shaysites are not to be taken as representing accurately the state of the people, and just as certainly the alarmist letters and pamphlets of interested persons on the other side are not to be accepted without discount."[74] At the same time Beard cited at length much of the important correspondence of Washington, Knox, Jay, and Higginson concerning the un-

---

72. Richard B. Morris, "The Confederation Period and the American Historian," in *William and Mary Quarterly*, 3rd. ser., XIII (1956), 139-156.

73. *Ibid.*, 147, 152. Morris noted that the terms "Antifederalist and pro-democratic are not necessarily equated."

74. Charles A. Beard, *An Economic Interpretation of the Constitution of the United States* (New York, 1935), 48. As Morris pointed out, the only evidence which Beard cited to prove that the general social conditions were prosperous was an essay by Franklin which was, at best, unconvincing propaganda, intended to refute the popular British view: "Your NewsPapers are fill'd with fictitious Accounts of Anarchy, Confusion, Distresses, and Miseries." Verner W. Crane, "Franklin's 'Internal State of America (1786),'" in *William and Mary Quarterly*, 3rd. ser., XV (1958), 214-225.

rest, and concluded that "by an increasing recognition of the desperate straights in which they were placed, a remarkable fusion of interested forces was effected."[75] He also acknowledged that members of the Society of the Cincinnati "were bitter in their denunciation of the popular movements in the states, particularly Shays' revolt. . . ."[76] Yet Beard failed to capitalize on the insurrection to demonstrate his argument that "social progress in general is the result of contending interests in society — some favorable, others opposed to change."[77] Perhaps Beard felt that highlighting the protests might weaken his single-minded thesis that personalty interests were the key motive behind the Constitutional Convention.

Forty years later Beard was excoriated by Robert E. Brown on his use of the rebellion for his own ends. Among Brown's other arguments, he pointed out that the unrest "was convincing evidence that farmers as well as personalty interests were hurt under the Confederation," undermining Beard's suppositions Brown wondered "how Beard could account for Shays' Rebellion as a manifestation of inertness and indifference."[78] Brown did not examine Beard's later repudiation of economic determinism, in which he described conditions during the Confederation period, as Morris put it, "in language which would have gratified Fiske and perhaps shocked Bancroft."[79]

Merrill Jensen's point of view was similar to the early Beard's in some respects, including its de-emphasis of Shays'

---

75. Beard, *Economic Interpretation*, 61.

76. *Ibid.*, 39-40.

77. *Ibid.*, 19.

78. Robert E. Brown, *Charles Beard and the Constitution: A Critical Analysis of "An Economic Interpretation of the Constitution"* (Princeton, 1956), 60, 61, 90. Brown also takes Beard to task on the question of Massachusetts' ratification: "If the contest in Massachusetts had been 'a sharp conflict between the personalty interests on the one hand and the small farmers and debtors on the other,' as Beard said . . ., Massachusetts would have stayed out of the Union." *Ibid.*, 185. See *Ibid.*, 150, 171-172, 186-187 for Brown's criticism of evidence Beard derived from Orin G. Libby's *The Geographical Distribution of the Vote of the Thirteen States on the Federal Constitution, 1787-8* (New York, 1894).

79. Morris, "The Confederation Period," *WMQ*, 3rd Ser. (1956), 150; Beard, *The Enduring Federalist* (New York, 1948), 27-30.

Rebellion as a catalyst for the Constitutional Convention. It is true, as Morris wrote, that "Jensen sees the radical party in the Revolution as comprising the town masses and the frontier groups" who "fought for an internal revolution. . . . Conservatives merely wanted independence from Britain."[80] It is also true that Jensen, like Beard, argued that "the dominating fact of the Confederation Period was the struggle between two groups of leaders to shape the character of the state and central governments. . . . The [true] federalists tried to strengthen the Articles of Confederation; the nationalists tried to create a new constitution. . . . [but to] avoid the method of change prescribed by the Articles. . . ."[81]

But Jensen's conclusions are also very different from Beard's, largely because of the greater depth and subtlety of its multifaceted analysis, compared to the blunt polemics of the unreconstructed Beard. Jensen recognized that the problems of this period of "post-war demobilization, of sudden economic change, dislocation, and expansion" were hardly phantoms of the imagination.[82] In a work published some years after Morris's essay, yet reflecting very much the same views as *The New Nation* and *The Articles of Confederation*, Jensen allowed that "the achievement of a convention owed much to the outbreak of violence in Massachusetts. . . . Not only the most dramatic, it was also the most frightening of any that had yet occured." He also cited Timothy Dwight, writing from Northampton as early as 1779, who reasoned that "without a gift of prophecy, I will venture to foretell that the movement which forces small farmers to sell their real estate for the purpose of paying taxes will produce a revolution."[83] This is incompatible with Beard's earlier pronouncements regarding

---

80. Morris, "The Confederation Period," *WMQ* (1956), 152.
81. Merrill Jensen, *The New Nation* (New York, 1950), 424, 428.
82. *Ibid.*, 422.
83. Merrill Jensen, *American Revolution in America* (New York, 1974), 163; Timothy Dwight to Samuel Parsons, 23 Apr., 1779, in Hill, ed., *Life and Letters of Parsons . . .*, 237. See also Merrill Jensen, *The Making of the American Constitution* (New York, 1963), 30, 34.

"the inertness, ignorance, and indifference of the masses."[84]

With regard to Washington, Jensen did state at one point that "Shays' Rebellion frightened him out of retirement and into politics," much as the Beards had declared in the twenties.[85] He did not follow through with this train of thought, however, to draw a logical connection between Washington's return to public affairs and the success of the Constitutional Convention.

Far and away the most exhaustive analysis of Shays' Rebellion came from Robert A. Feer in 1958, a work for which all future students of the protests must remain grateful. In almost six hundred pages of manuscript, Feer thoroughly scrutinized every aspect of "the historian's step-child," as he described the insurrection, starting with a close examination of the Constitution of 1780. It is hard to think of any relevant aspect of life in Massachusetts following the Revolution that Feer's narrative did not touch upon. If there is a weakness in his study of the causes of the rebellion, it is the insufficient emphasis he gave to the public debt, and its origins in the war, and the extent to which a large number of Massachusetts debtors were also creditors, who were owed military back pay and land west of the Ohio.

Writing just before the golden age of cliometrics, and fixing each factor of the unrest in its social and political context, Feer's comprehensive analysis leads him to the conclusion that "rebellion came, not simply because there were a specie shortage, high taxes, and a burdensome private debt, but because these conditions existed at the very moment that men and women expected and believed themselves entitled to the good life."[86]

Yet, almost paradoxically, Feer's enormous study of this small rebellion denies any clear connection between the unrest and the federal Constitution. In his dissertation, Feer devoted little space to the link between the insurrection and the

---

84. Beard, *Economic Interpretation*, 64.
85. Jensen, *New Nation*, 250; Charles A. Beard and Mary R. Beard, *The Rise of American Civilization*, rev. ed. (New York, 1933 [1st ed., 1927]) I, 307.
86. Feer, *Shays's Rebellion*, 69. [Feer's italics].

Constitutional Convention, Washington's decision to serve as its president, the Constitution itself, and its ratification: just seventeen pages, most of which are citations from Ferrand's *Debates*.

. . . Feer noted that other historians had suggested "that the Rebellion aroused conservatives to the need for a stronger central government."[87] While he did not deny this altogether, Feer insisted that Shays' Rebellion played only a minor part in Washington's decision to lend his prestige to the Philadelphia Convention: "Washington had already been convinced of the need for constitutional revision prior to the outbreak."[88] "A total of nine references, direct and oblique, during almost three months of debate suggests that Shays's Rebellion was hardly a major consideration in shaping the thinking of the delegates."[89] This is hardly evidence on a par with the rest of Feer's study. According to Madison's *Notes*, the question of fugitive slaves was brought up only once in the Convention, but that can hardly be taken as a full measure of the issue's significance, especially to slaveowners in the border states.[90]

"In Madison's hands," wrote Feer, "Shays's Rebellion was more a tool with which to rationalize a position which he already held than an experience which gave him new insights into the problems of government."[91] But Feer failed to explore just how powerful a tool the insurrection was in the hands of Knox, Higginson, Madison, Wilson, and others who had waited patiently for just such a crisis, to accomplish what they could not achieve without it — the rebirth of an already a moribund central government.

Feer published an essay eleven years his dissertation which proposed to answer the question: "*Would the Constitution have emerged when it did and in the form in which it did if Shays's Rebellion had not taken place in the winter of 1786-*

87. *Ibid.*, 486.
88. *Ibid.*, 490.
89. *Ibid.*, 496.
90. James Madison, *Notes of Debates in the Federal Convention of 1787* (Athens, Ohio, 1984 [2nd. ed., 1984]), 545-546.
91. Feer, *Shays' Rebellion*, 497.

1787?"[92] He had determined that this hypothetical question would meet Robert MacIver's criteria for social causation: "It must be shown, as being at least highly probable, that the prevailing conditions of public opinion were such that, but for the act of the leader, the tide would not then — or soon thereafter — have changed in this direction. . . . How would the situation have developed had it not been for the event?"[93] Feer also allowed that "if it can be shown that without Shays's Rebellion Washington would not have attended the Convention or have lent his name to the Federalists on behalf of ratification, then the Rebellion did help produce the Constitution."[94]

Feer's emphatic answer was that Shays' Rebellion was not a necessary cause of either the emergence of the Constitution or the presence of Washington at the Convention. Feer also proceeded to disavow the decisive impact of the rebellion upon Madison, Hamilton, King, Higginson, the state legislatures appointing delegates, and the entire process of ratification. "Although people talked about Shays's Rebellion and some were momentarily frightened by it," argued Feer, "there is no evidence that it changed in any significant way the thinking of the people who drew up and ratified the Constitution. The movement for Constitutional revision . . . was well under way prior to Shays's Rebellion."[95]

"Historians can say little, if anything, with complete certainty," Feer concluded, "least of all in the realm of causation. But, in all likelihood, the Constitutional Convention would have met when it did, the same document would have been drawn up, and it would have been ratified even if Shays's Rebellion had not taken place. If by a 'cause' we mean something necessary to the occurence of a particular event, Shays's Rebellion was not a cause of the Constitution of the United

---

92. Feer, "Shays's Rebellion and the Constitution," *NEQ* (1969), 389. [Feer's italics].

93. Robert M. MacIver, *Social Causation* (Boston, 1942), 180, 258, 264, as quoted in Feer, "Shays's Rebellion . . .," *NEQ* (1969), 389.

94. Feer, "Shays's Rebellion . . .," *NEQ* (1969), 395.

95. *Ibid.*, 410.

States."[96] The present study denies all of these contentions. The compromises forged in the Convention could not have been achieved merely to provide a prophylactic against the threat of social disorder: some destruction was a prerequisite to any deep-cutting political reform. Before the states would agree to fix the 'machine that would go of itself,' conclusive evidence was required that it was broken, and nothing less than violence against life and property would suffice. "What stronger evidence can be given," wrote Washington, "of the want of energy in our government than these disorders?"[97] The fact that the Continental government could not defend its arsenal from *its own citizens* without the assistance of private contributions was surely the final proof that some fundamental change was necessary — at least, before the next rebellion.

To speculate on how the Confederation Period might have ended had there been no insurrection, as Feer did, is to propose an unrealistic supposition. Shays' Rebellion was a part of the American Revolution, much as receiving the bill is a part of dining out. More than any other historian before or since, Feer was immersed in the facts and circumstances surrounding Shays' Rebellion; but that may have been exactly what blinded him to the powerful phantoms which the insurrection raised.

David Szatmary's *Shays' Rebellion: The Making of an Agrarian Insurrection* is the third and most recent full-length study ever to be published about the uprising and, as social history, makes a significant contribution. Szatmary succeeded admirably in his declared intention, to "locate the roots of the insurrection in a clash between a traditional, agrarian way of life and an ever-encroaching commercial society."[98] Quoting Halpern and Brode, he suggested that North American farmers of the revolutionary era may rightly be called peasants, since, "after all, many of them are only a generation

96. *Ibid.*
97. George Washington to James Madison, Mount Vernon, 5 Nov., 1786, *Writings of Washington*, XXIX, 52.
98. Szatmary, *Shays' Rebellion*, xiv.

or two removed from the European countryside."[99] According to Szatmary, "the rebellion represented a dynamic struggle between a largely subsistence, family-based, community-oriented culture of independent farmers, and an acquisitive, individualistic way of life dominated by merchants, professionals, speculators, and commercial farmers."[100] Szatmary gave scant attention to the problem of public debt, but placed a special emphasis — very convincingly — upon the 'chain of [private] debt' which stretched from western farmers who purchased, from Boston merchants, goods manufactured in England. "The resentment of British officials and the English people in general over their defeat" led them to extend the Navigation Acts to the United States, forbidding Americans from foreign trade with the West Indies, and to demand payment in specie.[101]

Because Szatmary perceived the rebellion exclusively as the result of a postwar society "in which rural tradition and commercial exapansion came into conflict," he failed to relate the unrest to the Revolutionary War and the ideology which was its motor — the same ideology which, in the eyes of the Shaysites, justified the insurrection and, in the eyes of the nationalists, required the establishment of a standing army.[102]

One ancient and fundamental element in that ideology was the right to satisfactory representation, which had long been established and experienced within town government: sharing in decisions was a familiar experience. Frontier representation had always been problematic, but, with the Massachusetts Constitution, had become critical. To the western eye, representation appeared less than satisfactory in the General Court, and demands for remedial measures appeared in different guises throughout the Shaysite petitions, which characteristically called for a say in the administration of the judicia-

99. Joel Halpern and John Brode, "Peasant Society: Economic Changes and Revolutionary Transformations," in *Biennial Review of Anthropology*, 1967, ed. Bernard Siegel and Alan Beals (Stanford, 1967), 58, as cited in Szatmary, *Shays' Rebellion*, 6.
100. Szatmary, *Shays' Rebellion*, xiv.
101. *Ibid.*, 23.
102. *Ibid.*, 1.

ry, the abolition of the Senate, the reduction of the poll tax, and even in the re-situating of the House of Representatives. Practical as they are, these demands are all rooted in the ideology that had fueled the war effort, not merely in economic self-interest or, as Szatmary would have it, in the defense of a subsistence-oriented culture. There was also, effectively, an absence of representation in the Continental Congress — that republican body which had first mustered Washington's Army, creating the debt for which the citizenry had recently been obliged to make an onerous supplementary payment. Because of the war, almost the entire male population had had transactions personally with the Continental government: now, that rarely meant even a quorum of representatives.

In short, Szatmary, like the majority of historians mentioned above, failed to note that ideology was actually an important component in the demonstrations, even though the effectual creed was no more revolutionary than "No taxation without representation," and its expression no more articulate than a band of veterans and farmers marching in step. But Szatmary was preoccupied with the important role that economic polarization played in creating the crisis, and felt no compunction to find causes for the demonstrations in ideology.

Szatmary insisted "it is clear that Shays' Rebellion played an integral part in the genesis and formation of the United States Constitution," and, in both its drafting and its ratification, "assumed an important role".[103] In the last dozen pages of his study, he offered not so much a thorough argument as a summary account of the nationalist movement, from Annapolis to ratification in Boston. While there is little to fault in his account, he has hardly provided the "careful analysis of the evidence to see in what way Shays's Rebellion influenced the Constitution" which Feer called for.[104]

Many other historians have contributed enormously to an understanding of Shays' Rebellion without having devoted

---

103. *Ibid.*, 120.
104. Feer, "Shays's Rebellion . . .," *NEQ* (1969), 388.

full-length works to the insurrection itself: Jackson Turner Main, Robert Taylor, and Van Beck Hall are among the most noteworthy, and their works are addressed throughout this study.[105] Still, the question posed by Feer has not been addressed: "whether, in fact, the Constitution might have been written and ratified when and as it was even if Shays's Rebellion had not occured."[106] To answer that question, one must begin by understanding what was evoked by the threat of civil war under republican government, and how the very language of liberty appeared to portend its own demise.

105. Jackson Turner Main, *The Social Structure of Revolutionary America* (Princeton, 1965), and *The Antifederalists: Critics of the Constitution, 1781-1788* (Chapel Hill, 1961); Taylor, *Western Massachusetts*; Van Beck Hall, *Politics Without Parties: Massachusetts, 1780-1791* (Pittsburgh, 1972).
106. Feer, "Shays's Rebellion . . .," *NEQ* (1969), 388.

BIBLIOGRAPHY

Manuscripts:

American Antiquarian Society, Worcester:
  Shays' Rebellion Folder.

Berkshire Athenæum, Pittsfield:
  Shays' Rebellion Papers.

Forbes Library, Northampton:
  Jonathan Judd Diary.
  Daniel Stebbins Notebook.
  Caleb Strong Papers.

Houghton Library, Harvard University, Cambridge:
  Sparks Manuscripts.
  William Manning Papers.

Library of Congress (microfilm):
  The Papers of the Continental Congress.
  The Papers of James Madison.
  The Papers of George Washington.

Massachusetts Historical Society, Boston:
  Henry Knox Papers.
  Theodore Sedgwick Papers.
  Shays' Rebellion Folder.

New-York Historical Society, New York:
Elbridge Gerry Papers.
Osgood Papers.
Shays' Rebellion Folder.

Springfield City Library:
Shays' Rebellion Papers.

Yale University Library:
Wetmore Family Collection.

Contemporary Newspapers:

Boston Gazette
Hampshire Gazette
Hampshire Herald
Independent Chronicle
Massachusetts Centinel
Massachusetts Magazine
Philadelphia Packet
Worcester Magazine

Primary Sources in Print:

A Collection of State Tracts, published during the Reign of King William III. 3 vols. London, 1706 [orig. publ. 1697].

Adams, Charles Francis, ed. *Works of John Adams.* 10 vols. Boston: Little, Brown. 1850-1856.

Adams, John. *The Diary of John Adams.* 4 vols. Cambridge, Mass.: Belknap Press, 1961.

Allen, W. B. *et al.*, eds. *The Essential Antifederalist.* Lanham, Md.: University of America Press, 1985.

Backus, Charles. *A Sermon, Preached in Long-Meadow, at*

the Public Fast, April 17, 1788. Springfield: Weld and Thomas, 1788 [Evans 20939].

Barnard, Thomas. *A Sermon, Delivered on the day of National Thanksgiving, February 19, 1795.* Salem, 1795 [Evans No.28239].

Bolingbroke, Viscount [Henry St. John]. *Letters on the Spirit of Patriotism; On the Idea of a Patriot King; and on the State of Parties, at the Acession of King George I.* Philadelphia, 1749 [orig. publ. London, 1749]. [Evans No. 6412].

Bowdoin and Temple Papers. 2 vols. *Massachusetts Historical Society Collections,* 7th Ser., VI, Boston, 1907.

Boyd, Julian P., ed. *The Papers of Thomas Jefferson.* 17 vols. Princeton: Princeton U.P., 1950-1965.

Burke, Ædanus [*pseud.* Cassius]. *Considerations on the Order or Society of Cincinnati.* Hartford, 1784 [Evans No.7862].

Burnett, Edmund C. *Letters of Members of the Continental Congress.* 8 Vols. Gloucester, Mass.: Peter Smith, 1963 [orig. publ. 1934, Washington, D.C.: Carnegie Institution, 1934].

Burroughs, Stephen. *Memoirs of Stephen Burroughs.* Hanover, N. H., 1798 [Evans No. 33478].

Chauncy, Charles. *Seasonable Thoughts on the State of Religion in New England.* Boston, 1748 [Evans No. 5151].

Commager, Henry Steele, ed. *Documents of American History.* 2 vols. Englewood Cliffs, N. J.: Prentice Hall, 1972.

Commager, Henry Steele, and Morris, Richard B., eds. *The Spirit of '76: The Story of the American Revolution as told by its Participants.* New York: Bonanza, 1958.

Croce, Benedetto. *The Philosophy of Giambattista Vico.* Collingwood, R. G., trans. New York: Macmillan, 1964.

Cushing, Harry A., ed. *The Writings of Samuel Adams.* 4 vols. New York: Octagon, 1968 [orig. publ. 1904-1908].

Dann, John C., ed. *The Revolution Remembered: Eyewitness Accounts of the War for Independence.* Chicago: University of Chicago Press, 1980.

Douglass, William. *A Summary, Historical and Political, of the First Planting, Progressive Imrovements, and Present State of the British Settlements in North America.* 2 vols. Boston, 1755 [Evans Nos. 6662, 6663, 6992, 7885].

Drake, Francis S. *Life and Correspondence of Henry Knox, Major-General in the American Revolutionary War.* Boston: Samuel G Drake, 1873.

_____. *Memorials of the Society of the Cincinnati of Massachusetts.* Boston, 1873.

Duclos, Charles Pinot. *The History of Lewis XI, King of France.* . . . 2 vols. London: Davis, 1746.

Elliot, Jonathan, ed. *Debates in the Several State Conventions on the Adoption of the Federal Constitution.* 5 vols. New York: Lippincott, 1888.

Farrand, Max, ed. *The Records of the Federal Convention of 1787.* 4 vols. New Haven: Yale University Press, 1937.

Fitzpatrick, John C., ed. *Writings of George Washington from the Original Manuscript Sources 1745-1799.* 39 vols. Washington: U. S. Government Printing Office, 1931-1944.

Foner, Philip S., ed. *The Complete Writings of Thomas Paine.*

2 vols. New York: Citadel, 1945.

Ford, Paul Leicester, ed. *Pamphlets on the Constitution of the United States*. New York: Da Capo, 1968 [orig. publ. 1888].

Richard, Fry. *A Scheme for a Paper Currency*. Providence: Standard Printing, 1908 [orig. publ. 1739].

Gaillard Hunt, ed., *The Writings of James Madison*. 9 vols. New York: Putnam, 1900-1910.

Gilbert, Benjamin. *A Citizen-Soldier in the American Revolution: The Diary of Benjamin Gilbert in Massachusetts and New York*. Rebecca D. Symmes, ed. Cooperstown, N. Y.: N. Y. S. Historical Ass., 1980.

Hamilton, Alexander; Madison, James; and Jay, John. *The Federalist Papers*. Franklin Center, Pa.: Franklin Library, 1977.

Handlin, Oscar and Mary F. *The Popular Sources of Political Authority: Documents on the Massachusetts Constitution of 1780*. Cambridge, Mass.: Belknap Press, 1966.

[Higginson, Stephen]. *Ten Chapters in the Life of John Hancock*. Boston, 1857 (orig. publ. as *The Writings of Laco*, 1789). [Evans No. 21886].

Hume, Edgar Erskine, ed. *General Washington's Correspondence Concerning The Society of the Cincinnati*. Baltimore, 1941.

Hutchinson, William T.; Rutland, Robert A.; Rachal, William, M. E., *et al.*, eds. *The Papers of James Madison*. 16 vols. Chicago: University of Chicago Press, 1977.

Hyneman, Charles S. and Lutz, Donald S., eds. *American Po-*

litical Writing during the Founding Era,1760-1805. 2 vols. Indianapolis: Liberty Press, 1983.

[Jackson, Jonathan]. *Thoughts upon the Political Situation of the United States of America, in which that of Massachusetts is more particularly considered. . . By a native of Boston.* Worcester, 1788 [Evans No. 21173].

Jameson, J. Franklin, ed. "The Letters of Stephen Higginson," in the *American Historical Association Annual Report 1896*, I (Washington, 1897), 704-841.

Jensen, Merrill, ed. *American Colonial Historical Documents to 1776*. New York: Oxford University Press, 1955.

Jensen, Merrill; Kaminski, John P.; and Saladino, Gasparé J., eds. *The Documentary History of the Ratification of the Constitution*. 16 vols. Madison: State Historical Society of Wisconsin, 1976-88.

Knox, Henry. *Plan for the General Arrangement of the Militia of the United States*. New York, 1786 [Evans 20076].

Luther, Martin. "The First Commandment," *The Large Catechism.*

Manning, William. *The Key of Libberty. Shewing the Causes why a free government has always Failed, and a Remidy against it. Adresed to the Republicans, Farmers, Mecanicks, & Labourers in the United States of America by a Labourer. Finished February the 20th, 1798*, reprinted in Samuel E. Morison, "William Manning's *The Key of Libberty*," *William and Mary Quarterly*, 3rd Ser., XIII (Jan. 1948), 202-254.

_____. "Some proposals for Makeing Restitution to the Original Creditors of Government and to helpe the Continant to a Medium of trade, Subscribed to the consideration of a

Member of the State Lejeslator of Masachusets February the 6th, 1790." MS Am 880.10, Houghton Library, Harvard University.

Massachusetts. *Acts and Resolves of Massachusetts* (1780-1789). 5 vols. Boston: Wright and Potter, 1890-1894.

_____. *Debates, Resolutions and Other Proceedings of the Convention of the Commonwealth of Massachusetts Held in the Year 1788 and Which Finally Ratified the Constitution of the United States.* Boston, 1808 [Shaw-Shoemaker 15516].

_____. *Massachusetts Soldiers and Sailors of the Revolutionary War.* 17 vols. Boston: Wright and Potter, 1896-1908.

McDonald, Forrest and McDonald, Ellen Shapiro. *Confederation and Constitution, 1781-1789.* Columbia, S. C.: University of South Carolina Press, 1968.

Morris, Richard B., ed. *Basic Documents on the Confederation and Constitution.* Malabar, Fla.: Robert E. Krieger, 1985.

Niles, H. *Chronicles of the American Revolution.* Vaughan, Alden T., ed. New York: Grosset and Dunlap, 1965 (orig. publ. as *Principles and Acts of the Revolution in America.* Baltimore, 1822).

Otis, James. *A Vindication of the Conduct of the House of Representatives. . . .* (1762). *University of Missouri Studies,* IV, No. 3. Mullett, Charles F., ed. Columbia, Miss., 1929 (orig. publ. Boston, 1762).

Paine, Thomas. *Common Sense.* New York: Penguin, 1976 [orig. publ. Philadelphia, 1776].

Pettit, Charles. *An Impartial View of the Rise and Progress of the Controversy Between the Parties Known by the Names of the Federalists & Republicans, Containing An Investigation of the Radical Cause of the Division. . . in a Series of Letters from A Partaker in the American Revolution (Charles Pettit) to a Junior Citizen.* Reprinted in *The Magazine of History 23.* New York: Abbatt, 1913, 324-349 [orig. publ. Philadelphia,1800].

Pocock, J. G. A., ed. *The Political Works of James Harrington.* Cambridge: Cambridge University Press, 1977.

"Proceedings at a Convention. . . holden at Hartford. . . the eighth day of November. . . 1780," *Magazine of American History,* VIII (1882).

Randolph, T. J., ed. *Memoirs, Correspondence, and Miscellanies from the Papers of Thomas Jefferson.* 4 vols. Charlottesville: F. Carr, 1829.

Shaw, Samuel. *The Journals of Major Samuel Shaw: the First American Consul at Canton.* Boston: Crosby and Nichols, 1847.

Smith, Adam. *An Enquiry into the Nature and Causes of The Wealth of Nations.* 2 vols. London: Methuen, 1904 (orig. publ. 1776).

Storing, Herbert J., ed. *The Complete Anti-Federalist.* 7 vols. Chicago: University of Chicago Press, 1981.

[Swan, James]. *National Arithmetick; or, Observations on the Finances of the Commonwealth of Massachusetts. . . .* Boston, 1786 [Evans No. 20016].

Syrett, Harold C., ed. *The Papers of Alexander Hamilton.* 15 vols. New York: Columbia University Press, 1961-1977.

Tappan, David. *A Discourse, Delivered to the Religious So-*

ciety of Brattle-Street, Boston. . . on April 5, 1798. Boston, 1798 [Evans No. 34627].

Taylor, Robert J., ed. *Massachusetts, Colony to Commonwealth: Documents on the Formation of Its Constitution, 1775-1780.* Chapel Hill: University of North Carolina Press, 1961.

Thornton, John W., ed. *The Pulpit of the American Revolution: Or, the Political Sermons of the Period of 1776.* Boston: Gould and Lincoln, 1860.

Trenchard, John and Gordon, Thomas. *Cato's Letters.* 4 vols. 3rd. ed. London: J. Peele, 1733 [orig. publ. 1721].

U. S. Continental Congress. *Secret Journals of the Acts and Proceedings of Congress.* 2 vols. Boston, 1821.

_____. *Journals of the Continental Congress 1774-1789,* Fitzpatrick, John C., ed. 32 vols. New York: U.S. Government Printing Office, 1968.

Warren-Adams Letters. . . . Massachusetts Historical Society Collections, LXXII-LXXIII. 2 vols. Boston, 1917-1925.

Warren, Mercy Otis. *History of the American Revolution.* Boston: Larkin, 1805.

Washington, George. "Sentiments on a Peace Establishment." Palmer, John McAuley. *Washington, Lincoln, Wilson: Three War Statesmen.* Garden City, N. Y.: Doubleday, 1930.

Winstanley, Gerrard, *et al. The True Levellers Standard Advanced: Or The State of Community opened, and Presented to the Sons of Men.* London, 1649 [British Museum, P. M., E. 552(5)].

Winstanley, Gerrard. *The Works of Gerrard Winstanley: Withan Appendix of Documents relating to the Digger Movement.* Sabine, George H., ed. New York: Cornell University Press, 1965.

_____. *The Law of Freedom in a Platform: Or, True Magistracy Restored.* London, 1651 [British Museum, P. M., E. 655].

Wolfe, Don M. *Leveller Manifestoes of the Puritan Revolution.* New York: Humanities Press, 1944.

Secondary Books:

Abernethy, Thomas Perkins. *Western Lands and the American Revolution.* New York; Russell and Russell, 1937.

Adams, Hannah. *A Summary History of New England. . . .* Boston, 1799.

Adams, Henry. *Documents Relating to New England Federalism.* Boston: Little, Brown, 1905.

Allen, Herbert S. *John Hancock: Patriot in Purple.* New York: Beechhurst Press, 1953.

Aldridge, A. Owen. *Thomas Paine's American Ideology.* Newark: University of Delaware Press, 1984.

Angermann, Erich; Frings, Marie-Louise; and Wellenreuther, Hermann, eds. *New Wines in Old Skins: A Comparative View of Socio-Political Structures and Values Affecting the American Revolution.* Stuttgart: Ernst Klett Verlag, 1976.

Appleby, Joyce Oldham. *Economic Thought and Ideology in Seventeenth Century England.* Princeton: Princeton University Press, 1978.

Bailyn, Bernard. *Faces of Revolution: Personalities and Themes in the Struggle for American Independence.* New York: Knopf, 1990.

_____. *The Ideological Origins of the American Revolution.* Cambridge, Mass.: Belknap Press, 1967.

_____. *The Origins of American Politics.* New York: Vintage Books, 1967.

_____. *Voyagers to the West.* New York: Knopf, 1986.

Bancroft, George. *History of the Formation of the Constitution of the United States of America.* 2 vols. New York: D. Appleton, 1883.

Bates, A.C. ed. *The Two Putnams, Israel and Rufus, in the Havana Expedition 1762 and in the Mississippi River Exploration 1772-73.* Hartford: Conn. Hist. Soc., 1931.

Beard, Charles A. *An Economic Interpretation of the Constitution of the United States.* New York, 1935.

_____. *The Enduring Federalist.* New York, 1948.

Beard, Mary R. *The Rise of American Civilization.* rev. ed., I. New York, 1933 [1st ed., 1927].

Becker, Carl L. *The History of Political Parties in the Province of New York, 1760-1776.* Madison: University of Wisconsin Press, 1909.

Beeman, Richard; Botein, Stephen; and Carter, Edward C. II, eds. *Beyond Confederation: Origins of the Constitution and American National Identity.* Chapel Hill: University of North Carolina Press, 1987.

Bellamy, Edward. *The Duke of Stockbridge*. Cambridge, Ma.: Belknap Press, 1962 [orig. publ. Boston, 1879].

Benton, William, ed. *The Annals of America*. Chicago: Encyclopedia Brittanica, 1968.

Berens, Lewis H. *The Digger Movement in the Days of the Commonwealth: As Revealed in the Writings of Gerrard Winstanley*. London: Holland Press, 1961 [orig. publ. 1906].

Blackburne, Francis. *Memoirs of Thomas Hollis*. London, 1780.

Blumin, Stuart M. *The Emergence of the Middle Class: Social Experience in the American City, 1760-1900*. New York: Cambridge University Press, 1989.

Bolton, Charles Knowles. *The Private Soldier Under Washington*. New York: Kennikat, 1964 [orig. publ. 1902].

Bonomi, Patricia U. *A Factious People: Politics and Society in Colonial New York*. New York: Columbia University Press, 1971.

Bonwick, Colin. *English Radicals and the American Revolution*. Chapel Hill: University of North Carolina Press, 1977.

Bradford, Alden. *History of Massachusetts*. Boston: Hilliard, Gray, 1835.

Brennan, Ellen E. *Plural Office-Holding in Massachusetts, 1760-1780: Its Relation to the "Separation" of Departments of Government*. Chapel Hill: University of North Carolina Press, 1945.

Brooks, Noah. *Henry Knox: A Soldier of the Revolution*. New York: Da Capo Press, 1974 [orig. publ. 1900].

Brown, Richard D. *Revolutionary Politics in Massachusetts: The Boston Committee of Correspondence and the Towns, 1772-1774.* Cambridge, Mass.: Harvard University Press, 1970.

Brown, Robert E. *Charles Beard and the Constitution: A Critical Analysis of "An Economic Interpretation of the Constitution."* Princeton: Princeton University Press, 1956.

_____. *Middle-Class Democracy and the Revolution in Massachusetts, 1691-1780.* Ithaca: Cornell University Press, 1955.

Burke, Peter. *Popular Culture in Early Modern Europe.* New York: New York University Press, 1978.

Burnett, Edmund C. *The Continental Congress.* New York: Macmillan, 1941.

Burns, James McGregor. *The Vineyard of Liberty.* New York: Knopf, 1982.

Bushman, Richard L. *King and People in Provincial Massachusetts.* Chapel Hill: University of North Carolina Press, 1985.

Callahan, North. *Henry Knox: General Washington's General.* New York: Rinehart, 1958

Carp, E. Wayne. *To Starve the Army: Continental Army Administration and American Political Culture, 1775-1783.* Chapel Hill, 1984.

Caruthers, E. W. *A Sketch of the Life and Character of the Rev. David Caldwell, D.D . . .Including. . . Some Account of the Regulation. . . .* Greenborough, 1842.

Cayton, Andrew R. L. *The Frontier Republic: Ideology and Politics in the Ohio Country, 1780-1825*. Kent, Ohio: Kent State University Press, 1986.

Colbourn, H. Trevor. *The Lamp of Experience: Whig History and the Intellectual Origins of the American Revolution*. Chapel Hill, N.C.: University of North Carolina Press, 1965.

Collingwood, R. G. *The Idea of History*. New York: Oxford, 1946.

Coolidge, Mabel Cook. *History of Petersham, Massachusetts*. Hudson, Mass., 1948.

Davis, David Brion. *Slave Power Conspiracy and the Paranoid Style*. Baton Rouge: Louisiana State University Press, 1969.

Douglas, William O. *Points of Rebellion*. New York: Vintage Books, 1970.

Douglass, Elisha P. *Rebels and Democrats*. New York: Da Capo Press, 1971 [orig. publ. 1955].

Dow, George Francis. *Every Day Life in the Massachusetts Bay Colony*. New York: Blom, 1935.

Dyer, A.M. *First Ownership of Ohio Lands*. New York, 1911.

East, Robert A. *Business Enterprise in the American Revolutionary Era*. New York: AMS Press, 1969 [orig. publ. 1938].

Ernst, Robert. *Rufus King, American Federalist*. Chapel Hill: University of North Carolina Press, 1968.

Fay, Bernard. *Revolution and Freemasonry, 1680-1800*. Boston: Little, Brown, 1935.

Feer, Robert. *Shays's Rebellion*. New York: Garland, 1988 [Harvard Ph. D. dissertation, 1958].

Fischer, David Hackett. *Albion's Seed: Four British Folkways in America*. New York: Oxford, 1989.

Fiske, John. *The Critical Period of American History, 1783-1789*. Boston, 1916.

Flexner, James Thomas. *George Washington*. 4 vols. Boston: Little, Brown, 1965-1969.

Foner, Eric. *Tom Paine and Revolutionary America*. New York: Oxford, 1976.

Force, Peter, ed. *American Archives*. 9 vols. Washington, D.C., 1837-1853.

Freeman, Douglas Southall. *George Washington*. 7 vols. New York: Scribners, 1948-57.

Gilje, Paul. *The Road to Mobocracy: Popular Disorder in New York City, 1763-1834*. Chapel Hill: University of North Carolina Press, 1987.

Glasson, William H. *History of Military Pension Legislation in the United States*. New York: AMS Press, 1968 [orig. publ. 1900].

Glasson, William H. *Federal Military Pensions in the United States*. New York: Oxford University Press, 1918.

Gras, N. S. B. *The Massachusetts First National Bank*. Cambridge, Mass.: Harvard University Press, 1937.

Greene, Evarts B. and Harrington, Virginia D. *The American Population before the Federal Census of 1790*. Gloucester,

Mass.: P. Smith, 1966 [orig. publ. 1932].

Greenleaf, W. H. *Order, Empiricism, and Politics*. London: Oxford University Press, 1964.

Gross, Robert A. and Allis, Frederick, eds. *In Debt to Shays: The Legacy of an Agrarian Rebellion*. Charlottesville, forthcoming.

Gurr, Ted Robert. *Why Men Rebel*. Princeton: Princeton University Press, 1970.

Gutteridge, G. H. *English Whiggism and the American Revolution*. Berkeley, 1963.

Hale, Richard. *The American Revolution in Western Massachusetts*.

Hall, Charles S. *The Life and Letters of Samuel Holden Parsons: Major General in the Continental Army and Chief Judge of the Northwestern Territory*. Binghamton: Otseningo Press, 1905.

Hall, Kermit L., ed. *The Formation and Ratification of the Constitution: Major Historical Interpretations*. New York: Garland, 1987.

Hall, Van Beck. *Politics without Parties: Massachusetts, 1780-1791*. Pittsburgh: University of Pittsburgh, 1972.

Handlin, Oscar and Handlin, Mary Flug. *Commonwealth: A Study of the Role of Government in the American Economy: Massachusetts, 1774-1861*. Cambridge, Mass: Belknap Press, 1969.

Harding, Samuel B. *The Contest Over the Ratification of the Federal Constitution in Massachusetts*. New York: Da Capo

Press, 1970 [orig. publ. *Harvard Historical Studies* vol. 2, 1896].

Harvey, Paul, ed. *Oxford Companion to Classical Literature.* Oxford: Oxford University Press, 1955.

Hatch, Louis Clinton. *The Administration of the American Revolutionary Army.* New York: Longmans, 1904.

Hayes, T. Wilson. *Winstanley the Digger: A Literary Analysis of Radical Ideas in the English Revolution.* Cambridge, Mass.: Harvard University Press, 1979.

Herder, J. G. *Ideen zur Philosophie der Geschichte*, 4 vols. Riga/Leipzig, 1784-1791.

Higginson, Thomas Wentworth. *Life and Times of Stephen Higginson.* Boston, 1907.

Hildreth, Richard. *The History of the United States. . .*, III. Boston, 1849.

Hill, Christopher. *Puritanism and Revolution: Studies in Interpretation of the English Revolution of the Seventeenth Century.* London: Seeker and Warburg, 1958.

_____. *The Century of Revolution, 1603-1714.* New York: Norton, 1981 [orig. publ. 1961].

Hobsbawm, Eric. *Primitive Rebels.* New York: Norton, 1965 [orig. publ. 1959].

Hoerder, Dirk. *Crowd Action in Revolutionary Massachusetts, 1765-1780.* New York: Academic Press, 1977.

Hofstadter, Richard. *The Idea of a Party System: The Rise of Legitimate Opposition in the United States, 1780-1840.*

Berkeley: University of California Press, 1969.

Hough, Franklin B. ed. *Proceedings of a Convention of Delegates From Several of the New Englasnd States, Held at Boston, August 3-9, 1780. . . .* Albany, 1867.

Hulbert, Archer B. *The Records of the Original Proceedings of the Ohio Company.* 2 vols. Marietta: Marietta Hist. Comm., 1917.

Humphreys, Frank L. *Life and Times of David Humphreys: Soldier, Statesman, Poet.* 2 Vols. New York: Putnam, 1917.

Huntington, Samuel P. *Social Change in a New Political Order.* New Haven, 1968.

Jay, William. *Life of John Jay.* 2 vol. New York: Harper, 1833.

Jensen, Merrill. *The American Revolution Within America.* New York: New York University Press, 1974.

_____. *The Articles of Confederation: An Interpretation of the Social-Constitutional History of the American Revolution, 1774-1781.* Madison: University of Wisconsin Press, 1963.

_____. *The Making of the American Constitution.* New York, 1963.

_____. *The New Nation.* Boston: Northeastern University Press, 1981 [orig. publ. 1950].

Johnston, Henry P., ed. *The Correspondence and Public Papers of John Jay.* 4 vols. New York, 1890-1893.

Jones, Douglas Lamar. *Village and Seaport: Migration and Society in Eighteenth-Century Massachusetts.* Hanover, N. H.: University Press of New England, 1981.

Jones, Samuel W., *Memoir of the Hon. James Duane*. New York: Keyser, 1852.

Kaufman, Martin, ed. *Shays' Rebellion: Selected Essays.* Westfield, Mass.: Westfield State College, 1987.

King, Charles R. *The Life and Correspondence of Rufus King, Private and Official, His Public Documents and Speeches.* 6 vols. New York: Putnam, 1894-1900.

Knollenberg, Bernhard. *Origin of the American Revolution, 1759-1766.* New York: Collier, 1960.

Kohn, Richard. *The Eagle and the Sword: The Federalists and the Creation of a National Military Establishment, 1783-1802.* New York: Free Press, 1975.

Kraus, Michael. *A History of American History.* New York, 1937.

Krooss, Herman E., ed. *Documentary History of Banking and Currency in the United States.* 4 vols. New York: Chelsea House, 1969.

Labaree, Benjamin W. *Patriots and Partisans: The Merchants of Newburyport, 1764-1815.* Cambridge, Mass: Harvard University Press, 1962.

Lafayette, Marquis de. *Memoirs. . . Published by his Family.* New York: Saunders and Otley, 1837.

Lesser, Charles H. *The Sinews of Independence: Monthly Strength Reports of the Continental Army.* Chicago: University of Chicago Press, 1976.

Libby, Orin Grant. *The Geographical Distribution of the Vote of the Thirteen States on the Federalist Constitution.* New

York: Burt Franklin, 1969 [orig. publ. 1894].

Lincoln, William. *History of Worcester, Massachusetts.* Worcester: C. Hersey, 1862 [orig. publ. 1837].

Lodge, Henry Cabot. *Life and Letters of George Cabot.* New York: Da Capo, 1974 [orig. publ. Boston, 1878].

Lossing, John Benson. *The Life and Times of Philip Schuyler.* 2 vols. New York: Sheldon, 1872-1873.

Lynd, Staughton, *Intellectual Origins of American Radicalism.* New York: Vintage, 1968.

Mace, George. *Locke, Hobbes, and the Federalist Papers: An Essay on the Genesis of the American Political Heritage.* Carbondale, Ill.: Southern Illinois University Press, 1979.

MacIver, Robert M. *Social Causation.* Boston: Ginn, 1942.

Maier, Pauline. *From Resistance to Revolution: Colonial Radicals and the Development of American Opposition to Britain, 1765-1776.* New York: Knopf, 1972.

Main, Jackson Turner. *Political Parties Before the Constitution.* Chapel Hill: University of North Carolina Press, 1973.

_____. *The Antifederalists: Critics of the Constitution.* Chapel Hill: University of North Carolina Press, 1961.

_____. *The Social Structure of Revolutionary America.* Princeton: Princeton University Press, 1965.

Malone, Dumas. *Jefferson and His Time.* 6 vols. Boston: Little, Brown, 1948-1981.

Marshall, John. *The Life of George Washington. . .,* 5 vols.

(1804-1807).

Martin, Joseph Plumb. *Yankee Doodle Dandy: Being a Narrative of some Adventures, Dangers and Sufferings of a Revolutionary Soldier*, Scheer, George F., ed. Boston: Little Brown, 1962.

Martyn, Charles. *The Life of Artemas Ward: The First Commander-in-Chief of the American Revolution*. New York: Ward, 1921.

Mattern, David B. *A Moderate Revolutionary: The Life of Major General Benjamin Lincoln*. Unpublished Ph.D. dissertation, Columbia University, 1990.

McDonald, Forrest. *E Pluribus Unum*. Boston: Houghton Mifflin, 1965.

_____. *Novus Ordo Seclorum: The Intellectual Origins of the Constitution*. Lawrence, Kansas: University Press of Kansas, 1985.

Melville, George Donald. "Evidences of Economic and Social Influences at Work in the Massachusetts Convention which Ratified the Federal Constitution." Unpubl. thesis, New Hampshire, 1920.

Miller, John J. *Sam Adams: Pioneer in Propaganda*. Boston, 1936.

Miller, Perry. *Jonathan Edwards*. New York: Sloane, 1949.

_____. *The New England Mind: The Seventeeth Century*. Cambridge, Mass.: Belknap Press, 1939.

Minot, George Richards. *The History of the Insurrections in Massachusetts in the Year 1786 and the Rebellion Con-*

sequent Thereon. Freeport, N. Y: Books for Libraries Press [prig. publ. Boston, 1788].

Morgan, Edmund S. *Inventing the People: The Rise of Popular Sovereignty in England and America.* New York: Norton, 1988.

Morgan, Edmund S. and Helen M. *The Stamp Act Crisis: Prologue to Revolution.* New York: Collier, 1963, rev. ed. [orig. publ. Chapel Hill, 1953 York].

Morison, Samuel Eliot. *The Life and Letters of Harrison Gray Otis, Federalist, 1765-184.* 2 vols. Boston: Houghton Mifflin, 1913.

Morris, Richard B. *Government and Labor in Early America.* New York: Northeastern University Press, 1981 [orig. publ. 1946].

Morse, Anson E. *The Federalist Party in Massachusetts to the Year 1800.* Princeton: University Library, 1909.

Morse, S. *Freemasonry in the American Revolution.* Washington, 1924.

Myers, Jr., Minor. *A History of the Society of the Cincinnati.* Charlottesville: University Press of Virginia, 1983.

Ollard, Richard. *This War Without An Enemy: A History of the English Civil Wars.* London: Fontana Books, 1976.

Parker, H. J. *Army Lodges During the Revolution.* Boston, 1884.

Parmenter, C. O. *History of Pelham, Mass. . . .* Amherst, Mass., 1898.

Parsons, Theophilus. *Memoir of Theophilus Parsons, Chief Justice of the Supreme Judicial Court of Massachusetts, with Notices of Some of His Contemporaries, by his son Theophilus Parsons.* Boston: Ticknor and Fields, 1859.

Patterson, Stephen E. *Political Parties in Revolutionary Massachusetts.* Madison: University of Wisconsin Press, 1973.

Pickering, Octavius. *The Life of Timothy Pickering.* 4 vols. Boston: Upham, 1867-1873.

Pitkin, Timothy. *A Political and Civil History of the United States. . .,* II. New Haven, 1828.

Pocock, J. G. A. *Virtue, Commerce, and History.* Cambridge: Cambridge University Press, 1985.

_____, ed. *Three British Revolutions: 1641, 1688, 1776.* Princeton: Princeton University Press, 1980.

Pole, J. R. *Political Representation in England and the Origins of the American Republic.* New York: Macmillan, 1966.

Putnam, Rufus. *The Memoirs of Rufus Putnam.* Buell, R., ed. Boston: Houghton Mifflin, 1903.

Rakove, Jack N. *The Beginnings of National Politics.* New York, 1979.

Riker, William H. *The Art of Political Manipulation.* New Haven: Yale University Press, 1986.

Robbins, Caroline. *The Eighteenth-Century Commonwealthmen: Studies in the Transmission, Development and Circumstance of English Liberal Thought from the Restoration of Charles II until the War with the Thirteen Colonies.* Cambridge, Mass: Harvard University Press, 1959.

Rohrbough, Malcolm J. *The Land Office Business: The Settlement and Administration of American Public Lands, 1789-1837.* New York: Oxford University Press, 1968.

Rossie, Jonathan Gregory. *The Politics of Command in the American Revolution.* Syracuse: Syracuse University Press. 1975.

Rossiter, Clinton. *The Political Thought of the American Revolution.* New York: Harcourt Brace, 1963 [orig. publ. 1953].

_____. *Seedtime of the Republic: The Origin of the American Tradition of Political Liberty.* New York: Harcourt Brace, 1953.

_____. *1787: The Grand Convention.* New York, Norton, 1987.

Rowland, Kate Mason. *Life of George Mason*, 2 vols. New York Russell and Russell, 1964 [orig. publ. 1892].

Royster, Charles. *Light-Horse Harry Lee and the Legacy of the American Revolution.* New York: Knopf, 1981.

_____. *A Revolutionary People at War: The Continental Army and the American Character,1775-1783.* Chapel Hill: University of North Carolina Press, 1979.

Rudé, George. *Paris and London in the Eighteenth Century.* Atlantic Heights, N. J.: Humanities Press, 1971.

_____. *The Face of the Crowd: Studies in Revolution, Ideology and Popular Protest.* Harvey J. Kaye, ed. Atlantic Heights, N.J.: Humanities Press, 1988.

Rutland, Robert Allen. *James Madison: The Founding Father.* New York: Macmillan, 1987.

_____. *The Ordeal of the Constitution: The Antifederalists and the Ratification Struggle of 1787-1788*. Boston: Northeastern University Press, 1965.

Schwartz, Barry. *George Washington: The Making of an American Symbol*. New York: Free Press, 1987.

Schwoerer, Lois G. *"No Standing Armies!": The Antimilitary Ideology in Seventeenth-Century England*. Baltimore: Johns Hopkins University Press, 1974.

Severo, Richard, and Milford, Lewis. *The Wages of War: When America's Soldiers Came Home — From Valley Forge to Vietnam*. New York: Simon and Schuster, 1989.

Shaw, Peter. *American Patriots and the Ritual of Revolution*. Cambridge, Mass.: Harvard University Press, 1981.

Smith, Barbara Clark. "The Politics of Price Control in Revolutionary Massachusetts." Unpublished Ph.D. dissertation, Yale University, 1983.

_____. *After the Revolution: The Smithsonian History of Everday Life in the Eighteenth Century*. New York: Pantheon, 1985.

Smith, J. E. A. *The History of Pittsfield, (Berkshire County), Massachusetts, From the Year 1734 to the Year 1800*. 2 vols. Boston: Lee and Shepard, 1869.

Smith, Page. *A New Age Now Begins*, 2 vols. A People's History of the United States. New York: McGraw-Hill, 1976.

_____. *The Shaping of America*. A People's History of the United States. New York: McGraw-Hill, 1980.

Sosin, J. M. *English America and the Restoration Monarchy*

of Charles II. Lincoln, Neb.: University of Nebraska Press, 1980.

Storing, Herbert J. *What the Anti-Federalists Were For.* Chicago: University of Chicago Press, 1981.

Sullivan, William. *The Public Men of the Revolution.* Philadelphia: Carey and Hart, 1847.

Szatmary, David. *Shays' Rebellion: The Making of an Agrarian Insurrection.* Amherst: University of Massachusetts Press, 1980.

Taylor, Alan. *Liberty Men and Great Proprietors.* Chapel Hill: University of North Carolina Press, 1990.

Taylor, Robert J. *Western Massachusetts in the Revolution.* Providence: Brown University Press, 1954.

Thacher, James. *Military Journal of the American Revolution.* . . . Hartford: Cottons and Barnard, 1862 (orig. publ. Boston 1823).

Thatsch, J. H. *Free-Masonry in the Thirteen Colonies.* New York, 1929.

Thomas, William S. *The Society of the Cincinnati, 1783-1935.* New York: Putnam, 1935.

Trumbull, James Russell. *History of Northampton.* 2 vols. Northampton, Mass., 1898.

Tudor, William. *Life of James Otis.* Boston, 1823.

Tyler, John W. *Smugglers and Patriots: Boston Merchants and the Advent of the American Revolution.* Boston: Northeastern University Press, 1986.

Welch, Richard E. *Theodore Sedgwick, Federalist.* Middletown, Ct.: Wesleyan University Press, 1965.

Weston, Corinne Comstock. *English Constitutional Theory and the House of Lords, 1556-1832.* New York: Columbia University Press, 1965.

Wills, Garry. *Cincinnatus: George Washington and the Enlightenment.* New York: Doubleday, 1984.

Winny, J., ed. *The Frame of Order.* Folcroft, Pa.: Folcroft Press, 1969 [orig. publ. London, 1957].

Wood, Gordon S., ed. *The Confederation and the Constitution: The Critical Issues.* New York: University Press of America, 1973.

_____. *The Creation of the American Republic, 1776-1786.* New York: Knopf, 1972.

_____. *The Radicalism of the American Revolution.* New York: Knopf, 1992.

Young, Alfred F. *The American Revolution: Explorations in the History of American Radicalism.* DeKalb: Northern Illinois University Press, 1976.

Secondary Articles:

Allen, Gardner Weld. *Massachusetts Privateers of the Revolution. Massachusetts Historical Society Collections, LXXVII* (Boston, 1927).

Appleby, Joyce. "The Social Origins of American Revolutionary Ideology." *Journal of American History* LXIV (March 1978), 935-958.

Bogin, Ruth. "Petitioning and the New Moral Economy of Post-Revolutionary America." *William and Mary Quarterly*, 3rd Ser., XLV, No. 3 (1988), 391-425.

_____. "'Measures So Glaringly Unjust,': A Response to Hamilton's Funding Plan by William Manning." *William and Mary Quarterly*, 3rd Ser., XLVI, No. 2 (1988), 315-331.

Boyer, Paul S. "Borrowed Rhetoric: The Massachusetts Excise Controversy of 1754." in *William and Mary Quarterly*, 3rd. Ser., XXI (1964), 328-351.

Brooke, John L. "To the Quiet of the People: Revolutionary Settlements and Civil Unrest in Western Massachusetts, 1774-1789." *William and Mary Quarterly*, 3rd Ser., XLVI (July 1989), 425-462.

Brown, Richard D. "Shays's Rebellion and Its Aftermath: A View from Springfield, Massachusetts, 1787." *William and Mary Quarterly*, 3rd Ser., XL (Oct. 1989), 598-615.

_____. "Shays's Rebellion and the Ratification of the Federalist Constitution in Massachusetts." Beeman, Richard; Botein, Stephen; and Carter, Edward C. II, eds. *Beyond Confederation: Origins of the Constitution and American National Identity*. Chapel Hill: University of North Carolina Press, 1987, 113-207.

Burrows, Edwin G. and Wallace, Michael. "The American Revolution: The Ideology and Psychology of National Liberation." *Perspectives in American History* VI (1972).

Bushman, Richard L. "Massachusetts Farmers and the Revolution." *Society, Freedom, and Conscience: The American Revolution in Virginia, Massachusetts and New York*. Richard M. Jellison, ed. (New York, 1976).

Cornell, Saul. "Aristocracy Assailed: The Ideology of Back-country Anti-Federalism." *Journal of American History LXX-VI* (1990), 1148-1172.

Crandall, Ruth. "Wholesale Commodity Prices in Boston During the Eighteenth Century." *Review of Economic Statistics XVI* (1934), 117-128, 178-183.

Crane, Verner W. "Franklin's 'The Internal State of America' (1786)." *William and Mary Quarterly*, 3rd Ser., XV (April 1958), 214-227.

Delmage, Rutherford E. "The American Idea of Progress, 1750-1800." *Proceedings of the American Philosophical Society LXXXXI* (Philadelphia, 1947), 307-314.

Davies, Wallace Evans. "The Society of Cincinnati in New England, 1783-1800." *William and Mary Quarterly*, 3rd Ser., V (Jan. 1948), 3-25.

East, Robert O. "Massachusetts Conservatives in the Critical Period." *Era of American Revolution*, Richard B Morris, ed. (New York, 1939), 349-391.

Feer, Robert. "Shays's Rebellion and the Constitution: A Study in Causation." *New England Quarterly* XLII No. 4 (1964), 388-410.

_____. "George Richards Minot's *History of the Insurrections*: History, Propaganda, and Autobiography." New England Quarterly XXXV, No. 2 (June 1962), 203-228.

Ferguson, E. James. "Currency Finance: An Interpretation of Colonial Monetary Practices." *William and Mary Quarterly*, 3rd Ser., X (April 1953), 153-180.

Fischer, David H. "The Myth of the Essex Junto." *William*

and Mary Quarterly, 3rd Ser., XXI, No. 2 (April 1964), 191-235.

Fowler, William M. Jr., "The Massachusetts Election of 1785: A Triumph of Virtue." Essex Institute, *Historical Collections*, CXI, (1975), 290-304.

Freeman, James. "The Character of Judge Minot. . .," *in Massachusetts Historical Society Collections 8* (Boston, 1802).

Green, Samuel. "Groton during Shays' Rebellion," in *Proceedings of the Massachusetts Historical Society* I, no. 3 (July 1884).

Greenough, Chester N. "Algernon Sidney and the Motto of the Commonwealth of Massachusetts." *American Historical Association Proceedings LI* (1917-1918), 259-282.

Gross and Allis, eds., *In Debt to Shays* (forthcoming).

Gross, Robert A. "Daniel Shays and Lafayette's Sword." *OAH Newsletter*, 15 (Nov. 1987).

Halpern, Joel and Brode, John. "Peasant Society." Bernard Siegel and Alan Beales, eds., *The Biennial Review of Anthropology, 1967* (Stanford, 1967).

Henderson, H. James. "Taxation and Political Culture: Massachusetts and Virginia, 1760-1800." *William and Mary Quarterly*, 3rd Ser., XLVII (Jan. 1990).

Hume, Edgar Erskine. "Early Opposition to the Cincinnati." *Americana, XXX* (1936), 597-638.

Kaplan, Sidney. "Pay Pension, and Power: Economic Grievances of the Massachusetts Officers of the Revolution." *Boston Public Library Quarterly*, III (1951), 15-34, 127-142.

_____. "Rank and Status among Massachusetts Continental Officers." *American Historical Review*, LVI (1951), 319-326.

_____. "Veteran Officers and Politics in Massachusetts. 1783-1787." *William and Mary Quarterly*, 3rd Ser., IX (1952), 29-57.

Kenyon, Cecilia M. "Men of Little Faith: The Anti-Federalists on the Nature of Representative Government." *William and Mary Quarterly*, 3rd Ser., XII (Jan. 1955), 3-43.

Ketcham, Ralph and Stein, Nathaniel. "Two New Letters Reveal Madison's Role, Unmask Ghost of Washington's Unused Inaugural." *Manuscripts* (Spring, 1959), 54-60.

Kramnick, Isaac. "The 'Great National Discussion': The Discourse of Politics in 1787." *William and Mary Quarterly*, 3rd Ser., XLV, No. 1 (Jan. 1988), 3-32.

Lord, Arthur. "Some Objections Made to the Constitution." *American Historical Association Proceedings*, L (Boston, 1917).

McDonald, Forrest. "The Anti-Federalists, 1781-1789." *Wisconsin Magazine of History, 46* (Spring 1963), 206-214.

Moody, Robert E. "Samuel Ely: Forerunner of Shays." *New England Quarterly*, V (Jan. 1932), 105-134.

Morison, Samuel Eliot. "The Struggle over the Adoption of the Constitution of Massachusetts, 1780." *American Historical Association Proceedings L* (Boston, 1917), 353-411.

Morris, Richard B. "The Confederation Period and the American Historian" *William and Mary Quarterly*, 3rd. ser., XIII (1956), 139-156.

_____. "Insurrection in Massachusetts." Daniel Aaron, ed., *America in Crisis* (New York, 1952).

Mutch, Robert E. "Yeoman and merchant in pre-industrial America: eighteenth-century Massachusetts as a case study." *Societas: A Review of Social History* VII (Autumn 1977), 279-302.

Noble, John. "A Few Notes on the Shays Rebellion." *Proceedings of the American Antiquarian Society* XV (1902-3). 112-121, 200-232.

Nobles, Gregory H. "The Politics of Patriarchy in Shays's Rebellion: The Case of Henry McCulloch." *Dublin Seminar for New England Folklife*, Annual Proceedings 1985, 37-47.

Pencak, William. "Samuel Adams and Shays's Rebellion." *New England Quarterly* LXI (1989), 63-74.

Persons, Stow. "The Cyclical Theory of History in Eighteenth-Century America." *American Quarterly VI* (1954), 147-163.

Pocock, J. G. A. "Machiavelli, Harrington, and English Political Ideologies in the Eighteenth Century." *William and Mary Quarterly*, 3rd. Ser., XXII (1965), 549-583.

Randall, Edwin T. "Imprisonment for Debt in America: Fact and Fiction." Mississippi Valley Historical Association XXXIX (March 1953), 89-102.

Robbins, Caroline. "Algernon Sidney's *Discourses Concerning Government*: Textbook of Revolution." William and Mary Quarterly, 3rd. Ser., IV (1947), 267-296.

_____. "The Strenuous Whig, Thomas Hollis of Lincoln's Inn." *William and Mary Quarterly*, 3rd Ser., VII (1950), 406-

453.

Robinson, William Alexander. "James Bowdoin." *Dictionary of American Biography*, Dumas Malone, ed., 20 vols. (New York, 1928-1936).

Skelton, William B. "The Confederation Regulars: A Social Profile of Enlisted Service in America's First Standing Army." *William and Mary Quarterly*, 3rd Ser., XLVI (Oct. 1989), 770-785.

Smail, Elmer S. "The Daniel Shays Family." *New England Historical and Genealogical Register*, CXL (Oct. 1986), 291-302.

Smith, Jonathan. "The Depression of 1785 and Shays' Rebellion." *William and Mary Quarterly*, 3rd Ser., V (Jan. 1948), 77-94 [orig. publ. 1905]).

Snell, Ronald K. "Ambitious of Honor and Places: The Magistracy of Hampshire County." Bruce C. Daniels, ed., *Power and Status: Officeholding in Colonial America* (Middletown, Ct., 1986), 17-36.

Stein, Nathaniel E. "The Discarded Inaugural Address of George Washington." *Manuscripts* (Spring, 1958).

Stone, Eben F. "Parsons and the Constitutional Convention of 1788." *Essex Historical Institute Collections XXXV* (1899), 81-102.

Tate, Thad W. "The Social Contract in America, 1774-1787: Revolutionary Theory as a Conservative Instrument." *William and Mary Quarterly*, 3rd. ser., XXII (1965).

Tatter, Henry. "State and Federal Land Policy during the Confederation Period." *Agricultural History IX* (1935), 176-186.

Thompson, E. P. "The Moral Economy of the English Crowd in the Eighteenth Century." *Past and Present*, No. 50 (1971), 76-136.

Vaughan, Alden T. "The 'Horrid and Unnatural Rebellion' of Daniel Shays." *American Heritage* XXVII, No. 4 (June 1966), 50-81.

Wade, Herbert T. "The Essex Regiment in Shays' Rebellion — 1787." *Essex Institute Historical Collections*, XC (1954), 317-349

Warren, Charles. "Elbridge Gerry, James Warren, Mercy Warren, and the Ratification of the Federal Constitution in Massachusetts." *Massachusetts Historical Society, Proceedings, LXIV* (1930-1932), 143-164.

Warren, Joseph Parker. "The Confederation and the Shays Rebellion." *American Historical Review*, II. New York, 1897, 42-67.

_____. "Documents Relating to Shays' Rebellion." *American Historical Review*, 2 (July 1897), 691-699.

Young, Alfred F. "English Plebeian Culture and Eighteenth-Century American Radicalism." *The Origins of Anglo American Radicalism*. Jacob, Margaret and Jacob, James, eds. (London, 1984), 185-212.

APPENDIX A

"On the Shais Affair in Maschusets,"
from William Manning's *Key of Libberty*[1]

A s I lived near wheir this afair hapned, & Received some
ffouns from the Acttors on both Sides of the Actt Because I was apposed to their Measures, I will Indaver to give
a More full But Impartial account of it.

At the Close of the Late war with Brittan, although our paper money had Dyed away, & left the peopel grately in Debt
by it, & a large publick Det on us by the war, yet their was
a large Quantity of hard Mony amongue us Sefitient for a
Medium. But for want of a proper Regulation of trade, & the
prices of Labour & produce being higher here than in other
Cuntryes, our Marchents Shiped it off Lode after Load by the
hundred thousand Dollars together untill their was but Little
Left, & taxes ware Extremely high. Some Countyes ware two
or three years behind, & the price of Labour & produce falling very fast - Creditors Calling for old Debts that they would
not take in paper Money, & those that had Money Demanding
30, 40, & Some 50 pursent Interest, Fee Officers demanding
Double, thribble, & Some 4 times So Much as the Law aiowed

---

1. William Manning, *The Key of Libberty. Shewing the Causes why a free government has always Failed, & a Reamidy against it. Adresed to the Republicans, Farmers, Mecanicks & Labourers in America by a Labourer* (1797).
Houghton Library, Harvard University, Am 880.3. The Houghton has three
copies in Manning's hand, with only insignificant variations between the three.
Also reprinted in Samuel E. Morison, "William Manning's *The Key of Libberty*," *William and Mary Quarterly*, 3rd Ser., XIII (Jan. 1948), 242-243.

them, and all of them so Crouded with bisness that it was hard to git any Done, & property Selling Every Day by Execution for Less than halfe its Value, & Jales Crouded with Debttors; & the peopel being Ignorant that all their help Lay in being fully and fairly Represented in the Legeslature, Many towns Neglected to Send Representitives in ordir to Save the Cost, so that the few ondly ware Represented at Cort, with an Aristrocratical Bodoin as Gouvenour at their head. Under all these Circumstances the peopel were drove to the gratest Extremity & Many Countyes took to Conventions, Remonstrances & petition to a Corte where they were not halfe Represented. But not being heard to or in some Instances Charged with Saditious Metings & intentions some Countyes ware So foolish as to Stop the Corts of Justis by force of armes. This Shook the government to its foundation, for insted of Fatherly Councals & admonitions, the Dog of war was Let Loose upon them & they ware Declared in a State of Insurrection & Rebellion. In these Circomstances, the few ware all alive for the Seporte of Government, & all those who would not be Continually crying Government — Government — or dared to Say a word against any of their Measures were Called Shasites & Rebels & thretned with prosicutions &cc. But a Large Majority of the peopel, thinking that their was blame on both sides, or Vueing one Side as knaves & the other as fooles, it was with Grate Difficulty & Delay Before a Sefitient number Could be Raised & Sent to Surpress them. But it was done with the Loss of but few lives.

This put the peopel in the Most Zelous Sarches after a Remidy for their greviences. Thousands & thousands of Miles ware Rode to Consult Each other on the afair, & they hapily Efected it in a few Months, Ondly by Using their priviledges as Electors. Bodoin was turned out from being govenour (& in a few years Sickened & Dyed) & Hancok was almost unanimously Chosen in his Rome. Many of the old Representitives Shaired the same fate, & a full Representation sent to Cort from Every parte of the of the State, which Soone found out Meens to Redress the Grevances of the peopel, though they were attended with the Most Dificult Circumstances. So that Everything appeared like the Clear & plesent Sunshine after a Most tremendious Storme. This is a Streiking Demonstration of the advantages of a free Elective Government, & Shews how a peopel May Run themselves into the gratest Difficultyes by Inatention in Elections & Retreve their circumstances again by attending theirtoo. This Shais afair neaver would have hapned if the peopel had bin posesed of a true knowledge of their Rights, Dutyes, & Interests, or if the government had Done their Duty according to the Oaths they ware under, & if they had have had Such a govenour as Hancok at that time. Even after the Corts ware stoped he would have Settled the hole afare for Less than a thousand Dollers. But as it was Maniged it Cost the State Seaveral hundred thousands Dollers, & this is always the way in wars. The few that are Imployed to Manage them Make them as Costly as posable & if the Mater was Sarched to the Bottom it would be found that Some of the ordir of Cincinaty have bin at the botom of all these wars, & Got into bisness & Grone Rich by them & the farmers & Labourers have yet the Cost to pay & So it will be again if we have a war with France. This Shais afair neaver would have hapned if the peopel had bin posesed of a true knowledge of their Rights, Dutyes, & Interests, or if the government had done their duty according to the oaths they ware under, & if they had have had such a govenour as Hancok at that time. Even after the Corts ware stoped he would have Settled the hole afare for less than a thousand dollers. But as it was maniged it cost the State seaveral hundred thousands dollers, & this is always the way in wars. The few that are imployed to manage them make them as costly as posable & if the mater was sarched to the bottom it would be found that some of the ordir of Cincinaty have bin at the botom of all these wars, & got into bisness Sr. grone rich by them & the farmers & Labourers have yet the cost to pay & So it will be again if we have a war with France.

APPENDIX B

Knox's Letter to Washington Regarding
Shays' Rebellion and the Constitution[1]

New York, 28 October 1786

My dear Sir, I have long intended myself the pleasure of visiting you at Mount Vernon, and although I have not given up that hope, and shall probably gratify it in the course of next month, yet. I cannot longer delay presenting myself to the remembrance of my truly respected and beloved general, whose friendship I shall ever esteem among the most valuable circumstances of my existence.

---

1. This is the draft of the letter which Washington received from Knox, from the Washington Papers, LC. The italics are Knox's; the passages in brackets are those which Washington copied verbatim in a letter to Madison as soon as he recieved Knox's. Every other printed version of this letter has been taken from the draft in Knox's letter-book, dated October 23rd, 1786, Knox Papers, MHS; that was the draft which Drake copied in *The Life and Correspondence of Henry Knox*, 91-93. The actual letter Knox sent, however, was dated October 28, making it all the more remarkable that Washington copied long passages to Madison as early as November 5. See above, Chapter VI. The dozen or so differences are not worth signalling. For example, in this final draft he has added quotation marks to: Their creed is *"That the property. . . ."* One can only speculate why five days passed before Knox copied the final draft to Washington; this in itself is unusual for Knox, and strongly suggests, despite the minor variations, that he spent a long time weighing his words. Did he, perhaps, consult with anyone concerning the first draft? Jay was in New York at the time, as well as Henry 'Light-Horse Harry' Lee; and Hamilton was certainly there by October 28, having attended the Annapolis Convention in September (see *Hamilton Papers*, Syrett, ed., Ill, 692).

Conscious of affection, and believing it to be reciprocal in your behalf, I have had no apprehensions of my silence being misconstrued. I know the perplexity accompanied by your numerous correspondents and was unwilling to add to it. Besides which, I have lately been once far eastward of Boston, on private business, and was no sooner returned here, than the commotions in Massachusetts hurried me back to Boston on a public account.

Our political machine constituted of thirteen independent sovereignties, have been constantly operating against each other, and against the federal head, ever since the peace, the powers of Congress are utterly inadequate to preserve the balance between the respective States, and oblige them to do those things which are essential to their own welfare, and for the general good. The human mind in the local legislatures seems to be exerted to pevent the federal constitution from having any beneficial effects, the machine works inversely to the public good in all its parts. Not only is State against State, and all against the federal head, but the States within themselves possess the name only, without the essential concomitant of government, the power of preserving the peace; the protection of the liberty and property of the citizens.

On the first impression of faction and licentiousness, the fine theoretic government of Massachusetts has given way, and its laws arrested and trampled under foot. Men at a distance, who have admired our systems of government, unfounded in nature, are apt to accuse the rulers, and say that taxes have been assessed too high and collected too rigidly — This is a deception equal to any that has hitherto been entertained. It is indeed a fact, that high taxes are the ostensible cause of the commotions, but that they are the real cause is as far remote from truth as light from darkness, the people who are the insurgents have never paid any, or but very little taxes — But they see the weakness of government; They feel at once their own poverty, compared with the opulent, and their own force, and they are determined to make up the latter, in order to remedy the former. [Their creed is, 'That the property of the United States has been protected from confiscation of Britain by the joint exertions of all, and therefore ought to be the common property of all. and he that attempts opposition to this creed is an enemy to equity and justice, and ought to be swept from off the face of the earth. . . .'] In a word, [they are determined to annihilate all debts, public and private and have agrarian Laws which are easily effected by the means of unfunded paper money, which shall be a tender in all cases whatever.]

[The number of these people may amount in Massachusetts to about one-fifth of several populous counties, and to them may be collected people of similar sentiments from the states of Rhode Island, Connecticut and New Hampshire, so as to constitute a body of 12 or 15000 desperate and unprincipled men. They are chiefly of the young and active part of the community,] more easily collected than kept together afterwards. But they will probably commit overt acts of treason which will compel them to embody for their own safety — once embodied, they will be constrained to submit to discipline for the same reason. Having proceeded to this length, for which they are now ripe, we shall have a formidable rebellion against reason, the principle of all government, and the very name of liberty. This dreadful situation has alarmed every man of principle and property in New England. They start as from a dream, and ask what can have been the cause of our delusion? What is to afford us security against the violence of lawless men? Our government must be braced, changed or altered to secure our lives and property. We imagined that the mildness of our government and *the virtue* of the people were so correspondent, that we were not as other nations, requiring brutal force to support the laws. But we find that we are men, actual men, possessing all the turbulent passions belonging to that animal, and that we must have a government proper and adequate for him. The people of Massachusetts for instance are far advanced in this doctrine, and the men of reflection, & principle are determined to endeavor to establish a government which shall have the power to protect them in their lawful pursuits, and which will be 'efficient in all cases of internal commotions or foreign invasions. They mean that liberty shall be the basis, a liberty resulting from the equal and firm administration of the laws. They wish for a general government of unity as they see the local legislatures must naturally and necessarily tend to retard and frustrate all general government.

We have arrived at a point of time in which we are forced to see our own national humiliation, and that a progression in this line, cannot be productive of happiness either public or private. Something is wanting, or something must be done, or we shall be involved in all the horror of faction and civil war without a prospect of its termination. Every tried friend to the liberty of his country is bound to reflect, and to step forward to prevent the dreadful consequences which will result from a government of events. Unless this is done, we shall be liable to be ruled by an arbitrary and capricious armed tyranny, whose word and will must be law.

The indians on the frontier are giving indisputable evidence of their hostile dispositions. Congress, anxiously desirous of meeting the evils on the frontiers, have unanimously agreed to augment the troops now in service to a legionary corps of 2040 men. The additions are to be recruited as follows

	Connecticut	180
Infantry and Artillery	R. Island	120
	Massachusetts	660
	New Hampshire	260
Cavalry	Maryland	60
	Viriginia	60
		1340

This measure is important, and will tend to strengthening the principle of government as well as to defend the frontiers. I mention the idea of strengthening government confidentially, but the State of Massachusetts requires the greatest assis-

356

tance, and Congress are fully impressed with the importance of supporting her with great exertions. . . .[2]

I am, my dear Sir, with ardent wishes for your permanent and perfect felicity your sincere friend, and much obliged humble servant

HKnox

---

2. The remaining three paragraphs of the letter concern unrelated business.

Made in the USA
Middletown, DE
28 December 2018